Critical Discourse in Bangla

This volume forms a part of the Critical Discourses in South Asia series which deals with schools, movements, and discursive practices in major South Asian languages. It offers crucial insights into the making of Bengali or Bangla literature and its critical tradition across a century. The book brings together English translations of major writings of influential figures dealing with literary criticism and theory, aesthetic and performative traditions, and reinterpretations of primary concepts and categories in Bangla. It presents 32 key texts in literary and cultural studies from Bengal from the middle of the 19th to that of the 20th century, with most of them translated for the first time into English. These seminal essays are linked with socio-historical events and phenomena in the colonial and post-independence period in Bengal, including the background to the Language Movement in Bangladesh. They discuss themes such as integrative aesthetic visions, poetic and literary forms, modernism, imagination, power structures and social struggles, ideological values, cultural renovations, and humanism.

Comprehensive and authoritative, this volume offers an overview of the history of critical thought in Bangla literature in South Asia. It will be essential for scholars and researchers of Bengali/Bangla language and literature, literary criticism, literary theory, comparative literature, Indian literature, cultural studies, art and aesthetics, performance studies, history, sociology, regional studies, and South Asian studies. It will also interest the Bengali-speaking diaspora and those working on the intellectual history of Bengal and conservation of languages and culture.

Subha Chakraborty Dasgupta is former Professor of Comparative Literature, Jadavpur University, Kolkata, India. She was Visiting Professor, University of Delhi, India, and Tokyo University of Foreign Studies, Japan. Her research interests and publications span the fields of cultural studies, gender perspectives, oratures, and translation. She has a book entitled *Bibliography of Reception: World Literature in Bengali Periodicals* (1890–1900) to her credit, and her most recent volume co-edited with K. Alfons Knauth is *Figures of Transcontinental Multilingualism* (2018).

Subrata Sinha is Assistant Professor of Bangla at St. Xavier's College, Kolkata (Raghabpur Campus), India. Earlier, he worked for the School of Cultural Texts and Records, Jadavpur University, and the Archives and Research Centre for Ethnomusicology, Gurgaon, India. His monograph *Adhunikatar Kavyatattva o Sudhindranath Datta* was published in 2019.

Critical Discourses in South Asia
Series Editors: Avadhesh Kumar Singh and Kiran Singh, AURO University, India

South Asia, and especially India, has a long and rich tradition of critical discourses in its languages. These discourses are unique in their own ways without being exclusive and they form an integral part of the regional intellectual traditions. Each critical discourse has its specificity, while it is also related with other critical traditions in an interlingual and interliterary way. However, there is a considerable amount of insulation among such critical traditions primarily because of lack of translation of seminal texts in major South Asian languages.

This series broadly deals with critical discourses in major South Asian languages representing various schools, movements and discursive practices. Each individual volume in the series brings together English translation of major writings dealing with theoretical formulations, literary criticism and theory, re-interpretations of critical concepts and categories and critical movements in the concerned language that go into the making of its critical tradition.

The volumes in the series not only offer a comprehensive picture of critical discourses in major South Asian languages but also facilitate a comparative understanding of critical traditions across the world.

Editorial Advisory Board:
G. N. Devy, Chairman, People's Linguistic Survey of India; Founder Director, Adivasi Academy, Tejgadh, Gujarat; and former Professor of English, M.S. University of Baroda, India.

Subha Chakraborty Dasgupta, former Professor of Comparative Literature, Jadavpur University, Kolkata, India; and former Visiting Professor, University of Delhi, India and Tokyo University of Foreign Studies, Japan.

Critical Discourse in Bangla
Edited by Subha Chakraborty Dasgupta and Subrata Sinha

Critical Discourse in Odia
Edited by Jatindra Kumar Nayak and Animesh Mohapatra

Critical Discourse in Telugu
Edited by K. Suneetha Rani

For more information about this Series, please visit: https://www.routledge.com/Critical-Discourses-in-South-Asia/book-series/CDSA

Critical Discourse in Bangla

Edited by Subha Chakraborty Dasgupta
and Subrata Sinha

Routledge
Taylor & Francis Group
LONDON AND NEW YORK

First published 2022
by Routledge
2 Park Square, Milton Park, Abingdon, Oxon OX14 4RN

and by Routledge
605 Third Avenue, New York, NY 10158

Routledge is an imprint of the Taylor & Francis Group, an informa business

British Library Cataloguing-in-Publication Data
A catalogue record for this book is available from the British Library

Library of Congress Cataloging-in-Publication Data
A catalog record has been requested for this book

ISBN: 978-1-138-63301-8 (hbk)
ISBN: 978-1-032-12470-4 (pbk)
ISBN: 978-1-003-22468-6 (ebk)

DOI: 10.4324/9781003224686

Contents

Acknowledgements

We express our deep gratitude to the late Avadhesh Kumar Singh for taking up this project and for his constant encouragement and help in the last few years. His vision continues to inspire us in this journey.

We are grateful to T.S. Satyanath for conceptualising and initiating the project with Avadhesh Kumar Singh. We received support from many distinguished scholars and individuals in the field, which helped us to move forward. Special mention must be made of Amiya Dev, Nabaneeta Dev Sen, Sukanta Chaudhuri, and Shamsuddin Chowdhury for their help and support. We received invaluable assistance with Sanskrit quotations from Pratap Bandyopadhyay and Probal Sen. Mitra Mukherjee Parikh, Probal Dasgupta, Nandita Basu and Sudeshna Datta Chaudhuri were always there for us with their constructive suggestions. Carol Charbonneau graciously read and commented on several translations. We were also enriched by Tapobrata Ghosh's comments on the translation of Jagadish Bhattacharya's essay. We thank all of them for their gracious help and encouragement.

We are grateful to Mahuya Dey Biswas, Chhanda Basu, Shouvik Panti, Anindita Bhaduri, Debdip Dhibar, Debalina Sen, Alakananda Guha, Rajib Chaudhuri, Anamika Das, Paramita Bhattacharya, Ritankar Mukhopadhyay, Ayan Chatterjee and Preeta Bhattacharya for their help in the preparation of this volume. Special thanks are due to Sucheta Ghoshal and Sayamindu Dasgupta for their care and assistance. We are also grateful to the librarian and all members of the staff of Sahitya Akademi Library, New Delhi; Central Library, University of Delhi; National Library, Kolkata, and Central Library, Jadavpur University.

Copyright holders were very generous with their permissions, and we thank each one of them for their kind cooperation. We are grateful to the late Sankha Ghosh, Alokeranjan Dasgupta and Debes Ray for valuable comments on the translation of their texts. We are also thankful to Sanghamitra Dutta Gupta, Ranjan Bhattacharya, Minakshi Datta, Jishnu Dey, Abul Hasnat, Satarupa Sengupta, Satadeepa Gupta, Tathagata Bhattacharya, Bishakha Roy, Abhijit Siraj, Dipankar Basu, Sushobhan Bhattacharyya, and Sanjida Khatun for their generosity. We also thank Samantak Das of

Hirendranath Datta Foundation and Pratap Kumar Mondal of Orient Book Company in this regard.

We gratefully acknowledge the constant support received from Kiran Singh and Shashank S. Sinha. Special thanks are due to Rimina Mohapatra for her patience and guidance at every stage and to Sathish Mohan, the copyeditors and all members of the Routledge team who were responsible for giving a final shape to the volume. And finally, this project would not have been possible without the hard work and commitment of all our translators. We will not thank them formally because this volume also belongs to them.

Translators

Debapriya Basu teaches English Literature at the Indian Institute of Technology, Guwahati, India. Her primary field of research is women's writing of the English Renaissance period and digital scholarly editing. Her other interests include translation, genre studies, and the philosophy of technology. She is a contributor in *Shaping the Discourse: Women's Writings in Bengali Periodicals 1865–1947*.

Sucheta Bhattacharya is Professor of Comparative Literature, Jadavpur University, India. Among her other interests are translations, realist literature of 19th century England and Bengal by 'non-canonical' women writers, and border studies with a focus on the life and culture of the people living on the Indo-Bangladesh border.

Parthasarathi Bhaumik teaches Comparative Literature in Jadavpur University, India. He is also Joint-Director of the School of Cultural Texts and Records, Jadavpur University. His recent publications include *Mahatma o Kabi* (Bangla translation of Letters and Debates Between Gandhi and Tagore: 1915–1941), 2020 and *Bengalis in Burma: A Colonial Encounter (1886–1948)*.

Tapan Chakraborty retired from the Audit Policy wing of the State Bank of India after spending over thirty-four years with the bank in various capacities. After retirement he worked with CINI, Jharkhand, India, for several years.

Paromita Chaudhuri teaches English Literature at Asutosh College, Kolkata, India. Her area of interest focuses on issues related to language studies.

Samantak Das is Professor of Comparative Literature and the Director of the School of Cultural Texts and Records, Jadavpur University, India.

Probal Dasgupta has taught linguistics and Esperanto in the United States, Australia, and India. He is President, Akademio de Esperanto (2016–2022) and President of World Esperanto Association (2007–2013). He has publications in Bangla, English, and Esperanto, concerning linguistics, literature, translation, and philosophy. His books include *The Otherness of English: India's Auntie Tongue Syndrome* (1993), *Inhabiting Human Languages: The Substantivist Visualization* (2011), and *Merur prarthana: bishuber uttor* (2015).

Anirban Datta is a marketing, communication and media professional in Kolkata, India, who took to translation in 2016. He translates world poetry and songs both from Bangla to English and from English to Bangla.

Sudeshna Datta Chaudhuri is Assistant Professor at KIIT, Bhubaneswar, India. Her areas of interest are speculative fiction, mythology, translation, and Hindustani Classical Music. Her translation of Ursula Le Guin's *A Wizard of Earthsea* (*Irasindhur Jadukar*) has been recently published.

Doyeeta Majumder is Assistant Professor of English Literature at Jadavpur University, India. Her primary research interests include early modern law and literature, political and juridical theory, and intellectual history. Her publications include *Tyranny and Usurpation: The New Prince and Lawmaking Violence in Early Modern Drama* (2019) and *Rajpurush* (2012), a Bangla translation of Machiavelli's *Il Principe*.

Sipra Mukherjee is Professor, Department of English, West Bengal State University, India. Her research interests are religion, caste, and power – areas in which she has published extensively. She has translated Manoranjan Byapari's autobiographical text *Itibritte Chandal Jiban* into English.

Sreemati Mukherjee is Professor in the Department of Performing Arts at Presidency University, India. Her areas of academic competence are feminist theory, narrative studies, postcolonial theory, and performance theories, and she has several publications in these areas. She also makes documentaries on subjects of contemporary cultural relevance. Her most recent publication is *The Many Dialogues of Sri Sri Ramakrishna Kathamrita* (2021).

Sujaan Mukherjee is a Ph.D. researcher at the Department of English, Jadavpur University, India, and works on urban space and colonial memory. He has also worked on the physical cultures of Bengal and is interested in museums as public cultural spaces. He co-edited with Sajni Mukherji a 1937 pamphlet by Humphry House titled *I Spy with My Little Eye* (2018).

Bimbabati Sen is a publishing and digital learning professional based in Delhi, India. She also runs 'Onubaad', a project that translates lesser-known Bangla texts to English.

Notes on transliteration and references

Transliteration

Diacritical marks in this volume have only been used in the case of Sanskrit words and those from *Charyapada*, where the conventions are slightly different. However, for a few common titles, like the *Ramayana*, and for names of characters diacritics have not been used.

For Bangla, the following format of equivalents has been used:

অ, আ = a, ই, ঈ = i, উ, ঊ = u, এ = e, ঐ = ai, ও = o, ঔ = au, স, শ = s, ষ = sh, ক্ষ = ksh, জ্ঞ = jn.

In certain cases, particularly in the context of poetry, deviations from the rule had to be made as for example in the transliteration of অ as 'o' and not 'a' to maintain rhythmic patterns. There may be certain other deviations as well, and we request the indulgence of readers.

Place names and proper names follow standard official forms. The words 'leela' and 'geeti' are also exceptions where convention has been followed.

Bangla names

The word 'Bangla' for the language instead of the anglicised 'Bengali' has been retained in the volume. In general, authentic Bangla forms of names have been kept rather than the anglicised versions – Bandyopadhyay and Chattopadhyay, for instance, instead of Banerjee and Chatterjee.

In Bangla, names are represented by first names and not by titles. Titles have been used in introductions while first names have been retained in translated texts.

References

References to quotations in the texts have been provided most often by the editors. On a few occasions, the versions cited are from a later date than the original articles as earlier versions were not accessible.

Introduction

Subha Chakraborty Dasgupta and Subrata Sinha

This volume presents essays related to Bangla literature, both in its scripted and non-scripted forms, within the larger project of 'Critical Discourses in South Asia'. The essays are chiefly from the mid-19th to the 1970s of the 20th century, but there are a few from a later date as well that either look back at the period or continue the discursive chain in an important manner. The essays primarily foreground expectations from *sahitya* or literature and performative modes in discussions regarding their reasons for being, their mode of existence, their critical interventions leading to new turning points in the history of literature, and their relations with the global literary community. However, the essays also lead to other pathways of reading and interpretation. They provide, for instance, a spectacular array of material details that constitute a particular space – in this context, both a pre-colonial and a postcolonial one. The force inherent in the materiality often inflects received ideas and concepts and, within the culture made up of many different strands, generates a discursive field that continues to remain distinctive within a larger shared human legacy. The tone of the essays varies, and efforts have been made to retain some elements of the tonality as tonal modulations also structure thought in significant ways.

With the world today in the grips of a pandemic affecting the lives of all and with the most fragile the worst-affected, certain realities demand precedence and urgency over others. It therefore becomes important to revisit the discursive area constructing the literary field in Bangla from certain perspectives. It is perhaps necessary to focus acts of reading on an aesthetics that is in a continuous process of emergence at the meeting point of several changing human and civilisational considerations – with imagination in its many modes contributing to the construction of affective communities and hence processes of justice and equality and, thereby, of inclusion of cross-cultural communicative efforts centred on enabling the humans across the globe, of the prioritisation of small, local viewpoints, of bringing back the non-humans as a significant part of the contemporary, and many such issues, however old they may be. Notes on the essays that follow are guided, to the extent possible, by such perspectives. It is important to mention that a

DOI: 10.4324/9781003224686-1

detailed engagement with the history of literary discourse in Bengal would take up several volumes. This volume merely presents some of the most relevant essays addressing the aforementioned perspectives.[1]

Texts on a few foundational cultural aspects

The background to the discursive field appears spacious and diverse in the first text by Shashibhusan Dasgupta, the noted scholar and literary critic, on Bengal in the *Charyageeti*. Charyapadas or songs of realisation by practitioners of the Buddhist Sahajiya cult, written sometime between the 8th and the 12th centuries, and *Srikrishnakirtan* by Boru Chandidas written between 1350 and 1400 CE were the only two manuscripts before 1500 CE that had been recovered. Dasgupta takes up *Charyageeti* as a cultural text of people speaking Bangla, Maithili, Asamiya, and Odia without losing sight of the esoteric nature of the songs expressed in the 'twilight' or shadowed language sheltering a silent unutterable realisation. The *dohas* are replete with images from the lifeworld of the indigenous people – their occupations, domestic arrangements, love lives, animals, rivers, mountains, trees, and flowers. These images are rendered into metaphors of *sadhana* along the Buddhist Sahajiya or simple path. Despite the sectarian content, the literary space in this early period linked with the lives and occupations of common people appears integrative. These early texts also suggest that the core of the 'literary' in the region holds a deep realisation that can only be hinted at through symbols and metaphors on the one hand, and on the other, the evanescent beauty and the drama of everyday life with both its power structures and its humanity. One encounters an irreducible space that at the same time is intricately entangled with social processes.

The second text by Upendranath Bhattacharya to some extent follows the first in taking up the tradition of the Baul singers in Bengal. Bhattacharya looks at the origin and early history of the Baul cult that he thinks emerged in the first half of the 17th century. The cult includes the Radha–Krishna or the Prakriti–Purusha union along with the spiritualism of the Upanishads and the Sufi tradition and, in practice, takes up elements from the Buddhist-Sahajiya and a transformed version of the Vaishnav-Sahajiya sects. The importance of performative music in religious cults of Bengal particularly among the Bauls and Fakirs for whom it is one of the most significant forms of expression to convey religious and philosophical thoughts is underscored in the text. The Baul tradition has travelled to the world today partly because of the Baul philosophy being based on an apparent simplicity of experience of a personal god, its syncretism, and its renunciation of a traditional way of life. It received a new impetus with Tagore's foregrounding of the Baul as an upholder of 'a free spirit' in his own works. Today, with a vitalised performative tradition, the Baul singer has found her place with others at the core of people's search for the meaning of 'freedom,' and through it to an alternative way of life and living.

The next text in the compilation by Dineshchandra Sen, one of the first historians of Bangla literature, moves over to Sri Chaitanya, the proponent of Gaudiya Vaishnavism, who lived in the latter half of the 15th century (1486 CE to 1533/1534 CE). His mode of worshipping the god Krishna with ecstatic song and dance and his piety linked with *bhaktirasa* led to a new age in medieval Bangla literature and was instrumental in giving rise to different genres in an emotional, performative mode. In the 16th century, Sri Chaitanya's life inspired a large body of hagiographic texts based on legend, hearsay, and various hermeneutic enquiries while his life provided inspiration for more than one hundred and fifty poets spanning over three hundred years from the 16th to the 18th century. The mortality of such a *bhakta* was not easy to accept, and the hagiographies suggested different ends for Sri Chaitanya. Dineshchandra Sen writing in the 20th century accepts the discourse of faith, engages with it, and then moves towards an empirical account of the passing away of Sri Chaitanya, marking an important moment in the framing of modern historiography. A hospitable dialogue between faith and reason is evident in the essay. In the context of literary historiography, it is important to mention the first attempt by Ramgati Nyayaratna in 1872/73 to write a history of Bangla literature entitled *Bangla Bhasha o Bangla Sahitya Bishayak Prastab* (Treatise on Bangla Language and Literature) where periods were divided into the ancient, middle, and the modern.

As stated earlier, the doctrine of devotion that had taken hold of Bengal with the emergence of Sri Chaitanya had a great influence on the religion, literature, and social life of the region. In the essay on the Gaudiya Vaishnav order, Bishnupada Bhattacharya states that 'such a complete evolution of devotion has not been seen in the history of any other race'. The statement has extensive implications suggesting the evolution of an attitude that had at its centre a surrender of the ego, which in turn had the potential to develop a non-anthropocentric approach to life, where man was not at the centre of the world, for a large number of people following the cult and for a still larger number coming under its influence through literature, music etc. In the context of *rasa*, the proponents of the school argued that the love of a devotee for his god was not a *vyabhicāribhāva* (transient feeling) as suggested by Bharata and accepted by others, but it was a *sthāyibhāva* (durable emotion) in its own right. In fact, they felt that love for the divine was the only sthāyibhāva of human life, and 'savouring it in its emotive-affective form through a surge of the *hlādini śakti* (the potency that rendered joy) seemed to be the prime goal of human life.' The 19th century would start looking at the phenomenon in a different manner. Bankimchandra Chattopadhyay, for instance, writes about the necessity of creating a literature different from the *Gitagovindam* type, which would incite men to action.[2] Rabindranath Tagore, while drawing extensively upon the Vaishnav literary tradition, in *Chaturanga* (1916) critiques the cult in its gradual change into a degenerative form where people may be kept in a perpetual state of idle ecstasy and sometimes as the victims of oppression of a self-seeking master. However, from today's vantage point, the worldview of a large section of the people with their lives centred on devotion and its concomitants deserves to be remembered and explored and not simply shrugged aside by the modern as symptomatic of a feudal social system.

Early texts, decolonisation, and visions of the future

The early years of the 19th century brought transformations in many areas of life, thought, and expression through initiatives taken up by William Carey and his group, Rammohan Roy, Iswarchandra Vidyasagar, and others. Literary discourse in the world of print gradually took shape primarily through journals. Critical writings on literature and book reviews were initiated in *Bibidhartha Sangraha* (1851), edited by Rajendralal Mitra and then Kaliprasanna Sinha, and in *Masik Patrika* (1854), edited by Pyarichand Mitra and Radhanath Sikdar, two of the earliest journals that stated their primary aim to be the welfare of the people.

Colonial issues, to some extent at least, were placed at the centre of critical discourse in Bengal by the mid-19th century. Rangalal Bandyopadhyay's lecture on Bangla poetry entitled 'Bangla Kabita Bishayak Prabandha' (An essay on Bangla poetry) in 1852 provides one of several entry points to the discourse. Bandyopadhyay is responding to an allegation that no poet was ever born in Bengal as the country was in bondage for such a long period of time. He takes up examples from Homer, Bhartṛhari, Tulsidas, and Jayadeva to argue against the statement by demonstrating that the poet was free in his innermost consciousness. He states that after Sanskrit it is Bangla that has the necessary foundation on which a rich poetic literature can emerge and appeals to the people to rise to the occasion and create a new body of poetry that will be a part of world literature for he thinks that the soil is fertile, the seeds are ready, provisions are there, and the only need is to find the farmer.[3]

Several years later, one would see the dazzling appearance of Michael Madhusudan Dutt's *Meghnad Badh Kavya* (1861) bringing in a kind of renaissance in Bangla literature. *Meghnad Badh Kavya* gives rise to several critical writings; issues are debated, and there is a gradual coming to terms with the phenomenon of modernity in Bangla literature, which at that point of time indicates moving away from tradition and questioning it. A new confidence emerges, despite controversies, and after the death of Madhusudan Dutt, Bankimchandra Chattopadhyay pays tribute to him in his journal *Bangadarsan* (August 1873) saying:

> If a European, proud of his modern wealth asks us, how can you be relied upon? – Has Bengal given birth to a human personality? – We will tell him we had Sri Chaitanyadev among preachers, Raghunath among philosophers, Sri Jayadeva and Sri Madhusudan among poets![4]

The construction of a tradition becomes an important agenda in some of the early texts in the journals, and this is evidenced in the earliest essay (1854) in this volume by Iswar Chandra Gupta on poets from the not-so-far-away oral tradition. In *Sambad-Prabhakar*, the newspaper edited by him, Gupta regularly wrote on the lives of ancient poets and *kabiwallahs*, or professional versifiers composing instant poetry on social occasions and often entering organised competitive sessions with other *kabiwallahs*. Gupta, as Bishnu Dey remarks in his essay in this volume, is the last of the poets looking back nostalgically to the past at a critical moment in history. The essay is a record of the problems faced by collectors of oral texts in the absence of any infrastructure. Gupta's style is an amalgamation of guilelessness, sophistication, and wit, which often provides a double-edged note to the discourse. He brings to the forefront many marginalised members of society who composed skilled verses in the common everyday language. He consciously points out their position as low castes who yet wrote with such spontaneous sophistication. The attitude is symptomatic of the gap that had firmly set in between the rising middle-class intellectuals and people from other sections of society.

The goals focusing on the welfare of the people receive a more crystallised dimension with an undercurrent of a still semi-conscious decolonising aspiration in the works of Bankimchandra Chattopadhyay. There is a projection into the future with both realist and utopic visions for a new nation. Pragmatic ends are evident in Chattopadhyay's manifesto entitled 'A Message to the New Writers of Bengal' (1886) anthologised in this volume. He states most emphatically that one should write only if one feels one is writing for the good of the people and the country or to create beauty. According to him a work which is not true, is against Dharma, and is written to disgrace or hurt others, or even to serve a selfish purpose, should be discarded. This however is a manifesto with its own generic dynamic, and it is important to look at his articulations on the purpose of art in some of his essays such as *Uttarcharit* (1872), where he asserts that the purpose of ethical wisdom and that of *kavya* is the same. 'The poets are the teachers of the world, but they do not teach through explanations of morals, nor through stories. They dictate the purification of the world's soul by creating beauty that is perfect.'[5] In a memorable statement, he also declares that that which is both in accord with nature and in excess of it is kāvya. What also needs to be pointed out is that the utopic visions cannot simply be conflated with nationalist goals because there is always an excess, both a concern for the immediate future that would be an agenda in the construction of a nation, sometimes bringing forward a revivalist spirit, as well as a functional ideal for a *longue durée*, a non-visible and probably ever-receding end. Chattopadhyay incidentally also points out in the introduction to his edited journal *Bangadarsan* (1872) the importance of writing for all classes of readers and maintains that the growing gap between the rich and the poor in all domains will continue to be a hindrance to the development of the region.

A significant number of periodicals such as *Bharati, Sahitya, Manasi o Marmabani, Bharatbarsha, Narayan, Dasi, Balak, Bangabani, Sabuj Patra, Basumati, Prabasi,* and *Bichitra* emerge in the late 19th and early 20th centuries. Pramatha Chaudhuri, the editor of *Sabuj Patra* (1914), a journal responsible for bringing in a new era in Bangla literary criticism facilitating the use of *chalit* or colloquial Bangla instead of the earlier *sadhu* or sophisticated written form, talks about the new spirit of life in evidence during the period and at the same time is critical of several illusions at work in society in his introduction. He sees the importance of drawing upon both tradition and Western culture iterating that a union of the two, and not their conflict, is necessary to move forward. Elsewhere, too, he not only acknowledges the gifts of English education, but also insists that a mere imitation of the colonial masters will not lead to any positive development. Learning has to be integrated with one's own environment. Chaudhuri is not in favour of literature that serves a programmatic end and is one of the first to uphold the aesthetic as a sign of the awakened mind. Bankimchandra Chattopadhyay's time is left behind in this new turn rejecting the utilitarian spirit in literature although Chaudhuri does comment that even if literature cannot provide for the livelihood of human beings, it can prevent them from committing suicide. Symptomatic of a new period or a postcolonial move is also the attempt to take the people out of their inertia that, Chaudhuri emphasises, acts as a driving spirit of the journal.

Dialogue with European literatures: affinities and bondings

An essay by Bankimchandra Chattopadhyay entitled 'Sakuntala, Miranda and Desdemona' (1876) is a point of beginning for a whole series of articles in Indian literary criticism comparing Kālidāsa and Shakespeare. Goals of comparison differ, and often two masters from cultures of the colonising and the colonised are evaluated. This piece, however, offers a study of vibrant affinities in the conceptualisation of *Abhijñānaśakuntalam* and *The Tempest*, both of which are 'poetic plays', as the author explains, and different from *Othello* that is 'drama' in the European sense. Differences, particularly in the cultural context, are highlighted, and the happy conclusion is that while the young Sakuntala is similar to Miranda, the more mature is comparable to Desdemona. The comparative perspective is that of a *sahṛdaya* in the best traditions of comparativism.

Haraprasad Shastri, the eminent multifaceted scholar, continues the tradition as he compares three popular writers in Bengal – Kālidāsa, Bankimchandra Chattopadhyay, and Byron – in his essay 'The Bengali Youth and Three Poets' (1878). His comparative approach is framed by the ruling paradigm of the period – literature's contribution to the formation of society and, in this case, its contemporary role in framing the character of the country's youth. His viewpoints regarding the *Ramayana* and the *Mahabharata*, as well as many of the popular authors of medieval and modern Western and

Indian literatures, demonstrate his substantially different attitude to tradition, eschewing both dogmatism and received notions, while opening up the field of reading. The larger theme of his text is the relation between the individual and society and the different ways of achieving happiness through this relationship in popular texts of different ages. Shastri's conclusion is that Chattopadhyay writes to evoke patriotism and Kālidāsa to generate love for all living beings, and in both cases the purpose is social happiness. Byron, the author states, writes for humanitarian reasons, and his purpose is to evoke happiness derived from breaking social norms. Byron's lessons are contemporary. The focus here, as also in Bankimchandra Chattopadhyay's manifesto, is on the urban, young, educated middle-class male: literature in print will continue to exclude large sections of people.

Dialogue with European literatures: towards the articulation of difference

A reading of the epic as genre in 1902 by Ramendrasundar Trivedi, the interdisciplinary scientist, in the volume is marked by an intrinsic difference from approaches to its classification in both Indian and European traditions. After a short introduction to the different Sanskrit and Bangla words in use for the word 'epic', Trivedi emphatically states that not all works designated as epic are worth the nomenclature. He thinks it is only the *Ramayana*, the *Mahabharata*, *The Iliad*, and *The Odyssey* that can be called epic. He compares the *Mahabharata* to the Himalayas with spectacular portrayals of its grandeur and, with a rhetorical flourish, upholds the spontaneous greatness of composition and the absence of a spurious art in the epic. He argues that what is deeply present in the consciousness of the people is the epic – it does not have to be read. One is aware of it without having read it and has knowledge of its characters and events. It is one of those rare 'texts' that belongs to all, and the author is careful to point out that the reading of the common person is in no way inferior to that of the scholar. Trivedi does not engage with the criteria for classification of the genre in any tradition but is content with projecting a strongly felt perspective on it and taking it to its logical conclusion. The perspective, in its difference, adds layers to the basic understanding of the genre.

In a similar manner, Mohitlal Majumdar in 1947 looks at the notion of 'tragedy' in the Western context and the absence of the realisation of its full potential in Bangla literature. He uses the word 'tragedy' in a general sense, linked with 'rasa' and not with the mode of enunciation. According to Majumdar, tragedy is the dramatic embodiment of the 'rasa' of sorrow, and unlike other modes it not only makes the *sahṛdaya* taste the rasa, but also leaves a forceful impact on her. The Greeks had a deep sense of proportion and harmony in life and nature, and they contemplated this harmony in terms of religion. A violation of nature or harmony led to tragic consequences and hence the presence of an unparalleled repertoire of tragedies in

Greek literature. Majumdar also speaks of the image of the crucifixion of Christ at the heart of Western culture and its many repercussions. In Bengal, he states, one is not completely overwhelmed by 'the cruelty of fate' – the system of beliefs does not allow the people to look at sorrow as a permanent state. Hence, Majumdar argues, in trying to give form to tragedy, Bangla literature has only been able to create poetic theatre marked by pathos and occasionally a fragmented form of a tragic poem as in Tagore's 'Parisodh' or narrative literature where variants are at work as in Bankimchandra Chattopadhyay's novels or where sorrow is finally transgressed as in Saratchandra Chattopadhyay's *Srikanta* (I–IV, 1917–1933). The position of the author shifting along a spectrum of different degrees of the insider–outsider leads to potentially new configurations of thought.

Sanskrit aesthetics, continuity, and reinterpretations

In Bangla literary thought, Sanskrit aesthetics, in particular *rasaśāstra*, was an all-pervasive phenomenon in concepts related to the nature of poetry and its ends during the 19th and the early 20th centuries. Its absorption into the literary field rendered its overt expression unnecessary, and there were also reservations on the part of a few authors such as Madhusudan Dutt and Bankimchandra Chattopadhyay about the relevance or adequacy of some of its formulations. Atulchandra Gupta's *Kavyajijnasa* (1928) based on themes of *dhvani* and *rasa* with illustrations from modern Bangla literature brings back the Sanskrit aesthetic tradition in literature as part of contemporary discourse. But a deep engagement with the tradition remains negligible because of a set of different social, individual, and aesthetic needs generating a different interpretative approach to literature, while some of its basic concepts continue to provide foundations for new poetic systems.

Writers during the period also draw upon Sanskrit poetics for different ends, and in the essay 'A consideration of Literature' (1852) by Rajendralal Mitra, the pathbreaking historiographer, it serves to contribute to the general objective of constructing an ideal society. Mitra does not write specifically about rasa or even *kāvya* but constructs three categories to define the several functions of utterance where there is an addressee, namely, to impart knowledge, to evoke rasa, and to influence or to change the direction of people's thought – the logical, the emotive, and the ethical. The last is important to him as it requires several skills, and, like Cicero, he is aware that persuasive utterance without a sense of the just may be dangerous. He does not state the matter categorically, but his purpose is evident from the title of his essay and from his enumeration of the possibilities of *doṣas* or blemishes in utterance drawing upon Sanskrit poetics where, anything that is employed in an improper or indecent manner is doṣa, and then again, the doṣas spring from logical fallacies. An attempt to create an order that is different from the fine but complex system of Sanskrit rhetoricians, and that is also more accessible, is evident in the short piece.

The second essay in the volume that deals with rasaśāstra is Rajshekhar Bose's 'Rasa and the Question of Taste' (1927) written in a humorous mode and with reference to Freud, whose works were being critically studied by his brother, the psychoanalyst Girindrasekhar Bose, at the time. Bose looks at the whole question of *auchitya* or propriety in literature, links it with taste, and then centres the question around desire and rasaśāstra's engagement with desire as the first durable emotion. He looks at the frailties of human beings and their circumstances bringing a taste of the contemporary and the mundane to literature. The essay also needs to be read against the background of the fervent debates on obscenity in Bangla periodicals at the time, reflecting norms and values of English Victorian society. Bose's tone is playful throughout with the hint of an attempt towards the retrieval of sanity. The essay falls in pattern with others of the period in the volume as Bose ends with the statement that the greatest poet is one who can overcome all complexities and contribute to the reconstruction of taste while keeping the common good in focus.

Rasaśāstra is absorbed into the modern tradition but not always in a seamless fashion, particularly when writers choose to engage with it in a conscious manner.

Towards Rabindranath Tagore and the aesthetics of interdependence

Jagadish Bhattacharya's text from a later date 'The Poetic Mind' (1979) tries to conceptualise the field of poetry in the late 19th and early 20th centuries with reference to Sanskrit poetics and to writers of the period. At the heart of his text is the central question of what constitutes the poetic mind, and evoking two phrases from Sanskrit aesthetics '*aghaṭanaghaṭanapaṭīyasībuddhi*', an intellect skilled in causing unusual occurrences, and '*apūrvavastunirmāṇakṣamāprajñā*', a wisdom capable of shaping unprecedented matter, he moves over to two Bangla writers, Madhusudan Dutt and Tagore. He engages with the response of Rabindranath Tagore in his essays on the significance and material of poetry where he focuses on the presence of wonder, love, and imagination that includes empathy in the poetic mind. Each of the words holds special significance in today's world with the potential for entering into relationships with both the human and the non-human world bringing in perspectives of justice[6] and also an ecological approach to aesthetics. In conclusion, Bhattacharya looks at the role of knowledge and practice along with genius in the formation of the poetic mind. His poem at the end of the essay can be taken to be an iconic representation of the figure of the poet with an amalgamation of tropes from classical, sectarian, and folk traditions.

The views of Rabindranath Tagore mentioned earlier are found in the three short seldom translated essays on the meaning, material, and the evaluating criteria of literature written in 1903. They represent certain central ideas of Tagore that take their full form in later works. His considerations on literature are based upon the premise of the self's relationship with the world, both as nature or even the cosmos, and with other human beings. In the essays, he talks of evaluating a writer with reference to his ability to make the outside world his own in a lasting and intense manner, and later in his talk on World Literature (*Visvasahitya* 1907), he speaks about a human being's worth measured in terms of his relationship with other human beings. The recurring statements in the three essays of the desire of the writer to make the external world intimately one's own and then to give it back to others in word-pictures and word-music to make it their very own unveil an integrative relationship with the world, which is echoed in the entire plan and design of Visva-Bharati University. Elsewhere in his lecture on 'What is Art' (1916), he juxtaposes the creative endeavours of artists with that of god. Just as god out of his surplus takes delight in creating the universe, so also human beings in their surplus break out of the bonds of functionality and self-preservation imposed on them by everyday life and create art. Art has its own purpose and delights in its creativity. The vision of some to integrate aesthetics and the commitment to build an ideal society in the late 19th century finds a fulfilling structure in the works of Tagore. The future in his case extends into time and not just the immediate future, and the imaginary of the globe extends to the planetary. The individual takes his place at the centre, but then the individual is also defined by his desire for bonding.

The conversation on the poetics of relation is continued in the text by Alokeranjan Dasgupta, a modern poet and critic, as he engages with Tagore's notion of world literature and his belief that what is universal in literature stands on the base of the local. Dasgupta feels that although Tagore draws upon Goethe's concept of world literature, he is closer to our times. His focus is on the relationship of the part to the whole, an aspect evident in Goethe to some extent but not foregrounded as such. This relationship is extended to rural or folk literature where Tagore suggests the presence of folk literature at the origins of elite literature. It is Herder and not Goethe, the author feels, who inspires him to find this model of a sustainable relationship between base and structure, the rural and the elite. Tagore is also looking for deep and close ties between the literatures of the East and West, the regional and the international, while Dasgupta himself with poet Sankha Ghosh in the introduction to their volume of translated poems *Sapta Sindhu Das Diganta* (1963) writes about modern poetry giving form to a universal poetic language, an act that they think is extremely necessary at a time of fragmentation witnessed by trends in high modernist poetry.

The many 'moderns' in Bangla poetic discourse: explorations and the carving out of new relations

One of the markers of modernist poetry in Bengal was a conscious attempt to move away from the influence of Tagore. In the first three decades of the 20th century, new journals such as *Dhumketu*, *Kallol*, *Kalikalam*, and *Sanibarer Chithi* emerged taking up the cause of modernist literature in different forms. The *Kallol* group in particular drew the attention of the literati with their conviction that Tagore's poetry was not adequate for them and their times. However, it was with the emergence of the journals *Parichay* and *Kavita* that a quite different kind of poetry, identified as modern, appeared in Bangla literature.

Buddhadeva Bose, one of the key architects of modern Bangla poetry and editor of *Kavita*, in the essay on Tagore and his successors (1954) in this volume, analyses why Tagore posed a 'problem' to young poets who were swept away by his genius and who by merely imitating the external forms of his creation were unable to create poetry of any lasting effect. He, of course, also underscores the important contribution of Kazi Nazrul Islam in demonstrating poetry's ability to incite revolt. Bose shows how modern poetry emerged by making meaningful use of Tagore's influence, with some stepping aside and others confronting him by 'assimilating him fully'.

Bose translates Baudelaire's *Les Fleurs du Mal*, poems by Rilke and Hölderlin, and also Kālidāsa's *Meghadūtam* following a long line of Bengali poets translating foundational texts from both foreign and Indian traditions. His long introduction to the translation of Baudelaire's text upholds Baudelaire as the modern poet par excellence who introduced the dark and the sinister as an integral part of the poetic universe. His point in choosing Baudelaire is also to look outside the world of the colonial masters. Elsewhere, in the preface to his translation of *Meghadūtam*, he highlights the importance of translating and rewriting ancient poetry in the context of the contemporary. The emergence of the 'modern' in Bangla literature and literary discourse linked with the general global anxiety of the period and the search for a new language to express the individual's sense of crisis have a clear stamp of European modernist literature. Yet, the socio-economic situation linked with European modernism is at a different stage in the country, the time scale is different, and the language of poetry and its related discourse bear marks of a different tradition of writing. Again, this particular kind of literature of avant-garde writers, often highlighted as the one and only kind of modernist literature in the region, brings in a distinctive gap between the 'popular circuit' and the 'cultivated circuit', leaving out the largest section of potential readers from access to the poems and the related discourse.

Poets often demonstrate an awareness of the issue. Sudhindranath Datta, the poet and editor of *Parichay* (1931), writes in his essay on 'The Liberation of Poetry' in the first volume of his journal that the first poets represented the community and its life in general, while the modern poet is merely a meteoric fragment, signifying the end of a journey. However, he upholds the heroism of the modern poet, as with a 'superhuman' effort linked with 'pure consciousness', 'authenticity', and 'a self-effacing resolve,' he continues to move on knowing that his creativity has even less meaning in a world which itself is of little significance. The poet from Bengal has on his own arrived at a site inscribed by Western modernity and its experience of an existential angst that he takes to the limit along with a matching density of language while still underscoring the affirmative strength of the poet. Datta also asserts that the link with the real and the question of authenticity have to be at the forefront of the poetic consciousness. In fact, the poet has to 'walk the streets' and enter the marketplace for there is no short-cut to poetry. No longer is there the projection into the future. The preoccupation with the present, a hallmark of modernist poetry, enters the landscape, and despite the call for moving into the marketplace, the diction remains distanced.

Jibanananda Das, often acknowledged as the greatest poet after Tagore, insists on the validity of imagination, and within imagination, he insists on intellect and experience nourished by poetic traditions of the past and the present in his essay 'On poetry' (1939) in this volume. He argues for an autonomous space for poetry in the modern world. Poetry, he asserts, questions all existing norms and creates a new world order that has an 'integral, subterranean' relation with life. It does not seek utilitarian purposes, and for poetry to enter the framework of society, the masses would need a 'change of heart' or else only third-rate poets would be appreciated. Das does not know who can catalyse that change, and he feels as long as that does not happen, the poet will continue to roam the streets, take refuge in nature and among the crowds, and strike out with the 'rebounding power of his imagination'. Das in his poetry seeks a dwelling in nature and brings a whole new range of sensibilities with the use of striking synaesthetic imageries. The future is not the immediate future, and the present is both isolating and non-isolating with its extension into time and place. The essay also works with several images from nature, making it an integral part of the modern. That remains the unique contribution of this poet whose poems remain accessible to all.

From a different viewpoint, Bishnu Dey, the socialist poet considerably influenced by Eliot, explores the meaning of the progressive in poetry, which he affirms is linked with a historical perspective in keeping with scientific approaches towards reality and with a focus on an integrated technique. According to Dey, a dedication to technique and an understanding of one's personal crisis as being part of a larger historical one allow the writer to stay away from static received notions of art. The centrality of the subject is questioned in his statement. The author then looks at the history of Bangla literature foregrounding writers who had kept faith with perspectives of the common people. The essay concludes by pointing out that writers are 'not mere craftsmen, nor inspired souls' but 'complete human beings, both socially and individually'. The language is intricate and complex while there is a return to the future and the foregrounding of a certain tradition of inclusion of common perspectives from the lives of people.

A different aspect of the modern is embedded in the compilation of the first collection of poems by Muslim poets from the early age to the present, entitled *Kavya-Malancha* (1945) and edited by Abdul Kadir and Rezaul

Karim. Rezaul Karim who writes the introduction demonstrates the significant contribution of Bengali Muslims in the development of Bangla language and literature. The poems selected for the anthology, he states, reveal a rare quality of beauty and craftsmanship and follow the art for art's sake dictum. There are a few exceptions that take up theoretical or spiritual themes. A different kind of relational poetics emerges from the author's illustration of the extent to which Muslim poets in the Middle Ages established a connection with the culture of the region, accepted its traditions, used the stories and metaphors of the land, and gave a new form to Vaishnav songs of Bengal by submitting them to the Islamic tradition. Such an anthology receives shape as the acknowledgement of a sad and grim reality, a marker also of the period of the modern in Bengal.

It is necessary to point out that texts on poetry in this volume do not go beyond the early 1950s after which there is a different phase of modernist poetry in the same decade and then again a radical and complex period in the 1960s with a profusion of 'little magazines' by various groups. Along with the inward turning of poets, there is often also a greater sense of commitment leading to a new consciousness of the poetic self. An example from Sankha Ghosh in whose poems there is a constant journey from the deeper layers of the inner world to social issues and everyday events that in their turn lead to a reawakening of the self may be pertinent here. He gives an example from real life:

> If a desperate girl comes out from her home to join a procession of hunger driven people and if the police take her beyond the line that cannot be crossed and kill her – at that moment her mother's face flashes before her: that death along with the pain of the entire country can be the words of poetry itself. But poetry at that same moment can be the poet's own birth, his awakening, the immense rise of his shapeless, aggrieved love, blessed by the sadness stretching from one horizon to another.[7]

The event Ghosh talks about leads to the famous poem 'Jamunabati'. In the works of other poets like Subhas Mukhopadhyay, one finds broken human beings reflecting the dying out of human possibilities and the struggle of a poet on a rehumanising mission.

The 1960s were again a turbulent period in the history of India with both internal and external crises. While the economic situation deteriorated further, a large section of the youth was enkindled with a new energy and the dream of freedom from struggle and poverty. Various new journals and manifestos of various groups of poets began to emerge right from the early years of the decade. *Satabhisha* and *Krittibas* from the 1950s were two of the most popular poetry journals. *Krittibas*, whose founder editor was Sunil Gangopadhyay, in fact, became the platform for a new kind of poetry. As the editor stated in the sixteenth volume, 'Intense, indifferent, insane, patient, angry, respected, hungry, peaceful, beatnik, fearful, immersed, clever, good, haunted, religious and dissatisfied poets'[8] received their shelter in its pages. There was a deep-seated rebelliousness in the poets of the times, linked with rebelliousness the world over, only in this case it was against the conformist pattern inherent in the writings of what the new poets designated as 'middle class.' The Hungry Generation of poets, severely non-conformist, with Malay Roychowdhury as the leader, brought out several manifestos under the influence of Allen Ginsberg and the Beat generation of poets. They wanted to write of a hungry, wild, and uncivilised truth, giving rise to a poetry of violence. Sankha Ghosh in an article entitled 'Dui Basante' in *Desh* in 1962 stated that in the last few years it seemed as if the poets were ready to enter into a new adventure. As a new venture, they naturally felt a little bewildered at first, but the very strong steps towards losing and then trying to find directions led to a preparation for the new in modern poetry. Some poets later left the group and found their powerful individual voices as in the case of Shakti Chattopadhyay, while a new strand of confessional poetry also emerged during the period. There were a host of other voices, some quiet but powerful like those of Utpalkumar Basu, Binoy Majumdar, and Bhaskar Chakraborty, while others gradually moved over to a different scenario altogether in the late 1960s and the early 1970s with the Naxalbari Movement and with the Muktijuddha or the Liberation War in Bangladesh. A few women writers like Kabita Sinha, Vijaya Mukhopadhyay, Nabaneeta Dev Sen, and others would also find their own voice during the period.

There are numerous levels of diffraction of motifs, topoi, and sensibilities circulating within global modernity that constitute the modernist phase in Bangla poetry. It is important to take a more detailed look at them to arrive at an understanding of the period and issues related to the specificity of the region that at the same time is also subject to hegemonic forces of global modernity.

Structuring elements of narrative literature: retrieving history, form, and word

During the middle of the 19th century, narrative literature in prose was gaining ground in Bangla literature with the satirical picaresque kind of writing known as *naksa* and then the novel. The idea of the novel was quite protean in many of the critical texts. The term 'upanyas' that later became synonymous with the term 'novel' was used interchangeably with many other terms denoting other modes of narrative. There was a consciousness not only of its Western links, but also of the Arabic–Persian tradition. The intercultural negotiations were rich and layered but eventually resulted in the erasure of the sketch or the '*naksa*' that was replaced by the novel. During the latter half of the 19th century, two striking observations emerge from discourses on the novel – the notion of 'kavya' or poetic literature on the one hand and a hard-core didacticism on the other where the colonial context sometimes brings a new meaning to didacticism.[9]

The novel in Bangla proceeded along varied lines of development including different kinds of discourse in its form. As genre, it could emerge only when individuals took responsibility for their own lives and did not depend on an erstwhile fate and when there was a change in certain norms of society. In Bibhutibhushan Bandyopadhyay's *Pather Panchali* (1929), for instance, the first section ends with the death of Indir Thakrun, the old widow in the family, and with the end of the *kulin pratha* where a man from an upper caste could marry as many wives as he pleased and where the man–woman relationship did not have space to crystallise. It also marked an end to the reign of superstition where the eldest son in a family would always die because of a curse related to a forefather's evil deed. The curse does not seem to work anymore. With the change in the social structure, one enters the domain of the *künstlerroman* – the life of Apu – the child of parents who have settled down together as husband and wife to start a family, an idyllic space indispensable to the early novel. This novel does not merely work with the relationship between the individual and society, but also between the individual and the cosmos.

In general, the space of the novel and the short story occasioned a reading of the everyday life of the people, a history with multiple nuances that again to some extent brought in differences to the very form of the novel. Tarasankar Bandyopadhyay (1898–1971), the novelist with an intimate experience of village society, declares in his *Amar Sahitya Jiban* (1953) that in the depiction of rural life in the works of Saratchandra Chattopadhyay, he sees social authority always 'occupying one corner of the triangle'. Its power is immense and its revenge terrible. In his diverse experiences, he finds it 'bereft of any strength', but 'because its shape and weight were once enormous it lay like the body of Ghatotkacha on the path of society's progress'.[10] Foreign imperialist powers also give it protection, and the task of the novelist, Bandyopadhyay thinks, is to remove it bit by bit.

Manik Bandyopadhyay whose short piece 'Why I Write' (1944) appears in the volume may be compared to Tarasankar Bandyopadhyay, as a writer in the realist mode with a sharp and succinct style that has not been encountered before. Bandyopadhyay's novels look deeply into the grim realities of social lives enmeshed within varied power structures. In this short piece, he lays out the logical, material dimensions of writing. He feels that the ability to write depends on the impassioned urge for mental experience, an intense desire to write, along with a focused effort on learning the skill. The writer for him is a 'pen-pushing' labourer, and that metaphor introduces a new phase in Bangla literature.

Included in this volume is a representative essay by Ashapurna Devi, an autodidact who became one of the most important writers of fiction in the mid decades of the 20th century. In late 19th century, women had entered the field of discursive writing, and what could or could not be written was determined by the larger patriarchal society even in journals for women for a considerable period. Within this framework, several women writers like Swarnakumari Devi, Sita Devi, Shanta Devi, Anurupa Devi, and others created a strong background for the emergence of the woman writer in a conscious independent form. In Begum Rokeya's novella *Padmarag* (1924), married women of various religions leave their oppressive homes and come together in an institution. A separate, independent discourse emerges in the pages of the novel where married life is not the only destiny available to a woman, and looking after the family not the sole religion. Ashapurna Devi while subscribing to many of the traditional values also demonstrates the struggle of women through generations to carve out a little space for themselves. Her essay in this volume entitled 'My Thoughts on Literature' (1978) upholds her intense urge to write of a rich, complex and intricate inner world that unfolds itself in all its minute details to one who is looking at life from within the four walls of her house. A faith that a better and more just world will prevail, particularly for women, giving them the freedom to choose the small liberties they desire, instigates her desire to write.

A quite different voice is represented in Mahasweta Devi's text 'I/My Writings' (1976). The Bangla novel went through various changes during and after the struggle for independence with the middle-class writer struggling with different kinds of crises. A few writers try to move out into the domain of non-script traditions as in the case of Satinath Bhaduri and his novel *Dhorai Charit Manas* (I–II, 1949–1951), where Gandhi is a central figure of authenticity. Bhaduri draws upon oral traditions and mixed languages inflecting mainstream language and consciousness. A critique of political and civil society from below, the novel calls for a new language of literary discourse. Mahasweta Devi follows this tradition and takes it further. She takes up the question of the writer's deep commitment to her people and her time. Her writing, she states, is a protest against the gross unimaginable exploitation of people by those in power, and her themes are lessons learnt from history. But the raw material of history, she insists, has to be transformed into artistic material. She uses the living language of the common people to bring in this transformation; and she does not want any label such as 'a woman writer' to be attached to her.

The figure of the postcolonial writer is again encountered in Debes Ray's essay 'In Search of a New Form of the Novel' (1994). Written much later in time than the others in this volume, the experience recounted belongs in general to the postcolonial writer conscious of his ambivalent position. Ray mourns the loss of traditional narrative forms that cannot be recuperated. Nevertheless, drawing upon Alejo Carpentier's *The Lost Steps* (1953), he underscores the necessity to rediscover and then to lose again what has been discovered. Without the rediscovery, writers would continue to remain 'parasites of a metropolitan culture,' and without the renewed loss they would remain a victim to eternal nostalgia alienated from the contemporaneity of existence. As a novelist he feels that his task is to strive for accord between sentence and meaning lost in the course of colonised existence and to strive for a situation where words are not fabricated and no intervention exists between the word and its meaning. The concept of the word yoked to meaning producing kāvya in Sanskrit poetics has new bearings now – a new weight is imposed on 'word' in the context of memory, oblivion, and experience in postcolonial society. Contexts of solidarities are also constantly woven into the discursive text.

The language of theatre and its engagement with people

Theatre in the second half of the 19th century in Bengal was negotiating with folk, classical, and European traditions. By the end of the century, the non-mimetic, stylised indigenous forms often framed by music gradually started giving way to the proscenium stage and to themes rooted in history and social realism retaining some elements from its early forms. Girish Chandra Ghosh (1844–1912) was a pioneer in giving form to this new theatre, and he was succeeded by Sisir Kumar Bhaduri who gave it a new orientation. Bhaduri in his text 'Form in Theatre' speaks about the early days of Bangla theatre, the relevance of the indigenous *jatra* form, its loss of popularity because of its excessive reliance on mythological stories, the demand for a more realistic presentation, the role of British theatre groups, and the final emergence of permanent theatre houses in Bengal. He points out that people in the world of theatre were not ashamed of their imitation of European theatrical forms for they felt that they could do what the Europeans did and that they could do it better. Bhaduri, who had tried very hard to establish a national theatre, is also of the opinion that one should look back to indigenous forms in conceiving of a national theatre for, among other reasons, the jatra form was designed to serve people who could not afford costly entertainment and therefore was more inclusive.

An article by the noted contemporary poet and critic Sankha Ghosh on 'Theatre Moments and the Search for Language' (1961) focuses on Tagore and demonstrates the nature of critical formulations that were available in the domain of performance studies during the period. Ghosh explains why Tagore was drawing on verse forms when his contemporaries in Europe were turning towards prose as a necessary vehicle of drama. The relation between language and dramatic conflict is worked out in the essay, and the conclusion is that as complexities and rifts deepened in the personality of Tagore in the last stages of his life, the possibilities of conflict in his plays became more intense giving form to a language of appropriate strength. It was then that Tagore discovered the music of words that was capable of integrating conflict, and there was no more the necessity for the creation of 'a dramatic garland through music' or 'a musical garland through drama' as in the days of his early plays. Verbal expressions, on which Tagore seemed to have been losing faith in the dramatic context, were replaced by the 'universal' language of music, along with dance, that resonated with all groups of theatre goers.

Theatre from the early days in Bengal was also seen as a means of making the people conscious of their real state of oppression under the British rule as in Dinabandhu Mitra's play *Nil Darpan* (1860). A new chapter in the history of theatre in Bengal emerged with the staging of Bijan Bhattacharya's *Nabanna* in 1944 by the Gananatya Sangha or the Indian People's Theatre Association (IPTA) in Bengal. It was based on the famine of Bengal and was performed both in the city and in rural areas. Earlier Bulletin No. 1 of the IPTA had declared that the task of the movement was to portray vividly and memorably through the medium of the stage and other traditional arts the human details of important facts of our people's rights and enlighten them about their rights and the nature and solution of the problems facing them and also that the 'productions should be simple and direct so that the masses can easily appreciate, understand and also participate'[11] in their creation and production. The Gananatya Movement brought together many well-known personalities from the cultural field, but within a few years it began to divide into several groups. The history is complex, and the reasons are diverse. The last Congress of the IPTA was organised in 1957–58 (December–January) in Delhi.

Meanwhile, the realistic trend continued to give sustenance to theatre in Bengal, and under the leadership of Shambhu Mitra (1915–1997), the group Bohurupee was formed. Its first production was Tulsi Lahiri's *Pathik* (October 1949), a play based on an imminent conflict between the owners and workers of a coal mine. The group gradually emerged as a leader of the Nabanatya or the New Theatre movement. It produced a whole range of plays by Ibsen, Sophocles, and Ionesco among others and opened the space of theatrical experience for the people. The tradition of the Gananatya Sangha, however, was continued by Utpal Dutt (1929–1993), the famous playwright and actor, in his People's Little Theatre. In a parallel stream, commercial theatre also continued to flourish.

Badal Sircar did not belong to any group. In his Third Theatre, he moved out of the proscenium into public spaces with minimum props and improvised dialogue. Sircar's deliberations on 'The Language of Theatre' (1981) focused on the extra-linguistic aspects of language – on gestures, movements, and tonal qualities, with an emphasis on the inclusion of the audience. For Third Theatre, the goal is to touch the audience, bring them out of their complacence, enact a change of consciousness, and take them to some stage of action. Language is performance in his theatre, and one can see the radical difference in the examples that he gives. His theatre, however, was critiqued by many of the prominent theatre personalities of the time in Bengal while Sircar critiqued their use of the proscenium. The authenticity of Sircar's engagement with folk forms was questioned as also was the nature of the 'indigenous' against the background of his involvement with Richard Schechner and other foreign theatre persons and groups. Yet, the intensity of the theatrical experience had a powerful effect in inscribing a set of values based on theatre-as-action. Theatre personalities in India over the years have acknowledged the contribution of Sircar's Third Theatre to theatre movements in the country.

The last text in the section on theatre is by Syed Mustafa Siraj written in the 1970s on Alkap, an indigenous comic satirical form of theatre dealing with local and contemporary issues and sometimes events of great national or global magnitude. Such forms sometimes gradually became extant, sometimes survived within a particular space and context, and often continued to exist by assimilating urban mass entertainment forms. Siraj affirms that the form in Alkap is inclusive of the audience, and without audience participation the performance cannot take place. A second element, he points out, is the incorporation of '*maya*' or endearing illusions in the fabric of the performance that is strongly woven around the harsh realities of life. The dream world of the people, presented in a humorous manner, is often represented through maya, which becomes the basis of its immense popularity. Sometimes, the laughter is arrested, and there is silence when, for instance, a hungry young boy sits with his father under a tree and dreams of his recently dead mother bringing him a plate of rice and then wakes up suddenly as he stumbles and falls while holding out an imaginary plate and calls out to his father in a hoarse voice. The actors are generally from the marginalised sections in society. This text from a master or *ustad* of the Alkap group offers several examples to suggest the meaning and implications of audience participation and the notion of theatre itself.

The Language Movement and its implications

The volume ends with an essay by Qazi Motahar Husain in 1947 in East Bengal, which takes up the issue of the state language and elaborates on the role of Bangla in the history of the formation of Muslim identity among the Bangla-speaking people. It may also be read as providing a background to the events that culminate in the Language Movement and the martyrdom of many in 1952. The significance of the role and function of language in the development of literature and culture and then to the overall progress of the people is worked out in the text. True freedom can arrive, Qazi Motahar Husain believes, only when one emerges out of a state of rapture, is able to determine for oneself, and can analyse issues and matters from an open perspective. Only a just engagement with the mother tongue can enable this, he demonstrates and adds, 'Whatever is beautiful, desirable or respectful in life, has to be attained through the mother tongue. No real progress is possible without this mother tongue.' This focus on the mother tongue and an analysis of its organic relation with the growth and progress of people become the culminating point in the quest for relevance.

The discursive space of literary criticism

The discursive material presented in the volume brings forward processes by which people came together; imagined spaces of beauty, truth, and freedom; critiqued dominant power structures; shared aspirations and ideals;

and tried to build solidarities with larger and larger groups of people in the world with a voice of their own. There were, however, inner ruptures, divisions among people based on caste, class, religion, gender, ethnicity, and geographical area, aggravated by colonising powers that became linked with economic and social disparities creating core areas of inequality in society, which were difficult to bridge and led to concentrations of power and hence exploitative situations. The discursive texts themselves also sometimes contributed to the divisive forces. However, the creative centre fortified by imagination seemed to be the only space that could continue to be affirmative in the face of overwhelming negative forces. Literary discourse, except in certain moments as in the period preceding independence or in the case of theatre, did not set out with a utilitarian agenda but had its purposiveness in building affective communities, enabling greater bondings and providing visions of a cultural ecology. As Mahasweta Devi commenting on the deep injustices of history states that 'The ceaseless vibration, changes in layers and transformations continue deep within my mind', and one may hope also perhaps a little in the reading community where discourse related to the literary may provide a 'force to shift underneath, beyond or on the side of the hegemonic order of things'.[12]

Notes

1 Some of the important writers contributing to the literary discursive field in the late 19th and the first half of the 20th century who have not been mentioned in the text are Bhudev Mukhopadhyay (1827–1894), Kaliprasanna Ghosh (1843–1910), Chandranath Basu (1844–1910), Shibnath Shastri (1847–1919), Ramesh Chandra Dutt (1848–1909), Chandrasekhar Mukhopadhyay (1849–1922), Thakurdas Mukhopadhyay (1851–1903), Priyanath Sen (1854–1916), Bipinchandra Pal (1858–1932), Brajendranath Seal (1864–1938), Asutosh Choudhury (1868–1924), Hirendranath Dutta (1868–1942), Sureshchandra Samajpati (1870–1921), Abanindranath Tagore (1871–1951), Abdul Karim Sahityabisharad (1871–1953), Aurobindo Ghose (1872–1950), Krishnachandra Bhattacharya (1875–1949), Rakhaldas Bandyopadhyay (1885–1930), Ajitumar Chakravarty (1886–1918), Radhakamal Mukhopadhyay (1889–1968), Sushil Kumar De (1890–1968), Kazi Abdul Odud (1894–1970), Dhurjatiprasad Mukhopadhyay (1894–1961), Kalidas Bhattacharya (1911–1984), Nirad Chandra Chaudhuri (1897–1999), Prabodh Chandra Bagchi (1898–1956), Humayun Kabir (1906–1969), Pramathanath Bishi (1901–1985), Gopal Halder (1902–1993), Niharranjan Ray (1903–1981), Subodh Chandra Sengupta (1903–1998), Jasimuddin (1903–1976), Annadashankar Roy (1904–2002), Abu Sayeed Ayyub (1906–1982), Hirendranath Mukhopadhyay (1907–2004), Nirendranath Roy (1896–1966), Saroj Acharya (1907–1968), and Ranesh Dasgupta (1912–1997).

2 See Bankimchandra Chattopadhyay, 'A Popular Literature for Bengal' (1870), in *Bankim Rachanabali*, Vol. III, Calcutta: Sahitya Samsad, 1969, pp. 97–102.

3 Rangalal Bandyopadhyay, *Bangla Kabita Bishayak Prabandha, Rangalal Rachanabali*, Santikumar Dasgupta and Haribandhu Mukhoti (eds.), Kolkata: Datta Chaudhuri and Sons, 1954, pp. 71–86. The essay was first published as a booklet in 1853.

4 Bankimchandra Chattopadhyay, 'Mrita Michael Madhusudan Dutta', *Bangadarsan*, 1873, 2(5): 209–214, 209.

5 Bankimchandra Chattopadhyay, 'Uttarcharit' (1872), in *Bankim Rachanabali*, Vol. II, Kolkata: Sahitya Samsad, 1954, p. 183.
6 See also Martha Nussbaum, *Political Emotions: Why Love Matters for Justice*, Cambridge, MA: Harvard University Press, 2013.
7 Sankha Ghosh, 'Pa Tola Pa Fela', in *Kabitar Muhurta*, Calcutta: Anustup Prakashani, 1987, p. 15.
8 Sunil Gangopadhyay (ed.), *Krittibas: Panhas bachhar: Nirbachita Samkalan*, Vol. I, Kolkata: Ananda, 2003, p. 138. Originally published in *Krittibas* XVI, 1963.
9 See Subha Chakraborty Dasgupta, 'Issues in Reception: A Case Study of the Early Bengali Novel', *New Comparison*, 1997, 23(Spring): 54–65.
10 Tarasankar Bandyopadhyay, *Amar Sahitya Jiban*, Kolkata: Paschim Banga Bangla Academy, 1997, p. 50.
11 Reprinted in Sudhi Pradhan (ed.), *Marxist Cultural Movement in India: Chronicles and Documents (1936–47)*, Vol. I, Calcutta: National Book Agency, 1979, p. 13.
12 Kathrin Thiele, 'Drifting in the Cracks: With-For-Against-Politics', *Position Paper Terra Critica IV*, http://terracritica.net/wp-content/uploads/pospaper_Thiele_London2019.pdf, accessed on 24 April 2020.

References

Anisuzzaman, *Muslim Manas o Bangla Sahitya* (1964), Dhaka: Charulipi, 2012.

Bandyopadhyay, Srikumar and Prafullachandra Pal (eds.), *Samalochana Sahitya Parichay*, Kolkata: University of Calcutta, 1960.

Bhattacharya, Bishnupada, *Sahitya Mimansa*, Kolkata: Visvabharati, 1948.

Bhattacharya, Sutapa, *Bangali Meyer Bhabnamulak Gadya: Unis Satak*, New Delhi: Sahitya Akademi, 2007.

Chattopadhyay, Suniti Kumar, *Nirbachita Rachana Samkalan*, Kolkata: Mitra o Ghosh, 2009.

Das, Dhananjay, *Marxbadi Sahitya-Bitarka* (comp. & ed.), Kolkata: Karuna, 2003.

Das, Pulin, *Banga Rangamancha o Bangla Natak*, vol. I&II, Kolkata: M.C. Sarkar & Sons, 1983–1991.

De, Sushil Kumar, *History of Sanskrit Poetics (1923–1925)*, Kolkata: Firma K.L.M, 1960.

Gupta, Atulchandra, *Kavyajijnasa* (1928), Kolkata: Visvabharati, 1941.

Kane, P.V., *History of Sanskrit Poetics* (3rd. rev. ed.), Delhi: Motilal Banarsidass, 1961.

Mukhopadhyay, Arunkumar, *Bangla Samalochanar Itihas*, Kolkata: Dey's Publishing, 1965.

Mukhopadhyay, Prabhat Kumar, *Rabindrajibankatha* (1959), Kolkata: Ananda, 1981.

Nyayaratna, Ramgati, *Bangalabhasha o Bangalasahitya Bishayak Prastab*, Part I, Hooghly: Budhoday Press, 1873.

Pal, Prasanta Kumar, *Rabijibani*, vols. I–IX, Kolkata: Ananda, 1993–2002.

Roy, Alok, Pabitra Sarkar and Abhra Ghosh (eds.), *Dusho Bachharer Bangla Prabandhasahitya*, vols. I–II, New Delhi: Sahitya Akademi, 2002–2006.

Sen, Dineshchandra, *History of Bengali Language and Literature*, Kolkata: University of Calcutta, 1954.

Sen, Sukumar, *Bangala Sahityer Itihas*, vols. I–V (1940–1958), Kolkata: Ananda Publishers, 1991.

Sengupta, Subodh Chandra and Anjali Basu (eds.), *Samsad Bangali Charitabhidhan*, Kolkata: Sahitya Samsad, 1976.

1 Shashibhusan Dasgupta: Bengal and the Bengali in *Charyageeti*

Introduction

Shashibhusan Dasgupta (1911–1964), an influential scholar in the field of Bangla literary studies, received his initial education in Philosophy and then obtained his Masters in Bangla literature from the University of Calcutta and became a professor. He completed his Ph.D. in 1939, and his thesis was subsequently published as *Obscure Religious Cults as Background of Bengali Literature* (1946), a work that is still regarded as seminal in the field. His later works in the field of ancient and medieval literature and philosophy include *An Introduction to Tantric Buddhism* (1950), *Sriradhar Kramabikas: Darsane o Sahitye* (1952), *Bharatiya Saktisadhana o Sakta Sahitya* (1960). Apart from that, he also wrote a number of texts on Sanskrit literature and its influence on Bangla literature, Rabindranath Tagore, Modern Bangla literature and a few volumes of poetry and fiction. The essay presented here was originally published in a periodical and later included in *Bauddhadharma o Charyageeti* (1957).

Haraprasad Shastri's discovery of the *charyapadas* from Nepal in 1907 and its subsequent publication in 1916 along with a Sanskrit commentary by Munidatta initiated a new era in Bangla literary studies. The monograph entitled *Hajar Bachharer Purano Bangala Bhashay Bauddhagan o Doha*, comprised four different manuscripts which Shastri found in Nepal. These texts were *Charyacharyabinishchaya*, *Sarahabajrer Dohakosh*, *Krishnacharypader Dohakosh* and *Dakarnava*. The language of *Charyacharyavinishchaya*, a compilation of 50 songs composed between the 8th and 12th centuries, is considered the earliest form of Bangla. Not only was the history of Bangla language and literature redefined, but an examination of its cultural past also became necessary. Earlier in the 19th century, the Buddhist canon of literature in Pali and Sanskrit was a phenomenon of a glorious past; now its philosophy became an integrated part of early Bangla literature, thus changing the perspective for its study quite radically. Scholars like Haraprasad Shastri and Prabodh Chandra Bagchi emphasised the crucial role of Buddhism in shaping Bengali culture and argued for an understanding of its syncretic nature on the basis of available literary evidence.

DOI: 10.4324/9781003224686-2

Shashibhusan Dasgupta provided a firm philosophical ground for the same in his pathbreaking work *Obscure Religious Cults* by discussing the interrelations between the Buddhist, Vaishnav and the Tantric *Sahajiya* cults and the numerous folk traditions, which also incorporated elements of Sufism and Islam in the course of time. In *Bauddhadharma o Charyageeti*, Dasgupta focuses on the relation between the religious doctrine of Buddhism and its philosophical implication in the late Mahayana period and how they shaped the religious practices of *Vajrayana* Buddhism in Bengal between the 8th and 12th centuries. He also provides an account of Bengali society and culture of the period as reflected in the songs. It may be mentioned in this context that Dasgupta identified a number of charya songs in Arnold Bake's collection of recordings from Nepal housed in the School of Oriental and African Studies and subsequently found a living tradition of such songs in Nepal.

*

Bengal and the Bengali in *Charyageeti*[1]

Shashibhusan Dasgupta

*

It is true today as it has been for thousands of years that literature has held up a mirror to life. The *doha*[2] and the *charyapada*[3], that is the poetry that was composed in Bangla a thousand years ago, retain signs of ancient Bengal and its inhabitants. There is also ample proof that these poets had true poetic genius though their compositions were based on religious tenets. All religions are made up of a philosophy and a passion, and both of them are amorphous; poetry emerges when these formless perceptions are given a form. Poets need metaphors and other rhetorical devices to do that otherwise where else would they find them apart from the surrounding life and living? These dohas reflect contemporary Bengal and its milieu at every step. The most complex philosophical thought and the most subtle of spiritual realisations had to be expressed in terms of images and expressions from gross material life. This discussion intends to acquaint the reader with the images of contemporary life and times of ancient Bengal in the poetry of the times.

As we discuss charyapada as Bangla literature, we must also disregard the East–West and North–South borders of Bengal arbitrarily put in place by the British government for their own benefit. This study is not about determining the geographical borders of ancient Bengal. Yet, from the information that we have, it is possible to say that the Bengal reflected in this poetry was a large tract of land, stretching from the west bank of lower Brahmaputra to the northern part of Odisha, and from eastern Bihar to Kamarupa or Assam. Overlooking this fact has led to some unnecessary debates in the discussion of the language of the charyapada. Some scholars have called this language ancient Odia, others ancient Bihari or Maithili or Bangla. The debate might end if we remember that the language of the charya is the language spoken from 10th to 12th centuries in what may now be called Greater Gauda.

We will discuss one by one what we come to know about the religion, social structure and milieu of contemporary Bengal from this poetry.

The poems composed by Buddhist Sahajiya poets should be taken into account as well because these are also Bangla poetry. Bangla poetry here does not mean poems composed in Bangla alone, but also poems composed in the land of Bengal by poets sharing a similar mentality. Many of the poems have been composed in the Apabhraṃśa[4] dialect used in the regions west of Bengal, though the subject and the expressions remain the same. Why did they use more than one dialect? The linguist Sunitikumar Chattopadhyay has said that, as the latter dialect was used by the aristocratic Rajput families, it picked up an air of nobility by association, and perhaps this was the reason why poets of Bengal aspired to compose dohas in that dialect. But that may not have been all. The doha is a genre of poetry much favoured and popular in the western regions, and it is possible that in adopting the genre, the poets of Bengal also adopted the language. The history of Indian literature too bears further proof of the fact that certain genres of composition and their languages gained popularity from time to time. The 'gatha'[5] in Pali literature was not composed in Sanskrit, nor in any Prakrit of that time, not in a local language either but in a 'literary' language, one that was used to create a particular genre of literature. The 'Brajabuli' that we have in later Bangla poetry is of a similar nature; it is neither from Mithila, nor from any other place, but just a popular literary medium invented for a particular purpose. Poets composing in that genre, whether from Odisha, Mithila, Bengal or Assam, might have been tempted to adopt this particular dialect as their vehicle.

*

Charyapada poets belonged to the Buddhist Sahajiya sect. They called the way or manner of their *sadhana*, that is pursuit of the ultimate end, 'sahaja', literally 'born with', the expanded meaning being 'uncomplicated' and 'straight'; any other means of sadhana, for them, was crooked. A crooked path only leads one astray, far from the truth. Sahajiyas criticised and discussed contemporary creeds and sects from this point of view. Their discussion gives us a glimpse into the popular creeds and sects of that time.

Charyapadas and dohas usually rebel against the Vedic creed. In one or two places, they mention *vedāgama* which is not a single or particular Veda per se, but the authoritative scriptures of the Brahminic faith, for example

Jāhera bāṇacihṇa ruba ṇa jāṇī|
So kaise āgama beẽ bakhāṇī||
[C 29][6]

If no one is able to discern the hue or the attribute or the aspect of it (the ultimate truth), how can the Vedas or the Agamas claim to explain the same?

Bengal had never been a land that followed the Vedic creed, which arrived here at a much later date. The Aryanisation of Bengal began at the time of the Gupta empire; yet, the stringent Vedic system could never gain much ground. It was only between the 10th and the 12th centuries that upper-caste Hindus invited proficient Brahmins from the western parts of India for conducting sacrifices and other rites and ceremonial recitation of the Vedas. The proof of this can be found in contemporary historical documents as well as legends and lore. Sarahapāda has a doha pertaining to this:

Bahmaṇo hi ma jānanta hi bheũ|
Ebai padiau e ccaubeu||
Maṭṭi [pāṇī kusa lai paṛanta|
Gharahī̃ baisī] aggi huṇantã||
Kajje birahia huabaha homẽ|
Akkhi uhābia kaḍuẽ dhūmẽ||
[D 1–2][7]

The Brahmins do not know the truth, but recite the four Vedas mechanically. They chant their mantra with water, earth and kusa grass in their hands, sit in the room and pour libations onto the fire. There is no visible result, but how the eyes burn from the acrid smoke of the oblations!

Sarahapāda has also mentioned Daṇḍi[8] ascetics in this regard.

Ekadaṇḍī tridaṇḍī bhaabā besẽ|
Biṇuā hoiai haṃsa uesẽ||
Micchehī̃ jage bāhia bhulle|
Dhammādhamma ṇa jāṇia tulle||
[D 3]

Various ascetics put on the garb of holy men and think themselves wise because of the advice they received from an enlightened guru. Their world spins on illusions; they have no knowledge of either dharma or adharma.

Brahmin pandits proud of their scriptural knowledge are mentioned in many texts as are Hindus with a belief in gods like Brahma, Viṣhṇu and Mahesvara. However, it must be noted that the texts mention faiths and creeds other than the commonly followed Hindu practices.

The Buddhist faith was widespread and well-established in Bengal at this time. This age may be called the Hindu-Buddhist age – it is difficult to determine which religion was predominant. But one cannot overlook the fact that

Jainism was also quite prevalent in Bengal. There is proof that long before 10th century CE, centres of Jainism were established in the northern and western regions of Bengal. Legend has it that when Mahavira came to Rarh that is Bengal, the uncivilised inhabitants of Rarh set their dogs upon him. Hiuen Tsang's accounts mention seeing Nirgantha Jaina monks in northern, southern and eastern Bengal and mention noticing many Digambara Jainas in Puṇḍravardhana and Samataṭa. From Sarahapāda's dohas, it seems that one could meet a Jaina monk in every street. Sarahapāda has described them thus:

> Dīhaṇakkha jai maliṇẽ besẽ|
> Ṇaggala hoi upāḍia kesẽ||
> Khabaṇehi jāṇa biḍiṃbia besẽ|
> Appaṇa bāhia hokkha ubesẽ||
> [D 6]

> These ascetics are long-nailed, wear faded clothes, and taking off their clothes they rip their hair off too. These Kṣapaṇakas[9] look as if they have gone astray and they carry themselves forward to their salvation.

Moreover, the Digambara Jaina sect used to maintain a certain set of beliefs and followed certain rites and rituals. Called Digambara (lit. 'sky-clad') because of their ritual nudity, they also ripped off their hair with both hands and carried fly whisks made of animal tail hairs or peacock feathers. They believed that their Tīrthaṅkaras could stay alive without taking any food. Sarahapāda observes them and says:

> Jai ṇaggā bia hoi mutti suṇaha siālaha|
> Lomupāḍaṇe atthi siddhi tā jubai nitambaha||
> Picchīgahaṇe diṭhṭa mokkha [tā moraha camaraha]||
> Uñchẽ bhoaṇe hoi jāṇa tā kariha turaṅgaha||
> [D 7–8]

> If nakedness brought salvation then dogs and jackals would also be saved; if removing hair made one reach siddhi, then a young lass's butt would be the prime candidate; if taking up a tail could bring *mokṣa*, the whisk made of peacock's feather would also receive it; and if knowledge was received by eating food left by someone, horses and elephants would also be blessed with it.

Mahayana was important in Bengal, but we may have a glimpse of Hinayana as well in the dohas. This one discusses Theravadi[10] Buddhists:

> Chellu bhikkhu je sthabira-uesẽ|
> Bandehia pabbajjiu besẽ||

Koi sutantabakkhāṇa baiṭṭho|
Kobi cinte kara sosai diṭṭho||
[D 10]

Chella and Bhikkhu (the initiate and the mendicant) take up the garb of renunciation only on the advice of their sthavira. Some stay in one place and explain *Sutrāntas* (in the hope of gaining material objects); some deliberately take up the opinions of the external world.

So one group became enamoured with the Agama and the Tarkasastra of Mahayana. Some pondered upon the Maṇḍala-Chakra, and yet some studied the Chaturthatattva.[11]

Aṇṇa tahi mahājāṇahi dhāvai|
Tahī sutanta takkasattha hai||
Koi maṇḍalacakka bhāvai|
Aṇṇa cautthatatta dīsai||
[D 11–12][12]

The Sahajiyas were against all these popular modes of Buddhism, so they never pursued the *dhyana–dharana–samadhi* (meditation–retention–ecstatic trance) way of sadhana. Neither dhyana nor samadhi permanently eradicated joy and sorrow, so they addressed their antecedents thus:

Saala samāhia kāhi kariai|
Sukha dukhetẽ nicita mariai||
[C 1]

What is the use of samadhi etc.? Joy and sorrow will only beget death.

Mahayana Buddhism passed through the way of the mantras to transform into Vajrayana. But the mantras and mediation held no charm for them, and the Sahajiyas vociferously rebelled against these in many ways.

Sarahapāda talks about yet another sect in his doha:

Airiehī uddulia cchārẽ|
Sīsasu bāhia e jaṛabhārẽ||
Gharahī baisī dīvā jālī|
Koṇahī baisī ghaṇṭā cālī||
Akkhi ṇibesī āsaṇa bandhī|
Kaṇṇehī khusukhusāi jaṇa dhandhī||
[D 4–5]

Aryan ascetics smear their bodies with ash, keep their hair matted as a sign of their asceticism, and pursue their rituals with burning lamps and ringing bells. They pretend to meditate by closing their eyes and sitting still in an asana and confuse the common people by whispering in their ears i.e.by initiating them into their sect.

The Tantrika Kapalik sect seemed to have much significance during that time. At times, even the Sahajiyas declared their wish to turn into Kapalik ascetics, although their idea of the Kapalik differed from the popular image of the Kapalik. According to them, 'kaṃ mahāsukhaṃ pālayatīti kāpālikaḥ', that is he who observes mahasukha is a Kapalik. With this thought in mind, they declared:

Ālo Ḍombī toe sama karibe ma sāṅga|
Nighiṇa Kāhṇa kāpāli joi lāga||
Tu lo Ḍombī hāũ kapālī|
Tohora antare moe ghalili hāṛeri mālī||
[C 10]

O Dombi,[13] I desire your company. I, Kāhṇa[14], have no repugnance for anything and that is how I shall become your consort, the naked Kapali Yogi. If you be my Dombi, I shall be your Kapali, I will garland myself with bones all for your sake'.

Elsewhere, we have discussed in detail the significance of this union between the Dombi and the Kapali according to the Sahajiya creed. What is to be noted here is the aspect of the Kapalik sect that remains outside the Sahajiya creed. There is another charya by Kāhṇupāda that spectacularly describes his Sahajiya way of life:

Nāṛī shakti diṛha dharia khaṭṭe|
Anahā ḍamaru bājae bīranāde||
Kāhṇa kapālī yogī paiṭha achāre|
Deha naarī biharae ekārẽ||
Āli kāli ghaṇṭā neura caraṇe|
Raviśaśī kuṇḍala kiu ābharaṇe||
Rāgadeśa moha lāia chāra|
Parama mokha labae muttāhāra||
Māria sāsu naṇanda ghare śālī|
Māa māriā Kāhṇa bhaia kabālī||
[C 11]

The power of the *nādi* or the cords[15] is held firmly in the Void. The *damaru* of *anāhata*[16] sounds in *vīra nāda*.[17] Kāhṇa the Kapali yogi enters his way of life. He turns wisdom and knowledge into his ankle bells, he wears the sun and the moon as rings in his ears.[18] His desire is burnt to ashes, as are his malice and his delusions. He will now be garlanded with the pearls of salvation. Now that he has killed[19] his mother-in-law and his sisters-in-law, Kāhṇa will become a true Kapali.

Leaving aside the mysteries of the sect, it is apparent that Kapalik ascetics used to play the Indian pellet drum, that is the damaru, wandered alone and wore ankle bells and large round earrings called *kundala*. They smeared themselves with ash and 'killed' their family to take to the Kapalik way of life. Like men, women too metaphorically 'devoured their husbands', that is left their homes and relatives and became initiated as yoginis or female ascetics. Sarahapāda says in a doha:

Gharabai khajjai sahajẽ rajjai kijjai rāa birāa|
Ṇiapāsa baiṭṭhī chitte bhaṭṭhī joiṇi mahu paṛihāa||
[D 85]

She devours the master of the house, dwells in the Innate,[20] attaches and detaches herself at will. She stays by my side, yet her mind goes elsewhere, this is how the yogini manifests herself to me.

The dohas and the charyas mention another ancient sect of ascetics called the Rasasiddhas who are the primitive form of the Nathasiddhas. This sect originated from the ancient ideals of Indian chemistry. They did not believe in salvation after death but tried to achieve salvation in life itself. They strove to transform the physical body into an unearthly body and finally a divine body and thus attain immortality or rather a kind of indestructibility. This was, in their minds, the achievement of a deathless and ultimate godhead. So, their first pursuit was to realise the possibilities of the physical body via the application of chemistry. The 'elemental rasa' or mercury of the Rasasiddhas became the 'soma rasa' secreted from the moon in the *sahasrāra* or the crownchakra for the Nathasiddhas.

Patañjali's *Yogasūtra* mentions ancient ascetic sects that believed that *rasa-rasayana*, or a culture of the vital juices, held the key to salvation. Patanjali has said that 'Janmauṣadhi-mantra-tapaḥ-samādhijāḥ-siddhaya', that is the siddhis or attainments come by birth, or from either stimulants, or mantra, spiritual pursuit, and the state of samadhi or ecstatic trance. *Vyāsabhāṣya* has clarified that 'Auṣad hibhiḥ asurabhavaneṣu rasāynetyevamādi', that is stimulants here mean chemical elements or compounds. Vachaspati too holds the same opinion. This thought came down through the Nathasiddhas to the 10th and 12th centuries to become a particular Saiva doctrine, which spread to Bengal as well. The Sahajiyas have expressed rather stern views against these Rasasiddhas. The Rasasiddhas believed in the reality of birth and death and wanted to transcend both and attain godhead. But Buddhist Sahajiyas recognised neither birth nor death and eschewed any concept of duality. Both 'is' and 'is-not' sprang from the idea of duality; and if there was neither birth nor death, what good were elements and compounds for? Sarahapāda says:

> Ahme na jānāhū achinta joi|
> Jāma maraṇa bhava kaisaṇa hoi||
> Jaiso jāma maraṇa bi taiso|
> Jīvante maile nāhi biśeso||
> Jā ethu jāma maraṇe bisaṅkā|
> So karau rasa rasānere kaṅkhā||
> [C 22]

> We who pursue the unthinkable, we do not know how birth, being and death occur. As there is birth, so there is death, and hence there is no difference between the living and the dead. Let those who fear birth and death, let them desire rasa-rasayana.[21]

*

Now we shall see something of the societal system as described in the charyas.[22] The question of *jati* arises first. The word jati is used for both race and caste, but I will use it in its earlier meaning as race. Bengal is primarily a non-Aryan country. From the 4th century CE, that is the time of the Gupta Empire, elements of language, civilisation and culture of the Aryans began to enter Bengal. However, their nature and extent never became so vast as to appropriate the local elements and transform them entirely. Bengal continued to keep its race and its culture distinct. If we refrain from tying Bengal up like a tugboat behind the mammoth and indistinct shape of Aryanism, we would be able to perceive Bengal's individuality more clearly.

Among the non-Aryan races who lived in Bengal before the Aryans trickled in, historians have attached much importance to the Kol tribe. Till this day, our race, civilisation and culture have significant Kol elements in them. Among the Kols, the Sabars, Doms, Pulindas and Chandals occupied a large part of the society when the charyas were composed. They certainly occupy a large part of the charyas. The charyakars themselves seem to be neither uninformed nor untaught – the charyas bear evidence to their level of perception and learning. When they repeatedly talk about the Sabar, Pulinda, Dom and Chandal while expressing the finer points of their sadhana, when they accord such importance to their lives, characters and dwellings, then it must be understood that these people were an important part of the society in Bengal at that time. Yet, they lived their lives far from the urban, 'civilised' community. That they gravitated to the lower rungs of the society at later times is also a fact corroborated by the charyas.[23]

The life of the Sabars is described in a couple of charyas. These Sabars used to live on top of the hills and knolls: Baragirisihara uttuṅga muṇi sabarẽ jahi kia bāsa| [K 25].[24]

Śavarapāda has a beautiful description in one of his charyas:

Ũcā ũcā pābata tãhĩ basai sabarī bālī|
Moraṅgi pīccha parahiṇa sabarī gībata guñjarī mālī||
Umata sabaro pāgala sabaro mā kara gulī guhāḍā tohouri|
Ṇia gharaṇī ṇāme Sahaja Sundārī||
Ṇāṇā tarubara moulila re gaaṇata lāgelī ḍālī|
Ekelī sabarī e baṇa hiṇḍai karṇakuṇḍalavajradhārī||
Tia dhāu khāṭa paḍilā sabaro mahāsuhe seji chāilī|
Sabara bhujaṅga ṇairāmaṇi dārī pehma rāti pohāilī||
Hia tām̐bolā mahāsuhe kāpura khāi|
Suna nirāmaṇi kaṇṭhe laiā mahāsuhe rāti pohāi||
Gurubāk puñcaā bindha ṇia maṇe bāṇẽ|
Eke śarasandhānẽ bindhaha parama ṇibāṇẽ||
Umata sabaro garuā roṣe|
Giribara sihara sandhi paisante sabaro loṛiba kaise||

[C 28]

There she lives, the Sabar girl, on top of those high hills. She wears peacock feathers around her waist and a garland of coral beads around her neck. O foolish Sabar, o passionate Sabar, please don't go astray in the commotion, I beseech you. I am but your woman, Sahajasundari by name. The trees have budded and bloomed, their branches reach the sky. The Sabar girl roams the forests alone, her ears adorned with rings. The Sabar made his bed out of three metals, where he and his woman spent a night of love, entwined like the Serpent and Nairamani, the force of self-annihilation. His heart as his tambula (betel leaf), his enjoyment his karpura (camphor), entwined with the Void, the ascetic attains *mahāsukha*, the Great Joy.[25] The word of the guru acts like a bow, and the arrow is one's own mind. A single arrow can pierce that ultimate beatitude of Nirvana. Crazed with anger, the Sabar enters the caves at the hilltop; will he be able to return?

Here, we see the Sabar couple living their lives away from human habitation. The Sabari dresses up in feathers and seeds, though there is a mention of earrings. The Sabar would get drunk and forget his woman, and the Sabari would have to call him back home. Their home and bed were simple, yet their pleasure intense. They had access to a few niceties like paan and camphor. Bow and arrows helped them hunt. Angry, the Sabar would trudge off into the hills, and the Sabari would wander alone, searching for him.

Another song by Śavarapāda says:

Gaaṇata gaaṇata tailā bāḍhī heñce kurāḍī|
Kanṭhe nairāmaṇi bāli jāgante upāḍī||
. . . .

Heri ye meri tailā bāṛī khasame samatulā|
Sukaḍae sere kapāsu phuṭilā||
Kaṅgucinā pākelā re śabara-śabarī mātelā|
Anudina śabaro kimpi na chebai mahāsuhẽ bhelā||
Cāribāse gaṛilāre diāṁ chañchālī|
Tahĩ toli śabaro ḍāha kaelā kāndai saguṇa śiālī||
[C 50]

The house reaches up to the sky. If you hack it off with an axe, *Nairātmā*[26] wakes up within. . . . With the clouds of cotton flowers blooming all around it, I see my house as part of the sky. The millet has ripened to the great delight of the Sabar couple. The Sabar lies inebriated day and night, his intoxication akin to the Great Joy. He fences everything in with strips of bamboo, then sets fire to it all, amidst the hoots and cries of vultures and jackals'.

So, they dwelt on hilltops, and they cultivated cotton and millet, which they protected from jackals and vultures with bamboo fences.

It is to be noted here that there are only two charyas which deal with the life of the Sabar, and both of them have been composed by Śavarapāda. Could he have been a Sabar himself?

One or two more charyas mention this kind of solitary living, such as 'Ṭālata ghara mora nāhi paḍibeśī' [C 33] etc.

The Kols are mentioned as Nishads in the charyas. The Nishads used to be hunters. Bhuṣukupāda has a charya where there is a striking description of a deer hunt:

Kāhere ghini meli acchahu kīsa|
Beṛhila hāka paḍaa caudīsa||
Apaṇā māṃsẽ hariṇā bairī|
Khanaha na chhāḍaa Bhusuku aheri||
[C 6]

Where are you hiding and with whom? The call of the hunters surrounds the stag. His own flesh makes him everyone's foe. The hunters never let Bhuṣuku the stag out of their sight even for a moment'.

The image of the terrified stag attacked from all around is remarkable.

Tiṇa na cchupai hariṇā pibai na pāṇī|
Hariṇā hariṇīra nilaa ṇa jāṇī||
Hariṇī bolaa suṇa hariṇā to|
E bana cchhāḍī hohu bhānto||
Taraṃgate hariṇāra khura na dīsai|
Bhuṣuku bhaṇai mūḍha hiahi na paisai||
[C 6]

The hart is afraid to eat and drink; nor does he know where the hind resides. The hind says, O hart, you must leave this forest. His hoof prints disappear when he runs at a full gallop. Bhuṣuku says, such words do not enter the heart of the ignorant.

In another pada Bhuṣuku says,

Jai tumhe Bhusuku aheri jāibẽ mārihasi pañcajaṇā|
Nalinībana paisante hohisi ekumaṇā||
Jīvante bhelā bihaṇi maela raaṇi (?)|
Haṇabiṇu māṁse Bhusuku padmabaṇa paisahili||
Māājāla pasariu re bāṁdheli māāhariṇī|
Sadgurubohẽ bujhire kānu kadini||
[C 23]

Should you go on a hunt, Bhuṣuku, then you must kill those five. Be determined to enter the lotus grove. Life is daylight, death is night. Bhuṣuku enters the lotus grove without any flesh. The elusive hind may only be caught using a net of illusions. Only the guru's advice will show the truth.

The Dombi are mentioned in quite a few songs. Even a thousand years ago, the Dombi lived on the outskirts of the city, considered untouchable by the shaven-pated Brahmins.

Nagara bāhiri re Ḍombī tohori kuṛiā|
Choi choi jāi so brāhma nāṛiā||
[C 10]

They travelled by boat and sold bamboo and cane bins and baskets wherever they touched land. Leaving aside their reed-boxes, people would buy the pretty objects sold by the Dombi.

Hālo Ḍombī to puchami sadbhābe|
Āisasi jāsi Ḍombī kāhari nābẽ||
. . . . .
Tānti bikaṇaa Ḍombī abara nā cāṅgeṛā|
Tohora antare chāṛi naṛapeṛā||
[C 10]

Even today, we may see people from these castes leading nomadic lives. They live in their boats and travel to places. They stop somewhere for a few days, weave beautiful objects with thin bamboo strips and sell them. People often buy these fancy objects setting aside their boxes and baskets. These women from low castes are often skilled at singing and dancing with which they captivate people's hearts. One doha describes the Dombi dancing atop a lotus with sixty-four petals:

Eka so padumā cauśaṭhṭhī pākhuṛī|
Tahĩ caṛi nācaa Ḍombī bāpuṛī||
[C 10]

Describing the Dombi's dance is just another way to let the readers know that the women were exceptionally skilled in music. Later accounts too attest to the skills of these women. Perhaps this made them capricious in character and that is how they made their way into the hearts of people from the upper crust of society. On the other hand, they also became partners of ascetics who renounced race and caste altogether. A song by Kāhṇupāda says as much:

> Well, Dombi, is this how you carry on? You play along with both the Kapali and the upper caste men. Some do say unwelcome words about you, but those who know never let you leave their side. Kāhṇu sings, you are *kamchandali*, desire itself, you are a minx above all others.
>
> [C 18]

Even now we may see a certain class of travelling singers in the towns and villages of Bengal, who make a primitive lute by attaching a cane and some strings to a gourd and sing along with it. The charyapadas mention exactly this class of singers in this way:

Suja lāu sasi lāgeli tāntī|
Aṇahā dāṇḍī eki kiata avadhūtī||
Bājai alo sahi Herua-vīṇā|
Suna tāntidhani bilasai ruṇā||
. . . .
Nācanti Bājila gānti Devī|
Buddhanāṭaka bisamā hoi||
[C 17]

> The sun is my gourd, the moon my strings, *anāhata* is the stem of my lute. It is the *avadhūtī* (the ascetic's partner) who brings them all together. Look, sakhi mine, how together they make up the great Heruka vīna! The Great Void reverberates with karuṇā (compassion).[27] . . . Hear Devi sing and see how Vajrācārya dances, turning the Buddha-nāṭaka upside down'.

'Buddha-nāṭaka' carries some significance here. These singers would depict an incident of special significance through such performances. Perhaps their performance gave rise to drama in Bangla; 'nata' and 'nataka' both are supposed to be derived from the Sanskrit word 'nṛtta'.

Another poem says that the hilltop house of the Dombi is burning and someone is trying to douse it with water. The fire has neither heat nor smoke but rises above the peak to reach the sky.

> Ḍāha Ḍombī ghare lāgeli āgi|
> Sasahara lai ṣiñcahū pāṇī||
> Nau kharajālā dhūma na dīśai|
> Meru śikhara lai gaaṇa paisai||
> [C 47]

Something else is stated here:

> Dāṛhai Harihara brāhmaṇa nāṛā|
> Phīṭai ṇabaguṇa śāsana pāṛā||
> [C 47]

Let us take the surface meaning here. Perhaps Harihara, the shaven Brahmin, was a neighbour of the Dombi and the fire reached his house too. Or perhaps he came to put out the fire and was burnt to death. In any case, once everything was burnt to ashes, the authority of the symbolic 'ṇabaguṇa', that is the sacred thread that represents Brahminical strictures, is destroyed too. 'Harihara brahmaṇa' here may also mean Brahma–Vishnu–Siva of canonical religion.

The Dombi also takes on the avatar of the ferrywoman who carries people across the water in her leaking boat:

> Gaṅgā Jaunā mājhẽ rẽ bahai nāi|
> Tahī buṛilī Mātaṅgī joiā līle pāra karei||
> Bāhatu Ḍombī bāhalo Ḍombī bāṭata bhaila uchārā|
> Sadguru pāapae jāiba puṇu jiṇaurā||
> Pāñca keḍuāla paḍantẽ māṅge piṭhata kācchī bāndhī|
> Gaaṇadukholẽ siñcahu pāṇī na paisai sāndhi||
> . . . .
> Kabaṛī na lei boṛī na lei succhaṛe pāra karai|
> Jo rathe caṛilā bāhabā na jāi kūle kūle bulai||
> [C 14]

She plies her ferry on the Ganga and the Jamuna. Dombi, Matanga's daughter, plunges playfully into the river to ferry the ascetic across. O Dombi, row quickly, or we will be delayed. Unless I am blessed by the lotus feet of my guru, I will not be able to reach Jinapura (mahasukha or the ultimate knowledge of the void). The boat has five oars, and there is a mooring rope. Let the sky be your bailer, so that water does not damage the joints of the boat. . . . Dombi takes no payment, not even the smallest coin; she ferries people of her own accord. Those who travel by cart on land, do not know what it is to be on a boat; their fate is to keep roaming on the banks'.

Clearly, these women used to earn quite a bit ferrying people from one side to the other.

The quarrel between the inhabitants of the eastern and the western parts of Bengal too seems to have its origins at that time. Sarahapāda's song says:

> Baṅge jāyā nilesi pare bhāgela tohara biṇāṇā||
> [C 39]

> You have taken a wife from Banga, no wonder your senses (vijnana) have taken your leave.

Here, Banga is the eastern part of Bengal, where mostly non-Aryan races dwelt. Intermarriage between the east and the south (Rarh) or the north (Barendra) of Bengal would invariably lead to the latter being denounced in society. Bhuṣukupāda has a song that says:

> Bājanāva pāṛī Pāuā khālẽ bāhiu|
> Adaa Baṅgāle kleśa luṛiu||
> Āji Bhusu Baṅgālī bhailī|
> Nija gharaṇī caṇḍālī lelī||
> [C 49]

> The thunder-boat (void or sunyata) has been taken to the Padma canal (the ultimate knowledge or prajna). Banga is a cruel land – it robbed me of all I possessed. Bhuṣuku has married the Chandali and turned into a Bangali today!

So, although Bhuṣuku crosses the river in his boat, robbers seize everything he has. But he has managed to become quite a Bengali by marriage!

The charyas describe several of the labouring classes of Bengal such as fishermen, weavers, cotton carders and carpenters. Bengal is a land of rivers, and their Kaibarta fishermen are famous from ancient times. This doha by Kāhṇupāda for example

> Tarittā bhavajaladhi jima kari māa suinā|
> Majha beṇī taraṅgama muniā||
> Pañcatathāgata kia keṛuāla|
> Bāhaa kāa kāhṇila māājāla||
> [C 13]

The fishermen cast their nets in mid-river and float along. All of a sudden as they row, they make a catch. Then they retrieve both the fish and the net, which is called a 'mayājāla', a magical net. It is clear now that this was the way of catching fish in the midst of the huge waves in mid-river even at that time.

A song by Śāntipāda speaks of a person carding cotton. It says,

> 'I've carded cotton till it became mere fuzz, and carded it still till nothing was left. In carding cotton, I embraced the Void and in embracing the Void I carded myself as well'.
>
> [C 26]

Charya 25 by Tantipa or Tantrīpāda is available only in a Tibetan translation discovered by Dr Prabodh Chandra Bagchi. He has also created a Sanskrit version of the charya. That doha explains everything through the metaphor of weaving. Kālapañcaka is the loom, the self is the source of the threads and the cloth thus woven covers the entire sky.[28]

A doha or two mentions carpenters and lumberjacks. When the poet says 'Jo taru cheva bhevau na janai', he points to a certain skill and knowledge required for the cutting down and processing of trees, known only to the artisan. Songs of boat-making also mention carpenters.

*

A profusion of rivers has left an indelible imprint upon the culture and civilisation of Bengal. All the charyapadas are full of descriptions of seas, rivers, streams and canals. Hence, all key philosophical thoughts and esoteric theories have been described in metaphors of running water.

> Bhavaṇai gahaṇa gambhīra begẽ bāhī|
> Duānte cikhila mājhẽ na thāhī||
>
> [C 5]
>
> The *bhavanadi*, or the stream of existence flows very deep. Its banks are muddy, and it is difficult to fathom.

Such extremely muddy banks are a characteristic of the rivers of Bengal. As the ascetic progresses towards the Great Joy of Nirvana, his journey is often compared to a boat's upstream passage on a river. This metaphor of the upstream passage is found in many other scriptures of India, and the three nādīs of the body are frequently compared to the rivers Ganga, Yamuna and Sarasvati. Still, it seems that the charyakars have used this metaphor because of the influence of the rivers of their own country. We have glimpsed the Dombi ferrying people for free and the fishermen fishing in mid-river. Śāntipāda has a song that says:

> Kūlẽ kūla mā hoi re mūṛhā ujubāṭa saṃsārā|
> Bāla bhiṇa ekubāku ṇa bhulaha rājapatha kanḍhārā||
> Māā moha samudāre anta na bujhasi thāhā|
> Āga nāva na bhelā dīsai bhānti na pucchasi nāhā||

Sunāpāntara uha na dīsai bhānti na bāsasi jānte|
Eṣā aṭamahāsiddhi sijhai ujubāṭa jāante||
Bāmadāhiṇa do bāṭā cchādī Śānti bulatheu saṃkeliu|
Ghāṭa ṇa gumā khaḍataḍi ṇa hoi ākhi bujia bāṭa jāiu||
[C 15]

The traveller must not travel on the banks but take the straight path, the Innate Way. If one cannot see the end or the beginning of the sea before him, if he sees no sign of another boat or raft, he ought to ask more experienced travellers. The empty sea shows no directions but the traveller must not give in to bewilderment and go on straight ahead. It is the straight road that brings attainment. Look neither to the left nor to the right; there is nothing to impede the traveller on his voyage.

Bāma dāhiṇa jo khāla-bikhalā|
Saraha bhaṇai bāpā ujubāṭa bhailā||
[C 32]

Saraha says, do not enter the streams and canals that go off to the right or to the left, but proceed straight ahead.

The boat was the main vehicle for transport in Bengal. The poets of charya have used the rowing of the boat as a significant metaphor in explaining the esoteric arts. A couple of dohas have detailed description of rowing, and the oarsmen and sailors find a place in these songs. One of Sarahapāda's poems says:

My body is my boat, my mind its oar. O my heart, steer by the advice of the guru. Concentrate and row, there is no other way to cross. As the steersman pulls on the mooring rope, so must you be pulled by your heart towards the Innate Way. There are robbers on the way and strong currents may upset your boat. Let the boat go upstream, till it vanishes into the point where the sea and the sky meet.
[C 38]

There is a doha by Kambalāmbarapāda, which describes a journey by boat. Boatmen in Bengal drive a mooring pole into the muddy banks to which they tether their boats. To set sail, the first thing that they do is pull up the mooring peg and loosen the rope, after which they bring the boats to the mid-stream and set their course. The doha repeats:

Khuṇṭi upāṛī melili kācchi|
Bāhatu Kāmali sadguru pucchi||

Māṅgata caṛhile caudisa cāhaa|
Keḍuāla nāhi kẽ ki bāhabake pāraa||
[C 8]

You have unpegged the boat and loosened the rope, now ask the guru and set your course, O Kāmali[29] (Kambalāmbarapāda)! Look around you as you take the road. You must have an oar to steer your boat.

Boats, perhaps more specifically barges, were the preferred vehicles for trade as well. People traded in gold and silver too. The aforementioned poem by Kambalāmbarapāda has a couple of lines at the very beginning:

Sone bharitī karuṇā nāvī|
Rūpā thoi nāhika ṭhāvī||
[C 8]

My boat of Compassion is filled to capacity with gold i.e. the Void, so that I have no more space to stow silver i.e. anything perceived in the outer world.

Here, *sona* (gold) is a play on the word *sunya* or the ultimate knowledge of the void and *rupa* (silver) on *rūpa* or phenomena.

Bridge-building was also a familiar activity in Bengal with its many rivers and canals. Cātīlapāda says in his poem that he has built a strong wooden bridge so that people may safely cross the river. The planks came from a great tree, and they were joined securely:

Dhāmārthe Cāṭila sāṅkama gaṛhai|
Pāragāmi loa nibhara tarai||
Phāḍia mohataru pāṭī joḍia|
Adaa diṛha ṭāṅgī nibāṇe koṛia||
[C 5]

*

The domestic life of Bengal is mentioned in the charyas. A song by Kukkurīpāda says:

Āṅgaṇa gharapaṇa suna bho biātī|
Kāneṭa cauri nila adharātī||
Susurā nida gela bahuṛī jāgaa|
Kāneṭa core nila kā gai māgaa||
[C 2]

Listen, O Avadhūtī,[30] to what happened in the courtyard of the house. At midnight, a thief entered and stole the young bride's earrings. The father-in-law is asleep, but the bride is awake. Where can she go and ask for it?

The words form a certain image. The bride had gone to bed still in her jewellery, and the thief stole it in the night. Her father-in-law knew nothing yet, but the bride could sleep no more. Where would she find the earrings she lost because of her own carelessness? Fear of the thief, fear of the in-laws and her grief over her loss, all kept her awake. The very next lines say:

Divasai bahuḍī kāgaḍare bhāa|
Rāti bhaile kāmaru jāa||
[C 2]

In the day, she screams in fear of a crow and in the night, she goes no one knows where.

This line points to the unchaste character of the bride. There is a similar Sanskrit śloka that we may be reminded of:

Divā kākarutādbhītā rātrau tarati Narmadām|
Tatra santi jale grāhā marmajñā saiva sundarī||[31]

It is evident that unchaste women were thought of in similar terms in ancient Bengal.

Thieves and robbers, as seen in the previous poem, find further mention in more dohas. People needed strong defences for their households. As Kāhṇupāda says:

Suṇa bāha Tathatā pahārī|
Moha-bhaṇḍāra lai saalā ahārī||
[C 36]

The Void has struck us with Tathatā (lit. 'suchness', implying the void) and looted all that was in the chest.

Strong locks featured in most houses. Sarahapāda's doha 'Jai pavana-gamaṇaduāre diḍha tālā bi dijjai' [K 22] hints at such locks.

Women were under strict authority and guardianship of men. The following dohas bear testimony to that:

Aisa uese jai phuṛa sijjhai|
Pavaṇa ghariṇi tahi ṇiccala bajjhai||
[K 24]

If one attends to such advice correctly, then the pavana-grihini may be stilled and killed.[32]

Ṇia ghare ghariṇī jāva ṇa majjai|
Tāva ki pañcabaṇṇa biharijjai||
[K 28]

Unless the wife at home mellows down, how may one dally within the five varnas?

Man and wife did not eat together; it would be contrary to the social customs of that time: 'Gharabai khajjai ghariṇi ehi jahi [desahi] abiāra' [D 84].

Kāhṇupāda provides a fine description of a wedding procession in one of his songs:

Bhavanirbbāṇe paṛaha mādalā|
Maṇa pavaṇa beṇi karaṇḍa kaśālā||
Jaa jaa dundahi sāda uchaliāṁ|
Kāhṇa Ḍombī bibāhe caliā||
Ḍombī bibāhiā ahāriu jāma|
Jautuke kia āṇutu dhāma||
[C 19]

The two drums are bhava-nirvana and the drumsticks are mana-pavana.[33] Amidst great shouts of triumph, and the booming of the big drum, Kāhṇa goes forth to marry the Dombi. I have destroyed all virtue of my birth by this marriage, but I have received the land beyond all realms as dowry.

We find here a pretty description of a wedding procession with the bridegroom. There are various kinds of drums, and people vociferously proclaim their joy. The Uttarakāṇḍa of Krittibas's *Ramayana* (Bangiya Sahitya Parishat edition) too has a similar description:

Jateka mahāpātra chāribhite sāje|
Sankha dundubhi singā chāripāshe bāje||
Singā dambura bāje kāngsya karatāl|
Padha mādal bheru dosar kāhāl||
. . . .
Karadā karadi bāje kundala kundali|
Benu banshi saramandal baje chandrābali||

The courtiers come together. Conch-shells, large drums and horns are heard on all sides. Cymbals, gongs, big and small drums join the trumpets. . . . Then there is the sound of rattle drums, lutes and flutes.

It seems that even in those days, the bridegroom received a fair amount of dowry from the bride's family and often married into a lower caste if the dowry was hefty enough. In the charya mentioned earlier, Kāhṇa says that he has destroyed his family name as well as the virtue of his birth in a higher caste, but he is very pleased with the dowry!

Chess was probably a popular game. Kāhṇupāda gives a detailed account of chess in one of his songs:

> Karuṇā pihāṛi khelahũ naabala|
> Sadguru-bõhe jitela bhavabala||
> Phīṭau duā mādesi re ṭhākura|
> Uāri uesẽ Kāhṇa niaṛa jinaura||
> Pahilẽ toṛiā baṛiyā māriu|
> Gaabarẽ toliā pāñcajanā ghāliu||
> Matiẽ ṭhākuraka parinibitā|
> Abaśa kariā bhavabala jitā||
> Bhanai Kāhṇu āmhe bhāla dāna dehũ|
> Cauśaṭṭhi koṭhā guṇiā lehũ||
>
> [C 12]

> Karuna (compassion) is the base on which I place my chessboard. Acting upon the advice from my guru, I won against my desires, and two of them were destroyed outright. The king should not be taken yet. Due to the advice of a benefactor, Kāhṇu has Jinapura within his reach. First, I moved the pawns, then took five of them with the rook ('gaja' or elephant in Bangla). I stopped the king with the queen, impeded his movements, and won over the force of existence. Kāhṇu says, I'm a good player, I am! I move along all the sixty-four squares.

The chess set, usually painted on a cloth, had to be spread on a base of sorts. The 'elephant' is the rook, which takes on a number of pawns. The 'minister' is the queen, which can corner the king and checkmate him.

A very realistic picture of the vintner's house and her business is evoked in a song by Birūpapāda:

> Eka se śuṇḍini dui ghare sāndhaa|
> Cīaṇa bākalaa vāruṇī bāndhaa||
> . . . .
> Daśamī duārata cihna dekhiā|
> Āila garāhaka apaṇe bahiā||
> Cauśaṭhi ghaṛiye dela pasārā|
> Paiṭhela garāhaka nāhi nisārā||
> Eka se ghaṛulī sarui nāla|
> Bhaṇanti Biruā thira kari cāla||
>
> [C 3]

> The wine-seller enters both the rooms. She uses a fermenting agent to prepare her wine. Her door bears the mark of her trade, which draws

her patrons in. The wine has been poured into sixty-four jars. All buyers fall silent upon entering her rooms. The wine-seller pours the wine through a narrow funnel. Birupa cautions her to be careful while pouring the wine.

Literature nowadays has no use for the clusters of curved tamarind pods, but it did honour the fruit then. A charya says, 'rukhera tentali kumbhīre khai', that is the crocodile eats the tamarind from the tree. We have also heard the following couplet in the *brata* of Maghmandal[34] when we were young:

Aam phale thoka thoka titail phale banka|
Chhaoal Surjai biya kare mayer jholay taka||

Mangoes ripen in bunches, the tamarind pods are curved. The boy Surjāi will be married today, and his mother will be richer.

The Santhals have songs which mention tamarind. A particular song says, 'The man I loved was dressed in gold, his ornaments were of silver. How can I forget that splendour? All his finery is now on top of that giant tamarind tree in our courtyard. Whenever I go to sweep the courtyard my eyes alight on the tree and I forget all else'.[35]

*

Elephants used to roam in the woods near the streams flowing down hills. As Sarahapāda says:

Mukkau cittagaenda karu ettha biappa ṇu puccha|
Gaaṇagirī ṇaijala pieu tahĩ taḍa basau saiccha||
[D 100]

Let loose the elephant of your mind, and do not ask for a choice. Let him drink from the rivers of the sky-mountain and let him live on its banks according to his own wish.

Kāhṇupāda says in a song [C 9] how a securely bound wild elephant breaks free by tearing apart the chains and destroying the pillars and enters the lotus grove nearby.

A song by Mahīdharapāda has exactly such a description:

Mātela cīa-gaendā dhāvai|
Nirantara gaaṇanta tusẽ gholai||
Pāpa puṇṇa beṇi toḍia sikala moḍia khambhāṭhāṇā|
Gaaṇa ṭākali lāgi re citta paiṭha ṇibāṇā||
[C 16]

My mind, the maddened elephant, rushes on towards the Void, destroying everything in its path. He has broken the chains of virtue and sin, he has upturned all the tethering poles, and he rests only when he has reached the summit of the sky (i.e. Nirvana).

A doha by Vīṇāpāda talks about the secret of catching an elephant – one must entice it with *sari*[36] songs:

Ālikāli beṇi sāri suṇiā|
Gaabara samarasa sāndhi guṇiā||
[C 17]

As the mighty elephant finds a place in the charyas, so does the little mouse that has always been a pest. It comes at night, rummages through the foodstuff, makes holes in the earthen floors and nibbles the aman paddy[37] stored in the loft or the granary:

Bhava bindāraa musā ṛṇaa gati|
Cañcala musā kaliāṁ nāśaka thātī||
Kāla musā uha ṇa bāṇa|
Gaaṇe uṭhi caraa (haraa?) amaṇa dhāṇa||
[C 21]

Translation: Sudeshna Datta Chaudhuri

Notes

1 Shashibhusan Dasgupta, 'Charyageetite Bangla o Bangali', in *Bauddhadharma o Charyageeti*, Kolkata: Orient Book Company, 1983, pp. 83–103.
2 'Doha' literally means a couplet.
3 *Charyacharyabinishchaya* (determination of the paths to be followed and not to be followed) is the first of the four manuscripts Haraprasad Shastri published in 1916 as *Hajar Bachharer Purano Bangala Bhashay Bauddhagan o Doha*. The padas or songs in the text are called *caryapadas*.
4 An interim stage of middle Indo-Aryan language, derivative of the Prakrits.
5 A long narrative tradition that emerged in early India.
6 The verse numbers with a C-prefix refer to the corresponding pada in *Charyacharyavinischaya* in *Hajar Bachharer Purano Bangala Bhashay Bauddhagan o Doha*, Haraprasad Shastri (ed.), Kolkata: Bangiya Sahitya Parishat, 1916. The Shastri edition of the text also includes emendations for each verse.
7 The verse numbers with a D-prefix refer to the corresponding verse in 'Sarahapādasya Dohākoṣah' in 'Dohakoṣa: With Notes and Translations', Prabodh Chandra Bagchi (ed.), *Journal of the Department of Letters*, 1935, 28: 1–180, 9–23.
8 Wandering mendicant ascetics, who carry a stick as a mark of their faith. They usually belong to the order of renunciates established by Adi Sankaracharya.
9 Mendicants of other sects.
10 The word is derived from Sthavira, meaning veteran, and refers to the oldest extant pre-Mahayana sect in Buddhism.

11 'Caturthatattva' is the fourth of four tattvas, viz. *vajra, bell, sosary and jñāna* or knowledge, regarding knowledge and control of the process of dying. See Vīryavajra's commentary on *Saṃpuṭa-tantra*, cited in Tadeusz Skorupski, 'The *Saṃpuṭa-tantra*: Sanskrit and Tibetan Versions of Chapter One', in *The Buddhist Forum*, Vol. IV, Tadeusz Skorupski (ed.), Tring: The Institute of Buddhist Studies, 2012, p. 213.

12 The edition does not have the complete text for these two verses.

13 Dombi literally means a woman from an untouchable caste that is commonly associated with the task of cremation. However, the word has a different connotation with reference to Sahajiya Buddhist rituals.

14 Kāhṇa or Kāhṇupāda, who is also referred to as Kṛṣṅācārya or Kṛṣṅavajra, is the composer of the highest number of charyapadas. Some scholars suggest that there were more than one poet who composed under the same name.

15 The Buddhist Tantric Sahajiyas imagine 32 cords in the human body. *Avadhuti* is the principal cord spread along the spinal column.

16 The sound unstruck; the primordial essence of creation.

17 One that reaffirms the *sadhaka* or the seeker's persistence in the path of the Void.

18 Implies that the sadhaka has mastered all dualities.

19 'Killed', that is they have become dead to him and his newly adopted way of life.

20 Sahaja or the ultimate knowledge of the Void.

21 Author's note: See also 'Are putto bojjhu rasa-rasaṇa susaṇṭhia abejja' etc. by Sarahapāda [D 51].

22 Author's note: Dr Sukumar Sen has briefly discussed this in *Prachin Bangla o Bangali*, pp. 36–38.

23 Author's note: Dr Niharranjan Roy mentions this in his booklet *Bangali Hindur Barnabhed*.

24 The verse numbers with a K-prefix refer to the corresponding verse in 'Kāhṇapādasya Dohākoṣah' in 'Dohakoṣa: With Notes and Translations', Prabodh Chandra Bagchi (ed.), *Journal of the Department of Letters*, op. cit., 24–27.

25 The couplet implies that the sadhaka has made his heart free of all worldly desires, like a betel leaf and the Void, free of all desire of attainment, like camphor, and has tasted them together while his mind is at the *visuddha chakra* at the throat – united with *nairamani* or the ultimate knowledge.

26 Nairatmā is a goddess in Tantric Buddhist Pantheon, also signifying the destruction of the 'atman', or the self-essence.

27 The path of a Mahayana Buddhist sadhaka is the union of the ultimate knowledge of the Void or *sunyata* and the path of the compassion or *Karuna*.

28 Author's note: See Prabodh Chandra Bagchi, 'Materials for a Critical Edition of the Old Bengali Caryapadas', *Journal of the Department of Letters*, 1938, 30: 1–156, 54.

29 Author's note: Wage labourers are still called 'kamula' (kamuliya or kamaliya) in the eastern parts of Bengal.

30 Avadhutas were among the practitioners of a yogic tradition that emerged in medieval India. In this context, *Avadhutī*, besides its primary meaning, refers to the central column of the nervous system through which the esoteric sect sought salvation.

31 Author's note: A variant of the sloka is also found elsewhere – 'Divā vibheti kākebhyo rātrau santarate nadīm|/Tatra nakrabhayaṃ nāsti taddhi jānanti tadvidaḥ||'. The story associated with the sloka has been narrated in *Prabodhachandrika* of Mrityunjaya Vidyalamkar. This is the variant that has been taken there.

32 Pavana-grihini or the air-wife here refers to the breathing of the sadhaka, controlling which may lead one to salvation.

33 Bhava is desire and Nirvana is going beyond desire, thus ending the stream of existence or suffering. The esoteric practice of the Tantric Buddhist Sahajiyas sought the path of salvation through rituals like controlling one's breath. Here the doha refers to the duality within existence and the path for salvation.
34 A fertility ritual in Bengal where the Sun god is worshipped during the month of Magh (late winter).
35 Author's note: 'Saontali Gan', collected by Santoshchandra Majumdar, *Visva-Bharati Patrika*, 1946, 5(2): 110–120, 112.
36 A traditional form of song commonly found in the eastern parts of Bengal, primarily among boatmen.
37 The principal rice crop of Bengal, usually harvested in autumn.

2 Upendranath Bhattacharya: The emergence of the Baul sect and the period of composition of Baul songs

Introduction

Upendranath Bhattacharya (1899–1970) was a noted scholar who worked on the Baul tradition and also on life of Rabindranath Tagore. He studied literature in Rajshahi College and Dhaka University, taught in different schools and colleges in Nadia and Calcutta, India, and became a professor at Rabindra Bharati University, Calcutta. His works on Tagore's poems and plays are entitled *Rabindrakavya Parikrama* (1952) and *Rabindranatya Parikrama* (1954). However, his most distinguished contribution to the field of literary studies is *Banglar Baul o Baul Gan* (1957), a compendium of nearly a thousand Baul songs, along with a detailed introduction.

The year 1916 was a decisive moment in the history of Bangla literary studies as two of its earliest forms were published for the first time in print. One of them was *Charyacharyavinischaya*, found in 1907 and subsequently published by Haraprasad Shastri, and the second was *Srikrishnakirtan* of Baru Chandidas, found by Basantaranjan Roy from a village in 1909.

While the mainstream of literary studies was trying to find the source of Bangla literature in ancient and medieval literature, there was a parallel stream that was tracing it down to oral and folk traditions. Shashibhusan Dasgupta's seminal work *Obscure Religious Cults* was published in early 1946 where he analysed the philosophy and the practices of the Baul sect, thus establishing a firm link between early written literature and the continuing practices of various esoteric sects of Bengal. He also discussed the two primary divisions of such practices, namely the Vaishnav and the Buddhist Sahajiya cults and other sectarian influences.

Upendranath Bhattacharya contributed to scholarship in this area not only by compiling one of the earliest and definitive compendiums of Baul songs, but also by providing an overview of the history of its practice right from the beginning. In the current selection which is a part of his introductory essay in *Banglar Baul o Baul Gan*, he tries to trace the emergence of the Baul tradition as an inclusive faith embracing tenets of Vaishnavism, Tantric Buddhism, and Sufism and how it arrived at its present state of being. One

DOI: 10.4324/9781003224686-3

may find his insights about the practice quite prophetic as the songs gained popularity among the rural as well as urban population, while their ties with the esoteric, sectarian tradition weakened over time.

*

The emergence of the Baul sect and the period of composition of Baul songs[1]

Upendranath Bhattacharya

The foundation of the Baul sect lies in harmony and synthesis. The basic spiritual pursuit of this sect is based on Tantric Buddhism. Other sects such as Saivism; the cult of Radha and Krishna; and the philosophies of the Vaishnav-Sahajiyas, Sufism, and Gaudiya-Vaishnavism have left their impressions on the religion. Combined with these, certain features specific to the faith have also developed to give it a distinct character. It will be discussed elsewhere.

It was particularly during the reign of the Pala dynasty (8th–12th centuries CE) in Bengal that Buddhism spread far and wide. Between the 9th and 12th centuries, Buddhism gained a foothold among the common people, assuming a particular Tantric form that was based on a set of practices. Agamasaiva, ancient Tantric Sivasakti beliefs, and Hatha-yoga practices came together with Prajna-Upayavada to constitute Vajrayana and ultimately gave a complete form to Sahajayana. The religion found mass acceptance, having synthesised earthly experiences with salvation. In Bengal, this Buddhist Sahaja religion spread particularly among the economically weaker sections.

The Senas ruled Bengal from the early 12th to the mid-13th centuries. The Senas (11th–13th centuries CE) were Vaishnavites. Prior to that, the *leelas* of Radha and Krishna were known outside of Bengal. During their reign, these tales spread within the kingdom as well. Noteworthy references are found in the 12th-century poet Jayadeva's *Gitagovindam* and in the works of contemporary poets who wrote of the leelas of Radha and Krishna. The Sivasaktivada of the Hindus had merged in some respects with the Buddhist Prajna-Upayavada during the reign of the Palas, and under the Senas the cult of Radha-Krishna established itself, harmonising *Prakriti* and *Purusha*. The earlier practices of religion included the merging with Prakriti and other unifying pursuits, and this was retained during the Vaishnav period. That basic form was preserved during the Vaishnav period. Thus, there was a synthesis of Buddhism and Vaishnavism, and the Buddha became an avatar in Hindu mythology. It is at this juncture that the Vaishnav-Sahajiya faith appears. Naturally, a large number of the common people converted from Buddhist-Sahajiya to Vaishnav-Sahajiya. The two sects were very similar in the fundamental spiritual practices. It would not be illogical to point out that the verse describing the unifying practice in *Srikrishnakirtan* supports this statement.[2] Even though the Vaishnav-Sahajiya sect emerged invigorated and with new characteristics after the rise of Chaitanya, its seeds had germinated earlier and had already started to spread.

The Muslim rulers established their domain in Bengal around the middle of the 13th century. State religions have a tendency of gaining primacy within society, and there can be different reasons for it. During the rule of the Palas, the religion of the rulers was Buddhism; during the Senas, it was Vaishnavism that held sway over the masses. There were exchanges between the two religions, which gave rise to a syncretic form. However, synthesis or negotiations with a religion of foreign origin proved impossible. These people of a different faith and race began to oppress the Buddhists. Under the new rulers, Odantapura and Vikramshila were destroyed, and many Buddhist monks and nuns lost their lives. When Islam was established as the state religion and started spreading, Brahmins and other high castes were forced to recede into their shells like tortoises to preserve their caste and religion. In self-defence, they took recourse to forming new rules, prohibitions, and social rituals as well as formulating new religious norms. This group of staunch and conservative upper-caste Hindus had kept a large section of backward and so-called 'low-caste' people outside all social transactions. A majority of these people belonged to the Sahajiya faith. They converted in large numbers to Islam after considering its social advantages and in order to escape the discrimination and oppression they faced at the hands of the upper-caste Hindus. Many became staunch Muslims, adopting the Sharia laws. Others became Muslim nominally to protect themselves and continued the practices of Sahajiyas. These people were the first fakirs of Bengal.

With the beginnings of Muslim rule in India, a religious sect known as the Sufis began to appear. The path of the Sufis was different from institutionalised Islam. The religion was in some ways similar to Vedantic philosophy, based on mysticism and the attainment of self-realisation. The aim of Sufi religious pursuit was to realise one's soul through the path of love to attain a luminous and complete perception of the self. It believed in accepting a guru, discarded rituals and performances of institutional Islam, and cultivated a tolerant view towards other religions.

Towards the end of the 13th century, Sufis started coming into Bengal, and they continued to spread unhindered until the 17th century.[3] Sufis do not recognise divisions between people, races, and religions – they preach a liberal, universal faith. They were able to gain the respect of both Hindus and Muslims.

Muslims who followed the Sahajiya path found a refuge with their arrival. Their faith bore certain similarities with Sufism. These similarities were in the acknowledgement of the presence of the absolute truth in the body, doing away with religious rituals and the inward turn in religious practices among other things. Muslim Sahajiyas took shelter in such similarities to protect themselves and live outside of Muslim society. They came under the influence of Sufism, and, consequently, the songs composed by later Muslim Bauls began to include Sufi phrases.

After the rise of Chaitanya, early followers of the Sahajiya-Vaishnav faith who had not converted to Islam and had barely succeeded in retaining their beliefs were inspired afresh by a new energy. This was aided by the dissemination of the Vaishnav Goswamis' doctrine of Chaitanya and texts like *Chaitanyacharitamrita*, which created a spiritual atmosphere of ideal love. In different verse forms, biographical accounts and chronicles, their religious views, and philosophy started being articulated around this time. The religions previously based on knowledge and on meditative performances were infused deeply with the spirit of love. The Vaishnav-Sahajiya cult received a firm foundation.

In the post-Chaitanya period, even the Muslim-Sahajiya Fakirs, who had adopted a superficial form of Sufism, were influenced by the Vaishnav-Sahajiya faith.

Following Chaitanya's death, when Gaudiya-Vaishnavism had begun to spread and Krishnadas Kaviraj's *Chaitanyacharitamrita* had appeared, we can see the emergence of the Baul sect, approximately around 1625 CE. The foundation and philosophy of the cult included the union of Radha–Krishna or the Prakriti–Purusha, the transcendental spirituality of the Upanishads and Sufism, and personal God, while their practices were based on those of the Buddhist Sahajiyas or a modified form of the Vaishnav Sahajiyas.

Whenever a new religious faith emerges, it comes with its own specific features. The faith of the Bauls, similarly, evolved with its own characteristics. These were maintained through the traditional relationship between the master and the disciple. In Bengal, their socio-religious practices were embraced by the humblest of the people. Their practices and rituals, religious dicta, and clothing did not fit in very well with societal norms, and, as a result, they were forced to go into hiding. They excluded themselves from mainstream society and stayed within their communities.

For various reasons, they did not codify their religious ideas and meditative practices in the form of manuscripts or books. They chose to express these, instead, through their songs. Their songs became vehicles for expressing their emotions, their imagination, and their religious experiences.

Buddhist Sahajiyas too expressed their religious beliefs and practices through different symbols and suggestions in their songs as in the examples of Charyapadas. The songs come with directives that suggest that they were meant to be performed and sung with the use of the classical modes of music, or ragas and raginis.[4] Haraprasad Shastri, the editor of the Charyapadas (composed between the 8th and 12th centuries CE), says that 'These padas are of kirtans. Sankirtans were performed even in those days and the verses were known as padas. Today we refer to the verses in *kirtans* as padas. Back then they used to be called charyapadas'.[5]

The bibliography of Buddhist Tantric texts prepared by Dr P. Cordier mentions a number of examples from Buddhist lyrical literature.[6]

Usually when we refer to padas we think of short verses, written with a particular spirit and feeling, to rhythms suited to singing. Verses of a spiritual or philosophical nature and descriptive poems also come under the label of padas. Short verses that are filled with emotion and feeling are also referred to as padas in Sanskrit literature. Jayadeva's *Gitagovindam* is also known as padavali[7] – a string of verses. Its form is structured to suit the demands of music. The term pada is also used in Vaishnav literature to describe verses of short length. Needless to say, these verses are meant for singing. The verses in *Srikrishnakirtan* were sung to various ragas and raginis,[8] and all subsequent compositions in the great tradition of Vaishnav padavali were also composed for the same purpose. They were not devoid of philosophical content either. So, we see that since the 9th or 10th century, short descriptive verses replete with spiritual philosophy and ideas have come down to us as songs. They inspired subsequent generations of songs to be composed in the same manner. That said, one might push the date even further back and look for inspiration in the suktas or religious incantations and hymns from the Vedic period. Many such hymns in the Vedas are dedicated to deities and contain devotional and philosophical elements in them. These suktas too would often be sung to music. The musical elements can be found in the Samaveda. A gradual transformation of these hymns is reflected in the Buddhist Sahajiya hymns and verses. The Vaishnav padavali demonstrates that all subsequent religious verses are, in fact, songs.

The fakirs who adhered to the Sufi path were also in the habit of gathering in secret circles to perform their songs and dances which carried religious and devotional messages. These practices are denoted as *Sama*. Following the emergence of Chaitanya, Bengal became steeped in a musical religious culture, where the chanting of the name and Vaishnav padavali-kirtans were prevalent. As a result, the idea that songs are an appropriate medium for expression of religious thought became widely accepted among the people. In fact, the members of the Baul sect accept music and song as the only medium of self-expression.

Having removed themselves from the mainstreams of society, Muslim fakirs and Hindu Bauls established separate spheres for themselves, where they were able to assemble and express their profoundest devotional feelings and religious ideas through music and song. Music was an essential part of their inner lives and their medium of self-expression.

It can be argued that Baul songs emerged around 1650. The evolution, development, and spread of the form continued into the late 19th century. We may extend this period of development into the first decades of the 20th century. By these calculations, we can consider a span of approximately two hundred and seventy-five years, between 1650 and 1925, as the period of emergence, spread, and evolution of this particular form. In the songs themselves, we see very little trace of the ancient traditions. There may have been some vestiges in the early days, but as the songs passed down orally, such signs were erased and replaced by contemporary symbols and ideas.

Of these, the song that appears to me to be the oldest dates back to the 18th century at the earliest.

The first quarter of the 20th century marks the beginning of the end of Baul music. The sect begins to shrink during this time and gradually moves towards extinction. The Bauls were unable to attract new members either among the Muslims or the Hindus. Thanks to a mounting pressure from those who upheld the Sharia, fakirs too started to disappear in the early 20th century. The surviving members continued to practice their faith. Committed to their beliefs, they were able to appreciate the true value of the results of their religious practices. We can rule out any possibility that these sects will spread any further – their extinction seems inevitable and irrevocable. The number of Bauls among Hindus has also decreased considerably. There are no new entrants to the faith. The reasons are many: societal, religious, moral, economical, and so on. No new *akhara* appears to have formed in the recent past, and those that existed are now inhabited by elder Vaishnavites. In the villages of Burdwan, I have noticed many an akhara where an elderly Vaishnav woman is spending her final years in solitude. It is difficult to find a Baul who has poetic abilities, knowledge of the philosophy, and is able to serve as a master. Today, we hardly ever come across new, original Baul compositions.

Translation: Sujaan Mukherjee

Notes

1 Upendranath Bhattacharya, 'Bauddhadharmer Abirbhab o Baulganer Rachanakal', in *Banglar Baul o Baul Gan*, Kolkata: Orient Book Company, 1957, pp. 126–132.

2 Bhattacharya refers to a verse in the last canto in *Srikrishnakirtan* called 'Radhabiraha' (the estrangement of Radha), where after Radha's repeated plea to Krishna to reunite with her, Krishna tells her that she no longer has an appeal for him since he spends his days and nights in practicing yoga: 'ahanishi yoga dheai'. The verse, set to Raga Mallar and Tala Rupak, describes Krishna's yoga practices.

3 Author's note: Enamul Haq, *Bange Sufiprabhav* (1935), Ch. III., 5th. Reprint, Dhaka: Ramon Publishers, 2006.

4 Author's note: Patmanjari, Gavada, Aru, Gunjari, Debakri, Desakh, Bhairavi, Kamode, Dhanasi, Ramakri, Baradi, etc.

5 Author's note: Introduction to *Hajar Bachharer Purano Bangala Bhashay Bauddhagan o Doha*, Harprasad Shastri (ed.), Kolkata: Bangiya-Sahitya-Parishat, 1916, p. 16.

6 Author's note: Caturavajragītikā (Advayavajra); Caryādohākoṣagītikā (Kaṅkaṇa); Dohākoṣagīti, Dohākoṣacaryāgiīti, Dākinīvajraguhyagīti (Saraha); Vajrāsanagīti, Caryāgīti, Dipaṅkara- Śṛjñāna -Dharmagītikā (Dipaṅkara-Śṛjñāna); Luipāda-Gītika (Luipāda); Virūpa-Gītikā, Virūpavajragītikā (Virūpa); Sahajagīti (Bhusuku); Mahāmudrāvajragīti (Śavara), etc.

7 Author's note: 'madhurakomalakāntapadāvalīm', *Gītagovindam* 1.3.

8 Author's note: 'Talshikshar puthi', 'Srikrishnakirtaner parisishtha', pp. 158–164; Manindramohan Basu, 'Srikrishnakirtaner pader nababishkrita puthi', *Sahitya-Parishat-Patrika*, 1932, 39(3): 176–194 and 'Baru Chandidaser pader nababishkrita puthi (2)' *Sahitya-Parishat-Patrika*, 1933, 40(1): 43–54.

3 Dineshchandra Sen: The termination of Sri Gauranga's *Leela*

Introduction

An erudite scholar and historian of Bangla literature, Dineshchandra Sen (1866–1939) was born in Dhaka. He studied English literature and taught in various schools in Sylhet and Comilla. He moved to Calcutta because of his ill health and in 1905 became an examiner in the University of Calcutta. He was a pioneer in the field of literary history with his work on Bangla language and literature entitled *Bangabhasha o Sahitya* (1896). His *History of Bengali Language and Literature* (1911) brought him an international recognition, and he was awarded the Ramtanu Lahiri Research Fellowship by the University of Calcutta in 1913, which facilitated his studies on *Mymensingh Geetika* (1923) and *Purbabanga Geetika* (1923–1932). He became the first Head of the Department of 'Bangla Language and Literature' at the University of Calcutta in 1919, a position he occupied till his retirement in 1932. A prolific writer, Sen wrote extensively for scholarly journals and popular periodicals and contributed towards shaping a general awareness of literary historiography. The essay presented here entitled 'The Termination of Sri Gauranga's Leela' was first published in *Bharatbarsha* (1929).

The advent of Sri Chaitanya (1486–1533) had a radical influence on the life and art of medieval Bengal. It brought a new lease of life to the Vaishnav *padavali* tradition and led to a large hagiographic corpus centred on the life of Sri Chaitanya and some of his followers. Vrindavandas' *Chaitanyabhagavat* was the first of such hagiographies, and Krishnadas Kaviraj's *Chaitanyacharitamrita* has been looked upon as a seminal text with one of the finest expositions of the philosophical treatises of the Gaudiya Vaishnav faith. Lochandas and Jayananda were also among the major poets who wrote on the life of Sri Chaitanya. There were also many tales and legends on the last phase of Sri Chaitanya's life in Puri, particularly regarding the nature and cause of his death. This aspect of his life remained shrouded in mystery and was of persistent interest to scholars of medieval Bengal and Vaishnavism.

For a considerable period, scholars of Bangla literature and historians engaged with the hagiographies, justifying or negating claims made by poets. A monumental work in this area is *Srichaitanyachariter Upadan*

DOI: 10.4324/9781003224686-4

(1938) by Biman Behari Majumdar. It is also the first doctoral thesis that is written in Bangla from the University of Calcutta. Sen's essay attempts a reconciliation of various contesting views and opinions regarding the demise of Sri Chaitanya from textual and legendary sources alike. His approach is primarily rationalist and based on evidence, but he does not shy away from giving importance to the devotional overtones on the debate.

*

The termination of Sri Gauranga's *Leela*[1]

Dineshchandra Sen

We shall not attempt to resolve the thorny issue of whether Sri Gauranga[2] was a full incarnation, a partial one, or merely a devotee of the divine. What purpose could possibly be served by inflicting the materialist's complex web of logic upon those who surrender themselves at his lotus feet, seeing in him the fruition of true godhead? The keys of the spiritual kingdom are entrusted to the faithful. Even were their faith destroyed, we can offer nothing in place of the heavenly peace and contentment that is their prerogative. A few well-aimed hammer blows might demolish the Taj Mahal of their faith, but would dry and arid materialism be able to quench the thirst of their soul?

Let us set this matter aside. Whether a god or the *avatar* of one, Chaitanya came into the world in the form of a man and was subject to every natural law that binds corporeal beings. He caught fever on the way to Gaya, thorns pricked in his flesh drew blood – he could not escape the clutches of human ailment. He was born of the womb of Sachimata. He had siblings,[3] a wife, and an affectionate father like the rest of us. We can therefore consider the events of his life as earthly *leela*. The leela of divine love we observe in him is of course celestial – marvellously unprecedented – there is nothing like it in the world. His tears are more precious than the Kohinoor or the Kaustubh,[4] and the intensity and ardour of his passion are not of this earth. If we analyse this ecstatic tendency, we shall discern in him such spiritual beauty and such a divine pleasure of the lotus of love that opens wide the very gates of heaven to the world and makes the suprasensible accessible to the senses. Nevertheless, we shall consider him a corporeal being. He has roared as a wild boar,[5] revealed physical forms resplendent with six or eight arms,[6] planted a mango tree and made it bear fruit instantly,[7] ingested the food of twelve men in a day yet remained whip thin,[8] – we will skirt the devotion with which various accounts of Chaitanya's life narrate such matters and refrain from expressing any opinion about them. The birth of Vrindavandas was shrouded in profound mystery, a fact for which some would condemn him. He vociferously proclaims how he was able to overcome the laws of nature and attain supernatural spiritual powers upon Lord Chaitanya's command. He has threatened to kick those who would not believe him on their heads. But it is useless to employ threats of physical violence; the educated youth of our times will not have any confidence in these supernatural theories. The story that Lord Chaitanya summoned Lord Vishnu's celestial discus to severe the heads of the wicked brothers Jagai and Madhai and that immediately the weapon could be seen whirring over them has been narrated by Vrindavandas as though he were an eyewitness. We do not scoff at these stories, but we must point out that if Chaitanya had really been an *avatar* of Lord Vishnu, he had not really appeared in this age to intimidate people with the Vishnu-chakra[9] but rather to conquer the world with the unprecedented power of his loving tears. Even conservative Vaishnavs would perhaps not penalise me for saying this.

Several absurd stories about his demise are popular in Vaishnav circles, and these form the focus of my discussion today. Some Vaishnavs say that Lord Chaitanya was absorbed into the body of Lord Jagannath; others assert that he entered the thigh of the Gopinath idol and was united with it. The Gopinath idol has a golden dot beneath its skirts. The priests are regularly persuaded to remove the skirt and show the spot to the devotee against a donation of one rupee to the temple. There is no dearth of visitors, so the priests derive as much profit from, and take as great care in, the exhibition of this tiny spot regarded divine for the great passage of Lord Sri Chaitanya as pilgrims derive satisfaction from viewing it.

What is surprising, however, is that the most prominent of the accounts of Lord Sri Chaitanya's life make no mention of the circumstances of his demise. *Amritabazar Patrika*'s office has printed Murari Gupta's poetic work *Sṛkṛṣṇacaitanyacaritāmṛtam*. It is not possible to establish the authenticity of every part of it, since, despite having been written in 1503, it incorporates many incidents that took place at a later date. This biography of Chaitanya does not mention his passing. Kavi Karnapur, who knew the Mahaprabhu in person, composed the play *Caitanyacandrodaya* in 1572. He, too, refrains from mentioning the Mahaprabhu's demise. Krishnadas Kaviraj, who wrote the *Chaitanyacharitamrita* in 1582, is also silent in this regard, only remarking at the beginning of the book that the Lord attained his heavenly abode in 1455 Saka era (1533). Vrindavandas wrote the *Chaitanyabhagavat* probably in 1575, and the text does not talk about the Mahaprabhu's death. Neither do Nityanandadas' *Premavilas* (1640) nor Narahari Chakrabarty's well-known 1708 book *Bhaktiratnakar*.

It seems as though Vaishnav biographers have come to a mutual arrangement in this matter. Was this collective adjustment prompted by the sensibility that it is unseemly to talk about things that are too painful? Vaishnav teaching, after all, does prohibit the writing down of similar distressing incidents. Could this be the reason for all of these writers steadfastly protecting the facts of Chaitanya's demise? But then, how was Krishnadas, who wrote the *Chaitanyacharitamrita*, able to describe the eternal rest of Haridas, or the author of the *Chaitanyabhagavat* able to narrate the demise of Jagannath Mishra? *Bhaktiratnakar* mentions the passing of many Vaishnav luminaries such as Dasgoswami and Rupa-Sanatan. The Mahaprabhu's demise is recorded in that text, but it is a fleeting reference: not a hint is offered about how that great bereavement actually came to pass. We only know from the *Chaitanyacharitamrita* and other seminal texts that he was born on the full moon night of the month of Baisakh (April–May) in Saka era 1407 (1485–1486) and left the earthly abode on the seventh day of the fortnight of the waxing moon in the month of Asarh (June–July) in Saka era 1454 (1533–1534). The theory that the facts regarding the demise of Chaitanya were deliberately suppressed by the chroniclers of his life due to the terribly painful nature of the event may be partially correct, but it cannot offer a complete explanation. There were certain other reasons why conservative Vaishnav society hid the facts around Chaitanya's earthly diversions. His sportiveness in the world is eternal. It would be a transgression to describe any end to it. 'To this day Gora Ray performs his leela/And only a fortunate handful can see his whimsy.' The dissolution of this endless diversion is beyond the imagination of these chroniclers. The masses knew him as Jagadbandhu[10] incarnate. The story of him being assimilated into the body of Lord Jagannath was bruited about the country by the priests of that deity. While established authors did not wish to hurt mass sentiment by challenging such rumours, they were also loth to slander truth by lending their support to this view. By then, Vaishnav society had established strong roots with its own rules and laws, and its members agreed upon the same theories regarding the Mahaprabhu. During those days, only with the sanction of the Goswamis of Vrindavan[11] could a new book be disseminated among the Vaishnavs. A few, such as Jayananda's *Chaitanyamangal* and Gobindadas' *Karcha*, managed to escape this circle of influence; but it was for this reason that, despite being replete with novel historical facts, several books are not considered legitimate accounts in dogmatic Vaishnavite circles. The Goswamis of Vrindavan were at great pains to establish the handful of broad precepts that were thought to constitute Chaitanya's life. Thus, those books that did not adhere unfailingly to those origins, precepts and opinions were not recognised by them. There was a felt need to establish with the help of a variety of scriptural authority that Lord Sri Chaitanya and Lord Sri Krishna were one and the same. Vrindavan has always drawn parallels between Chaitanya's life and Krishna's, and the composer of the *Chaitanyacharitamrita* has followed its lead. In childhood, Sri Chaitanya had lain on a python,[12] he had repeatedly partaken from the rice offered to a Brahmin guest,[13] a thief had tried to kidnap him but had returned him home overcome by his charisma – these stories told about Chaitanya are exact replicas of the life of Krishna of the *Bhagavatam*. So much so that Vrindavandas has even compared Chaitanya's early tutor Gangadas to Sri Krishna's guru Sandipani.[14] He has compared the student Chaitanya in a class at the village *tol*[15] to the young scholar Krishna surrounded by learned ascetics in *Naimisharanya*. However far-fetched this might sound, conservative Vaishnavs would accept nothing else. They were also at pains to prove that Chaitanya's companions were nothing but *avatars* of Radhika's maiden companions and wrote variedly and extensively in Sanskrit and Bangla in order to establish the theologies of Krishna and Chaitanya as identical.

Needless to say, the *Chaitanyabhagavat* and the *Chaitanyacharitamrita* were the two volumes that expended the most labour to prove Lord Sri Chaitanya's status as an *avatar*. I do not mean to imply that the historical grounding of these texts is slack. I only note that the value that they have given to establishing the *avatar* theory is less than the attention paid in them as far as historical significance is concerned. The importance of religious scriptures the world over is not exactly due to the value of their argumentative, logical, or analytical qualities. The demand of each of these texts on the reverence of their readers is mostly based upon something similar to blind religious faith.

But we have wandered quite far from our stated topic. There are three speculations about the ending of Sri Chaitanya's leela. We have indicated two of them before: (1) melting into the body of Lord Jagannath and (2) dissolving into Gopinath. The third belief is very modern and suggests that Lord Chaitanya had fallen into the sea and thus perished. This story has been spread across the country by few modern educated writers. This theory is completely without foundation. After some research, certain newly educated individuals found that there were no books that described the ending of Chaitanya-leela; at least no texts or documents had come to their hands when they had the matter under consideration. They could not, of course, believe the stories about Chaitanya dissolving into the bodies of Jagannath or Gopinath. Therefore, when it came to their notice that at one point in the *Chaitanyacharitamrita*, it is described how Sri Chaitanya, being in a state of ecstasy, perceived in the moonlight-inscribed blue waters of the Bay of Bengal the eternal amorous sport of Radha and Krishna and immediately prepared to jump into the water to become one with that divine leela, these writers instantly decided that Chaitanya must not have escaped the clutches of the deep waters, and in this anecdote was to be found the true cause for the termination of his own leela.

However, the incident happened like this. The ocean at Puri looked bewitching on a certain moon-drenched night. The moon had crested the rippling waves with diadems of light. The entire ocean seemed to be heaving with the divine pleasure of the cosmic dance of Radha and Krishna. Chaitanya thought to himself: 'Behold! Here is the leela of Krishna with his *gopis*.' In moments the delusion grew stronger, imagination became insight – 'Mahaprabhu was engulfed in that play' – and he surrendered to Radha and Krishna's divine leela and plunged into the water.

Swarup and his other devotees could not find him. They thought he must be in the Jagannath temple or at any other shrine – maybe at Lord Jagannath's maternal aunt's house at Gunjabari[16] or at the sacred tank of Narendra Sarovara or 'in Chatak Parvat or Konark.'[17] On full moon nights, when the gleaming radiance of nature would trace the fields of Radha–Krishna's leela in his eyes, Chaitanya would roam the night away, sometimes going as far as Konark, the more profoundly to experience the divine dance. Not finding him anywhere, his devotees reached the seashore and were afraid that he might have been taken by the waves.

But a fisherman had caught him in his net. His limbs would become limp and bones disjointed towards the end of these bouts of ecstasy. This time the same thing had happened. The fisherman did not recognise him – he said, 'I have seen the Lord many times, this is not his handsome form, this is a distorted image!' But when Swarup loudly chanted the names of Hari, his limbs reknitted, and he woke up. This is nothing new – in his later life he was frequently prone to such fits of mystic stupor. Upon regaining consciousness, he said, 'I thought I was watching Krishna perform his leela with the gopis on the banks of the Yamuna.'

He was still alive approximately two and a half months more after this incident.

The *Chaitanyacharitamrita* has recounted many tales that took place afterwards. Gauranga became increasingly impatient in his separation from Krishna. Gobinda and Swarup had a difficult task restraining him at night. If they dozed off for a moment, he would start running, and once he even got lost in a flower garden. Where would this man go, chanting the names of Hari, arms uplifted, dancing to some sublime inner melody? Where would this mystic madman roam? What if he fell into water or got lost in the forest? His devotees grew increasingly anxious. Then a pundit named Shankar started keeping watch, serving at his feet throughout the night. Swarup, Gobinda, and Shankar were the three who kept keen vigilance on him round the clock.

After this, on a full moon night in the month of Baisakh, he visited the Jagannatha Vallabha garden and made Swarup sing Jayadeva's 'Lalitalavangalatāpariśīlana-komalamalayasamīre'[18] and danced all night in ecstatic bliss. During this time, he would recite verses nonstop from Vidyapati, Chandidas, *Jagannathaballabha Natakam*, and the *Srikrishnakarnamritam* and pass the night away propounding their meaning to Swarup.

Krishnadas Kaviraj ends his work at this point. He has written that the leela of the Mahaprabhu is endless – how could he hope to explicate it? The poet's powers are limited, 'language inept' – he could not say anything else. The *Chaitanyacharitamrita* ends here.

So now we notice that Sri Chaitanya did perform more leela after being rescued by the fisherman. No legend in Puri or elsewhere has it that he gave up his life by falling into the ocean. Finding no other sign of the Mahaprabhu's demise, newly educated writers leaped to the conclusion that falling into the sea marked his end. But why would this be the end? The one who has inscribed the incident has himself noted how a fisherman had brought Chaitanya back to shore and has also recorded many of his other leela after this incident. What could one possibly have to say about writers who ignore these facts and scoff at other evidence and only accept the veracity of a stray figment of their imagination? Such is the method for discerning authenticity as employed by these modern-day travellers on the path of truth! This account of a watery demise has grown quite widespread, yet it contains not a grain of truth.

It is now left to tackle the legends about becoming one with the Jagannath or Gopinath idols.

We do not come across the Gopinath legend in any written sources. However, Vaishnavs sometimes recite the following verse: 'Where shall we go, oh what shall we do?/ We have lost Gorachand in the house of Gopinath.'

Some Vaishnavs say that on a full moon night in the month of Magha (January–February) (possibly seven months after the passing of Chaitanya), Gadadhar winessed a supernatural vision. It was as though Chaitanyadev descended from the sky exuding divine effulgence and entered the temple of Gopinath, upon which the temple idol immediately enfolded the mass of light into itself. This vision appeared to Gadadhar with such clarity and lucidity that he was persuaded to believe that Lord Chaitanya had truly reappeared and then become one with the Gopinath idol. Some therefore indicate the verse given before as Gadadhardas' utterance.

Gadadhar passed away on the new moon of the month of Jaishtha (May–June). He was an intimate of the Mahaprabhu and is even considered an *avatar* of Srimati Radhika. He went to his eternal rest in the Gopinath temple, and Chaitanyadev himself had stayed quite some time there. The legend of the Mahapraphu melting into the Gopinath idol gained currency possibly due to these causes. However, no ancient texts or documents survive that indicate this. The priests of the Gopinath temple used the rumours of the Mahaprabhu entering the idol to their advantage. About the third legend – the Mahaprabhu entering the body of Jagannath – there exist a handful of texts contemporaneous to Chaitanya – surviving in manuscripts two or two and a half centuries old – which are relatively less valued than the Vaishnav *charits* or hagiographies that are particularly honoured in Vaishnav society. In three of them, we find some tenuous support for the third thesis. Ishan Nagar was a trusted follower of the Mahaprabhu. In his *Advaita-Prakash*, he writes that once the Mahaprabhu went to Jagannath. the doors of the temple closed on their own. The devotees waited anxiously outside: 'the door opened by itself after some time/ everyone realised that Gauranga was there no more.' *Advaita-Prakash* ends in 1568.

Lochandas wrote the *Chaitanyamangal* in 1575. This text also mentions that the Mahaprabhu became one with Jagannath on a Sunday of 1455 Saka era (1533) on the seventh day of the waxing moon in the month of Asharh (June–July).

Jayananda composed his *Chaitanyamangal* in 1540. This text also mentions that Chaitanya disappeared at Gunjabari on the seventh day of the waxing moon in the month of Asharh.

Thus, three major texts hint at this thesis, and none of them was written very long after the Mahaprabhu's passing away. As has been mentioned earlier, 1540, 1565, 1575 were the respective years during which Jayananda's *Chaitanyamangal*, Ishan Nagar's *Advaita-Prakash*, and Lochandas' *Chaitanyamangal* were composed. Ishan Nagar and Jayananda were alive at the time of Gauranga's passing away in 1533. Jayananda's *Chaitanyamangal* was written merely seven years later, Ishan Nagar's *Advaita-Prakash* was written thirty-five years later, and Lochandas' *Chaitanyamangal* was written forty-two years after this event. Therefore, the rumours of the Mahaprabhu becoming one with Jagannath are contemporaneous with the lamentable fact of his passing – and at that time there were no rumours other than these. However absurd or supernatural this legend might sound, it is very old, born during the time of Chaitanya's demise, and thus it would not be untenable to deduce some truth from it.

Several more questions and complex ones as well are entangled in the rumours of the Mahaprabhu's disappearance in this way, and we shall now undertake a discussion of these.

In two of the aforementioned sources, it is noted that upon the Mahaprabhu's entering the temple, its doors firmly closed. Both Lochandas and Ishan Nagar mention this.

Lochandas writes that devotees thronged the barred doors of the building and pleaded pitifully with the priests to open them. 'Seeing the priests, the devotees cry/ Remove the doors, we wish to see the Lord.'[19] Lochandas' account suggests that among his devotees, Sribash, Mukunda Datta, Gauridas, Basu Datta, Srigobinda, and Kashi Mishra were present at the time.

Jayananda writes – when Chaitanya danced with abandon on the occasion of Jagannath's Ratha Yatra[20] celebrations, a piece of brick got lodged in his foot. After this, he bathed in the Narayana Sarovar, but on the sixth day of the waxing moon the pain in his foot increased. Then, having lost the ability to move, he took refuge in Gunjabari. It was the time of the Ratha Yatra, and the idol of Jagannath was there. Next day was the seventh day. Lochandas writes – the doors of the temple are closed, many devotees jostle at the gates waiting to see him. But the priests did not open the doors. Ishan Nagar also mentions the barring of the temple doors. Lochandas continues to say that after a great deal of appeal and entreaty the doors opened, and a priest approached the throng to say:

> The Lord has become invisible at Gunjabari/ Our eyes saw the union of the Lord and Gaur/ Hear us and know it as certain truth/ The disciples raise their voices in great lament/ Never shall we see the moonlit beauty of his face again.[21]

Jayananda writes that garlands of a variety of flowers began to be brought to the temple after the sixth day when the Mahaprabhu took his rest at Gunjabari due to his painful foot.

Jayananda, however, does not write that the Mahaprabhu became one with Jagannath. He says that a chariot came down from the skies to bear him away to heavenly Vaikuntha. He boarded a chariot with a Garuda pennant and was taken to heaven. However, we will turn our attention to another of the poet's verses, viz. 'The illusive corporeal body was there left behind.'[22] Therefore, this does not prove that Chaitanya was dissolved into the body of Jagannath. Rather, he makes it quite clear that his body was left at that place. But where did the body that was like the pure and eternal ideal of love go? Jayananda is silent on this.

The date harbours no confusion. On Sunday, the seventh day of the waxing moon in 1455 Saka era (1533), the Mahaprabhu left this earthly abode. Lochandas has written how on that day, he achieves union with Jagannath and Gunjabari temple's gates remain barred for a long time. The *Advaita-Prakash* notes how on that day the Mahaprabhu 'disappears' (i.e. is no longer perceived). His account also mentions that the temple gates had needed to be barred. Jayananda has recounted how on that day the Garuda-pennanted chariot bore him away to heaven and how his earthly body remained below. These proofs establish that on the Sunday of the seventh day of the waxing moon of the month of Asharh in 1455 Saka era (1533), Chaitanya disappeared in proximity of the Jagannath idol. There is no reason to question the validity of this claim. At this time, the Jagannath idol was at Gunjabari – this is the time of the Ratha Yatra celebrations – and the image of Chaitanya leaving his earthly abode in a chariot in Jayananda's account might owe some of its creativity to the Ratha Yatra being organised at the time.

Now, at one point, Jayananda mentions the term 'tota.' This we have deduced as Gunjabari because he has also mentioned that during Jagannath's holy chariot progression, the idol remained at Gunjabari. Chaitanya bathed in the Narendra Sarovar immediately after the brick shard inflicted injury upon his lotus foot. Narendra Sarovar is not far from Gunjabari. 'Tota' means 'garden' or 'country house.' These old 'totas' of Puri have been mentioned in many old texts. The place where Gunjabari now stands used to be called as 'aai tota' – 'aai' denoting the jasmine flower. There also used to be the 'Yameshwar tota' and 'Gopinath's tota,' among others. In Jayananda's *Chaitanyamangal*, we have 'Sriharidas Thakur he remained in Neelachal/Built he a tota on the shore of the sea.'[23] In the 'Antya-parva' of the *Chaitanyacharitamrita* too, we find 'suddenly seeing the sea from a tota.' Puri was a land of 'totas' once with many pleasure gardens. In Murari Gupta's *Charitamrita* too, Gundicha has been called 'house of flowers' ('tota'). Lochandas has clearly stated that Jagannath was present in Gunjabari during the time of the Ratha Yatra. This gives us the day, date, and place of Chaitanya's passing with certainty. There need no longer be any doubt or uncertainty about this.

There still remains some uncertainty, however, regarding the time of death. Lochandas writes that Chaitanya merged with the Jagannath idol on Sunday on the third hour. Jayananda has the time of his passing as the tenth hour on Sunday night. Thus, according to Lochandas, the Mahaprabhu passed away around 4 p.m. while Jayananda has him breathing his last around 9 p.m. We shall try to resolve this difficulty later.

Now, we know clearly from Jayananda's *Chaitanyamangal* that a brick shard pierced Chaitanya's foot as he danced with mystic abandon during the Ratha Yatra in the month of Asharh (June–July). The pain terribly intensified when he bathed in the Narayan Sarovar immediately afterwards. And on the sixth day of the waxing moon, he told his companions about his imminent demise. The two manuscripts of Jayananda's *Chaitanyamangal* from which Nagendra Basu has prepared the aforementioned edition are respectively two hundred and fifty and two hundred and eight years old. Under these circumstances, there is no reason whatsoever for disregarding these old witnesses. Those who require some supernatural story for believing everything might be averse to giving history its due, but the impartial critic would certainly concede that Jayananda had no self-interest to serve by concealing the truth.

If Lord Chaitanyadev really merged into the Jagannath idol, then what might be the justification for so many of these old textual witnesses talking about closed doors? We see that the doors of the temple were carefully barred for a very long time. This is exceedingly strange! Why should the main entryway to the Gundicha temple be barred in this way during the Ratha Yatra festivities? This does indicate that some secret activity must have been taking place within the temple for a long period of time. What might this activity be? Jayananda writes that many flower garlands were brought to the temple (perhaps by the back entrance). He also writes that Chaitanya's mortal frame was left behind at the temple. What, then, happened to the earthly body?

It is easy to surmise that Chaitanya must have been interred in the Gundicha. Why else were devotees kept waiting outside for such a long time? If the Mahaprabhu's earthly remains were relocated, it could have been achieved in very little time, but in which case some amount of uproar and a bit of crowding would have been unavoidable. Despite powerful attempts at secrecy, it would not have been possible to suppress some outbursts of grief wherever those remains might have been sought to be transported. Therefore, it seems most likely that Chaitanya's sacred form was interred within the temple premises, and the spot was covered with stone and repaired, which would have taken a very long time. The news of the dissolution of Chaitanya's leela was certainly given to Prataparudra.[24] Perhaps he had been secretly present in the temple and arranged for matters to be like this. The Mahaprabhu's leela is eternal and never-ending. Ishan Nagar has written 'Even if Chaitanya is not unrevealed to his devotees/ Hearsay makes them greatly afflicted.'[25] Imagining an end to this leela is unbearable to the Vaishnav soul. This is why the matter of Chaitanya's demise was cloaked in secrecy.

Now, hints in support of the proposition that the Mahaprabhu was secretly laid to rest in Gundicha may be found in Kavi Karnapur's play *Caitanya-candrodaya*. Later in the play, Prataparudra's plaintive lament during Ratha

Yatra is heartrending. Looking at Gunjabari he says 'so'ayaṃ nīlagiriīśwarah sa vibhavo yātrā ca sā guṇdicā/ te te digvidikāgatāh sukṛtinastāstā/ ārāmāṣca ta eva nandana vana ṣrīnāṃ tiraskāriṇah/ sarvvānyeva mahāprabhuṃ vata vina śūnyāni manyāmahe.'

Briefly translated it goes thus:

> There lies the Lord of the Blue Mountain, there the holy chariot procession and the Gundicha. Pure hearted devotees have come from far and away and stand waiting in throngs. That pleasure garden is more beautiful than the garden of Nandanvana, Yet today my heart finds all of it empty in mourning for the separation of the Mahaprabhu.

That great bereavement of the Mahaprabhu's leela ending in the world is intimately and pitifully connected to the Gundicha temple. It is not surprising that Prataparudra would feel like this when he came to the place.

We have thus reached several conclusions regarding the end of Chaitanya's earthly leela, which appear to be correct. He received a wound on his foot while dancing in Jagannath's Ratha Yatra procession on a day in the waxing lunar fortnight in the month of Asharh. This wound grows serious on the sixth day of the waxing fortnight, and on the seventh day he attains his heavenly abode. A long time after his passing, the doors of the Gundicha were closed, and devotees could not gain access despite copious cries and entreaties. When the doors finally opened, some priests said that Chaitanya had merged into the body of Jagannath while others said that he had ascended to the heavens in a Garuda-pennanted chariot. These accounts clearly indicate that the priests had probably, following Prataparudra's wishes, laid him to rest inside the Gundicha, and having hidden that loving body, they required a great deal of time to carry out repairs at the site of interment. This was the reason for the temple's gates being barred for a long time. Now, Lochandas says that the Mahaprabhu passed away on Sunday at 4 p.m.; but Jayananda writes that the moon of Nabadvip set at around 9 in the evening. How can we reconcile this difference?

I believe that this is not a very great difficulty, and a solution is easily at hand. Lochandas reports that the Mahaprabhu was brought to Gunjabari on Saturday when the pain in his foot became unbearable. From early morning of the following day, his condition was critical. The gates were then closed fearing the end of his leela at any moment. He passed away at 4 p.m., and after laying him to rest, it took another 5 to 6 hours to repair the spot. Thus, after everything had been accomplished, the doors of the temple were opened at around 9 in the evening. The priests who reported truthfully gave the time as 4 p.m. Those, however, who believed the time of the unbarring of the gates to be same as the hour of the Mahaprabhu's passing have written the hour of his being hidden from mortal sight as 9. This is the reason for two separate times being propagated for his passing. We believe that

4 in the afternoon is the actual time of the Mahaprabhu's demise, and 9 the time when the doors of the temple were opened upon the completion of his interment.

One more question remains – where exactly in the temple was his body laid to rest? Could the body of the man thought to be Jagadbandhu Krishna be relinquished to total obscurity? If that were so, wouldn't hundreds and thousands of feet unknowingly trample upon the sacred resting place of his corporeal remains? Were those who laid his body to rest prepared to allow the defiling of the holy spot by indiscriminate crowds? Did they not retain any sign of that sacred location? I went to the temple and saw a couple of big bridges made of sandalwood. There is a shrine for the temporary rest of Jagadbandhu beside the idol of the lady aunt. But there is no place dedicated to the Mahaprabhu within the tiny chamber of the inner temple. Deeply disheartened, I was about to leave the temple when I caught sight of the footprints of the Mahaprabhu adorned by hundreds of lotus blossoms displayed at one end of the doorway of that inner chamber. It was beside the doorway, beyond which there was the many-pillared splendour of the Gundicha temple's open pavilion – this was the same pavilion the gates of which had been closed by the priests when they interred his body and they had possibly added these footprints as a sign of the place of his *samadhi* or grave. His footprints were found by the Garuda-pillar upon which the Mahaprabhu had rested his arm watching the *arti* ceremony of Jagadbandhu's worship in the Puri temple in the course of eighteen years. Recently, some Vaishnavs have shifted the footprints to the top of a pillar to apparently increase their glory. We are unclear about whether this is inducive to or detractive of the value of their devotion. But now travellers freely tread that spot on which the Mahaprabhu had stood watching the worship of the Lord every morning and evening for eighteen long years. No one would have set foot on the spot if the footprints were left there. Similar footprints can be seen in the Gopinath temple too. There, too Lord Chaitanya was prone to stand and contemplate the face of Lord Gopinath.

We are of the conviction that these footprints in the Gundicha indicate the place of his interment. The priests have noted that for some unknown reason, thousands of Vaishnavs throw themselves upon those footprints in the Gundicha temple weeping disconsolately. Although the Mahaprabhu's demise is a deeply opaque thing – it has been shielded from the public eye as much as possible – nonetheless, does the enactment of such terrible grief over these footprints point a feeble finger at some ancient instinct long since lost? It is my belief that the feet icon illuminates, as in faintly flickering lamplight, the last signpost of the Mahaprabhu's final remains. We have heard that the leading Vaishnav devotee Ramdas Babaji wept copious tears over these feet last year. Does this announce the spontaneous expression of some unknown passion inherited from a past life? Or was it merely an uncontrolled overflow of his Vaishnav piety?

I feel that I have been able to resolve several thorny questions in the matter of Lord Chaitanya's passing. If there should arise any comments in this regard, I shall always be open to further discussion.

Translation: Debapriya Basu

Notes

1 Dineshchandra Sen, 'Srigauranger Leelabasan', *Bharatbarsha*, 1929, 16.2(3): 321–329.
2 Sri Chaitanya, major Vaishnav saint and founder of Gaudiya Vaishnavism. He is variously referred to as 'Sri Gauranga,' 'Gauranga,' 'Chaitanya Prabhu,' 'Mahaprabhu,' 'Chaitanyadev,' 'Lord Chaitanyadev', and so on in the text.
3 Author's note: 'Mahaprabhu had eight sisters, but all of them fell into the jaws of death in infancy.'
4 Legendary gemstone worn by Lord Vishnu in Hindu mythology.
5 Author's note: 'The Lord adopted the form of the boar/ Murari looked on, dazzled by that unprecedented sight.' *Chaitanyabhagavat*, Madhya-khanda III.
6 Author's note: *Chaitanyabhagavat*, Madhya-khanda, II and III.
7 Author's note: *Chaitanyacharitamrita*, Adi-khanda.
8 Author's note: *Chaitanyacharitamrita*, Madhya-khanda XV, śloka 90 and Madhya-khanda III, śloka 49.
9 Author's note: 'caturddasa ṣatābdānte pancaviṃṣati vatsare/ āṣāḍa sita saptamyāṃ granthohayaṃ pūrṇatā gatah.' ['This book has come to fruition on the seventh white day in the month of Asharh at the end of the 14th century's twenty-fifth year'].
10 'Friend of the World,' one of the names of Krishna.
11 Six disciples of Chaitanya, who spent lives of renunciation in Vrindavan in the 16th century disseminating Gaudiya Vaishnav Bhakti, were responsible for the major corpus of treatises. They are Rupa Goswami (*Ujjvalanīlamaṇih, Bhaktirasāmṛtasindhu*); Sanatan Goswami (*Bṛhatbhāgavatāmṛta, Haribhaktivilāsa*), Jiva Goswami (*Gopālacampu* and the six *Sandarbhas*, viz. *Tattva, Bhāgavata, Paramātma, Kṛsṇa, Bhakti and Prīti*), Gopal Bhatta, Bhatta Raghunath, and Raghunthadas Goswami, to whom a number of prayers are attributed.
12 Author's note: *Chaitanyabhagavat*, Adi-khanda III.
13 Author's note: *Chaitanyabhagavat*, Adi-khanda. Repeated partaking defiles the food for the Brahmin.
14 Author's note: *Chaitanyabhagavat*, Adi-khanda.
15 Sanskrit grammar school.
16 Although the author uses 'Gunjabari' and 'Gundicha-griha' interchangeably, only Gunjabari has been retained in translation.
17 Temples in Puri, Odisha, India.
18 'Soft sandal mountain winds caress quivering vines of cloves', Ashtapadi 3, *Gītagovinda* by Jayadeva. Trans. reproduced from *Gitagovinda of Jayadeva: Love Song of the Dark Lord*, Barbara Stoller-Miller (trans.), New York: Columbia University Press, 1977.
19 Lochandas, *Chaitanyamangal* (Final canto), Ramnarayan Bidyaratna (ed.), Baharampur: Radharaman Press, 1892, p. 340.
20 Ratha Yatra, or the Chariot festival of Jagannath, Balabhadra, Subhadra, and Sudarshan, happens in the month of Asharh (June–July) every year, when the idols of the deities are brought out of the sanctum of the temple to carry them to Gundicha temple for a brief period.

21 Lochandas, *Chaitanyamangal* (Final canto), pp. 340–341.
22 Jayananda, *Chaitanyamangal*, Biman Behari Majumdar and Sukhamay Mukhopadhyay (eds.), Kolkata: Asiatic Society, 1971, p. 234. The text also offers a variant of the line from another manuscript.
23 Jayananda, *Chaitanyamangal*, Uttarkhanda, Biman Behari Majumdar and Sukhamay Mukhopadhyay (eds.), op. cit., p. 234.
24 Gajapati Prataparudra Deva, one of the principal followers of Chaitanya, ruled in certain parts of Orissa between 1497 and 1540.
25 Ishan Nagar, *Sri Sri Advaita-Prakash*, Ch. 21, Satish Mitra (ed.) (1926), Kolkata: Manasi, 2015, p. 281.

4 Bishnupada Bhattacharya: The Gaudiya Vaishnav order: Its treatises on rhetoric and *rasa*

Introduction

An eminent Sanskritist and rhetorician, Bishnupada Bhattacharya (1921–1990) taught Sanskrit in various colleges and universities in India and was the Principal of Sanskrit College, Kolkata, India (1969–1983). Although his principal area of scholarship was Sanskrit poetics and semantics, he contributed significantly towards editing and translating a number of Sanskrit texts. Such volumes include *Dhvanyāloka of Ānandavardhana* (1956–7), *Vyaktiviveka* of Mahimabhaṭṭa (1957), and 'Brahma Kānda' from *Vākya-Padīya* of Bhartṛhari (1991). His monographs on poetics include *Prachin Bharatiya Alamkarsastrer Bhumika* (1953), *Sahitya-mimamsa* (1960), *Gaudiya Vaishnav Sampraday: Bhaktiras o Alamkarsastra* (1993), and *Kalidasa o Rabindranath* (1960).

Bharata's *Nāṭyaśāstra*, the earliest available Sanskrit doctrine on poetics, enumerated the possible *sthāyibhāva* or permanent emotions as eight, and Abhinavagupta (10th century CE), added a ninth one as *Śama*. However, the ancient rhetoricians did acknowledge the influence and impact of Bhakti or *Bhagavad-rati* (love for God), even if they did not accept it as a sthāyibhāva, which can be inferred from the celebrated verse by Ānandavardhana (9th century CE), which stated that poets were tired of describing the world and its ways, but as far as Bhakti was concerned they remained enchanted with its bliss and could not find anything comparable. The principal contribution of the 15th-century Gaudiya Vaishnav scholars known as the Goswamis was to establish Bhakti as a permanent emotion, complete with its corresponding *Madhurarasa*. Bhattacharya's essay delves into aspects of Sanskrit poetics and its relation to the ideals of Bhakti. The current essay was first included in Bhattacharya's *Prachin Bharatiya Alamkar-Sastrer Bhumika* (1953) and subsequently elaborated and published as the introductory essay in *Gaudiya Vaishnav Sampraday: Bhaktiras o Alamkarsastra* (1993).

*

DOI: 10.4324/9781003224686-5

The Gaudiya Vaishnav order: its treatises on rhetoric and *rasa*[1]

Bishnupada Bhattacharya

So far, we have discussed a few significant systems of ancient Indian rhetoric. But the history of the development of Indian rhetoric will remain incomplete unless we discuss the most notable ideology of the philosophers of the Gaudiya Vaishnav order. The unique doctrine of devotion that flooded Bengal (then Gauda) in 15th and 16th century AD with the emergence of Sri Chaitanyadev left an everlasting impression on the religion, literature, and the social life of greater Bengal. The huge corpus of padavali literature grew up centred around the extraordinary personality of Chaitanyadev. The manifestation of devotion that was seen in his divine life was also infused into the lives of his devotees. Such a complete expression of devotion has not been seen in the history of any other personality. Those who came in direct contact with him considered him the embodiment of divine devotion. They came to understand that devotion was the *puruṣārtha* or one of the prime objectives of human life – compared to devotion, all other paths were immaterial, insignificant, withered. Under the inspiration of their newly discovered insight, the companions of Sri Chaitanya began to expound upon the true form of devotion. The books composed by the Goswamis of Vrindavan are the result of that effort.

While discussing Bharata's theory of rasa, we have seen that Bharata considered only nine[2] sthāyibhāvas or stable emotions and established only those as evoking rasa (*rasībhāva*). According to him, the love of a devotee for his god or the love of parents towards their child are vyabhicāribhāvas or transitory emotions. They cannot attain fulfilment of the form of rasa (*rasarūpatā*). Almost all the masters have humbly accepted Bharata's conclusion. Even Jagannatha, the independent exponent of poetics and author of *Rasagaṅgādhara*, has been unable to go against Bharata's opinion and consider love for the divinity as a sthāyibhāva. His opinion is quoted here:

> Atha kathameta eva rasāḥ, bhagavadālambansya romāñcāśrupātādibhiranubhāvitasya harṣādibhiḥ paripoṣitasya bhāgavatādipurāṇaśravaṇasamaye bhagavadbhaktairanubhūyamānasya bhaktirasasya durapaṇhavatvāt? bhagavadanurāgarūpā bhaktiścātra sthāyibhāvaḥ | na cāsau – śāntarase'antarbhāvamarhati, anurāgasya vairāgyaviruddhatvāt| ucyate – bhakterdevādiviṣayaratitvena bhāvāntargatatayā rasatvānupapatteḥ –
>
> Ratirdevādiviṣayā vyabhicārī tathāñjitaḥ|
> Bhāvaḥ proktaḥ . . . ||
>
> iti hi prācāṃ siddhāntāt | . . . bharatādimunivacanānāmevātra ras abhāvatvādivyavasthāpakatvena svātantryāyogāt | . . . rasānāṃ

navatvagaṇanā ca munivacananiyantritā bhajyeta iti yathāśāstrameva jyāyaḥ |

So why these alone are treated as rasa? The bhaktirasa has God as its fundamental determinant, the signs of its manifestation are horripilation, tears, etc.; it is nourished by joy and similar emotions and is experienced by the *bhaktas* while listening to texts of the Purānas such as the *Bhāgavata*, etc. and hence cannot be denied the status of rasa. The permanent mood in this rasa is devotion, that is love for God. It cannot be included in *śāntarasa* for love is incompatible with detachment. It is said that devotion being love for God and the like falls under the category of *bhāva*, and hence incapable of attaining the state of rasa because early writers (such as Mammaṭa) state, 'The sentiment of love towards God etc. and the transitory mood (vyabhicāribhāva) rightly manifested are called bhāva; when not rightly manifested they become the mere appearance of rasa and bhāva.' It should not then be argued that since love is the same in both *rati* and bhakti, the sentiment of love or rati for a woman should be treated as bhāva, or bhakti for God should be considered as a permanent mood (worthy of being called rasa) and the love of a woman should be admitted as bhava and so on since there is hardly any argument to support either of the two – rasa and bhāva. The words of sages like Bharata are vested with ultimate freedom for ascertaining the state of rasa and bhāva, or else why should not the love for a son be of the nature of a permanent mood (of śṛṅgārarasa) or why should not aversion, grief be treated as pure bhāva (vyabhicāribhāva)? If one subscribes to this, the whole philosophy of aesthetic realisation would become futile. The number of rasas as nine is determined by the words of the sage (Bharata); hence it is wise to follow the scripture.

However, those who witnessed the singular madness of bhakti in the divine life of Sri Chaitanya were unable to label that bhakti as a transitory emotion. For them, it would have been a sheer denial of truth and therefore impossible. They realised that the love for the divine is the sole stable emotion of human life, and savouring it in its emotive–affective form of bhakti rasa through a surge of the *hlādinī śakti* (literally, the potency that renders joy) seemed to be the prime goal of human life. Compared to that, śṛṅgāra and all other rasas propounded by Bharata are transitory.

According to rhetoricians, vyañjanā or suggested meaning awakens the latent or unexpressed desires (rati) in the human heart, and makes it favourable for experiencing rasa; similarly, the masters of the doctrine of devotion say that the natural joyous dispensation of the divinity i.e. hlādinī, awakens dormant or unexpressed feelings of desire towards the divine in the hearts of men creating a favourable situation for them to experience the rasa divine. The theory of devotion comes to the conclusion that this inclination towards the divine is a natural attribute (dharma) of all human beings. The divine is joy (ānanda) personified, and it is hlādinī śakti that makes one experience one's own soul as the image of joy, as well as makes all creatures experience it. Since hlādinī perpetually exists within the divine as its true form, it must be recognized that the desire for the divine is a natural characteristic of all creatures.[3]

Thus, love for the divine is the only stable bhāva, and devotion is the only rasa – this is the singular ideology of the Gaudiya Vaishnavas. The Goswamis of Vrindavan composed several philosophical treatises to establish this precept. Two such authoritative texts of Vaiṣṇava theory are Sri Rupa Goswami's *Bhaktirasāmṛtasindhu* and *Ujjvalanīlamaṇi*. In *Bhaktirasāmṛtasindhu*, Rupa Goswami has indicated *śānta, prīti, preyaḥ, vatsala*, and *ujjvala* (peaceful, respectful, companionable, parentally affectionate, and amorous) as the principal rasas, yet expounded fully and clearly in his *Ujjvalanīlamaṇi* that *ujjvala rasa* or *madhura rasa*, that is the rasa of devotion based on love for Krishna was the most sublime. It was the 'rasarāṭ', that is the rasa supreme. Not all are fit to experience this rasa – those who are averse to the love of Krishna, under the impression that this is nothing but lust, are not fit for this rasa. It is both unfathomable and inaccessible for them. Rupa Goswami has clearly stated that *Bhaktirasāmṛtasindhu* only summarises this theory:

Nivṛttānupayuktatvād durūhatvādayaṃ rasaḥ |
Rahasyatvāccaḥ saṃkṣipya vitatāṅgo'pi likhyate ||[4]

Ujjvalanīlamaṇi explains the same in detail:

Mukhyaraseṣu purā yaḥ samkṣepeṇodito rahasyatvāt |
Pṛthageva bhaktirasarāṭsa vistareṇocyate madhuraḥ ||[5]

Rupa Goswami has divided this natural stable bhāva (the desire to attain Krishna) into three distinct categories, based on intensity – *sādhāraṇī* (or universal), *samañjasā* (or congruent), and *samarthā* (or capable).

Ratiḥ svabhāvajaiva syāt prāyo Gokulasubhruvām |
Sādhāraṇī nigaditā samañjasā cāsau samarthā ca |
Kubjādiṣu mahiṣīṣu ca Gokuladevīṣu ca kramataḥ ||
Maṇivaccintāmaṇivat Kaustubhamaṇivat tridhā'bhimatā |
Nātisulabheyamabhitaḥ sudurlabhā syādananyalabhyā ca ||[6]

Thus, samañjasā is superior to sādhāraṇī, and samarthā is superior to samañjasā. Samarthā rati is the greatest *rati-bhāva*, since this when incited turns into the great state or the *mahābhāva*.[7] The *Gokuladevis* are the fittest vessels for this. But those devotees following the *rāgānuga-mārga* or the way of divine eros enter into the bhāvas of Gopinīs and experience the love of Krishna. They may also attain the greatest *mahābhāvadaśā* or the state of the supreme emotion:

Iyameva ratiḥ prauḍhā mahābhāvadaśāṃ vrajet |
Yā mṛgyā syāt vimuktānāṃ bhaktānāṃ ca varīyasām ||[8]

Rupa Goswāmi has also described the six stages of the desire for Krishna:

Syād dṛḍheyaṃ ratiḥ premā prodyan snehaḥ kramādayam |
Syānmānaḥ praṇayo rāgo'nurāgo bhāva ityapi ||
Vījamikṣuḥ sa ca rasaḥ sa guḍaḥ khaṇḍa eva saḥ |
Sa śarkarā sitā sā ca sā yathā syāt sitopalā ||
Ataḥ premavilāsāḥ syurbhāvāḥ snehādayastu ṣaṭ |
Prāyo vyavahriyante'mī premaśabdena sūribhiḥ ||[9]

Just as sugarcane is transformed to sugar through six stages of increasing sweetness and intensity viz. *rasa, guḍa, khaṇḍa, śarkarā, sitaśarkarā*, and *sitopalā* (sugarcane juice, molasses, solidified molasses, unrefined sugar, refined sugar, and crystallised sugar), similarly the same desire for Krishna, that is the stable bhāva goes through the stages of *sneha* (endearment), *māna* (respect), *praṇaya* (affection), *rāga* (passion), *anurāga* (love), and *bhāva* (or *mahābhāva*) to become the most delightful and culminative experience. The ultimate stage of that mahābhāva is *divyonmāda* or transcendental madness:

Etasya mohanākhyasya gatiṃ kāmapyupeyuṣaḥ |
Bhramābhā kāpi vaicitrī divyonmāda itīryate ||[10]

Sri Chaitanya's divine temperament embodied the essence of that same mahābhava that was attainable only by the *brajadevis* and its eventual state of transcendental madness. Krishnadas Goswami's description of Sri Chaitanya's state of transcendental madness in the *Antyaleela* canto of *Srichaitanyacharitamrita* is a jewel of Gaudiya Vaishnav literature and truly melts the reader's heart. The two ślokas by Raghunathdas from *Stabābalī* quoted as follows depict Chaitanya's state of transcendental madness splendidly:

Anudghāṭya dvāratrayamuru ca bhittitrayamaho
Vilaṅghyoccaiḥ kāliṅgikasurabhimadhye nipatitaḥ |
Tanūdyatsaṃkocāt kamaṭha iva Kṛṣṇoruvirahād
Virājan Gaurāṅgo hṛdaya udayanmāṃ madayati ||
'Svakīyasya prāṇārbudasadṛśagoṣṭhasya virahāt
Pralāpādunmādāt sakalamatikurvan vikaladhīḥ |

Dadhad bhittau śaśvad vadanavidhugharṣeṇa rudhiraṃ
Kṣatotthaṃ Gaurāṅgo hṛdaya udayanmāṃ madayati ||[11]

The scholar of Vedanta Madhusudan Saraswati's book *Bhaktirasāyana* is another magnificent treatise on the rasa of devotion. The wonderful synthesis of *jñāna* (knowledge) and bhakti (devotion) in his life is astonishing. In the first śloka of the first ullāsa, that is the first section of *Bhaktirasāyana*, Madhusudan says:

Navarasamilitaṃ vā kevalaṃ vā pumartham
Paramamiha mukunde bhaktiyogaṃ vadanti |
Nirupamasukhasaṃvidrūpamaspṛṣṭaduḥkhaṃ
Tamahamakhilatuṣṭyai śāstradṛṣṭyā vyanammi ||[12]

Apart from these, other treatises like *Ṣaṭsandarbha* by Sri Jiva Goswami, *Bhaktirasāmṛtasindhubindu* and *Ujjvalanīlamaṇikiraṇa* by Visvanath Chakravarty, *Alaṃkārakaustubha* by Kavi Karnapur, and *Kāvyakaustubha* and *Sāhityakaumudī* by Baladeva Vidyabhushan also discuss the various topics of rasa theory and rhetoric. However, the Vaisnav rhetoricians and philosophers have demonstrated their distinct intellectual capacity best to establish the primacy of the emotion of bhakti. In determining other doctrines of rhetoric, they have merely opted for a restatement of the theories of their predecessors.

Translation: Sudeshna Datta Chaudhuri

Notes

1 Bishnupada Bhattacharya, 'Gaudiya Vaishnav Sampraday: Alamkar o Rasasastra', in *Prachin Bharatiya Alamkar-Sastrer Bhumika*, Kolkata: Sanskrit Pustak Bhandar, 1953, pp. 77–84.

2 The number of sthāyibhāvas and their corresponding rasas in Bharata's Nāṭyaśāstra is eight, as described in its sixth chapter. However, some of the later scholars like Abhinavagupta and Jagannātha have argued that a ninth sthāyibhāva as well as rasa may have been implied in the said text by the use of the words śama (Ch. I) and mokṣakāma (Ch. XXIV). Bhattacharya draws upon this argument in this context. For a detailed exploration of the subject, see V. Raghavan, *The Number of Rasa-s*, Madras: The Adyar Library and Research Centre, 1974.

3 Quoted from Pramathanath Tarkabhushan, *Bangalar Vaishnavdharma* (Adharchandra Mukherjee Lecture), Calcutta: University of Calcutta, 1939, pp. 111–112.

4 'Those who are averse to the love for Krishna, are unworthy of this rasa and the rasa is inaccessible to their understanding, and is concealed from them; thus it is being summarized here, though it is, as a matter, vast.' Rupa Goswamin, *Bhaktirasāmṛtasindhu*: Madhurabhaktirasa (2), Kolkata: Sri Chaitanya Research Institute, 2008, p. 473.

5 'Among the primary rasas, madhura or bhakti, "the rasa supreme", which has been discussed in brief before, will be considered in detail in this text.' See Rupa

Goswamin, *Śrīśrīujjvalanīlamaṇih* 1.2, Haridas Das (ed.), Kolkata: Sanskrit Book Depot, 2017, p. 2.

6 'The rati of the Gopinīs is almost always inherent. This inherent rati is found in Kubjā et al, the wives of Krishna and the Gopinīs as sādhāraṇī, samañjasā, and samarthā respectively. Like the diamond, the philosopher's stone and the Kaustubha, these are correspondingly *anatisulabhā* (not easily attainable), *sudurlabhā* (very difficult to attain), and *ananyalabhyā* (attainable to only a few).' See Rupa Goswami, *Śrīśrīujjvalanīlamaṇih* 14.42–44, Haridas Das (ed.), op. cit., p. 252.

7 A state of supreme, eternal bliss, attainable only by the *Brajadevi* like Radha. The nectar-like state attracts the mind and becomes one with it: 'Baramrtaswarupasrih svam swarupam mano nayet.'

8 Rupa Goswami, *Śrīśrīujjvalanīlamaṇih* 14.57, Haridas Das (ed.), op. cit., p. 254.

9 Ibid., verses 59–61, p. 254.

10 Ibid., verse 190, p. 254.

11 'He who has transcended the three walls without opening the three entrances, he who is immersed in the fragrances of Kalinga, he who has lost all sense of physical mortification, it is he, Gauranga, who has emerged in my heart due to the viraha of Krishna and entranced me, just as Vishnu had appeared within the turtle. He whose learning has fled before the transcendence of all, due to his madness emanating from the delusions of his separation from his own true form, he who has rubbed his beautiful face on the walls and smeared them with his blood, it is he, Gauranga, who has emerged in my heart due to the viraha of Krishna and entranced me.' Raghunāthadāsa, 'Śrī Gaurāṃga Stavakalpataruh' 5–6, in *Stavāvalī*, Berhampore: Ramnarayan Bidyaratna, Radharaman Press, 1888 (date not cited), pp. 16–18.

12 'The nine rasas, whether taken together or integrated as puruṣārtha, are considered to be the bhakti-yoga to Krishna. The true self of this bhakti, which is an experience of incomparable happiness without the faintest touch of sorrow, will be narrated now according to the scriptures.' Madhusūdana Saraswatī, *Bhaktirasāyana* 1.1, Durgacharan Samkhyavedantatirtha (ed.), Kolkata: Surendranath Bhattacharya, 1933, p. 1.

5 Iswar Chandra Gupta: The early poets

Introduction

Iswar Chandra Gupta (1812–1859) was one of the most important authors of Bangla prose and also an eminent poet of his time. His most remarkable achievement was to edit and publish *Sambad Prabhakar*, which appeared as a weekly journal in 1831 and was converted into a daily in 1839. The journal nurtured a host of eminent authors and critics like Rangalal Bandyopadhyay (1827–1887), Dinabandhu Mitra (1830–1873), Bankimchandra Chattopadhyay and Michael Madhusudan Dutt (1824–1873) who shaped the course of the literary history of Bengal in the pre-Tagore era. It was in the pages of *Sambad Prabhakar* that Iswar Chandra Gupta brought to light the lives and works of great literary figures of the late medieval and early modern Bengal such as Bharatchandra Roy (1712–1760), Ramprasad Sen (1720–1781) and Ramnidhi Gupta or Nidhubabu (1741–1839). He also brought major composers of *Kabigan* before the reading public, such as Ram Basu, Nitaidas Bairagi, Horu Thakur, Gonjla Guin, Rasu Nrisingha and Lalu Nandalal. They were popular performers in urban cultural sites in the late 18th and early 19th centuries, who bridged the gap between the prevalent rural and the emergent urban ethos. 'The Early Poets' (1854) anthologised in this volume is one of the early essays in the series.

The first half of the 18th century witnessed a few major debates in the sociocultural realm in Bengal, which eventually determined the course of cultural history of the land under the British colonial regime. The first such major debate came up regarding the practice of Sati, which was legally abolished in 1829 through the initiative of Raja Rammohun Roy. Iswar Chandra Gupta was a young man of 18 at that time. Twenty-five years later, when Iswarchandra Vidyasagar advocated Widow Remarriage and the Act was established in 1856, the year before the First War of Independence, Iswar Chandra Gupta was already an eminent editor with conservative ideas regarding Hindu society and British rule. Even as he opposed the Hindu Widow Remarriage Act and was not in sympathy with the First War of Independence, he was investing much of his time in finding obscure data on the lives

DOI: 10.4324/9781003224686-6

and works of poets from earlier as well as contemporary periods. His essays are path-breaking studies of popular performative art forms which were already in decline along with a search for the right method.

*

The early poets[1]

Iswar Chandra Gupta

We have placed our soul and subsistence, even our very existence, at stake in the procurement of the works of early poets like Ram Basu. We have renounced almost all the joys of the quotidian and flouted every rule of rest and nourishment. We rush from pillar to post, over land and water, supplicating a variety of individuals. No sooner do we hear that 'Mr. X of Y has poem Z' than we exert ourselves to liberate the said song from his possession by any means available. Failing this, we have no recourse but to invoke the almighty in lamenting our fate. Only the omniscient lord of creation knows the state of my mind in recent days. No worldly pleasure gives me delight – nothing takes my interest – no other work tempts my soul. Thoughts of ancient verses are the only occupants of my mind. Singing a song worth the name gives me limitless joy, and in that moment I feel, perchance, I have encountered divine bliss.

If only we had embarked on this path earlier, we might have achieved half our goal by this time. As it is, my enterprise encountered great difficulties as soon as I started as my body grew host to a terrible disease. Having been forced to take to my bed for a couple of months, I have finally spent two months on water, endlessly voyaging from place to place. I have not, however, desisted for a moment from the project of collecting verses even in this most terrible time. I may have abandoned hope of life in the midst of the agonies of disease, but never have I forsaken the quest. The satiety of sleep is almost unknown now, and in dreams I think I see my work nearing its desired fulfilment.

It does not appear that we can complete this important work to our satisfaction in our own lifetime. Funds are scarce, and the body's growing frailty signals the approach of death. There would be no need for this regret if there were wealth sufficient unto the needs of the project since there is no work that cannot be completed provided there is enough money. Many might be eager to ensure the attainment of our hearts' desire when tempted with remuneration. But what can we do? No money seems to be available for this. We have spent and are still spending beyond our means, and we will continue to do so as far as we are able. If any individual offers the entirety of ancient verses in exchange for our press, we would not be averse and gladly suffer this penalty. When one has pledged the most precious gem of all, one's own life, what value can mere riches hold?

A few wealthy patrons had promised monetary support according to their abilities prior to the commencement of this work, but those vows have dispersed like the scudding clouds of autumn. Indeed, why should one need to bemoan the state of affairs at such length if men of means took the slightest interest in this matter? We are all subject to Mammon. Who will not do the work if offered payment? There is still time, but it will be impossible to achieve success if there is even a slight delay, for who will provide the songs when all the old people are gone? All of Kuber's gold will not benefit us then.[2] As it is, connoisseurs of the ancients have mostly left this world. The few who are still living do not have much longer to wait. They know about some of the material we are seeking. If these gentlemen become unavailable, all this knowledge will be irretrievably lost. None of them has written these verses down, having kept them alive in oral practice, which has frustrated the purpose. Written material can be tracked down and recovered, but the entire project fails with the passing away of the oral practitioner.

Although it is true that only funds and physical labour will not ensure a comprehensive collection, whatever degree may be achieved is good nevertheless, and the smallest portion of the good is more than enough! A mere drop of butter or rich milk will satisfy the palate. The faintest blush of light will have to illuminate the pitch-dark chamber. When all seems to be on the verge of being lost, whatever little comes to hand should be regarded as the greatest fortune. Following this example, we have gathered our courage and fallen for succour at the feet of the goddess of enterprise. If we do not take steps in this matter and spend the next five years in slavery to sloth, not only will the songs of these poets never be printed in this country, but also their very names will be in danger of extinction. I do not wish to talk about century-old things; it would need an entire book to properly describe the qualities of the wondrous verses that have been composed by poets in Bengal as recently as in the past 40–50 years. It would suffice to glance at a few among those presented in this chapter to appreciate their value.

We publish here songs of Nitaidas Bairagi and Ram Basu only due to space constraints, but other poets will follow and you shall be amazed by them all.

Some songs are extant only in fragments, which is a fact that sears our soul with flames of sorrow. For example, this one of Ram Basu:

> If fire, should it have true might, water would quench it;
> Nor serpent death, should the body bite, mantras revive it.

O readers! Consider for yourselves how curiously the poet might have expressed his emotions in subsequent lines. It is a matter of no ordinary grief that they shall remain unuttered for ever. Alas! How the appreciative reader's soul is set aquiver by the loss of those words! My distress at being thwarted from completing these verse-fragments is a thousand times greater than the agitation of the bee unable to drink from the blooming lotus; the chataka[3] unable to sip its celestial drink from rain-dark clouds; the chakora[4] failing to imbibe the nectar of the full moon's beams; the serpent interrupted in enjoying the softly blowing cool southern breeze; the king prevented from occupying his beloved throne; the devoted wife frustrated in the throes of desired union; the wise man hampered in savouring good conversation; or the miser kept from his money. Only if the almighty lord takes pity on me and fills this lack can my spirit gain tranquillity, I cannot see how else I can calm its perturbation.

When we first pledged ourselves in our minds to this great cause we did not have any confidence in a successful outcome. However, at this moment, it seems that the divinely merciful is not averse to looking kindly upon our endeavour. Several unimaginable and inconceivable events have come to pass. A perfect stranger has suddenly arrived offering help and assistance. Wishes have been granted by an individual from whom help in this matter was never expected. Many people at home and abroad have been equally supportive and encouraging, helping with labour and effort. The more enthusiasts we get, the closer shall we be to our goal. This task is not for an individual. If many equally committed persons come together, only then can we easily confound all confusion. Is there any doubt that renown always follows anything that holds the interest of a crowd? Hear our repeated humble entreaties: let us avoid calumnious attitudes towards this cause and instead nurture it with care and then we shall be able to achieve our goal.

Never think that your support is meant to help only us. We have never preached this in our campaign while beseeching favour. Those who help us shall be profited far more than us and will bind those who are inferior to them in goodwill by virtue of their act. They shall be considered benefactors of the nation as long as the sun and the moon endure. With the publication of these poems, formerly dead poets shall rise and have new careers of fame on this earth. The nation's honour shall be protected, and the perfume of its glory shall float far and wide. The towering arrogance of the unskilled poets of our time shall come tumbling to the ground! Those who have embarked upon the path of poetic composition shall have the means of achieving success ready to hand.

How can a handful of youth, who are habituated to Western tastes and have studied only foreign poetry through alien art, be true connoisseurs of Bangla poetry? They cannot help being like this because, right from the beginning, their training has not included these things: they have heard nothing. They hate and ridicule our songs based on the smattering of inferior verses they hear in the marketplace and from the lips of common itinerant performers. We cannot blame them for lacking culture: how can they appreciate the completely unfamiliar? We have recently urged these gentlemen to look upon their native poetry with greater favour. They will surely derive much pleasure through a proper understanding gained from a patient and careful study of these poets. They will easily be able to see with what felicity our early poets have expressed contemplative, aesthetic and amorous moods in their poetry. Look with what curious skill they have illuminated their thoughts such that each reveals the truth of its nature! Look at the sweetness of the turns of phrase! Look at the deep significance of meanings! Wonderful! Wonderful! Nowhere in this bounty can any dearth be observed. These poets have figured forth with great exactitude each mood they have attempted. The more we experience the distinct aesthetic moods of these early poems, the more they seem to swell with flavour, wave upon wave, until the very ocean of literary delectation is overwhelmed.

We have printed here poems of only two authors. Try to read or sing a couple of the heroes' and heroines' dialogues and you will immediately see how these men and women or groups of maidenly companions seem to hold animated conversations of various moods and in diverse ways right before our eyes. Especially see the works of Ram Basu, whose effortless simplicity of expression no one has been able to surpass. This is not to say that the other authors are lesser, there are merely slight differences in degree!

The more we pursue our researches into the past, the greater is our satisfaction. It is impossible to tell how many volumes will be sufficient to contain the material of olden times. I shall desist from going back more than two hundred years past. Approximately one hundred and forty or one hundred and fifty years ago, there was an individual named 'Gonjla Guin' who formed a 'professional' group to sing in the homes of the wealthy. We have not been able to determine whom he had his competitions with. In those days, they used to be accompanied on the 'tikera.'[5] The bards 'Lalunandalal, Raghu, and Ramji' were pupils of the said 'Gonjla Guin' and others. Raghu hailed from Farasdanga. He was born to a family of weavers and was good at composing, writing songs and setting them to music. Not much is known till date about Lalunandalal and Ramji. These are the three ancient bards. The 'kara'[6] was used to keep the rhythm in their time. In the age of Haru Thakur and his contemporaries, the 'shorkhai' and subsequently the 'dhol' were introduced as accompaniments.[7]

Haru Thakur was the disciple of Raghu, Ramji's disciple was Bhabane Bene, and Nite Baishnab was Lalunandalal's pupil. The practice of these greats then was to speak about their respective 'ostad' or master upon the completion of the performance. Around the time Lalunandalal and others formed their groups, a shoemaker by the name of Krishna, whom common people called 'Keshta Muchi,' achieved great fame for composing poetry. His songs received much veneration from discerning patrons. Prominent companies of 'ostadi' players came to him for the songs they sang in their poetic entertainments. This shoemaker defeated Haru Thakur many times in poetry contests. We have not spared any effort in trying to recover the work of this Keshta. Unfortunately, a thorough survey of the entire region has yielded only one, given here:

Mahara[8]

'O Hari,[9] who can fathom your capriciousness! Look at the love you have got for yourself!

You are Lord of the world, master of fortune,[10] yet in possessing your crooked hunchback maiden you forget the lovely Radha.

Chiten[11]

O dusky one, you have indeed adorned yourself well. Where have you concealed your humble cowherd's habit, O omnipotent lord of all senses?
Vanquisher of kin you have given prosperity to the cowherds but[12] have let Gokula[13] be swept into the shoreless currents of uncertainty.

The rest of this poem could not be recovered. The age of this song will be near seventy years. Ah! Such purity, such exquisite taste in the nectar of musical composition! Who will call this author a mere 'cobbler'? See also in this context how, apart from this poet, there was another important composer by the name of 'Nime Sunri.'[14] How vastly superior would the men of gentle birth have been in a land whose weavers, vintners, cobblers and sweepers were such accomplished artists.

We give here a song of Nitai Das' master Lalunandalal collected by us:

Mahara

Such is the joy love has given me   My life has passed in tears

Chiten

Shame and scandal is my inevitable lot, and exile from kin.
I thought I would dip into the waters to see how deep they run.
Alas, this is how it ended – my helmsman fled and the boat floated away.

Antara[15]

The one refuge to whom I surrendered all my wealth, heart and soul, this bloom of youth,
Yet, O ladies, winning his heart is an impossible task.
Desire frustrated, separation imminent, I am only left with false calumny in the world.'

This song is not less than eighty years old. One cannot but praise this composition.

The date of composition of Gonjla Guin's songs is very probably the far side of one hundred and forty years earlier. Fragments from two of his songs have been recovered thanks to the generosity of a certain friend, and we present them here with gladdened heart for general perusal:

1.

Come my celestial beauty[16] do not turn me away from this treasure.
We are of the same body, you the lotus and I am the bee,[17]
I am sure I must be the serpent and you the jewel on his crown.[18]

2.

We two are but one form, I am body and soul, you are the lustrous reflection,[19]
The mighty animated spirit I, and you sweet illusion. O think upon this in your mind.

Again:

Seeing you, O my dearest life, all my cares are ended,
The fire of separation grows cool and my soul's chakora bird is soothed.

How wonderful is the first of these songs! It has dispelled the darkness of the soul using language as assured as the canonical truths of the Vedāntas. Oh Guin, what manner of man wert thou! What irony that a mind capable of straddling the vast expanses of infinity answered to the name of 'Gonjla!' Can a mere handful[20] do justice to a full figuring of talent such as this Gonjla's? I shall be captive to your melody, style and allusive power for the rest of my existence.

During this time songs did not usually begin with the chiten refrain. The mahara preamble would initiate the song, followed by the chiten and antara stanzas.

Translation: Debapriya Basu

Notes

1 Iswar Chandra Gupta, 'Prachin Kabi', in *Iswar Gupta Rachanabali*, Santikumar Dasgupta and Haribandhu Mukhoti (eds.), Kolkata: Datta Chaudhuri & Sons, 1954, pp. 106–110. The essay was first published in *Sambad Prabhakar* in November, 1854.
2 Kuber is the Hindu god of wealth.
3 Identified as the pied-crested cuckoo and thought to be a harbinger of the monsoon due to the time of its arrival. In Indian mythology, the chataka is a symbol of spiritual thirst as it eschews all earthly water sources.
4 A bird in Indian mythology whose only food is moonlight. Identified as the chukar partridge.
5 A tikara or kettle drum.
6 A kind of drum beaten only at one end.
7 Percussion instruments.

8 The initiating couplet, the proposition. Literally, 'face.' These are examples of alliterative poetry with extensive wordplay and punning. This polysemy is obviously lost in translation. Therefore, secondary (and further) meanings have not been noted unless particularly relevant in context. Names of gods have been retained in the first instance; all subsequent names have been translated for example 'sripati' (as given in endnote 10).
9 One of the names of the Hindu god Vishnu.
10 Puns on 'sripati,' one of the names of the god Vishnu, also meaning 'husband of fortune or Goddess Lakshmi.'
11 Chiten, primary phrase of a fixed melodic composition and a refrain. Used in contexts of music/poetry competitions. See the final paragraph of this essay for explication of this unusual placement of the initial refrain.
12 Krishna killed his maternal uncle Kansa.
13 Childhood dwelling place of Krishna. Literally cow-pen or herd of cows.
14 Sunri: vintner, distiller and seller of alcoholic beverages (lower caste occupation). Connotes very low social status.
15 Usually second verse stanza of song.
16 Literally 'moon-limbed' or a woman whose physical beauty is like the moon.
17 Puns on the double meaning of bhringa: 'bee' and 'libertine.'
18 In mythology, the rare jewel that the cobra was supposed to carry on its head. Imbued with spiritual significance.
19 In original lineation, 'you are shadow' is printed in the next line.
20 Wordplay on 'anjla' or 'fistful' that rhymes with the poet's name and the handful of recovered lines attributed to him.

6 Bankimchandra Chattopadhyay: 'A Message to the New Writers of Bengal' and 'Sakuntala, Miranda and Desdemona'

Introduction

Bankimchandra Chattopadhyay or Bankim Chandra Chatterjee (1838–1894) was one of the leading figures of the Bengal Renaissance. He was the first major novelist in Bangla, and his novel *Durgeshnandini* (1865) is generally identified as the first novel in the language. Chattopadhyay was one of the first two students to graduate from Calcutta University. For many years he was a Deputy Collector and a District Magistrate. He sometimes wrote in a humorous form underlying which was a scathing satire on contemporary issues. He broke new grounds in many areas of discourse.

In 1872, Bankimchandra Chattopadhyay brought out *Bangadarsan* that became one of the most important journals of the 19th century. The introduction to the first volume stated that he wanted to serve the cause of education that was restricted either to an English-speaking elite or to a handful of Sanskrit scholars and so, divorced from the people, did not serve any purpose. Apart from literary texts, *Bangadarsan* published essays on science, philosophy, sociology, anthropology, economics, education, music and political science. Chattopadhyay was joined in his venture by several eminent thinkers who were still in their early stage of writing, and he himself wrote many of the articles in the journal anonymously. Deeply influenced by the Utilitarianism of Jeremy Bentham and John Stuart Mill along with the Positivism of Auguste Comte, Chattopadhyay combined the different strands of thought with some of his religious principles. His larger aim was to serve humanity as he stated repeatedly. In the later period of his life, he studied and analysed religious texts although even there *samaj* or community had a privileged place. In the preface to *Krishnacharitra* (1886, revised 1892), a text that recorded the essence of his thoughts on *dharma*, he spoke about humanism as the practice, expansion and fulfilment of human potentials or general inclinations. These inclinations were directed towards erudition, a refined capability of judgement, eagerness to work, a religious propensity, a sense of humour and a healthy physique. He wrote 13 novels that have a special place in the history of Bangla fiction. Some of his collections of essays are *Lokarahasya*

DOI: 10.4324/9781003224686-7

(1874, revised 1888), *Kamalakanta* (1875–1885), *Bigyanrahasya* (1875), *Samya* (1879) and *Dharmatattva* (1888).

The two essays compiled in this volume, 'A Message to the New Writers of Bengal' and 'Sakuntala, Miranda and Desdemona' are taken from 'Bibidha Prabandha' in *Bankim Rachanabali* (Vol. II). The first essay demonstrates the unhesitant clarity of the author on the overall purpose of literature and a system of values linked with it. The second is one of the first essays in the language to foreground a comparative aesthetics that reveals the horizon of sensibility within which Bangla texts operate.

*

A Message to the New Writers of Bengal[1]

Bankimchandra Chattopadhyay

1 Do not write for fame. You will then neither have fame nor will your writing be good. If you write well, fame will naturally follow.

2 Do not write for money. Many people in England today write for money, and they get money; their writing is also good. But we will have to wait for such a situation. Now if we try to write for money, our desire for entertaining people will become very strong. If we take into consideration the taste and education of our common readers and try to entertain, our writing will become distorted and harmful.

3 If you think you can contribute to that which is for the good of the country or for the people or to create beauty by writing, you must write. Those who write for any other purpose can be compared to *jatrawalas* or to crude businessmen.

4 That which is not true, which is against dharma, that which is written to disgrace or hurt someone or to serve a selfish purpose can never be good for anyone, and hence such writing needs to be discarded. Truth and dharma are the goals of literature. It is a great sin to take up the pen for other objectives.

5 Do not publish as soon as you write. Keep it aside for some time. After a while, correct your writing. You will then find many faults in the writing. Poems, plays and novels gain perfection when they have been kept aside for a year or two and then corrected. Those who devote themselves to topical writing cannot keep to this rule. Hence, topical writing is regressive for the writer.

6 If you do not have proficiency over a subject, you have no right to meddle with it. This is a simple statement, but in topical writing this rule is not valid.

7 Do not try to demonstrate your knowledge. If you have knowledge, it will get expressed naturally, without your effort. It is very annoying to the reader when one tries to show off one's knowledge, and it is also particularly harmful to the harmony of the text. I see a large number of quotations from

English, Sanskrit, French and German in essays written today. When you do not know a language, never quote from it on the basis of another text.

8 Do not try to introduce figures of speech or humour. Figures of speech and irony are sometimes necessary in a text; if the writer has them in his store, they will come naturally when needed – no effort can bring them if they are not there. There is nothing as ugly as bringing in figures of speech or humour from an empty stock or in the wrong place.

9 An ancient rule states that where a figure of speech or humour appears delightful, you delete it. I am not saying that. But my advice is, read that section to your friends again and again. If it is not good the writer will realise that after a few readings – he will feel ashamed to read it to his friends. He will then erase it.

10 Simplicity is the best of all ornaments. One who can in simple words carry across his feelings to the reader with ease is the best writer. This is because the purpose of writing is to make the reader understand.

11 Do not imitate anyone. In imitating, the faults get imitated, not the virtues. Never think that such and such English, Sanskrit or Bengali writer wrote in a particular fashion, and I will write similarly.

12 Do not write that which you cannot prove. It is not always necessary to demonstrate your proof, but it must be kept ready.

Bengal is dependent on Bangla literature. If writers of Bengal adhere to these points, Bangla literature will develop rapidly.

Translation: Subha Chakraborty Dasgupta

*

Sakuntala, Miranda and Desdemona[2]

Bankimchandra Chattopadhyay

One: Sakuntala and Miranda

Both Sakuntala and Miranda are daughters of sages; Prospero and Visvamitra are both princes. As daughters of sages, Sakuntala and Miranda are helped by superhuman powers. Miranda is protected by Ariel, Sakuntala by Apsaras.

Both are raised by sages. Both are forest vines, and both defeat the vines in their beauty. Dushyanta is reminded of the pallor in the beauty of those confined within the palace when he sees Sakuntala.

> If the beauty of maids who dwell in woodland retreats cannot easily be found in the recesses of a palace, the garden flowers must make room for the blossoms of the forest, which excel them in colour and fragrance.[3]

Ferdinand, also on seeing Miranda, thinks in a similar manner:

> Full many a lady
> I have ey'd with best regard; and many a time
> The harmony of their tongues hath into bondage
> Brought my too diligent ear: for several virtues
> Have I lik'd several women; . . .
>   . . . but you, O you,
> So perfect and so peerless, are created
> Of every creature's best![4]

Both Sakuntala and Miranda are raised in the forest and are experts in the magic that there is in innocence. The beautiful, simple and pure feminine nature gets distorted while living in the company of human beings – who is going to love me, who will call me beautiful, how will I conquer a man – such desires, pleasures and delusions, like the moonlight hidden by the cloud, darken its loveliness. This darkness is not present in either Sakuntala or Miranda: because they are not brought up in the company of human beings. Sakuntala spends her days wearing the bark of a tree and watering plants here and there from her small pitcher that she carries in her arms; she herself is pure, untainted, joyous, spreading her fragrance to far horizons like the wet *mallika* flowers washed by drops of water. Her sisterly love is for the new mallika flower; she loves the mango tree like a brother, and she has a maternal love for the motherless fawn; she is in tears and sad and depressed as she takes leave from them while leaving for her husband's home. Sakuntala speaks to them; she is happy mocking a tree, caressing one or taking a vine to its destination. But despite being simple, she is not uneducated. Her modesty is her sign of education. Her sense of modesty is very strong; very often she lowers her face when she is with Dushyanta – her modesty does not allow her to express her deep love, even to her companions. Miranda is not like her. She is so simple that she does not even have modesty. How could she have modesty? She had never seen any man, except her father. She does not know what he is when she first sees Ferdinand:

> Lord, how it looks about! Believe me, sir,
> It carries a brave form: – But 'tis a spirit.[5]

All the prejudices of society are there in Sakuntala, Miranda has none. She has no qualms in praising the beauty of Ferdinand to her father – it is like someone praising a picture.

> I might call him
> A thing divine; for nothing natural
> I ever saw so noble.[6]

And yet the purity that is natural to a woman, that which is modesty within modesty, is very much present in Miranda, and hence, the novelty and sweetness of her simplicity are greater than that of Sakuntala's. When she sees her father trying to berate Ferdinand, she says,

> O dear father,
> Make not too rash a trial of him, for
> He's gentle and not fearful.[7]

Miranda, hearing her father speaking negatively of the beauty of Ferdinand, says,

> My affections
> Are then most humble; I have no ambition
> To see a goodlier man.[8]

We then know that Miranda is without prejudice, but she is pained by the sorrows of others; Miranda is caring, and she is not modest. However, she has a purity that is the essence of modesty.

Miranda's heart has never been touched by love before her meeting with the prince; for she has never seen any man since her childhood, except her father and Caliban. When Sakuntala sees the king, her heart too is empty, for she has seen no men except the sages. Both saw the heroes in the midst of groves, those of Kanva and Prospero, and immediately fell in love. But watch the wonderful art of poets; they had not consulted each other as they started drawing the characters of Sakuntala and Miranda; yet it seemed as if a single person had drawn two pictures. If the same person had drawn both characters, how would he have differed in drawing the nature of love in Sakuntala and in Miranda? He would have understood that Sakuntala partook of the prejudices of society, she was modest and hence her love would be expressed not in words but only through signs; however, Miranda was free of prejudice and did not know of societal modesty, and hence the signs of her love would be more pronounced. The different poets did just that in their portraits. Sakuntala is in love; she does not reveal a word about her new obsession, not only to Dushyanta, but even to her companions, until they plead with her. They see her stricken state and understand it all through feelings. She merely reveals a few signs:

> when she cast her eyes even upon her companions, they sparkled with tenderness, when she moved her graceful arms, they dropped, as if languid with love; when her friend remonstrated against her departure, she spoke angrily – All this was, no doubt, on my account. – Oh! How quick-sighted is love in discerning his own advantages![9]

When Sakuntala goes to leave Dushyanta, her bark gets caught in trees and blades of grass prick her feet. But Miranda has no use for any of it – she does not know them; on their first meeting, Miranda without any inhibition declares her love before her father,

> This
> Is the third man that e'er I saw, the first
> That e'er I sigh'd for: . . .[10]

And seeing her father about to persecute Ferdinand, she tries to appeal to his kindness by talking of him as one who is close to her. She gives herself to Ferdinand in the very first instance.

The first expression of love between Sakuntala and Dushyanta is a kind of hide-and-seek game. 'Friend, why do you hold the king back?' – 'So let me go away' – 'Let me hide behind this tree –' Sakuntala has all these 'pretensions'; Miranda has no pretension. Sakuntala behaves in a manner that is expected of a modest girl in the community, but Miranda is not a modest community girl – she is a bird of the forest – she is not shy of singing out with the rising of the sun; she is a flower on a tree, she does not feel shy of blossoming out with full radiance in the evening breeze; finding her hero, she is not shy of saying,

> . . . but my modesty,
> (The Jewel in my dower,) I would not wish
> Any companion in the world but you;
> Nor can imagination form a shape,
> Besides yourself, to like of:. . .[11]

Then again,

> Hence, bashful cunning!
> And prompt me, plain and holy innocence!
> I am your wife, if you will marry me;
> If not, I'll die your maid: to be your fellow
> You may deny me; but I'll be your servant,
> Whether you will or no.[12]

We wanted to quote the entire first dialogue of love, but that is not necessary. Everyone has the texts of Shakespeare, and they can all read the original versions. They will find that this is no less powerful than the dialogue of Romeo and Juliet in the garden, famous all over the world and memorised by all college students. Miranda is aglow with the same lofty feelings as Juliet when she says – my gift is infinite like the ocean, my love as deep as that ocean. In a similar situation, in the leafy bower, where Sakuntala first opens her heart-bud before the rays of the sun and smiles, the conversation between Dushyanta and Sakuntala does not have the same glory, nor does one see at its core the restless brimming waves extending to the whole expanse of human nature. The spoken words alone are there and nothing more – Sakuntala finds it shameful, she wants to leave and it is only a game of hide-and-seek – there is just a little guile, such as, 'When I was halfway gone, I realised that this lotus-fibre bracelet had fallen from my hand and I returned' etc. There is a little directness, as when Dushyanta says, 'Is not the bee around the lotus flower content with its fragrance?' Sakuntala responds, 'What does it do if it is not satisfied?' She only says this and no more. This is not a weakness but a virtue in the poet. Little Sakuntala is lost in the shadow of the glorious Dushyanta. Ferdinand and Romeo are small people, almost of the same age as the heroine, and of a similar standing, without fame, but how important is Sakuntala before Dushyanta who is the emperor of all the oceans and the world? The large shadow of the great tree Dushyanta has covered the blossom Sakuntala – she cannot open up completely. This is not a lover's address – this is a princely sport where the lord of the world desires to come to a garden to play a game resembling love and, like a mad elephant, lifts the lotus bud Sakuntala with his trunk, indulging fully in the forest adventure. Will the lotus bud blossom there?

One will not be able to comprehend the character of Sakuntala if one does not remember this. Sakuntala did not flower in the same spray of water in which Miranda and Juliet flowered. In the love-stricken Sakuntala, we saw a young girl's restlessness, her fears, her modesty, but a seeming lack of a woman's seriousness and her affections. Some will say that is because of the difference in behavioral norms in different countries. But it is not because of a difference. It is not as if Sakuntala was stricken by modesty because she was a village housewife, and Miranda and Juliet displayed their feelings because they were shameless Westerners. Minor critics do not tell you that differences in time and place lead to external differences alone, whereas the human heart remains the same in all places and in all times. In fact, of the three characters, it is Sakuntala who is the most brazen. That is proved by her question 'What does it do if it is not satisfied?' That is the Sakuntala who, a few months later, would chastise Dushyanta in the king's court and say, 'Unworthy king! You take everyone to be like yourself?' Sakuntala remains a child in the creeper bough, and that is not because of her modesty as a country girl. It is because of the expanse of Dushyanta's character. Sakuntala is a wife, a queen about to gain the status of a mother when she is deserted in the court and then she is a woman; in the garden, she is the daughter of a sage, who erringly desires a king's grace. Who is she in this place? She is just a lotus on a stem. I have tried to show that the poet of *Sakuntala* is not of lesser merit than the poet of *The Tempest.*

Two: Sakuntala and Desdemona

We have compared Sakuntala with Miranda and shown that Sakuntala was quite unlike Miranda. But a part of Sakuntala's character can be understood only when compared to Miranda's. We have to understand the other half of Sakuntala's character, and I wish to do so by comparing her with Desdemona.

Sakuntala and Desdemona are both similar and dissimilar. They are similar, because both surrendered themselves without consulting their elders. Gautami's words to Dushyanta regarding Sakuntala could apply to Desdemona with reference to Othello,

> She waited not the return of her spiritual father; nor were the kindred consulted by thee. You two only were present, when your nuptials were solemnized: now, therefore, converse freely together in the absence of all others.[13]

The two characters are comparable because both gave themselves to a valiant person, and in both cases the 'long climbing creeper of hope' entwined itself round a giant tree to move up. But the attraction to valour that is so evident in Desdemona is missing in Sakuntala. Othello is dark, and hence for the Italian girl it is not the appearance of the man but rather his valour that serves as a greater attraction. The great poet, who made Draupadi value Arjuna among her five husbands thus preventing her bodily ascendance to heaven, knew this: the one who created Desdemona expressed this subtle fact.

The two characters are comparable because the 'long climbing creeper of hope' fails them both as both are forsaken by their husbands. The world is full of neglect and tyranny. It also often happens that those deserving love are subjected to the utmost neglect and oppression. This is not really bad for human beings: because the higher faculties that exist in human nature receive an overall impetus in such circumstances. These are the seeds of positive lessons – the chief components of literature. Those mental faculties were about to blossom in Desdemona either because of a virtue or a fault in her destiny, and it was the same for Sakuntala. Hence, all conditions are there for the comparison of the characters.

The two characters are comparable because of their great affection and chastity. But most women are affectionate and chaste. All heroines of all commonplace and mediocre writers in plays, novels, new novels and ghost novels are affectionate and chaste. But these chaste women forget their husbands even when their pet cat comes to them, and Sakuntala who was immersed in thoughts of her husband did not hear the fearful utterance of Durvasa. All are chaste, but who can penetrate the depths of the firm belief of Desdemona that there is no unchaste woman in the world and that no woman can be unchaste? If the unwavering devotion to a husband remains firm even after being beaten, tortured, rejected and dishonoured, and if that is a sign of faithfulness, then Desdemona is greater in character than Sakuntala. Sakuntala rebuked her husband raising her head like a snake about to strike when she is rejected by him. When the King mocked Sakuntala by saying that she was full of clever wiles despite being uneducated, Sakuntala in rage and pride changed her former suppliant, shy, sorrowful demeanour. She said, 'Unworthy prince, you look upon others in the likeness of your own self?' In response, the king retorted in a stately manner, 'Lady, everybody knows the character of Dushyanta'. Then, Sakuntala with great sarcasm proclaimed,

> You kings are in all cases to be credited implicitly: you perfectly know the respect which is due to virtue and to mankind; while females, however modest, however virtuous, know nothing and speak nothing truly.[14]

This anger and the sense of being hurt and this sarcasm are not there in Desdemona. When Othello struck Desdemona in front of all and sent her out, she just said, 'I will not stand and disturb you anymore'. She was leaving, but when she was called back, she responded, 'Lord', and returned. When Othello insulted her gravely for no fault of hers, even then Desdemona just said, 'I am innocent, God knows'. Even after that, deprived of her husband's love, conscious of an emptiness in the world, she called Iago and said,

> O Good Iago,
> What shall I do to win my lord again?
> Good friend, go to him; for, by this light of heaven,
> I know not how I lost him. Here I kneel: –[15]

And so on. When Othello like a brutal demon stood before the beautiful lady sleeping at night saying that he would kill her, then too there was no anger – no sense of hurt – no lack of courtesy or affection. Desdemona merely said, 'Then let God save me.' Even when in fear of death, Desdemona prayed for a day's, a night's, a moment's time, and the stupid man paid no heed, there was no anger, no sense of hurt, no discourtesy, no loss of affection. When Emilia saw her dying and asked who was responsible, Desdemona said, 'Nobody; I myself; Farewell: Commend me to my kind lord; O, farewell!'[16] Even then Desdemona did not tell people that her husband had killed her for no fault of hers.

Hence, I was saying that Sakuntala both is and is not comparable to Desdemona. She is not comparable because different kinds of substances cannot be compared. This play by Shakespeare is like an ocean, while the one by Kālidāsa is like a garden of paradise. A garden cannot be compared to an ocean. That is not possible. This garden has an abundant, profuse and immeasurable collection of whatever is beautiful and graceful, fragrant and mellifluous, pleasant and gratifying. And all that is deep, expansive, restless and rumbling belongs to this ocean. This unique ocean-like play by Shakespeare is full of swirling, aggrieved waves rising from the heart, and driven by restless anger, hatred and other strong passions. Its strong force, its reckless turbulence and the restless play of waves – and then again, its pleasant blue expanse, its infinite projection of crushed particles of light, its radiance and shadow, its jewels and soft music are all rare in the literary world.

And so Sakuntala and Desdemona are not comparable. Different species are not comparable. I will explain why I am speaking of a different species.

A play (*natak*) in India is not exactly synonymous with what is called a play in Europe. In both parts of the world, a play is a *dṛśyakāvya* or a poetic work that is seen, but European critics bring a little more to the notion of a play. According to them, there are poetic works that are presented as *dṛśyakāvyas* but are not really plays. It is not as if they would be counted as inferior forms because they are not plays – there are some among them that are excellent as Goethe's *Faust* and Byron's *Manfred* – but whether superior or inferior, they are poetic works and not plays. Shakespeare's *Tempest* and Kālidāsa's *Sakuntala* belong to such a genre, that is, they are excellent narrative poems in the form of plays, but are not plays. It is not slanderous to say that they are not plays – for such poetic narratives are extremely rare and almost matchless in the world. In India, we can designate both as plays, for all the traits that critics identify in plays are present in these two kavyas. But according to European critics, the elements that ought to be there in a play are absent in these texts. *Othello* has an abundance of such traits. *Othello* is a play, and from this perspective *Sakuntala* is a narrative kavya. The result is this that Miranda and Sakuntala lack the clarity of Desdemona. Desdemona is full of life, Sakuntala and Miranda are meditative. In the words of Desdemona, we hear her piteous, distorted voice and see the drops of tears that flow down her cheeks; the trembling upward glance of this long-limbed beauty enters our heart. We do not see Sakuntala's eyes turning red except when we hear of it from Dushyanta,

> She looks indignant; her eye glows; and her speech, formed of harsh terms, falters as she utters them. Her lip, ruddy as the Bimba fruit, quivers as if it were nipped with frost; and her eyebrows, naturally smooth and equal, are at once irregularly contracted.[17]

We do not see the expanse of Sakuntala's sorrow, its motion or its force – all that is very clear in Desdemona. Sakuntala is a portrait sketched by a painter, and Desdemona is a lifelike form moulded by a sculptor. Desdemona's heart is fully revealed and laid bare before us: Sakuntala's is expressed only in signs.

Hence, as Desdemona's narrative is more radiant, Sakuntala cannot stand before her. But they are both internally similar. Sakuntala is half-Miranda and half-Desdemona. The full-formed Sakuntala is similar to Desdemona and the immature Sakuntala is similar to Miranda.

Translation: Subha Chakraborty Dasgupta

Notes

1 Bankimchandra Chattopadhyay, 'Bangalar Nabya Lekhakdiger Prati Nibedan', in *Bibidha Prabandha II*, *Bankim Rachanabali*, Vol. II, Jogeshchandra Bagal

(ed.), Kolkata: Sahitya Samsad 1954 (Rep. 1998), pp. 236–237. The essay was originally published in *Prachar*, 1886, 1(7): 252–255.

2 Bankimchandra Chattopadhyay, 'Sakuntala, Miranda ebang Desdemona', in *Bibidha Prabandha I, Bankim Rachanabali*, Vol. II, Jogeshchandra Bagal (ed.), op. cit., pp. 179–184. The essay was originally published in *Bangadarsan*, 1876, 4(1): 1–9.

3 Kālidāsa, *Sacontalá; Or, The Fatal Ring: An Indian Drama* (1789), Act I, William Jones (trans.), www.columbia.edu/itc/mealac/pritchett/00litlinks/shakuntala_jones/ accessed on 19 June 2019. All Sanskrit quotations from Kālidāsa's *Abhijñānaśākuntalam* are cited from this translation.

4 William Shakespeare, '*The Tempest*, Act III, Sc. i', in *The Dramatic Works of Shakespeare*, Vol. I, revised by George Steevens, London: John and Josiah Boydell, George and W. Nicol, 1802, p. 48.

5 Ibid., Act I, Sc. ii, p. 21.

6 Ibid.

7 Ibid., p. 23.

8 Ibid., p. 24.

9 Kālidāsa, *Sacontalá*, Act II.

10 William Shakespeare, *The Tempest*, Act I, Sc. ii, pp. 22–23.

11 Ibid., Act III, Sc. i, p. 48.

12 Ibid., p. 49.

13 Kālidāsa, *Sacontalá*, Act V.

14 Ibid.

15 William Shakespeare, '*Othello* Act IV, Sc. ii', in *The Dramatic Works of Shakespeare*, Vol. IX, revised by George Steevens, op. cit., pp. 104–105.

16 Ibid., Act V, Sc. ii, p. 124.

17 Kālidāsa, *Sacontalá*, Act V.

7 Pramatha Chaudhuri: Preface to *Sabuj Patra*

Introduction

Pramathanath Chaudhuri (1868–1946) was born in a land-owning family in Pabna district, which is now in Bangladesh. He studied Philosophy and English Literature and then pursued a degree in Law and briefly practiced in the High Court of Calcutta. Chaudhuri was a noted poet with collections such as *Sonnet Panchasat* (1913) and *Padacharan* (1919). An eminent fiction writer, his works include *Char Iyari Katha* (1916), *Ahuti* (1919) and *Nillohit* (1932). However, his principal fame rested on his experiments with prose. His major contribution to Bangla language and literature was the periodical *Sabuj Patra* that he brought out in 1914 and that worked towards bridging the gap between the verbal and the written forms of Bangla prose.

Bankimchandra Chattopadhyay's plea to the authors of Bangla literature was focused on subject matter and the purpose of writing. Chaudhuri, on the other hand, as one of his principal followers Annadashankar Ray once put it, taught us 'how to write'. *Sabuj Patra* was able to bring together a group of authors who wanted to disseminate knowledge through the mother tongue and gradually adopted a prose style that was closer to the colloquial form of the language. Rabindranath Tagore was one of the principal contributors to the periodical.

The 'Preface' to the first issue of *Sabuj Patra* in April–May 1914 tried to justify the publication of a new journal where many already existed. Chaudhuri, on the one hand, wanted to single out his journal by a few negations – by denying any space to 'unsolicited articles meant for women and children, those meant for schoolbooks and those that were unreadable' and by a refusal to preach. On the other hand, he promised to nurture in his periodical the living energy of the creative individual – one that allowed the cultivation of ideas, both indigenous and foreign, in a language that was rooted in its own culture and tradition. In a period that he recognised as intrinsically barren, he concentrated on keeping the mind from becoming dormant and dedicated *Sabuj Patra* to that very spirit of life that he wanted to perceive in literature.

*

DOI: 10.4324/9781003224686-8

Preface to *Sabuj Patra*[1]

Pramatha Chaudhuri

Om prānāya svāha[2]

'Do something new' was the advice given by the late Dwijendralal Roy (1863–1913) to the Bengali community. It will not be entirely correct to say that following his advice, we ventured into publishing a new monthly journal. This world is quite old; hence, doing anything new with it is very difficult, especially in India. If ever anything new is achieved with considerable effort, it either tends to become obsolete within a short span of time because of the environment, or it is taken over by the ancient. Because of this condition in our country, we cannot vouch that we have enough confidence or courage to start anything new either in word or in deed.

We will not be able to respond positively if someone asks us why and to fulfil what needs we are launching a new journal when there are already so many; because not being able to keep one's commitment is not regarded as courteous even in literary circles. To introduce oneself and to sing one's own praise before having proved oneself have become 'literary' norms accepted by all, and we are constrained to break the rule. We are unable to gather enough courage to boast that we shall not falter at times in our effort to gather material for twelve monthly instalments. Moreover, fulfilling a particular need or accomplishing a certain goal for one's own society or one's own country is neither the duty nor the dharma of literature; that is a concern of the field of work. The narrowness that creeps in while taking up a particular cause as one's purpose is not favourable to the joyous flowering of literature. Work requires combined effort from all. We can have Literary Conventions but not literature by working in groups, and this is because in order to accomplish a task with the help and association of others, one has to suppress one's own liberty to a great extent. If ten of us share eighty percent of thoughts and ideas, then keeping aside the twenty percent, we can work together for a cause equally desired by all. It is only when there is this eighty percent agreement in a large section of the people of a nation, an era and a society that social work can be performed satisfactorily, and not otherwise. But literature is the expansion of personality. Hence, the value of the twenty percent that is the individual's own is greater than the readily available eighty percent for literature because it is created and rendered stable by that twenty percent alone. Those who are mentally in total accord with society have nothing to say. While agreeing, the mind falls asleep and wakes up with the touch of dissent. And it is this wakeful state of the mind that is responsible for the genesis of all prose, philosophy and science.

This would perhaps make people say that writing that does not fulfil even a single need in a country with so many needs on so many fronts is not literature but a mere hobby. It is like flying a colourful kite of imagination, and the sooner the kite string is cut-loose, and it disappears, the better. Of course, there is a sense of fulfilment in flying a kite. A kite at least teaches man to look upwards. Nevertheless, it is true that bereft of any connection with human life, literature is mere jugglery of words and not worth its name. Based on life, literature is born and nourished; but that is not the everyday life of human beings. Literature cannot readily provide for food and clothing for mankind. Some words may be of no use, but there are others that have a hold over one, and the common definition for that class of words is literature. The power of words is limitless. The darkness of night and the buzz of mosquitoes put people to sleep (provided they sleep inside mosquito nets), but the light of day and the call of crows and cuckoos wake them up. We may not be fully aware of the deep signification of what we call life, but its chief symptom is clear, prominent and obvious. It is the state of being awake. On the other hand, slumber is the sister of death. Words put us to sleep or wake us up – and that is why we either live or die in words. I am not sure whether snakes can be charmed by mantras, but the whole of India is proof that mantras can charm human beings. Bangla literature is proof of the fact that Sanskrit words are capable of resisting reform. Human minds are partially awake and partially dormant. We take that part of our mind which is awake as constituting the whole, and we do not believe in the existence of its dormant section because we do not know it. Literature is the main support of human lives because its chief effort lies in gradually leading the mind out of the clutches of sleep into a state of awakening. If the early morning birds of Bangla literature alight on our green leaf-covered new branches, we would be able to fulfil the greatest need of the Bengali community to some extent. And that need is knowledge of a full picture of what is lacking in our minds and characters. We have not been able to comprehend our shortcoming in any significant way, and that is reflected in the manner in which, through our speeches and writings day in and day out, we declare and try to demonstrate our poverty as glory, inertness as piety, laziness as detachment, extreme apathy as transcendental joy, fasting as festive and the idler as a passive being. The reason for this is clear. Deceit is the strength of the weak. One who is weak deceives others in self-defence and deceives oneself to gain self-esteem. There is nothing more self-destructive than self-deception. Literature cannot arrange for the livelihood of human beings but can prevent them from committing suicide.

I cannot dare say that we shall be able to awaken, to some extent, the mind of the nation because one's good intentions are not enough to create the kind of literature that is required for this – what is necessary is God's will or an other-worldly talent at the source. It is not the kind of wealth that can be got by begging. However, it is within our capacity to ensure that the mind of Bengal does not become more dormant. The capacity to stir humanity is found in all, to some extent, but its implementation depends on one's inclinations. There is no denying the fact that our natural tendency is towards arousing others and ourselves for Europe is regularly shaking us up and disturbing our sleep. The touch of European literature and European philosophy is not soft but forceful. And regardless of whether European civilisation is nectar, wine or poison, its creed is to excite the mind and not let it rest. English education and culture have made all our countrymen restless and eager to move along a certain direction, whatever it may be, and make others do so as well. Some want to move westwards, others want to move back towards the east, some are searching for god's spirit up in the skies and yet others for his image on the earth. In short, whether we are progressive or regressive, we are all moving forward and we do not remain static. With the touch of Europe, we have attained mobility if not anything else, or, in other words, we have received some deliverance from all kinds of mental and physical inertia. The genesis of our new literature is in the joy that is there in this freedom. Just as flowers had blossomed in Hiramalini's withered garden with the arrival of Sundar,[3] flowers of literature blossomed in our country with Europe's arrival. Although we do not know what the result will be, our firm opinion is that this blossoming of flowers should not be stopped. Hence, we shall encourage anyone who is capable of cultivating flowers.

We gained the wonderful knowledge from Europe that one may bring seeds of ideas from anywhere, but they must be cultivated in the soil of the country. It is a futile exercise sowing them in a pot containing Chinese soil. This newly acquired knowledge has taught us to identify India's extensive past as the appropriate field to take up the study of new ideas. It is because of English education that we have taken it upon ourselves to resurrect our ancient history. That is the reason our heart with a single leap has crossed about a thousand and five hundred years and, moving across Bengal, gone back to Aryavarta. Our ancient poet is Kālidāsa and not Kasidas, our ancient philosopher Shankar and not Gadadhar, our specialist in sastras is Manu and not Raghunandan and our rhetorician Daṇḍin and not Visvanātha. For us, Navya Nyaya, recent schools of philosophy and *smriti* are very old, and those which are chronologically very old have returned in new forms. The reason for this is that modern European literature may not be similar in form to ancient Indian literature, but there is an inner resemblance that consists of a vitality – both are full of life. Although a paper rose may resemble a rose in nature, their difference is akin to that between the living and the dead. But a rose in the garden and a lotus in water are similar – because both have life. Therefore, the new education of our new life is a resource both for our country and for foreign lands. That which reflects this new life is literature – other writings are either utilitarian or unworthy.

We have taken up this effort to publish this new journal as we have discovered an easy way to discard writings that are not literature. We have set out not for the sake of doing something new but in order to clearly demonstrate the novelty that has arrived in the life of the Bengali.

It is not difficult to ascertain why, after being inspired with a new life, Bangla literature has come up with new leaves and not flowers. If one has both inner and external visions to some extent, one would easily be able to see both sides of why that is so.

Literature has not yet become a part and parcel of business in this country. It is difficult to say whether the writer or the reader is to be blamed for this. As a result, we are mere amateurs in the literary world. Nothing in this world can attain perfection in the hands of non-professional people – this is a fact known to all. For most of us authors, writing is neither work nor play but just meaningless toil; for the good health and ease that is there when we play is absent in writing, nor is there the care and attentiveness present in work. Absent-mindedness is reflected in every step of our writings because we produce literature during the leisure that we do not have. We want to create literature naturally, and therefore we have no option but to depend on supernatural talents. All authors need to remember that those who write to please Saraswati may not be blessed with her gifts. This is one of the reasons why Bangla literature instead of blossoming is getting covered with leaves. Forests grow naturally, but flowers must be cultivated. Mammoth monthly journals are bound to accept the weed to fill their pages and to indulge their growth as well. Being aware of this, and out of fear, our journal is small in size. This difference in size will be reflected in the content as well. We shall be obliged to ignore many writings in our small journal. We shall be able to redirect unsolicited articles meant for women and children, for school texts, and those that are unreadable to their respective places as we have very little space. In other words, we will not have to publish articles meant for teaching. The benefits of this will be better understood by the person who knows that the religion of a pedagogue consists in repeating what has been said a hundred times before. That which does not bear the imprint of the writer's mind is not literature.

Again, the life-force that I mentioned earlier did not appear from within us – it came to us from outside, from a distant time or a distant space. This force is still lying in a distraught manner within us and in our society. It will not help our literature to blossom or our lives to be fruitful unless we bring it within our control. In order to reflect this new life in literature, we must first reflect it in our minds. But Europe's strong impact has confused most of our minds. Nothing can be reflected in the mind unless it is made clear. However, only when the present restlessness and scattered thoughts and feelings are integrated in the mind's mirror can they find reflection in the mirror of literature. We hope that our small journal will help writers to frame their thoughts in a more compact and integrated manner. We do not want external rules to frame literature; we just want self-restraint. The only way to be restrained in one's writing is to keep oneself within limits. In our periodical, we shall endeavour to demarcate such limits.

My last word on this is that there is new life in the country and the desire to create literature because of the impact of education, and yet because of the faults in that very education system we have not been able to achieve the ability to convert our desire into results. Caught between modern

Europe and ancient India, we have almost forgotten Bangla. Our learning is in English, and our writing in Bangla where the burden of Sanskrit remains. Although the seeds of English education were first sown in the field of ancient Indian studies, the saplings need to be transplanted to the soil of Bengal or else flowers of our own literature will not blossom. The seeds of thought that the life-giving breath of the west brings are not able to spread their roots in the country's soil, and, as a result, they are either drying up or becoming parasitic. That is why *Meghnad Badh Kavya* is the flower of a dependent plant. It may have the glorious colour and form of an orchid, but it lacks fragrance. Although of a limited aspiration, *Annadamangal* (1753) is kavya because it is rooted to the soil, and *Britrasamhar* (Vol. I: 1875, Vol. II: 1877), because it does not belong anywhere, is not an epic although it has an expansive aspiration. Bharatchandra, matching words and feelings and with self-control, expressed himself clearly like a blossoming flower, and that flower, however small, had both life and fragrance. The future of our literature and society rests on the combination of the two vital forces: the past of our nation and the present of the foreign country and not on their conflict. We hope that the untilled land of Bengal will be the point of union of the two forces. Flowers of literature will blossom on this piece of untilled land made fertile, and they will eventually turn into fruits of life. For this, art is essential, because it is art alone that can bring in vitality. We expect that this small journal of ours will help writers in this regard. The aim of art is to hold the great within the small. Musical masters say that the Gaud Saranga is not an expansive ragini, but its rendition is difficult – 'just as it is difficult for an elephant to pass through a narrow door, so it is difficult to put a river into a small pitcher'. However difficult it may be, because of its situation, Bengali society must try to sing the Gaud Saranga. We shall have to try to make the elephant of our ancient India pass through the narrow back-door of Bengal, and we shall have to try and hold the seven seas within the earthen pot of our language. This pursuit is of course difficult, but we are unaware of any easier method to seek the salvation of our own people.

Translation: Tapan Chakraborty

Notes

1 Pramatha Chaudhuri, 'Mukhapatra', *Sabuj Patra*, 1914, 1(1): 1–11.
2 A mantra of dedication to the energy of life.
3 Refers to *Vidyasundar*, a traditional story narrated by Ramprasad Sen, which also occurs in the *Annadamangal* of Bharatchandra Roy. Vidya and Sundar are the two main characters.

8 Haraprasad Shastri: The Bengali youth and three poets

Introduction

Haraprasad Shastri (1853–1931) was one of the principal figures of the Bengal Renaissance. As a student of Sanskrit College and Presidency College, he had an acquaintance with such renowned scholars such as Prasannakumar Sarvadhikary, Maheshchandra Nyayaratna, and Ramnarayan Tarkaratna, and later, he came in contact with Rajendralal Mitra, from whom he acquired an interest in Indology, textual scholarship, and Buddhist studies. An erudite scholar, he wrote in various Bangla journals like *Bangadarsan*, *Bangiya Sahitya Parishat Patrika*, and *Narayan*. He found the earliest extant specimen of Bangla literature in the royal library of Nepal, which he subsequently edited and published to redefine the history of Bangla literary traditions. He was well acquainted with Western literary and philosophical canons. He also worked towards a clear understanding of his contemporary society and culture, and that is exemplified in the essay presented in this volume from an 1878–1879 issue of *Bangadarsan* edited by Bankimchandra Chattopadhyay.

In the present essay, Haraprasad Shastri begins with a detailed list of authors – ancient and modern, Indian as well as Western – to give a very general idea about what people read and gradually formulates a principle for assessing the social relevance of literature. Although he limits the scope of his essay to the urban youth educated in English schools and colleges, a section of it may be read as a chronicle of the changing taste of the reading public linked with historical contexts. The author also invokes a comparative paradigm of criticism in his essay by identifying Kālidāsa, Byron, and Bankimchandra Chattopadhyay as having a major formative influence on the reading public and arrives at a sociology of literature in the course of his analysis.

*

DOI: 10.4324/9781003224686-9

The Bengali youth and three poets[1]

Haraprasad Shastri

The Bengali youth is faced with a large body of English, Bangla, and Sanskrit literature the moment he moves from school to college. He can now enter the world of poets such as Chaucer, Spenser, Shakespeare, Milton, Dryden, Pope, Shelley, Byron, Wordsworth, Tennyson; Kālidāsa, Bhababhūti, Bhāravi, Māgha, Naiṣadha, Bhaṭṭi; Vālmīki, Vedavyāsa, composers of the Vedas and Puranas, Kasidas, Krittibas, Bharatchandra, Michael, and Hemchandra, as well as prose writers such as Addison, Goldsmith, Scott, Lytton, De Quincey, Thackeray; Daṇḍin, Bāṇabhaṭṭa, Viṣṇuśarmā; and Hutom (Kaliprasanna Sinha), Dinabandhu, and Bankimchandra. For a few days, he roams around in this beautiful literary orchard. However, this orchard is unending – all the trees are pleasant, everyone is happy. His young soul is not yet burdened with worldly concerns. He has eyes only for this world's beauty. The inclinations of his heart are not yet distorted nor have they hardened. He gradually tastes all kinds of literature, but in this ocean of literature, only three poets become his favourite. These are the only three that can help mould his character and morality. Copious lectures by priests, instructions by teachers, and various efforts by parents have so far failed to teach him the lessons that he learns from these three writers (who will never meet). They manage to soften the young man's soul, change his ideas, and make him empathetic and compassionate towards others. They have an impact on him during his years in college, and the lessons will remain with him. Life will bring him many trials and tribulations, but he will not forget what he has learnt.

The *Ramayana* and the *Mahabharata* framed young characters before the advent of English education in India, and the current development of Bangla literature determined the formation of young characters. The lessons learnt from bards, from his teachers, and from Krittibasa's *Ramayana* would seep into the young man's bones and stay with him till his last days. He would worship Rama or Yudhishthira as gods all his life, trying to imitate their actions. When old, he would impart the lessons to his grandchildren. The *Ramayana* and the *Mahabharata* would teach them to respect gods, elders, and the Brahmins; they would teach him to love his brothers and to walk down the prescribed, religious path of life. They would sift through these two massive epics in order to determine the course of their lives. The Bengali youth nowadays does not read the *Ramayana* or the *Mahabharata*. And even if he does, he does not let Rama or Yudhishthira reign supreme. The supreme emperors of his heart are Lord Byron, Kālidāsa, and Babu Bankimchandra. All three of these authors have an undeniable attraction for our youngsters. Their books move young hearts, taking them along paths chosen by them.

Familial ties were very important at the time when the *Ramayana* and the *Mahabharata* were composed. Hence, the chief advice of these two epics is fraternal and familial love. Historically, this was the time when human beings had just started to come out of their nomadic, uncivilised stage and settle down to build civilisations. Therefore, belief in the rules of the society is the second lesson that these epics impart. The third lesson is a deep distrust and animosity towards those who disrupted the norms of society. The main purpose of these epics is to curb all the base urges of human beings and lead them towards a peaceful life. Vālmīki and Vedavyāsa, along with their respective translators Kasidas and Krittibas, were so successful in imparting these lessons that the Bengali youth was diligently following the rules even forty years ago. Uncivilised, animal instincts had more or less been banished from their minds. Three or four generations liked to stay together in joint families. They were slaves of gods and Brahmins, with a deep-seated hatred and mistrust of people from other religions – no matter how socially peaceful and helpful. The strength of the Bengali youth was decreasing even as baser animal instincts were being curbed. The boisterous, disruptive Aryan youth was bewitched by the heart-rending, insane, majestic poetry of Vālmīki and Vedavyās to become as placid as sheep. Bengal's power, independence, and spirit were gone – it had become just a part in a factory machine. Just as steam makes the numerous cogs of a machine run tirelessly from 6 in the morning till 6 in the evening, so also thousands of Bengalis went through their lives from birth to death. Who controlled them? Which steam-powered machine had such power? Just as sweet music mollifies and domesticates rampaging elephants, likewise the invincible people fall to the hypnotic powers of Vālmīki and Vedavyāsa's creations. The Bengalis, thus, were bound to come under their power.

The main problem with ancient societies is that human beings do not like to be ruled by anyone, and most people want to do whatever they want. However, obedience is the first trait needed to bind society. Therefore, people who created the earliest social bonds tried to impart the lesson of obedience to many. Proud humans cannot be brought under someone else's control within one generation. We need 10 to 15 generations living with the same rules before human beings become inherently docile and obedient. The *Ramayana* and the *Mahabharata* were written for this specific purpose. For ages, Hindus have followed the actions of Rama and Yudhishthira, automatically obeying all the rules of the society. As a result, social bonds have strengthened. However, pure social ties are not what humans ultimately strive for. Social ties are but paths to an end. Human beings are supposed to use the path to climb the steps of civilisation. They are supposed to use social ties to gradually start controlling the physical world to expand the comfort and happiness of their own kind. First, a human being is supposed to serve the needs of his own race, then those of his country, then of all people, and finally of the entire living world. The path can only be meaningful if with the help of the physical the living world attains happiness, a long life, and a peaceful death. Or else what is the use of making pathways in a jungle?

Social ties were created, but there was no purpose of them in society. Human beings calmed down by imitating Rama, Lakshmana, Bharata, and Shatrughna. But they had no idea what to do with all that peace. This resulted in some people getting addicted to worldly pleasures, while some abandoning the same diligently pursued the pleasures of the afterworld. There were some who spent their time with beautiful women and alcohol in warm homes in winter, around cool pleasure gardens and fountains in summer, on rooftops on full moon nights, and swimming in lakes on sunny days and thought that these were the ultimate aims of life. There were others who felt that if they spent their lives meditating while hanging upside down over fiery pits, they might be surrounded by the likes of Urvasi and Menaka[2] and all kinds of sensory delights in the heavenly gardens, and that would be the greatest human pleasure. Some found heaven in charity, others in pleasurable showers. Ultimately all sought sensual pleasures – some on earth and some in heaven. No one explained that the chief purpose of human society was to establish control over the inanimate world – for no one could survive outside society. We are reaping the benefits of structures and systems that our previous generation created and bequeathed to us, and so it is our responsibility to leave something more for our descendants by increasing our control over the physical world. Man is but a leaf in the tree of society. Just as leaves take in air and contribute to the growth of a tree before falling off – sacrificing themselves so that the future leaves sprout well and move higher – likewise human beings grow and nurture society and change it for the better with new discoveries before passing away. Future generations reap the benefits of these changes and take society forward.

No one explained these points to our ancestors, and so their lives went on calmly following the paths prescribed by the *Ramayana* and the *Mahabharata*. The epics had now fulfilled their aims, but there was nothing that could replace them. Therefore, they continued to be our national *kavyas*.

Forty years ago, when English studies began in earnest, the moral lessons of the *Ramayana* and the *Mahabharata* were discarded as old and irrelevant. Critics may praise the incomparable poetic prowess of Vālmīki, archaeologists may write on ancient Indian societies as depicted in the epic, hundreds of readers may surrender themselves to the joy of the *Ramayana*, but no one will imitate the character of Rama, less so of Yudhishthira. The lessons imparted by the *Ramayana* and the *Mahabharata* have been replaced with those by certain foreign examples, historical texts, and reflections on books and contemporary events. In such civilised times, a single figure or a book cannot entirely determine the character of a young man. Yet, soft-hearted young men retain something of what appeals to them in the books that they read. Whatever is retained often emerge through action, moulding one's character in the process.

A young Bengali reads a large number of texts, and Shakespeare has a primary place among them. But perhaps Shakespeare does not play any role in moulding his character. Since Shakespeare's intention is 'to please', his villains are as attractive as his heroes. The feelings generated by these two kinds of characters cancel out one another. Milton, on the other hand, is full of the 'puritanic spirit'. No one will dare imitate his creations. In fact, many people might want to imitate the devil, but no one will be willing to take on the mantle of Jesus Christ or Samson (*Samson Agonistes* 1671). There's nothing to imitate or follow in the works of Dryden and Pope. *An Essay on Criticism* (1711) is full of moral instructions that one can forget as in the case of lessons by a schoolteacher. Chaucer and Spenser's writings are full of strange spellings, scaring away most readers. Furthermore, Chaucer's stories are from other times and do not suit the taste of our contemporary readers. They may be liked by the older readers but not by the younger group. Spenser's ideal lies in Europe's dark medieval centuries. It does not appeal to the modern man. Lessons that always rely on specific metaphors are not suited to civilised times. Shelley is a brilliant poet, but his creations are too complex and his ideals too high to be imitated. Tennyson's aim is to present the old in a favourable light and that does not contribute to character building. Wordsworth, be it good or bad, had the unwelcome tendency to repeat himself into annoyance. If he is talking about a flower, he will go on to describe every petal, every filament, and every grain of pollen. Now we are left with Byron, who is a friend of the oppressed, an enemy of the oppressor, a vessel of love, an epitome of youth, immensely powerful, and constantly active; he is perpetually enraged with laziness and the oppressions of society. Byron possesses all the traits that can attract the youth. Therefore, among numerous great English authors, only Byron has a role in shaping the characters of young Bengalis.

In Sanskrit poetry, the *Ramayana* and the *Mahabharata* are ancient and outdated. The average man does not study the *Vedas* and the *Puranas* anymore. Even if these were being studied, no contemporary person certainly would want to imitate Garga, Visvamitra, and Agastya. Let alone college students, even learners at the *tols*[3] do not aspire to be Vasishtha, Visvamitra, or Vedavyāsa. Bhāravi's Arjuna (*Kirātārjunīyam*), Māgha's Krishna (*Śiśupālavadha*), Naiṣādha's Nala (*Naiśadhacharita* by Śrīharṣa), Bāṇabhaṭṭa's Tarapira (*Kādambarī*) – all of them are outdated and ancient, and none of them is to our taste. Critics are better qualified to deal with the craft of description in the works of Bhāravi, Māgha, and in *Naisādha*. These do contain certain interesting, good portions – but most of them are obsolete. Our average brains are not equipped to appreciate them. Even if we can, our characters are not formed by reading Bhāravi. The young Bengali reader loves Bhababhūti (*Uttararāmacarita*), who sometimes has an impact on his character. However, this influence is quite small and can be disregarded in this argument. Apaharavarman, a character in *Daśakumāracaritam* (Daṇḍin), is not only great and fascinating, but he is also a dacoit and a thief and so on! Even if a young Bengali man is inspired by Apaharavarman, he will try to hide it to maintain his prestige. We are now left with Kālidāsa, whose writings are so delightful that they fascinate us the moment we read them. Many young people love his characters so much that they imitate them in real life. Therefore, Kālidāsa also has a great influence on the Bengali youth.

We have definitely received a great deal from authors in Bangla literature. The chief among them is Bankimchandra Chattopadhyay. His books are read and loved by so many that some parts from all his books have definitely become part of their identities. People also learn Dinabandhu Mitra's jokes, memorise Hutom's songs, and sometimes imitate Michael Madhusudan Dutt. However, the average person cannot come to terms with some of the unusual words in their writings. Everyone knows Hemchandra Bandyopadhyay's *Bharatsangeet* (1870) by heart; no one knows how *Britrasamhar* will influence the reading public today. Let alone imitating, many people do not even read Bharatchandra out of embarrassment. Apart from these, there are many other authors and poets with limited abilities.

Now, let us do a comparative examination of the three poets. We are not evaluating the quality of their creations. We are just trying to understand how good and rich their writings are in inspiring and moulding the character of the youth. These poets are from England, Malava, and Bengal, respectively. One of them received his education during the French Revolution, another lived during the glorious days of the Hindus, and the third was educated in British India's education system. One of them teaches us to break the shackles of society and change oppressive societal rules; he teaches us the kind of pleasures that are gained from leaving society behind. Another poet teaches us how we can gain the utmost pleasure by living within society. The third one teaches us how to be happy while helping as well as opposing society.

All three are poets of love – though the idea of love may differ in each of them. All three impart lessons intended to make us appreciate the beauty of that which is natural. All three are captivated by natural traits and can make people partake of their sense of appreciation. Bengal does not have hills or mountains but has undulating, lush green fields interspersed with winding, wide rivers and clear or cloudy skies. As such, one might come to think that Bengal does not have much by way of natural beauty, but every line written by Bankim expresses the exquisiteness of Bengal. He is the first to have looked at Bengal's loveliness with a poet's eye, and it is our good fortune that we are able to experience the beauty of Bengal as reflected in his heart. In those days, the feeling for the beauty of nature was expressed in the worship of gods. The holy river Ganga was god; the sky was the abode of the sages; Chandra was the moon god; Surya was the sun god; Bankim internalised all these various divinities and showed us only the pure beauty of the land, asking us to see the same. He has shown us almost all beautiful aspects of Bengal. From the drawings of birds in the walls of Hira's house to the intricate painted abode of Suryamukhi[4] – he has written about everything. There is nothing unclean about the pictures he draws with his words. Everything is clear and pure.

Kālidāsa has described the entire Indian subcontinent. From the Sinhala Island to the mountains of Kailasa – he has written about them all. His descriptions are not just clear but also bright and glittering – as if lit up by electric lights. India provides a microcosm of natural beauty, and Kālidāsa has gone to the depths of it all. However, it is not his job to show everything in detail – for that one needs Wordsworth. Kālidāsa makes choices, showing only the best. It is not just beauty that he depicts, but also the otherworldly aspect in it as in the description of the chariot Pushpaka of Rama (*Raghuvaṃśam*, Canto XIII) and the cloud messenger (*Meghadūtam*). However, his *Ṛtusaṃhāra* describes the pure beauty of nature in the brightest of colours. Here the otherworldly aspect is absent and so is a distinction between what is clear and what is not. However, whether the described objects are clear or not, the attraction of the descriptions remains the same.

Byron describes Europe. He includes almost anything that is worthy of any description in Europe – ranging from the Alpine peaks to the waters of the mighty Rhine, the islands of Greece, the paintings of Michelangelo, and the ruins of Venice and Rome. Anything that is great in art and nature finds place in his works. His ability to describe historical scenes is unparalleled, and the largeness of his heart is fully reflected in the depictions of the Battle of Waterloo, the place where Rousseau lived, and the church of Balder. It is not surprising that the lessons that accompany such descriptions are etched in the hearts of the youth forever.

The reader might ask why we need to discuss descriptions of nature in order to understand how young characters are shaped. He might feel that it is out of context. That is because such descriptions can also impart moral lessons, and it is comparatively easy to show this. Let us see what instructions we gain from these before attempting to look at other kinds of instructions.

First, Kālidāsa's words and descriptions are all peaceful and pleasurable. They fill our minds with peace. While Brahmin priests, foreign preachers, and Brahmo missionaries constantly talk about the sorrowful world carrying the burden of sins as being on the brink of disaster, one can read such a text and feel that the world is really not so full of sorrows. This is not an insignificant lesson to learn. Bankim's nature descriptions do not necessarily invoke such untainted peace – his works have an extra layer of youthful excitement and joy. There is no peace in Byron's descriptions either. He is constantly shifting his attention to newer things, constantly changing from this to that and from that to this, without being satisfied, as if there is an emerging discontent, or as if the pleasure that he is seeking in natural beauty remains absent. Moving on with a curious thirst, he goes to see and sees whatever is beautiful, and he is satisfied, but that satisfaction does not remain for long.

In short, there are three kinds of purpose in the descriptions of the authors that may be shown in a different way. Kālidāsa sits above, looking down and showing us the beauty below with pure joy. He looks at the endeavours of human beings, their songs and dances from above. Mountains and hills look somewhat tiny to him, the river seems to lie like a single necklace, and he shows his readers something that he loves in the surroundings. It is as if the *Purusha* of *Saṃkhya* was watching the play of *Prakriti* from his seat of detachment.[5] Kālidāsa states that we need to rise above the human in order to realise the joy that is there in the beauty of nature. He has great hopes. For Bankimchandra, human beings are at the centre of natural beauty, be it Nagendranath or Amarnath (*Bishabriksha* or *The Poison Tree* 1873), Gobindalal (*Krishnakanter Will* 1878), or even Bankimchandra himself. He too watches with detachment, looks at the beauty of nature from within, and, if there is anyone near, shows how beautiful and deep it is. Let the earth and the sky overwhelm people with the love of God. But this is not so for Byron. If you want to observe natural beauty, move out from your home, but will you be satisfied with whatever comes before you? That is not the case. Let's go where there are beautiful objects – one has to go to those places. How can you see all if you are detached? Why will you sit at home watching the ways of the world and enjoy peaceful pleasure? Human life is short, see and hear as much as you can; for the more you observe, the more you gain knowledge and happiness. And this is true happiness, everything else is sorrow and tyranny – the tyranny of love and of society and of one human being on another. Everything else is suffering, and the joy of nature is supreme.

So, one of these authors is observing nature from above, another is observing from within, and the third one is going around in frenzy. One thinks that there is greater happiness in life beyond the human. The second claims that this world also provides us with sufficient happiness. And for the third, everything is associated with this world.

Byron was born during the French Revolution of the 19th century. Therefore, he has no respect for contemporary society. He firmly believes that there is nothing but tyranny in contemporary society. The best characters portrayed by him are outside society. They are all angry with society. Some of them are even enemies of society – they are either rebels or misanthropes. They detest all conventional rules of this society. Conrad, Lara, and Don Juan's hatred for society is indirectly evident in their words all the time.

The society inhabited by Kālidāsa has not changed from the time of Manu. According to him, everyone is happy in such a social structure.

Bankimchandra's society is one of educated Bengali youth. He has shown how one can never be happy by acting against society. Such acts eventually make one repentant. Nagendranath's (*Bishabriksha*) adultery leads to his spiritual perversion; Saibalini's (*Chandrasekhar* 1875) adultery results in extreme atonement in a mountain cave. Even Gobindalal and Rohini's (*Krishnakanter Will*) unhappy end strongly proves this very point.

Byron's characters as well are none too happy. They do experience otherworldly, wondrous happiness at times, but misery is their normal state of being. But they know as long as society remains as it is, their sorrows will not end. Therefore, they do not want to repent and come back. Their amusement lies in berating society. Some are always looting and plundering, some in solitary prison are crying out and calling for a demolishment of society while others are searching for an opportunity to break all social rules. They are sad but not helpless in misery; and as human society is the cause of their sorrow, they wish to take revenge on society and all those who steer it. Byron's characters are all angry with human society. But they are sympathetic towards human beings, towards women, and those who are weak. They want to love, but repressive social conventions do not let them love the way they desire. Happiness makes them angry. Kālidāsa's characters occupy a higher plane. They are either partially divine or avatars of gods or gods themselves; some are *apsaras* or celestial nymphs, some are daughters of apsaras, some sages, and some are kings. Sages and kings are human beings but possess more superhuman powers than Byron's characters. In Kālidāsa's works, they are moving up to heaven, then again coming back to earth, and circling the world in the blink of an eye. They are fighting with the gods and falling in love with apsaras. However, they are always consciously abiding by the societal laws prescribed by Manu. These human beings have immense power but do not use them indiscriminately.

Jñāne maunaṃ kṣama śaktau tyāge ślāghā biparyayaḥ[6]

The sloka describes the ideal of these characters to some extent. Their powers are unending and their mental strength incredible. They also have the ability to channel their powers into a life of honesty, and hence their lives are free from sadness and misery. Their desires are not free, but just like rigid natural laws, they think that social norms are also unbreakable. There is no attempt to break laws, hence no sorrow and no repentance.

Bankimchandra's characters, educated Bengali young men, are all social beings. An educated young man's life is full of infinite struggle. He gets two kinds of education – one in school and one at home. These two are often quite opposite. Hence, there are often contradictions in the character of the educated young man. Bankimchandra's characters show this contradictory trait as well, though not always. Wherever they do appear, they are quite vivid. Bankimchandra's characters are home-bred Bengalis, innocent and good. They possess all the characteristics and traits loved by Bengalis. They are intelligent, cunning, kind, social, graceful, and have feelings. Analysing the thoughts and traits of such people in detail is a pleasurable act and a learning experience. Bankimchandra has drawn his characters in a similar light.

The primary lessons imparted by ancient texts such as the *Ramayana* and the *Mahabharata* include obeying one's parents, loving one's siblings, and behaving cordially with relatives. However, none of these three reigning authors of our hearts has much to say about parents. Bankim had shown us

Gobindalal's mother but, apprehending trouble, promptly sent her to live in Kashi. None of his heroes or heroines has brothers, and only one or two have sisters. Gobindalal's cousin Haralal lives in Calcutta as well. Byron is also not quite in touch with his parents or brother. Don Juan never even talks about Donna Inez. And there is no need to mention Azo and Parisina. Kālidāsa's works also seldom mention parents, but at least they are there. Sometimes even there are occasional encounters of pure fraternal and parental love – but as we said before, these glimpses are rare.

Our authors and poets have replaced all these familial bonds with marital love. But why do we speak of marital love? Byron has nothing to do with marriage. Let us then refer to it only as love. Byron therefore has nothing of familial love. Bankimchandra's works, on the other hand, show pure marital love. He has replaced other kinds of love with the love of one's country, and Byron has replaced them with love for entire humanity. One has taught us to cry for our tortured land, while the other has taught us to take up weapons in order to save our tortured humanity. Byron has taught us to applaud people who free others from the tyranny of oppression.

Kālidāsa's society has not changed since the time of Manu. Everything there follows rules and logic without any deviation. Thus, his works are free of temptation. Between sin and virtue, there is very little sin, and all is virtue. There is no room for desire. Thus, his books paint pictures only of happiness and of uninterrupted, pure, spiritual pleasure. Byron is loath to admit that sin and virtue have two distinct existences. Thus, he does not admit the existence of what is popularly known as temptation. According to him, anything an individual does on his own volition is correct, and whoever he loves on his own is lovable. Therefore, human beings depend on their own desire for happiness, and sometimes they are successful and at other times they are not and they do not want to follow instructions by others or adhere to societal rules. The current social structure wants to repress these self-willed individuals, and so they turn into enemies of society. They desire a new society that will not oppose their desire, and when that does not happen, they go violently against society.

Bankimchandra has Kālidāsa on one side and Byron on the other. However, he is more influenced by the former. Hence, he wants society to follow ancient norms. He wants the same control over the senses, the same happiness and peace, but sometimes desire becomes all-powerful and this is where Byron comes in. He shows that when there is no control over desire, people fall a prey to danger at every step. He sometimes places temptations before his characters: he shows that everyone succumbs to temptation, but some keep their feelings to themselves and practice restraint. These are the people who have gained victory over their senses, such as Pratap (*Chandrasekhar*). However, characters such as Saibalini and Nagendranath are unable to control their own desires. People who gain control over their desires are happy, courageous, and admired by all. Others who do not gain such control are sad, cowardly, and full of self-loathing.

There are no temptations in works of Kālidāsa. Byron's works are full of temptations, but there is no desire to overcome them. There are temptations in works of Bankimchandra; there is sorrow in them, and there is happiness in overcoming them. Therefore, Bankimchandra's works in contemporary society give us higher moral lessons.

Byron does teach us to love humanity, but he has not given us clear instructions anywhere. He has criticised modern society and expressed sympathy for the oppressed, and that tells us of his intentions. However, the patriotism portrayed in Bankimchandra's works is of a different kind. Some of his characters like Ramananda Swami (*Chandrasekhar*) are human embodiments of the love for one's country. They have amazing characters. They have given their lives for the good of others. No matter what the religion of the oppressed – Muslim, Hindu, or Christian – they are ever-ready to lend a helping hand. They hold little esteem for their lives and are ready to give them up for others. Ramananda Swami is the epitome of a morally evolved character, while Kālidāsa shows us another kind of love – the love for all beings that exist. It is probably derived from Buddhism. Even though Buddhism as a religion was almost extinct by the time of Kālidāsa, it remained strongly present to a large extent in the minds of Hindus. However, in our country, the non-vegetarian youth do not much relate to the idea of love for all. According to them, love for humanity is the prime religion.

Kālidāsa's Sakuntala is deeply in love with the flora and fauna of the forest. We sometimes plant flowers and keep cows and calves but we do not love them as equals. Unlike us, Kālidāsa's heart cries for animals as well. Bankimchandra's Nagendranath loves his subjects like his children. That is as far as our love can go. Byron feels affection for all mankind. His deep anguish for the unfortunate Greeks and his sincere attempts to influence people to alleviate their suffering are proof of the fact.

Let us note another point. Are their methods of imparting lessons similar? According to Sanskrit rhetoricians, the advice we gain from the Vedas are orders, that from the *Puranas* are as well-meaning suggestions from friends, but that which we gain from poetry is similar to that which is given by our beloved. She wins us over by talking about various different things before imparting the lesson, and that lesson is infallible. The poet described the battle between Rama and Ravana; showed us numerous fascinating events, made us laugh and made us cry, and then eventually taught us that complete surrender to our desires might lead to unwelcome developments in the future and even, as in the case of Ravana, the destruction of an entire clan. All three authors that we discussed essentially impart the same lesson with just a few differences.

Kālidāsa's manner of imparting advice is the same. He never preaches – just talks about everything that comes up in his poems, without imparting lessons. Byron has an underlying lesson in each of his portraits. A description of beauty is always followed by a criticism of social exploitations in contemporary times. Everywhere in his work, one is sure to find one or two pieces of sarcastic advice. Just as one remembers gravestone inscriptions that one comes across while walking in graveyards, likewise Byron's chiselled words remain with us. The reader will never forget the profound moral insights brought to light by Byron while marvelling at the beauty of the Rhine or the majesty of the Alps or even while witnessing the nightly courtship between Haidee and Juan. Byron does sometimes preach. But Bankimchandra has too high a level of preaching. His *Kamalakanter Daptar* (1875) is a repository of sermons. One can learn innumerable moral lessons from that novel. He even creates characters for this – all the sanyasis in his works are always giving moral advice. The soliloquies of his characters like Nagendranath are nothing but sermons. Haradeb Ghoshal's (*Krishnakanter Will*) letter has discovered several profound psychological theories.

Some people feel that there is no moral lesson to be learnt from Byron, for he is an obscene poet. Byron does not impart any lesson to such people. Their morals are ancient, while Byron's moral lessons are contemporary. He is a follower of Rousseau's school of thought. All human beings are equal. Social structures and rules are determined by only a few, who with their tyranny and exploitative powers render the rest of humanity weak and impotent. This state of things needs to change. This is incessantly present in Byron's poems. Even if the characters from his works apparently seem misanthropic, and even if that is what young readers and others get from his works, a deeper reading will make it clear that his anger is only with contemporary society and underneath it all, there is profound sympathy for humanity.

Bankim's thoughts on philanthropy expressed in his books are not less strong than those of Byron's, but they are mostly expressed as pure patriotism. Hence, we assert that the purpose of his works is to arouse love for the country.

In closing, we can state that Bankim writes to evoke patriotism and bring in social happiness, Kālidāsa writes to enkindle love for all living beings and for social happiness, and Byron writes for humanitarian reasons and for the happiness that is derived from breaking social norms.

Translation: Bimbabati Sen

Notes

1 Haraprasad Shastri, 'Bangiya Jubak o Tin Kabi', in *Haraprasad Shastri Rachana-Samgraha*, Vol. II, Satyajit Chaudhuri et al. (eds.), Kolkata: Paschimbanga Rajya Pustak Parshat, 1981, pp. 475–492. The essay was originally published in *Bangadarsan*, 1878, 6(9): 435–449.
2 Urvasi and Menaka are apsaras or celestial nymphs.
3 Traditional Bengali schools for instruction, predominantly in Sanskrit.
4 Both Hira and Suryamukhi are characters from Bankimchandra Chattopadhyay's novel *Bishabriksha*.
5 Samkhya is the only school of Indian Philosophy which acknowledges the epistemic authority of the Vedas but does not believe in God. It is a dualist school

which looks at the universe as consisting of two realities, viz. *Purusha* and *Prakriti* (lit. man and nature), signifying consciousness and matter.

6 He (king Dilip) 'would stay silent despite his knowledge, be merciful while holding power, he will relinquish all without any pride'. The śloka is from *Raghuvaṃśam*, 1.22.

9 Ramendrasundar Trivedi: The sign of the epic

Introduction

Ramendrasundar Trivedi (1864–1919), a versatile scholar, was one of the principal figures of what is known as the 'Bengal Renaissance'. He studied science at Presidency College and University of Calcutta, India, and then studied law for a while before joining Ripon College, Calcutta, as a professor where later in 1903 he also became the principal. He started writing for journals in the 1880s and played a crucial role in popularising science to the readers of Bengal. A thoroughly secular scholar, Ramendrasundar Trivedi was deeply interested in the Vedas and translated the *Aitareya Brāhmaṇa* into Bangla.

Trivedi devoted his life to the nationalist movement of his time and played an important role in the foundation of the Bangiya Sahitya Parishat (Bangla Academy of Letters) in 1894 and was associated with it in various capacities for the rest of his life. In 1905, he called for *arandhan* or a day of fast to protest against the attempts at dividing the Bengal Province by the then British Raj and wrote *Bangalakshmir Bratakatha* to nurture communal harmony. His primary field of work was the promotion of learning through Bangla. In this volume, we have taken up his idea of the epic in society.

The *Ramayana* and the *Mahabharata* were at the centre of the various emerging discourses of nationalism in the late 19th and early 20th centuries. There were a large number of editions and translations of the texts along with a renewed attempt at understanding 'Indian' life through these epics. Kaliprasanna Sinha's translation of the *Mahabharata* and Hemchandra Bhattacharya's translation of the *Ramayana* rekindled the possibilities of experiencing the epics anew in the 19th century. Bankimchandra Chattopadhyay worked on the epic hero Krishna between 1876 and 1892 and published *Krishnacharitra* in 1886. Apart from that, numerous other Sanskrit texts tracing their origin from the epics were being translated during the period. Many folk performative traditions drawing on the epics were also popular. Trivedi tries to look at the function of the primary epic as the principal cohesive force in society and arrives at a very original definition of the literary genre: that which need not necessarily be read to be experienced.

DOI: 10.4324/9781003224686-10

He emphasises the unadorned primeval nature of its expression and the impossibility of its re-emergence in modern civilisation.

*

The sign of the epic[1]

Ramendrasundar Trivedi

The English term 'epic' is usually translated as *mahakavya*,[2] but it is not clear whether all the elements of the latter are congruent with those of the former. I have no personal knowledge whatsoever of Sanskrit rhetorical theory, but it is my understanding that Sanskrit rhetoricians had formulated the characteristics of the mahakavya in great detail, and hence poets were never in any difficulty. The epics of Kālidāsa, Bhāravi, and Māgha that prevail in the country presumably conform to the rhetorical prerequisites in their composition. The *Ramayana* and the *Mahabharata*,[3] however, present a vigorous controversy at the very outset regarding their status as epics. They are identified as epics in English publications, but our own pundits are not always unanimous in their views in this matter. First, these two books have excessively transgressed the rules of rhetorical ornamentation. Second, calling them epics runs the risk of diminishing their glory. Terms such as *itihāsa, purāna*, and *karmaśāstra*[4] are possibly better suited to the protection of their majesty. The term mahakavya reduces their prestige.

The glory is indeed diminished. The *Ramayana–Mahabharata*[5] are not epics in the same terms as the *Kumārasambhava* or *Kirātārjunīya*.[6] They differ in level and degree. If the first two are named epics, the others cannot be validly called the same.

Even with full confidence in the historicity and the religious authority of the *Ramayana–Mahabharata*, we are forced to concede that they contain the poetic flavour in full. Whatever the authorial intentions of the sages Vālmīki and Kṛṣṇadvaipāyan, a great deal of poetry may be found in the works that they chanced to write. The poetic elements might have crept in probably without the author's knowledge, but it is undeniable that they did.

If one were to acknowledge the poetry in the *Ramayana–Mahabharata*, one would have to call their creators epic poets and these works epics. This is because our language cannot offer any other appropriate name. Thus, we are inclined to accept the *Ramayana–Mahabharata* as epics, striking off *Kumārasambhava–Kirātarjunīya* from the list.

Macaulay had somewhere commented that poetry and civilisation share a predatory relationship: civilisation engulfs poetry or the creeper of poetry cannot thrive within the constrictions of civilisation. Needless to say, like many of Macaulay's remarks, this too has been scoffed at by the learned. The flowering of poetry in Europe in the past century despite the aggressive ostentations of civilisation is proof enough of this. No further argument is required.

Nevertheless, it is our belief that Macaulay's remark does contain a grain of truth. Civilisation might not nibble at the poet's brain, but it definitely swallows the epic completely. I repeat here that I do not use the term epic in the sense the rhetoricians did. In this context, I do not consider *Raghuvaṃśam*, *Kumārasambhava*, and *Paradise Lost* as epics. I call epics those compositions that are of the stature of the *Ramayana–Mahabharata*. So many poets have gained fame by their creations in this world, but those works that I call epic were written long before them, and these feats have not been repeated since. Not much is known about the writers in poetic genres in the West, but one suspects that no work apart from the two Homeric compositions may be granted the status similar to the *Ramayana–Mahabharata*. No one can assert that poetry has declined with progress in the Western world. Nevertheless, even with Shakespeare's name in mind, one can state without fear that the European continent has not given birth to more than one Homer.

In fact, Vālmīki, Vyāsa, and Homer appeared in the history of world's literature and civilisation in the very remote past; since then, many thousands of years have passed, without the appearance of any other epic. One wonders why this happened, but it is not within the ability of this writer to discover the reason. But it seems at times that the present state of human society is not conducive to the production of similar epics.

The picture of human society that we see depicted in the Homeric poems and the *Ramayana–Mahabharata* cannot be called civilised in the modern sense. We do not know whether society will return to those conditions, but it is certain that the events that routinely occurred in those times could never take place in the current state of affairs. We cannot imagine a scenario in which the President of the United States, having accepted the hospitality of a European kingdom, carries off the queen of the land in his steamer at the end of his visit, and European leaders seeking vengeance sitting outside Washington for a decade in siege.[7] We hardly expect a telegram with the news of de la Rey traversing the South African veld with a captive Lord Methuen tied to the wheels of his cart.[8] Bismarck might have overcome Napoleon in the Battle of Sedan, but he did not feel the need to rip open his enemy's chest to drink his blood.[9] It is true that a war far more terrible than that of Lanka took place in the land of the Boers long after the end of the 'Treta yuga,'[10] but none of the victorious brave was required to use a tail in the campaign.[11]

The barbarism of those times is indeed repugnant to us, although there is another aspect of the society of those times that is conspicuously absent in ours. Burke, in one of his sublime moments, had said 'the age of chivalry is gone.'[12] This indefinable thing called chivalry is the unprecedented fruit of the union of naked barbarism and undisguised humanity. It is true that in our age, human beings do not wish to drink the blood of other humans, but one cannot say with any certainty that a man of our time would be able to honour his elder brother's gesture of restraint and control himself when faced with his wife's very public humiliation.[13] Today's kings do not gird their loins to join the fray with their clubs, but it is doubtful how many of them would willingly exile themselves to the Fiji islands to honour their vow to a senile father.[14] Asvatthama showed relentless cruelty in massacring the peacefully sleeping sons of the Pandavas, but he did not feel any need to gather assemblies and write newspaper editorials to justify the unspeakable act. The dejected Pandavas, despairing of hope of victory in the war, did crawl to Bhishma in the enemy camp with Krishna's assistance, begging him to sacrifice his life in their cause, but they did not carry a bunch of currency notes under their iron armour to bribe his sacrifice.

While human society has outwardly changed a great deal in the last four thousand years, it is difficult to say if it has changed in its inward nature. The outer coverings of human beings have changed significantly, but they remain much the same inside. The kings of the past would probably not have shied away from appearing in the public assembly in a loincloth if the occasion so demanded, but the hungry workers of our times are forced to cover their pale and malformed bodies under the cover of their clothes. Cruelty, barbarism, brutality was real in those times, and they were present in all nakedness. There was no covering, polish,[15] or wash of colour to hide them. In these times, cruelty, barbarism, and brutality perhaps remain the same as in those times, but an artificial layer of hypocrisy has been laid over these to conceal their hideous nature. Given the devastation that the united forces of Europe have recently wreaked on China, the spirits of Attila or Genghis Khan need no longer hang their heads in shame.

It is indeed correct to say that in the past four thousand years, human nature has not altered in any significant manner, but the configurations of society have undergone a sea change. It is no surprise, therefore, that the structure of the kind of poem that reflects such changes should also have become altered beyond recognition. Whether wondrous things are present or absent, no Vālmīki, Vyāsa, or Homer has appeared or is likely to appear in modern times. The age of literary epics has perhaps gone forever. As time is endless and the world vast, there will hopefully be no dearth of great poets and glorious poems, but if the conditions of ancient society do not reappear, the revival of epic poets and epic poetry does not seem likely.

Truly, revival is not possible. There is a certain openness and natural spontaneity in the epic that is impossible to recapture. The competent artist can construct the Taj Mahal in these times, but the days of building pyramids are gone forever. We can compare epics to the towering uniqueness of pyramids. At times, one almost feels that instead of comparing them to the fruits of human artifice, one should liken them to works created by nature's hand.

It is sometimes tempting to compare our Indian *Mahabharata* to the Indian Himalayas. As that mountain protects our land in the shelter of its vast lap of rocks, likewise the vast body of the *Mahabharata* has nurtured the literature of our land for thousands of years. Hundreds of eternally nourishing streams flowing out of the immense breast of the Himalayas have moistened India's soil, producing a richly fertile land – so have the numerous narratives flowing out of the *Mahabharata* in the form of stories, tales, and legends, flowing through the nation's literature in myriad clear streams, keeping the field evergreen and the nation's life nourished and glowing. Just as the geologist rescues the bones and fossils of wondrous lives through a careful analysis of the stratification of the Himalayas from the lost memory of the dark chambers of time, likewise the anthropologist mines the complex layers of this vast text to discover forgotten signs of the ancient history of people of India.

The geologist sees with the mind's eye into that period on the other shore of time when in the earth's history, the great *Mahakala*[16] himself extended his mighty arm to centre the stupendous power in the molten womb of the earth, and soon the gathered force ripped open the earth's breast and asserted itself. Tremendous earthquakes, one after another, shook the land. The waters of the sea swelled in sympathy, only to retreat timidly. Splitting the earth from the eastern seaboard to the sands of the western coast, rose the magnificent rock-bodied Himalayas. Tornadoes roared around the sunlit peaks of his snow-clad horns. Chains of lightning spurted from smoke-hued clouds. Peak upon peak came crashing down; depression in the valleys swelled into plateaus, and plateaus turned to depressions; forests kindled, and a hush fell upon the animal kingdom as Mahakala danced his great *tandava*[17] and the skies rang with the sound of his divine mirth.[18]

We do not know why, but, just as the demented tandava dance of Mahakala can be perceived at specific moments in the history of nature, so can the reverberations of his laughter be heard in the chronicles of human society. Although the events of the *Mahabharata* took place among the inhabitants of a particular place and a specific society, we may consider it to be a picture of a time of upheaval in the human community as a whole. When enviousness, ambition, vengefulness, and other hideous and uncontrollable desires of the human heart come together, intensify, grow ponderous and seek outlets for their release and extend their flame-tongued gaping maws to spread their blazing flame within society, virtue, piety, love, and goodwill are withered at the source. The bedrock of society is shaken by the multiple earthquakes of one revolution after another. Subterranean forces tear the very fabric of society into a thousand pieces and scatter it to the winds. Thousands of years of accumulated beauty are incinerated in that liquid firestream. We are arrested and crestfallen by the faint echoes of the demented laughter of Mahakala, which we can hear in the incidents described in the *Mahabharata*. This is the chronicle of the eternal revolution of human society that recurs in a cyclic progression throughout ages, which lifts seabeds to plateaus and throws plateaus into the ocean and rubs mountain tips together to ignite the fires of apocalypse. In those flames, lush woodland becomes desert, and living beings lay their bones down on the earth and disappear into the dark dungeons of time. This is that eternal triumph of evil that oppresses, torments, and shrivels all righteousness bringing in the need for a reappearance of the glory of the greatest divine being who would initiate the revival of *dharma* in the world – when the intimidated and amazed human spirit under the illusion of its glittering wealth surrenders itself at his feet.

The story of the *Mahabharata* is the history of a revolution in human society. To enquire whether this kind of revolution took place at all in the history of the Indian subcontinent is the task of historians and anthropologists. Perhaps the epic poet, in a moment of contemplative reflection, dreamt of this revolution in the affairs of men from the fading memory of some small regional conflict and thus he sketched for the edification of future generations the picture of that ultimate revolution, this mighty battle between good and evil, which was attained in a meditative dream. The power lodged in the core of the earth, which the Himalayas harnessed to climb out of its depths, is now pacified for having attained an equilibrium. His slopes are covered in verdant growth, deep springs from his broad breast nourish the verdure of the fertile land, and, far above them, the milky brilliance of Dhavalgiri and Gaurishankar excite the viewer's wonder.

The very memory of the hurricane of unrest that blew over ancient India thanks to the social upheaval and rise of *adharma* has been almost obliterated by the establishment of dharma. The storm has been calmed, the clamour of the tidal waves silenced, and the roar of the wildfire hushed. Now the numerous literary streams flowing out of that *Mahabharata* have sprouted branches and leaves, fruits and flowers and ensured its thriving life, while we gaze from afar in ecstatic wonder upon the robust, proud, and shining forms of Bhima–Arjuna, Karna–Duryodhana, Bhishma–Drona, and Ashvathhama–Kritavarma[19] standing on the distant horizon of the Indian social life like so many snow-crowned scintillating mountain peaks.

The Himalayan metaphor has perhaps tried the reader's patience enough, but I cannot desist from pointing out something else. In considering the *Mahabharata* as the ideal epic and comparing it with the Himalayas, this writer has chanced upon a characteristic element or mark of the genre. Needless to say, this discovery will create a great turmoil among rhetoricians! Nevertheless, I shall dare to present this finding to my readers, hoping that their dazzling brilliant perspectives will not compel the author to run away before the battle has begun.

In the view of this author, a poem which does not need to be read is an epic. We can experience the *kavyarasa* of the epic to a great extent without reading the text. A large section of readers will hopefully not protest if we claim that the majority of the 24,000 *slokas* or verses of the *Ramayana* and the 100,000-odd slokas of the *Mahabharata* have never been read. Nevertheless, the readers will never accept the claim that they do not know the two epics. Most of us have never managed to penetrate the deep groves of the epic to touch Rama, Krishna, Lakshmana, Karna, Ravana, Duryodhana, Bharata, and Bhishma as characters. We have merely inspected them from a distance; yet, they have inspired awe and amazement in us. One might very well ask that where is that unfortunate – that inert being – who, having been born in Indo-Aryan society, has not had the nectar of the tales of the *Ramayana* and the *Mahabharata* flow in his spiritual life, electrify his nerves like lightning, and strengthen his very marrow and muscles like mother's milk? Doubtless, many of our millions of Hindu sons are not equipped to quench their thirst from the pure wellspring of this river simply due to constraints of language, but how many do not have standing before their eyes the living paradigms of the ideal brother in Lakshman, the model servant in Hanuman, the exemplary grandfather in Bhishma, and the noblest foe in Karna? In our own Bengal, most men and women have heard tales about the burning of Lanka and Lakshman's fast from their mother's lips; been entertained by the exaggerated anecdotes of Manthara's humiliation[20] and Ravana's exchange with Angada[21] by minstrels and singers; shed tears at the reunion of Bharata and the exile of Sita enacted in songs and folk plays; and whiled away moments of leisure with a Krittibas's *Ramayana*[22] in hand before finally departing from the world to the sound of the chanting of the name of Rama. Yet, they have never had the good fortune to be acquainted with the immortal writing of the original poet. Nonetheless, if you who are wise, you pundits, you connoisseurs of art, you critics, you who have gone through the sea of Sanskrit literature, you who have memorised the entire seven cantos of the *Ramayana*, if you believe that you can appreciate the excellence of Rama's story better than that unlearned old village lady, I must submit that you are sorely mistaken.

Indeed, it is my belief that the primary characteristic of the epic is that it does not need to be read from beginning to end and word for word. How many in the world have read Homer in the original? How many scholars have perused even a synopsis of Homer's work? Most have merely heard Homeric tales. Yet, even now we see, as though painted before our eyes, Agamemnon's tremendous[23] army thronging the beach before the walls of Troy. There we see the towering, broad-chested, wide-shouldered, living, breathing forms of Achilles, Ajax, and Diomedes stride through that vast battlefield. Years pass, but the impregnable walls of the city stand strong, and slowly the envy and resentment that are intrinsic to the human heart surface like smoke. From that smog, sparks begin to fly. The Greek heroes lose sight of their purpose and start quarrelling among themselves. Scarcely has Patroclus' funeral pyre died out that the next act rises with the sudden intensity of Achilles' fury, flames of wrath blazing in his incandescent form with roars of rage. See how the mighty Hector's inert body mangled by that great warrior's chariot wheel drenches the battlefield in rivers of blood as men on earth and the gods in heaven stand wide-eyed and mute before the unspeakable act.

This writer would consider it a great misfortune if by this the reader believes that Krittibas yields the same profit as reading Vālmīki, or that looking through the songs and verses[24] which Kasidas[25] consulted in his narrative of *Mahabharata* makes Dvaipāyan's work redundant. Doubtless, pilgrims who have crossed hill and dale to visit the Badrinath temple, negotiated the perils of the Niti Pass at altitudes of 16,000 feet on their way to mount Kailash, and even those who have merely strolled along the glittering promenades of Darjeeling or Shimla have been privy to Himalayan vistas that are inconceivable to those who dwell in the foothills or plains. Nevertheless, one suspects that however enchanting the unique beauty of the various aspects of the Himalayas may be, that is its *kinnari*-haunted caverns,[26] sal-encrusted plateaus,[27] ruddle-tinctured meadows, bamboo groves vibrant with the flute song of the passing breeze,[28] or mountain streams attended by ice-bearing winds, the single visions of a particular landscape and the regional charms do not provide a comprehensive view of the mountain. Just as we need to look upon its range of peaks from afar for a true appreciation of its vast glory, so does the epic require a perusal of the many *khaṇḍakāvyas*[29] which comprise its body. Doubtlessly the soul is enraptured when, having ploughed through many jungles and thickets and having clambered over rocks and screes up and down steep slopes, one manages to drag one's exhausted frame to that vantage point from which the string of khaṇḍakāvyas can be comprehensively viewed. Doubtlessly, the similes and ornamentation employed by these semi-epics are rare and cannot be experienced elsewhere. A discussion of these poems, however, is not quite conducive to an understanding of the greatness of the true epic. It seems advisable to stay at some distance in order to really apprehend the majesty of the epic. It is far more appropriate to remove the distracting charm of the episodic series from our eyes and turn to the colossal breadth of the mahakavya.

Many among us have not read the original epic but have seen it from a distance. All of us have only looked upon the sublime personalities of Bhishma–Drona–Karna–Asvatthama like a range of snowy mountain peaks, and yet we appreciate the glory of the epic. The situation is slightly different among European critics. European criticism of the *Ramayana–Mahabharata* disappoints us. They have not been able to experience the rapture of looking upon the epic from a distance nor have they been able to approach it in close study. Especially noteworthy is the physical fatigue they experience on the trek uphill through the undergrowth and rocky slopes, which tries their patience and tests their resolve. The critic who manages by good fortune to visit a particular region and enjoy its beauty thinks it is enough to simply describe its local charm. No doubt the narratives of Sakuntala, Nala, Savitri, and other khaṇḍakāvyas embedded within the *Mahabharata* are deserving of acclaim in their unique attractions,[30] and European critics eulogise them. But we know their beauty cannot hold a candle to the immense beauty of the epic. Yet, the felicity with which the European's pen shows the worth of these *khaṇḍakāvyas* is lost when it comes to the appreciation of the epic as a whole.

A work of literature that does not demand to be read is an epic: the significance of this defining marker is probably clearer by now. One may not read the epic, but one cannot possibly not read that which is not an epic. Kālidāsa is a great poet, probably greater even than Vyāsa-Vālmīki, but he has never written an epic poem. In order to comprehend the *Kumārasambhava*, it is simply not enough to know its story or even to read a translation. We need to sit down with the text like a schoolboy and read every detail with commentaries, or the *Kumārasambhava* will not be read. One cannot hear anything of Kālidāsa's language, his rhythm and cadences, without going close to him; nothing is audible from a distance. Kālidāsa is an artist. He has placed stone upon stone to build his mansion; he has carefully joined perfect white marble bricks one by one to erect his wall and set vibrant jewels in it in a curious tracery of vines and creepers to adorn it. He has crafted the Taj Mahal; he has built the Alhambra. The detailed artistry of it demands to be perceived at close quarters. Everyone cannot see this beauty; it gives access only to the connoisseur's eye and the critic's taste. It cannot be seen or understood otherwise.

Shakespeare is perhaps a greater poet still, and his status is possibly higher than Homer's; yet, even he has never written an epic. We have never seen the Greek poet's heroine Helen and only heard tales about her; yet the blazing beauty that reduced Troy to ashes still dazzles our imagination. It is, however, never enough to know the stories or read a translation to feel the beauty of Shakespeare's heroines. We must draw close and look at them with our own eyes, with the eyes of the connoisseur. We cannot hope to apprehend Shakespeare's language, his rhythm and cadences, without drawing near. It does appear at times that from within each of Shakespeare's plays, one can hear the ocean's roar, the rumbling of seismic convulsion, or the growl of the forest fire; but one cannot hear the sense in the sound without a close approach. Shakespeare may be the great poet of our times, but he has not written any epic.

It is not fruitful to compare the beauty of natural objects with that of artificial ones. Their respective aesthetic value cannot be weighed on a scale of comparison. Human genius occasionally seems to surpass even divine creation. It is therefore not advisable to place the natural and the artificial side by side to judge which is greater or the lesser in glory. What the artificial possesses is absent in the natural and vice versa. They are of separate categories. Mahakavyas did not emerge from the four mouths of Chaturanan.[31] They were doubtless fruits of human endeavour, but they contain a naturalness that is lacking in better and more sophisticated achievements of humanity. They might very well contain impassable undergrowth and be filled with steep rocky inclines; yet, they have an innate grandeur that is unmistakable even at a distance. Their tales enthral the mind, and they do not demand specialised skills of appreciation or rigorous training. We do not need glasses; our native eyes are adequate for grasping their meaning and recognising their worth. The single most distinctive characteristic of the epic or mahakavya is nothing but this unadorned, unclothed, and free artlessness. Human civilisation, at least in our modern times, is a highly artificial construction.

I do not denounce this artificiality. Perhaps artifice is the most distinctive marker of humanity, and perhaps contrivance is indistinguishable from the condition of being human. At any rate, we may safely assert that the artificial is precisely that which distinguishes the human from the animal. To condemn artifice will merely malign the intrinsic nature of human beings, and thus I do not wish to criticise it. I would not be surprised if unnaturalness were considered to be the special glory of human beings. I would be ready to admit too that the greatest expression of humanity lies in artifice. I would further grant that the crafting of beautiful objects constitutes the acme of human fame. Nonetheless, crafted art is artificial. There is elegance in it, careful construction and expertise as well as an attempt in its intentional imaginative fabrication – the 'design'[32] if you will – to suggest the human creative genius. That which is natural does not possess elegance or structure and is born without control from an extravagant and haphazard jumble of rain-drenched and tempest-tossed large objects. Modern civilisation is tremendously contrived. For this reason, the absence of artlessness that is the primary sign of the epic blocks its emergence in our times. Modern civilisation is not an obstacle to poetry, but it perhaps is an impediment to the epic. Today's human being, whirling in the work machine, has to fill the sparse moments of respite he somehow acquires in a life of endless toil with the agonies and ecstasies of *khaṇḍakāvyas* and portioned-out beauty. He has no time to gaze upon the monumental material to enjoy its magnificence as a whole. It is perhaps due to this that a Shakespeare and a Kālidāsa has been born in this society, but neither Homer nor Vālmīki. The author has not the leisure to calculate whether this is a matter of profit or loss to the human race. We must be content with our lot. We do not have the power to reverse the currents of the world. We might try a thousand times today but will not be able to produce an epic poet in our midst. Yet, time is infinite and the earth boundless, so we shall not be greatly surprised if the temporal stream witnesses the rebirth of the epic poet at some point in the future.

Translation: Debapriya Basu

Notes

1 Ramendrasundar Trivedi, 'Mahakavyer Lakshan', *Bangadarsan* (New Series), 1902, 2(9): 479–490.
2 Mahakavya, literally 'great poem.'
3 Indian epics traditionally ascribed to the Hindu sages Vālmīki and Kṛṣṇadvaipāyana Vedavyāsa (or Vyāsa), respectively. In Sanskrit literature, the *Ramayana*, which tells the story of the divine prince Rama's campaign to rescue his wife Sita from the demon king Ravana of Lanka, is considered to be adi-kāvya or 'first poem.' It predates the *Mahabharata*, which narrates the Kurukshetra war between the Kaurava and the Pandava dynasty and is thought to be not older than 400 BCE.
4 The *Ramayana* and the *Mahabharata* are considered *itihāsa* or historical chronicles in Sanskrit literature. The puranas are a discrete collection of sacred texts on Hindu myths, legends, genealogies, and other traditional lore. A *karmaśāstra* is

a text which reveals the causal workings of karma (physical and spiritual action) in human life.

5 Trivedi uses this composite title for the *Ramayana* and the *Mahabharata* consistently throughout the essay, and as such this formulation has been retained in translation.

6 Narrative poems composed by Kālidāsa and Bhāravi respectively.

7 The siege of Troy, the subject-matter of the *Iliad*.

8 Paul Methuen, third Baron Methuen (1845–1932), was captured in the Battle of Tweebosch in 1902. He broke his leg after his horse fell on him during the battle. Boer General Koos de la Rey released him due to the severity of his injuries, providing his personal cart to take Methuen to hospital in Klerksdorp. See Carl Jeppe, *The Kaleidoscopic Transvaal*, Cape Town: J. C. Juta, 1906, p. 243. In the *Iliad* (Book XXII, 367–404), Achilles ties Hector's corpse to his chariot wheels and drags it to the ships.

9 Battle that took place in 1870 in the Franco-Prussian War, leading to the capture of Napoleon III and French defeat. Bhima splits open Dushasana's chest and drinks his blood in the 'Karna Parva' of the *Mahabharata*.

10 Second of the four *yuga* or ages of mankind in the Vedic–Puranic chronology, containing three avatars of Vishnu, including Rama.

11 Refers to the ape god Hanumana. In the 'Lanka Kanda' or 'Yuddha Kanda' of the *Ramayana*, Hanumana's tail is set on fire on Ravana's orders, but he escapes and sets the whole of Lanka ablaze with his burning tail.

12 Edmund Burke (1729–1797), *Reflections on the Revolution in France*, London: James Dodsley, 1790.

13 The game of dice in the 'Sabha Parva' of the *Mahabharata* in which King Yudhishthira lost his kingdom, brethren, and wife. The raging Bhima restrains himself in obedience to his elder brother.

14 Refers to Rama's exile in the *Ramayana* at the behest of his father and manipulated by his stepmother.

15 In English in the original.

16 Literally Vast or Great Time, epithet of the god Siva in his destructive form.

17 Term used to describe Siva's cataclysmic dance of simultaneous creation and destruction.

18 Authorial note: 'Students of Lyell need not be alarmed by this imaginary account of the birth of the Himalayas. Regional catastrophes are entirely opposed to Lyell's view.' The reference is to Sir Charles Lyell (1979–1875), one of the foremost champions of uniformitarianism (the idea that slow incremental changes created all of the earth's geological features) as opposed to catastrophic theories (which held the view that all geological changes were a result of sudden cataclysmic shifts) of the geological evolution of the planet.

19 Names of heroes of the *Mahabharata*.

20 The hunchback wet nurse of Kaikeyi (king Dasharatha's wife and Rama's stepmother) who was involved in the plotting of Rama's exile.

21 One of the Vanara or monkeys who helped Rama rescue Sita from Ravana's clutches. He acted as Rama's emissary to Ravana.

22 A fifteenth-century rendition of the *Ramayana* story by Bengali poet Krittibas Ojha (1381–1461).

23 The word used here is 'Akshauhini' that indicates a complete army consisting of 109,350-foot soldiers, 65,610 cavalry, 21,870 chariots, and 21,870 elephants; alternatively, signifying a hundred trillions.

24 The terms used are *panchali* and *payar*. A panchali is an oral narrative form of songs and stories (including its metre) in Bangla. The payar is the principal metre of medieval Bangla literature.

25 Kasiram Das is a sixteenth-century Bengali poet famous for his influential retelling of the *Mahabharata*.

26 Kinnari are mythical creatures with the upper body of a woman and the wings, tail, and feet of a swan said to inhabit the Himavanta (the legendary forest that surrounds the base of Mount Meru in Hindu mythology). They are renowned for their dancing, singing, and poetic skills and are symbolic of the feminine graces.

27 The sal tree (bot. *shorea robusta*). Deciduous tree with straight slender trunks found on Himalayan plateaus at 3,000–4,000 feet above the sea level.

28 The original uses Marut, the storm deity in Hindu mythology. The imagery literally describes the wind blowing through gaps in the bamboo groves, making a flute-like sound.

29 Rhetorical term for one of the three principal branches of kavya in Sanskrit, the others being *mahakavya* and *muktak*.

30 Sakuntala was the wife of Dushyanta and the mother of Bharata, the tale of whose dynasty is the subject matter of the *Mahabharata*. Nala is the king of Nishadha who lost his kingdom in a game of dice and abandoned his wife Damayanti under the influence of the demon Kali. Savitri, daughter of King Asvapati of Madra, is the ideal devoted wife who engages with Yama, the god of Death, in a battle of wits to win back her husband's life. She is considered a character, similar to Draupadi in the text. These embedded narratives occur in the 'Adi Parva' (Sakuntala) and the 'Vana Parva' (Nala–Damayanti and Savitri–Satyavan) respectively.

31 Chaturanan, 'one who has four faces,' an appellation of Brahma, the original creator god in Hindu mythology, as well as the creator of the Vedas, the oldest of Sanskrit texts.

32 In English in the original.

10 Mohitlal Majumdar: Tragedy in Bangla literature

Introduction

One of the greatest critics in the history of Bangla literature, Mohitlal Majumdar (1888–1952) resisted modernist trends and defended an idealistic perception of literature. A poet himself, his major contributions include *Swapan-Pasari* (1922) and *Smaragaral* (1936). However, Majumdar's principal area of contribution was literary criticism, and he was a prolific critic. A professor of Bangla literature at the University of Dhaka (1928–1944), Majumdar wrote on Michael Madhusudan Dutt, Bankimchandra Chattopadhyay, and Rabindranath Tagore in works such as *Adhunik Bangla Sahitya* (1936), *Kavi Sri Madhusudan* (1947), and *Sahitya Bichar* (1947). He was associated with the literary movement foregrounded by the group around *Sanibarer Chithi*, a literary journal edited by Sajanikanta Das. The group was critical of literary trends initiated by the *Kallol* group of authors advocating realism and naturalism in literature. The essay presented in this volume appeared in the second edition of his collection of critical essays titled *Sahitya Bitan* (1949).

Mohitlal Majumdar was known in the field of Bangla literary criticism for his persistent quest for method. A self-professed proponent of a 'historical' method of criticism, Majumdar used various critical tools in his writings. In this essay, Majumdar begins with an attempt to understand tragedy in the Western context and the absence of the realisation of its full potential in contemporary Bangla literature. He tries to find his answer in the historical and legendary sources of Indian and Western traditions and points to the sacrifice of Christ as the perennial source of tragedy, which not only draws tears, but also asks for redemption in immortal glory. He goes on to show how, through the influence of the Western canon, Bankimchandra Chattopadhyay becomes the first great author of the tragic in Bangla literature although with variants. He argues that the legacy is followed by Rabindranath who fails to create the tragic in drama but gives it a fragmented form in his poem 'Parisodh'. Similarly, despite the pervasive sense of tragedy in Saratchandra Chattopadhyay's novel *Srikanta*, it eventually ends with a sense of rest and

DOI: 10.4324/9781003224686-11

refuge. Majumdar shows that the Indian system of belief did not allow people to look at sorrow as a permanent state.

*

Tragedy in Bangla literature[1]

Mohitlal Majumdar

The famous saying by one of the greatest poets of Western European literature – 'Our sweetest songs are those that tell of saddest thought' – is repeated so often because it is true. If the poet meant that the song which is tinged most heavily with sorrow is the loveliest, then it is understandable why most people would agree. But one must ask – what is this message of sorrow that acquires such loveliness in poetry? Surely it does not comprise tumultuous confrontations or tempestuous conflicts, self-declarations or consolidations of personalities; neither the public, nor chaos? If there is something at the heart of it, it is an agonised longing, like the memory of a dwindling day in a lonely heart in the sad twilight; like the memory of another incarnation, an unsaid but keenly felt separation – the dilemma between being together and separated. This yearning is without consolation but is so deeply pleasurable that one does not desire to be consoled. In reality, this is the rasa of lyrics; the essential rasa of the 'songs' referred to by Shelley. Literature enters our minds as a metaphor for the rasa of life itself, and this rasa is loveliness; therefore, Shelley's utterance is true in the sense that every great work of art will reveal this note of sorrow at its core. This is something that is easily comprehensible to all of us. The connoisseurs of rasa might be able to access this core of loveliness even in the manifestations of horror and wrath; nevertheless, the rasa of sorrow remains our favourite – it enriches not only our aesthetic sensibilities, but also our mind. But even here, there are degrees of excellence among the various formal manifestations, and this is why in Western Europe the genre of tragedy emerged as a new form of poetics. This was nothing but the dramatic form of the rasa of sorrow. Tragedy helps us visualise the sorrow that lyric can only make us feel. And this distinction is a significant one. 'Feeling' is an emotional state that does not involve questions; a lyric can achieve that emotional state based on a slight action or an insignificant set of circumstances or a momentary unsettling of the heart; it is as if one were playing one's flute sitting at the edge of the ocean of life; the roar of the stormy seas drifts in from the horizon in the form of a melody that emanates from the flute. But in a play we are too close to – nay, perhaps even amidst – the roar of the turbulent, rocky seas; the image of sorrow that we witness is not a mere reflection but its actual presence. It strikes us not just with melody, but with real force; we are not mere partakers of rasa here – we are struck by its plaint, its petulant questioning. I have discussed elsewhere why this particular manifestation of the rasa requires the greatest degree of poetic skill; I have also explained why tragedy, the genre which has given a dramatic shape to the rasa of sadness, is an unrivalled creation of Western European literature. In this piece, I will discuss in some detail the reason why tragedy has not achieved the same status in our literature, and why, if at all, it has acquired some glory in modern Bangla literature.

In this essay, I will consider the term tragedy in both its restricted and larger sense; both are equally crucial because the word has acquired a wide currency in our everyday lives beyond its classical definition. This is because, in our lives, we have become used to encountering this representation of sorrow in various piecemeal forms. Whether in life or in literature, wherever we encounter a sorrowful fate we call it 'tragedy'. Our close encounter with the canon of European literature and European philosophy has taught us to hold tragedy in special regard, and therefore it has become increasingly important to come up with an accurate translation of the word. But since we have not been able come up with an adequate substitute yet, we are having to make do with this foreign term.

What is the reason for this? The inherent poverty of the Bengali language? Sanskrit is not an impoverished language. To answer this question properly, one will have to come to terms with the fact that we have not been able to assimilate the essence of the tragic rasa as yet, so how can we articulate it in language? The inner life of a people is after all inextricably linked with language and expression. If an emotion fundamentally contradicts the way our life, mind, and psyche are structured, then regardless of how deeply it enters our consciousness, we can never fully accept it. That we have not been able to come up with a name for tragedy bears testament to this fact. Our Indian or Hindu consciousness has instilled in us a way of experiencing feeling, that, even while it facilitates an easy grasp on the emotion of sorrow, it simultaneously shields us from being absolutely overwhelmed by the cruelty of fate. Our system of beliefs – about this life and this world, about our immortal soul and its afterlife – does not allow us to consider any form of grief as insurmountable or permanent. Everything is fine, no irregularities or injustice anywhere, no sorrow is entirely uncalled for or is meaningless; in fact, if seen from the point of view of knowledge or devotion, sorrow has no existence at all. We shed tears because it is our biological function to do so, but there is consolation in such tears. In our consciousness and our unconscious mind, the indispensability of this consolation has become deeply rooted.

European cultural life is the exact opposite of this – sorrow is truly felt and ever-present, its power is boundless, and not even the Almighty can cope with its evil. Sorrow is so potent that even Jesus himself, the Son of God, was struck by its force. The lasting memory of his crucified, blood-covered body, his face distorted by pain, his eyes half-open, still, and bereft of light enveloped Europe in a nightmarish vision. While the cruelty of the death meted out to him won him his immortal glory, it also reaffirmed the image of sorrow in the European consciousness. Nothing else fascinates the European as much as the sorrow; it is also why, perhaps, they love cruelty. Deep down the European mind is unchristian. Christ's message and the fathomless ocean of kindness and charity which underlie his sacrifice are not easily assimilable for the European; the virtue of kindness is not at one with their lives. Sorrow has made them harsher instead of kinder, and it has invoked their aggressive egotism. The vigour that enables humans to cope with misery and pain is what constitutes his manhood; thus in plays and novels, this kind of sorrow will not only impel the audience to shed tears of commiseration, but also expose to ridicule every weakness and shortcoming and thereby invoke a feeling of hard contentment and peace. This rasa is the rasa of tragedy.

This rasa is not native to Indian or Hindu literary culture; there is no room for this rasa in our lives. The reason for this, as I have explained before, is that it is a form of deification of sorrow. In order to put a finger on the pulse of human greatness, one needs to focus single-mindedly on sorrow. There is no desire to decode the deeper meaning of life and no desire to access the truth achieved from the balance of joy and sorrow, life and death. Indians have embraced sorrow, death, joy, and immortality as truth, and even the sage Buddha has been defeated by this realisation. The flower of tragic poetry has never taken root in the Indian mind. They do not deny the existence of sorrow – no one can, really; but they cannot fully accept that unconquerable human fortitude can be annihilated by death or sorrow, and therefore tragedy as a genre remains meaningless to them; even in literary fiction, the abyss of death is navigable, so the rasa of tragedy is eschewed because it is redundant.

*

A few examples, now, to clarify the point I have been making. Two examples of European tragedy and of the idealism of the Indian literary imaginary have had me in their thrall, right from the inception of my literary career up to this day. One is Victor Hugo's immortal romance *The Toilers of the Sea*, a supreme tragedy of love and sexual desire which makes Shakespeare's *Romeo and Juliet* seem juvenile in comparison – a tragedy in the form of a novel in which the author has shown us the extent of love's strength and sacrifice, while also incorporating the inevitable ending in death and destruction that is the inalienable characteristic of a tragedy, which has imbued the work with pathos. The greatness of love on the one hand and the cruelty of human destiny on the other have inflected the work with fine but deep imprints, which seemed tremendously appealing to my youthful heart. Hugo's imagination and literary craft is well known to all; in this work, they are manifested along with a degree of lyrical depth and artistic finesse that, according to me, makes it one of the finest creations of French narrative poetry. I am biased towards this rasa; I must admit this weakness that the way European literature fascinates me, its Indian counterpart does not. My soul, moth-like, is drawn towards these healthy and robust flames of human desires and yearnings rooted in the body. What do we have to offer to counter the heroism and life-enabling, self-destructive hunger of European poetry? But I also understand that whatever the nature of Indian poetry, Indian philosophy is deeper, truer – true in the sense of being whole. This gaze is such that it surpasses the vocabulary of our bodies and minds. In literature, as in the other arts, this thirst for metaphysical rasa is unable to create the superficially sensual beauty of Hellenistic culture. But besides being Indian, I am also Bengali; I need body as well as soul, the physical along with the metaphysical; human senses and the human body are for me the locus of the Almighty, I say therefore:

> Here in the flesh, within the flesh, behind,
> Swift in the blood and throbbing on the bone,
> Beauty herself, the universal mind,
> Eternal April wandering alone,
> The god, the holy ghost, the atoning lord,
> Here in the flesh; the never yet explored.[2]

To resume, the Indian way of life is unique; its rasa is a taste of that which frees the body and soul of bondage and creates a joy of unprecedented freedom. The lover of literature will say that this kind of tragedy is a distraction, it cannot be called rasa; here love itself is a thirst, and in order to glorify this thirst, one resorts to fraud and glorifies death. As far as literature is concerned, I acquiesce to this but contradict it at the same time – for reasons already stated. But right after I read Hugo's novel, I read two articles on two ancient Indian tales in a Bengali monthly. I can recall neither the names of the author nor the titles of the articles, but the portrait of love depicted in these two stories is vividly etched in my memory. One of those two tales I still remember, and I will try to summarise it from memory. The tone of the narrative is typical of ancient Indian tales – the familiar question of Betal or the Brahmapisach (Vetālapañcaviṃśati); the tone has fit the narrative like a glove. The story goes thus:

The great forest of the South was once stricken by a terrible drought. All the birds and animals ran around desperately looking for water and eventually began to die in hordes. A doe and a deer had walked miles in search of water, and at last when they were about to drop dead from thirst and exhaustion, they found a tiny puddle of water in a dry river bed. It was just about enough to slake the thirst of one but not of both. They kept pleading each other to drink the water, but both stubbornly refused to save their own life by sacrificing the other's. In the end, the deer said to the doe that since she was pregnant, by drinking the water it would save two lives and spare the deer the guilt of being responsible for its own child's death – finally, with great pain and reluctance, as if being sentenced to a terrible punishment, the doe drank the water, and the deer died. Having finished this story, the

Brahmapisach asked the scholars of the royal court – of these two, who loved the other more? If he did not get the right answer from them, the Pisach would break his fast by eating one of them. Despite long deliberations on logical proof of the superiority of the doe or the deer, none of the scholars could come up with a satisfactory answer. The Pisach laughed at both parties and asked to eat one of them. By this time, the king had become thoroughly embarrassed at this display of incompetence among his scholars; he had already made a pact with the Brahmapisach and felt unable to go back on his word now. One of the king's courtiers rescued him from this quandary – the bird which perched on a golden rod on the king's right side was no ordinary bird. This omniscient, clairvoyant bird, endowed with human speech, addressed the Pisach in a sombre voice:

> All this controversy for this simple question? Neither of those two was a true lover, if they were then neither of them would have died. That little puddle of water was sufficient, one of the two would drink the water and save its own life, the joy of saving its partner's life would save the other. No need to drink water separately to slake its thirst, this joy itself is life-giving. This is the nature of love, and it does not permit the existence of death. The doe and deer did not truly love each other, what they had was deep attachment that could not transcend its own mortality.

You can gauge the extent of the idealism that characterises Indian thinking from this tale. In its literal sense, the moral is false, but it is true in an emotional sense. In this context, the story of Savitri and Satyavan also deserves a mention, another iteration of this motif of rescuing one's partner from the clutches of death. One can gather from all this that the impediments of literal reality do not limit Indian thinking; it must always pierce through that reality and not give up until it discovers something greater beyond nature and destiny. Actions performed on the stage of this world do not satisfy it but the deeper mysteries enacted behind the scenes keep its senses alert.

This is why in our modern dramatic tradition, while trying to create tragedies in the European model, we have ended up only creating musical theatre drenched in pathos. The heroes and heroines of these plays must be such that we can put our arms around them and have a good cry; the severest of sorrows are rendered pathetic in this mode and mocks the virility of man. These plays showcase the torments of fate and destiny, but there is no rebellion against their vagaries, no deeper engagement with the cause of sorrow, because such a character would not appeal to our sensibilities. In trying to compose European tragedies, we have created dramas of spectacle in the pathetic mode.

Nevertheless, there was a time when our literature was deeply impacted by European Romanticism, and our poets and dramatists had begun writing in the romantic manner. Numerous tales were written in this spirit – most of them are lost now. The laments of unrequited love in these novels made our feeble and transient youth dream impossible dreams. The impossibility of desire supplied the rasa of tragedy for our poems. All of those poems and novels were forgotten almost immediately, because what we had found in European tragedy could not be recreated in our own literature. We were enthralled, amazed, and agitated by the rasa of that foreign poetic culture but could not fruitfully internalise it. I have been trying to reiterate the reasons for this failure.

*

In modern Indian literature, only one author has shown himself capable of mastering that rasa and the craftsmanship allied with it in a way that no other writer has – in Bankimchandra's novels, the core of European tragedy has been captured in a new way, and only in these prose narratives can we catch a glimpse of the Shakespearean spirit of romantic tragedies. But tragedies of that sort are not immediately palatable to our native literary tastes, and the wonder of novelty is the only yardstick by which we tend to measure quality. Bangla literature at the present time has only been the happy site of the scholar's pity and the fool's joy. Thus, as soon as Bankim's novels lost their novelty in the eyes of the readers, they were banished from the libraries of scholars and fools alike. Bankim's novels defied the modern definitions of the genre, thus they cannot be characterised as such; any just evaluation of his works has to approach them by way of the best romantic tragedies, and even in so doing his own unique imagination and inspiration have to be kept in mind. But that is outside the scope of this discussion. I am speaking of the existence and spread of tragedy in our literature.

Bankimchandra, having internalised the rasa of European tragedy, manifested it in a dramatic form in his tragedies. But even he, midway through his works and overcome by Indian or Hindu prejudices, often failed to adhere to the European ideals or did not wish to do so anymore. While it is true that the structural principles of his works are indebted to European tragic forms, he too has focused on the conspiracies of destiny, the evil plots of a villain, the self-destructive nature, or overwhelming desire leading to the fall of man – but his predilection for tragedy was also gradually becoming less vehement. The core of inspiration his tragedies draw upon reinstates the belief in man's glory as a manifestation of his own soul that even one who has lost all still has the assurance of some higher treasure and can remain totally unaffected by the vagaries of nature. Till *Bishabriksha,* he had displayed his full faith in the European way of writing tragedies; *Krishnakanter Will* onwards his imagination has followed a different trajectory, although in *Sitaram* (1887) and *Rajsingha* (1886, 1893), it seems he has resorted to new incarnation of European tragic imagination. The terrible games played by fate in *Sitaram*, its cruelty and destruction made manifest in the figure of the loving, chaste wife, and in *Rajsingha*, where the great hero Mobarak was reduced to a mere plaything in the hands of destiny – no system of spirituality or justice could illuminate the darkness of these tragedies. I do not know what came over the author during the writing of *Sitaram*; perhaps he could not bring himself to ignore either man's spiritual nature or his blind instincts – but due to his bias towards spirituality, in this work he has admitted defeat to his own self. In no other work has he created such a glorious blaze of destruction. Who knows, perhaps he was struggling with some personal crisis at this time, that is why the imagining of total decimation gave rise to some cathartic pleasure.

Nevertheless, in Bankim's work, we see a variant of the uncorrupted principle of European tragedy. His faith in human greatness was of a religious kind, but that greatness does not just belong to man – it is derived from being part of a higher power. To discipline one's self is to discipline that higher power. The fantasies of the weak heart erupt in a hundred colourful flames in the theatre of this life and this world; that which is essentially false is still capable of rendering that canvas of life so diverse, so abundantly beautiful. The poet in Bankim views even this falsity with a gaze of wonder but has not given it primacy. If truth is *Siva*, then that falsity is no less than *Sivamohini* or that which charms Siva; keeping Siva before him, Bankim has immersed himself in the beauty of that Sivamohini. The worship accorded to Prakriti[3] in Western tragedies is different – no higher power of truth is foregrounded there; according to Bankim, Prakriti is a temptress but one that grants benediction. In the garden of the five senses, her beauty holds man in thrall. If we are denied the partaking of that rasa, we are deprived of an entirely necessary beguiling of our hearts. The pain inflicted by this beauty is the ladder that leads to higher truth; we must remember not just the fire but the sacrifice that is engulfed by its flames. Once the flames are satiated by the sacrifice and the remnants consumed, the worshipper becomes one with the deity.

After this, two other great writers appeared on our literary horizons: Rabindranath and Saratchandra. Rabindranath's novels are a different thing altogether, but in his early verse we witness his attempts at recreating the rasa of tragedy. We see the effects of Bankim's influence in his first two novels *Bauthakuranir Hat* (1883) and *Rajarshi* (1887) and particularly so in the first one. Rabindranath's own unique poetic genius, whether in novels or plays, has never succeeded in creating the tragic or, for that matter, the theatrical. Undoubtedly one of the greatest lyric poets in the world, Rabindranath had written two plays called *Raja O Rani* (1889) and *Bisarjan* (1890). These plays are coloured by the musicality of his own youthful dreams. If we were to evaluate the theatrical merits and demerits of these works in this context, it would be doing grave injustice to both the poet and his creations. Nevertheless, for the benefit of the readers, I will say a few words to delineate the tragic or theatrical features thereof. Rabindranath, being the poet that he was, lacked the kind of objectivity that is required in writing a novel or a play, and this was entirely natural. This is why the characters created by him are nowhere to be found in the outside world; they are inhabitants of his own mind. Udayaditya of *Bauthakuranir Hat*, Jaysingha of *Bisarjan*,

Kumarsen of *Raja O Rani,* and even the king himself is the reflection of the poet's own psyche. The emotional universe of these works is so far removed from reality, that the love or hate depicted between men and women does not manifest itself in actual battles fought – that love is not a product of life, but of the mind. Rabindranath's lyric inspiration failed to capture the heart of tragedy. The blazing flames that lie at its core – converting people into steam-driven boilers in human shape eluded Rabindranath. The fire that burns in the blood vessels of the human body is absent in his work. What is there in his poetry is a distant gleam of that fire or the distilled essence of that burning. In *Bisarjan*, we see the lyric poet's unabashed self-expression. In this work, the excessive seriousness of his poetry has been revealed to us time and again, on the other hand, the poet's intense desire to put his own self on display has resulted in turning the main characters to ash. *Chitrangada* (1892) and *Bisarjan* – in both of these works, the poet's excessive eagerness to make an ideological point led to a gross violation of formal and generic principles, even as these poems were engulfed by the poet's youthful self. In *Chitrangada,* the issue was women's right to self-determination; and in *Bisarjan,* it was the establishment of a religious viewpoint – in either case, these ideological concerns fragmented the poet's inspiration. Thus, none of the characters of these works was theatrically convincing, that is, in keeping with nature and society. King Govindamanikya is no monarch but a devout seeker. The warrior-prince Jaisingha is no son of Rajput but a poet and a philosopher. Somewhat like Hamlet, but not quite him either, in the final act he could not express Hamlet's inevitable royalty. Raghupati, too, is not the Shakta priest of a Hindu temple. To fit into the poet's vision, he has been made cruel, power-hungry, godless, and shrewd, a stereotypical Egyptian or Phoenician votary. He is the symbol of all idolatrous sects in the world, and the keepers of these religions deceive the people and mock their blind faith. In *Rajarshi*, the Bengali Brahmin worshipper of Shakti has been morphed into such an unlikely character just to serve the poet's purpose. Most notably, none of the characters of this play is a tragic character – they are all excessively weak and overwhelmed by the excess of emotions. Jaisingha's suicide is not driven by ordinary human motives; similarly Raghupati's end, too, is akin to the explosion of a bomb of sentiments. It is as if his terrible oath and his arrogance were not organically part of his character but a sort of mask, as if he were in some sort of a trance – and the tragic shattering of that dream manifested itself in a melodrama.

The same applies to *Raja O Rani.* This play can be seen as a tragedy of love, but that love is also of the lyric kind wherein Ila and Kumarsen have exhausted their lyric passion. But as far as the hero (Raja) and heroine (Rani) of this tragedy are concerned, the hubris of this love turns into a conflagration. The tragedy therefore is not a tragedy of flesh and blood but that of emotions. 'Raja' and 'Rani' are both self-involved 'egoists' – their love is devoid of sacrifice. 'Raja' is in love with himself or rather a particular emotion of his mind; 'Rani, too, is not in love with 'Raja', but the ideals of truth and justice which exist in her soul.' These are not real human beings but personifications of virtues. Thus, this tragedy has turned into a lyric in which the beauty of his poetry and the depth of the emotions shine through. This is all about Rabindranath's poetry for now.

*

The transformation undergone by tragedy in the Indian context described in this essay makes it undeniable that tragedies in the European mould are alien to us. I have posited that this lack is rooted in our cultural and collective behaviour. The greatest literature produced by a people is usually the fullest flowering of their artistic sympathies. The Greeks were the original creators of tragedy. Their life philosophy led to the invention of that rasa. Whatever evidence there is of Greek mental life it tells us that this tangible, visible world was adequate for their thinking and their poetic imagination. No deeper spiritual contemplation has been able to disturb this deep appreciation for nature and human life. The senses of proportion, harmony, and regulation that they found in nature were accepted by them as principles of formal beauty with the seriousness of religion. They have regarded the violation of these principles in human life with fear and abhorrence. Whenever man has been led astray from those principles – either from an autonomous sense of right and wrong, or from a sense of compassion – these very principles then assume the form of fate and punish the erring individual. That punishment has been called by various names, whether it be 'Nemesis' or 'the Furies'. The simplicity of this philosophy, which is basically the inviolability of natural principles, the extreme frightening vision of human life, the nakedness of human nature, the inevitable progression of events, and their relentless unavoidable consequences, all of this endowed their theatre with a unique beauty.

Thus, to write tragedies in this manner, a mental life of this kind is required. This dilemma and conflict of human nature and their sad consequences are part of our everyday reality, but not all people view them in the same manner. In fact, the successors of Greeks, the people of latter-day Europe, have been unable to keep the Greek spirit of tragedy intact. Human life and fate, the dilemmas produced in nature, and the sins and sorrows of humans have been reimagined in myriad ways, and the problem has acquired a mysterious spiritual depth. India, from the beginning, has viewed the world and human life from a different perspective, so our experience of rasas has also progressed in a different direction. It has not acknowledged this visible world as the be all and end all of existence, and probing deeper into life it has found itself unable to deny that the sorrowful dénouement is not the whole truth – all conflict, all sorrow is transient. This is the reason why Indian literary imagination has sought to incorporate the scope and variety of the external world and all the complexities of life into one unified rasa consciousness. Thus, at its core, the literary rasa of India is always that of the lyric. If that rasa is served to us in the mimetic mode, it will still be lyric – it can become a tableau of spectacles but never theatre. Rabindranath was essentially an Indian poet and he realised his limitations while attempting to write a tragedy in the European mode; in his later plays, he did correct this impulse.

Nevertheless, this inability is a serious lack. Philosophy is not the main prop of literature, however exalted Indian philosophy is, why should it become an obstacle in the creation of literature? This is because the tenets of this philosophy are also part of our lives. They exert such an influence on our social behaviour that we do not distil philosophy from our life, our life begins from philosophy. Shakespeare's immortal tragedies bear testimony to the fact that particular facets of this philosophy can be reincarnated into a rasa. The philosophy that shines through his work could be seen as an aspect of Hindu philosophy. The power of this rasa is one with life, and it is not derived from externalities, such is the rasa of Shakespearean tragedies. This tells us that the European way of life had moved considerably away from the Greek ethos, culminating in this great philosopher-poet's vision, which is not opposed to the Indian literary rasas. Even if fate has a part to play in Shakespeare's plays, fate is not the master of man. Thus, the same human life has been seen as transitioning from comedy to tragedy and from tragedy to comedy – sometimes it is like the sunlit waves of the calm ocean, at other times it is like the tempest ridden seas. It is the same strength that can indulge in laughter, mirth, and humour and can also embrace the ground in grief with dishevelled hair. All this diversity of moods is the play of the 'one' who resides in all humans; the 'one' who decks her own bridal boudoir and simultaneously builds her own funeral pyre. The clouds of destruction which darken the horizons of a Shakespearean tragedy are not related to an external moral structure, which is why it does not seem as terrifying; on the other hand, they overwhelm our hearts by invoking the wonders of some eternal mystery. Shakespeare experienced the play of Purusha and Prakriti, of human and natural elements, as a conflict. In most instances, it resulted in the defeat of man but not a permanent denigration. Even if the Purusha had received greater prominence in *Hamlet* and the Prakriti in *Antony and Cleopatra*, in the final analysis each has succeeded in mesmerising the other. Neither element was showed in ill light at the expense of the other. Europe is ignorant of this play between elements, which is why the critical debates surrounding Shakespeare's plays are still raging.

Even if fate or destiny plays a part in Shakespeare's plays, that remains peripheral. And the protagonists imbue the play with vitality despite the inhibitory presence of fate. In this sense, the governing rasa of these plays can be termed 'Romance of Character'. If the hero's tragic destruction seems inevitable, it is not because of the insurmountable edicts of fate, rather it seems as if the limitlessness of human potential manifests its glory in this manner by transgressing the boundaries of human life. This is why destruction is inevitable. A learned critic has phrased this very argument in the following manner:

> The purest reality, the purest beauty, the purest love, cannot, by its own nature, manifest itself here on earth without disaster, but in disaster it can.

The fullest potential of man is this 'purest reality'. If we add our Indian way of thinking to this, we can say that there is no reality outside of this. 'But in disaster it can' means that if human beings choose to reveal their fullest potential, it can only end in disaster. This is the core of Shakespearean tragedy.

Nevertheless, if we must accept fate, then we would do well to be guided by the German scholar's dictum: 'Character is Fate'. This, too, is in keeping with Hindu philosophy, which holds that the 'character' of man is nothing but the palpable form of the immaterial body created out of his own accumulated karmic earnings. He is the creator and therefore also its sole master. This philosophy, when seen through the lens of rasa, is Shakespeare's works in a nutshell. In this context, it must be mentioned that modern tragic imagination has no need for the villain – that one rascally fellow who is responsible for wreaking havoc in the world of the play. Modern tragedy is constructed around graver principles, as a contemporary English poet and novelist has noted:

> In tragic life, God wot,
> No villain need be! Passions spin the plot:
> We are betrayed by what is false within.[4]

This is also what Hindu philosophy propagates, and if this is what tragedies are made of then what are obstacles in the way of our writing tragedies?

I was talking about the principles of writing tragedy and their particular application, and let no one draw the conclusion that the tragic poets render these principles in dramatic form. If a philosophic principle touches the poet's soul, it no longer remains a principle, and it becomes a touchstone of poetic inspiration. In the recent past, such philosophical principles have gained an unprecedented degree of influence on the psyche of poets. As a result of this in the works of a particular English novelist and poet, tragedy has become the vehicle of philosophy. This, too, dovetails partially with a specific strand of Indian thinking. German philosopher Schopenhauer, taking his cue from Indian thought, infused the philosophy of pessimism with a neo-Buddhist strain. The English author Thomas Hardy has given a literary incarnation to this. In his novels, a blind but alert and relentless destiny seems to be constantly thwarting every human endeavour. In the presence of that power, truth, justice, and love, nothing has any significance. Man's glory has been razed to the ground. In this new kind of tragedy, there is no capacity to explore man's internal joyousness, and what should one call this new poetic rasa? But this is not the only question. What I want to say is this: whatever the rasa of this new tragedy, the thought governing these works is not new to us; if not to Vedanta philosophy, then at the very least it bears a familial resemblance to Buddhist nihilism. But even this kind of tragedy is missing from our literary tradition. The reason is this: even this kind of philosophy is experienced directly as rasa, we do not let it linger in our lives, and as a stable emotion it becomes the creative principle behind lyric poems of various lengths. That kind of theatre in general, and tragedy in particular, keeps eluding us.

*

Thus far I have only discussed formally conventional tragedies and the principles underlying these. But if we take the word 'tragedy' to mean something wider, then whatever its theatrical form, we keep catching sudden glimpses of its rasa in life. There is a reason why the word 'tragedy' has become a part of everyday conversations. It is unanimously acknowledged that life's sorrow is various and terrifying. Even if that sorrow does not appear to us in the form of a particular rasa, or follows a specific concrete literary formula, the truly tragic character who is able to bear that sorrow is often encountered in our lives, and this is reflected in modern tragic poetry and novels. These days, a slight hint is enough to trigger the experience of rasa in the soul of the sensitive reader, who is more thoughtful than ever. Not everything has to be enacted; a lot of the tragic narrative can be constructed in the mind of the reader with the help of these hints. Tragedy has acquired this fragmented form in contemporary literature. I will end this present discussion by citing a few examples of this and showing how our Indian way of thinking has responded to it.

A fantastic example of this is Rabindranath's poem 'Parisodh', a part of *Katha o Kahini*. The tragic imagination of this poem is reminiscent of the lyric form; nevertheless, the dramatic event that has lent a unique depth to this lyric-tragedy has revealed itself in a brief gesture towards the very end – like a flash of lightning. This has been enough to serve his purpose. It has cut through the lyric atmosphere of the poem and declared in thunderous tones:

> The young boy,
> Uttiyo was his name, maddened by
> unrequited love for me. At my entreaty,
> taking the blame of thieving upon his shoulders,
> has given his own life.[5]

The lyric poet does not need any more than this. The terrifying nature of this event frightens him. The tragedy of the main poem is different, and that is what the poet chose to focus on. That tragedy was crude, while the heroine's tragedy is more refined. In spite of that, it seems to be the central tragic preoccupation of the poem, as even in its limited form it takes up most of the space, and this is why the effect of the main poem fades in comparison. Here too, Rabindranath has viewed the boy's impatient, mad love as the manifestation of unconquerable earthly passion; however sad its dénouement, it is seen as bereft of higher moral truth – which is why he is attracted towards the more intangible tragedy. The lamentation of this transcendental tragedy is imbued with the glory of moral penitence, whereas in the other one we only encounter the gaping nihilistic abyss of European tragedy.

Now I will cite another instance of such tragedy from Saratchandra's greatest work, *Srikanta*. Right from the very first volume of *Srikanta*, the looming presence of tragedy overwhelms the imagination. Yet, that it is not merely a product of imagination is evident from the author's writing style and from his own voice. To him too, it manifests itself as a revelation or a divine vision of sorts. The incident is connected to the character called Annada didi. This tragedy is no less than the previous poetic example; in fact, a deeper consideration of the two brings out their essential similarity. In both cases, we find the same frustration and the same sense of supreme hopelessness. Works such as these have neither space, nor need for the technical skill and formal aspects of theatrical composition. But even so, in this narrative, the relative verisimilitude of the events depicted has helped to heighten the theatricality of the characters involved. Still, this tragedy is written in the lyric mode – its inspiration is not Shakta but Vaishnav. The story exemplifies the essential Indian-ness, indeed the Bengali-ness, of the author's spirit.

The steely female figure created in this story is imbued with the unrelenting force of tragedy, and this is why the Indian author could not bear it, and he had to make some moral meaning out of it. Annada didi's unforgiving self-denigration inspires respect and awe in him, but he could not unquestioningly accept her tribulations and destiny's utter contempt towards her greatness. Such power and sacrifice could not go without truth, beauty, and goodness. This desire stems from the tenets of philosophical thinking and is the purest form of spiritual desire. In literature, this desire can only manifest itself in the form of lyric inspiration. This is the force that drove Srikanta, indeed Saratchandra himself. He remains relentless in his quest for satisfactory answers to such questions all through his life; like a meteorite, he rushes through the world while every other thing becomes transient and insignificant. The pain of that crucified woman and her contentment in the face of such disaster follow him like a nightmare. The one person who remains unperturbed is Indranath. He is Annada's spiritual sibling; both characters made from the same other-worldly material. This is why Annada could accept Indranath's charity but felt compelled to reject Srikanta's offerings. While she felt affection for Srikanta's foibles, she regarded Indranath as her equal. Indranath's nature is the personification of the Indian mental life – what we understand by 'tragedy' could not touch his consciousness. He is the man freed from the ties of this world; he feels pity but not sentimental affection; and he feels love but not dependence. If Srikanta were to be like Indranath, then he would have been a totally different person. Srikanta being a Bengali, is affectionate and sentimental; again, being an Indian, he wants a resolution to this anxious yearning he feels. Till he finds that resolution, he can neither reject the suffering nor accept it as the final word. Saratchandra, in the guise of Srikanta, reveals the fruition of this essential Bengali-ness of spirit in the fourth volume. The wanderer-protagonist's travels have finally ended in the *akhra* at Muraripur. His troubled soul has finally been calmed by the Vaishnavi Kamallata's love.

Even Annada's tragedy cannot agitate his being any longer; however sorrowful, however deserving of empathy, it loses its tragic character and acquires a different significance altogether. Indian idealism transforms that tragedy of love – and once infused with Bengali spirit, even unrequited love becomes the dream of the love bowers of Vrindavan. This Vaishnavite view of eros is essentially Bengali – that which emerges from 'churning the nectar of the Bengali heart.' It is the panacea for all heartaches, and this is what crystallises between Srikanta and Kamallata and finally puts a balm on his anxious suffering. What the regal Rajlakshmi could not achieve, this ascetic Vaishnavi did. Eventually he would then cease to feel sorrow for Annada and finally comprehend that she could not possibly rest before her final sacrifice at the highest shrine of beauty and love. In this journey, hitherto, she had been misled, which is why her quest could not end. But no amount of deception could shake that faith and love inside her. The directionless fiery river of love would one day find its destination inside her own self – in Kamallata, Srikanta finally comprehended the nature and culmination of that quest. Annada didi was a little behind him, nevertheless a sojourner on the very same path. The obstacles in the way of life and love acquire the form of tragedy, but that is not the whole truth and the reason why tragedy is fundamentally mendacious. It obstructs the body not the soul. This, too, is one way of saying:

> The purest reality, the purest beauty, the purest love, cannot, by its own nature, manifest itself here on earth without disaster, but in disaster it can.

This is the fundamental truth of Indian nature, despite having witnessed the cruellest manifestations of sorrow, the people of the subcontinent feel bound to reject it in their beings. They are resolved to defeat that sorrow somehow. The weak will accept defeat and shed tears – but still never fully believing it, they will try to evade it and not look upon it squarely. The strong will either consume the passion of that sorrow like Indranath did, or, like Kamallata, they will transform it altogether and decorate the altar of their soul in the light of that flame. Modern poets and artists have harnessed the creative force of this sorrow but limited themselves to its lyric beauty: 'Our sweetest songs are those that tell of saddest thought'. They have neither the need nor the power to do more than this. There is no need because if sorrow is rendered sweet, then in practical terms it does not remain 'sorrow' anymore. Rather, it is proved thus that even sorrow is not sad but a rasa in itself. This is why our poetic inspiration is bound to be primarily lyrical. What becomes a unanimously accepted principle of philosophy in the realm of ideas acquires a unique musicality in the world of rasa. The greatest modern Indian poet, Rabindranath himself, has corroborated this:

> All the kings and emperors of this world,
> Those who were once, where are they now
> Joy, sorrow, and shame bloom in the morning
> Only to wither by evensong;
> In the midst of all this plays a single tune
> Fathomless, vast, deep, and dulcet,
> Pervading the whole of eternity,
> Filling up the skies.[6]

This is why tragedy has never realised its full potential in our literature. The realities of life, with its conflicts and complexities, are never accorded the kind of significance required to establish them in literary imagination with the full splendour of tragic glory. The two fragmented tragedies I have discussed are then adequate for us. The tragic stage in these is internal to our consciousness, however, it can be brought out and externalised to a certain extent – as the second text does. The essential Bengali poet as Srikanta remains the most effective example of the kind of alchemy required to do this.

Translation: Doyeeta Majumder

Notes

1 Mohitlal Majumdar, 'Bangla Sahitye Tragedy' (1947), in *Sahitya-Bitan*, Kolkata: Vidyodaya Library, 1949 (2nd ed.), pp. 236–252.
2 John Masefield, *Sonnets*, Sonnet V, New York: The Macmillan Co., 1916, p. 6.
3 The feminine principle as in Purusha and Prakriti, but the author is also referring to human nature in the context of Bankimchandra's novels.
4 George Meredith, *Modern Love*, Stanza XLIII, New York: Mitchell Kennerley, 1909.
5 Rabindranath Tagore, 'Parisodh', in *Katha*, Kolkata: Adi Brahmosamaj, 1900, pp. 39–40. The narrative was converted into a dance-drama in 1939, where the lines are almost similar. See *Shyama*, Kolkata: Visvabharati, 1939, p. 20.
6 Rabindranath Tagore, 'Puraskar' (The Prize), in *Sonar Tari*, Kolkata: Kalidas Chakraborty, 1894, p. 163.

11 Rajendralal Mitra: A consideration of literature

Introduction

Rajendralal Mitra (1822–1891) was one of the most prominent figures of 'the Bengal Renaissance' and a pioneer in the field of studies in ancient and medieval Brahminical and Buddhist scriptures. A librarian at the Asiatic Society of Bengal from 1846, Mitra went on to be its first Indian President in 1885. He was trained in Sanskrit, Persian, and Urdu and brought out edited volumes of numerous manuscripts and their translations. He edited, among others, an illustrated monthly magazine called *Bibidhartha-samgraha* or a compendium of miscellaneous subjects that included legends, history, zoology, art, and literature. Fashioned after the *Penny Magazine*, it was published under the aegis of the Vernacular Literature Society. The present essay, 'A Consideration of Literature,' was published in the eleventh issue of the magazine in 1852.

Scholars had been engaging with Sanskrit poetics for a very long time, but it was not quite the critical norm of the mid-19th century. On the one hand, the educated Bengali came under the influence of Europe in the realm of thoughts, and on the other hand, the need for an English-oriented education was promoted by both the Bengalis as well as the British East India Company rulers. The British formulation came out clearly in the 1835 minutes drafted by Thomas Babington Macaulay, who believed that 'a single shelf of a good European library was worth the whole native literature of India and Arabia'. Macaulay believed the common dialects lacked literary and scientific information and were so 'poor and rude' that they required enrichment from other sources to carry translations of valuable works. However, it was necessary to reach out to the masses in their language – no matter how inferior it was, for the sake of governance, to maintain law and order, and to deliver justice. The following essay focuses on the question of language and its function, rather than on overtly aesthetic concerns. He also underscores the flaws or *doṣas* in the use of language, presumably following the *guṇa* school of Sanskrit poetics and, to some extent, the Western schools of rhetoric. Mitra's triad of types of utterances – logical, emotive, and ethical – also reminds us of Bankimchandra Chattopadhyay's later division of human

DOI: 10.4324/9781003224686-12

faculties into a triad of *jnanarjani, karyakarini,* and *chittaranjani*: to gather knowledge, to act rightly, and to please the mind, respectively.

*

A consideration of literature[1]

Rajendralal Mitra

An utterance is never made without intent, and such an utterance is of two kinds: first, one that is expressed yet not addressed to anyone, that is, an utterance made to oneself with the intent of expressing one's own thought. Second, the one expressed and addressed to someone, that is, an utterance with a purpose directed towards an individual or a group. The text that determines the rules of sequential implementation of such utterances is called literature, that is an effective treatise on utterance. An utterance replete with rasa is called kavya or poetry. A related series of such poetry may be termed literature but perhaps only to suggest the excellence of the poetry.

The first kind of utterance needs no regulation because the speaker may utter these non-sequentially or at random order yet may be perfectly able to comprehend his own utterance, and that completes and fulfils the purpose of the utterance. Others need not comprehend such an utterance, so there is no point formulating regulations for it.

In the second kind of utterance, a speaker expresses his intent to another. If these utterances are coherent and pleasing, their intent is easily accomplished, so they need particular rules and regulations, and such rules develop into the function of literature. Cohesion between the utterances depends upon grammar. It stands to immediate reason that the speaker himself can determine and regulate the applicability or non-applicability of his own utterances and that this needs no specific rule. We get angry utterances from a person expressing anger, not compassionate ones. Similarly, expressions of other feelings have corresponding utterances. Furthermore, this natural arrangement provides results when applied to the expression of internal thoughts. In the matter of inspiring rasa, rules followed should be the ones traditionally tested and proven to be the most effective. When the poet has to illustrate the rasa frozen within, especially while composing poetry, he needs to make a conscious effort to learn the rules to evoke the said rasas. It is not that such efforts ask only for rules, but the reasons behind those rules and the innate principles of such rasas must also be investigated. Distinction in poetry is rarely achieved otherwise.

It has been stated before that an utterance is not made without intent. With reference to intent, utterances may be of three types: (1) logical, that is, an utterance used for argument, information, or enlightenment; (2) emotive, that is, an utterance which inspires rasa in the audience; and (3) ethical, that is, an utterance that can persuade or motivate the audience to change its mind or pursue a definite course of action, such as calming anger with gentle words. As intent differs, so does the manner of composition; imposing the manner of one upon the intent of the other does not yield a beneficial result. The manner of composition of an emotive utterance will not yield similar results for a logical one. Emotive utterances need to use rhetorical devices like assonance, alliteration, and metaphor. Their use in a logical utterance might result in the possibility of misinterpretation and would not help the primary premise in any way.

Rhetoric is absolutely forbidden in the teaching of mathematics. If one needs to prove that 2, 3, 5, 7, and 9 together make 26, then it is best that they add the numbers up thus: 2 and 3 make 5, 5 and 5 make 10, 10 and 7 make 17, and finally, 17 and 9 make 26. This makes the intent of the speaker clear and therefore well expressed, which would not have been simple or unproblematic had there been the use of rhetoric. Thus, rational disciplines like logic and mathematics, and counsel or instruction of any sort, should forego rhetoric and concentrate on the unambiguous expression of intent.

This is not to say that other disciplines have no need for clarity. In fact, all disciplines ask for clarity of expression. It is considered one of the very best attributes in any composition. No composition that wants clarity may be truly admired, and all authors must strive towards its attainment. Thus, in our previous statement, we meant that mathematics needs clear unambiguous utterances free from rhetorical devices. Such clarity is essential in documents pertaining to the law courts as well. There, rhetoric is of no consequence but rather incurs a chance of misunderstanding. The *Mitākṣarā*[2] says that a claim letter must not be unpleasant or meaningless or full of conflicting words; the words should be short, few, moderate, and consequential. It is the inability of the current-day employees of the law-courts to compose such claim letters, which has given rise to the practice of jotting down the gist of the matter in the margin. Apart from mathematics and rules and regulations, other fields might include some rhetoric after careful consideration, but that too should be restricted to similes and other common rhetorical figures; illuminating figures like the metaphor would not be welcome.

The second type of utterance is called emotive. The intent of this is to evoke pathos and other, emotions in the audience and thus entertain them. With that intent, an emotive utterance must be clad in suitable rhetorical devices and held up before the mind's eye. A prime example of such composition is poetry. Rhetoric is used in many ways in poetry, and hence poetry and emotive fiction are its fittest vessels. In fact, an ethical utterance too does not bar the use of rhetoric.

An utterance that can influence and persuade a person to leave one course of action and pursue another is called persuasive or ethical, and its prime example is public speech. It is more difficult than the other two types of compositions. The first two have a single intent each. It is enough to preserve logic and clarity in a persuasive utterance. An emotive utterance seeks primarily to entertain, and that remains its main object. A persuasive utterance has a twofold purpose – first to establish a matter and second to engage the audience's attention. So, reason, clarity, and emotion must be evoked – and unless all three work in harmony, the purpose is never truly served; and the speeches that successfully combine these features are both admired and effective.

So far, we have been categorising compositions on the basis of differences of intent. Similarly, these might be categorised on the basis of usage of rhetoric as well, such as *sādhāraṇī* (common), *vṛttagandhinī* (metrically tinged), and *utkalikā* (having ornate words). However, we are not inclined to concentrate upon that at this point of time. The attributes and misattributes pertaining to the components of the composition must be considered first, and rhetorical devices may be classified later. Determining differences in methods in compositions will be easier when both concepts become clear.

Word, syllable, utterance, meaning, rasa – these are the five elements of composition. Rhetorical devices are just ornamentation, and they are susceptible to error. Literary theorists have determined fourteen error types in words.

1. Discordant – that which is jarring to the ear;
2. Obscenity – that which induces embarrassment;
3. Inelegance – use of a grammatically incorrect word;
4. Inapplicability – use of a word not used by eminent authors despite being grammatically correct;
5. Vulgarity – use of a non-standardised or dialectal word;
6. Non-recognisability – use of a word previously used only in one text;
7. Equivocation – use of a word with double meaning;
8. Implication – use of a sentence, not overtly necessary, in an obscure manner in order to fulfil the demands of the metre;
9. Futility – use of an unnecessary sentence only to fulfil the demands of the metre;
10. Obscurity – use of a word in its secondary or minor meaning;
11. Non-connotative – use of a word that does not convey the intended meaning;
12. Complexity – use of a word that needs a lot of effort to be comprehended;
13. Contradiction – use of a sentence where the intended meaning of a word gets contradicted;
14. Ineffectiveness – use of a word that does not clearly convey the intent of the author.

Translation: Sudeshna Datta Chaudhuri

Notes

1 Rajendralal Mitra, 'Sahitya Bibek', *Bibidhartha-samgraha*, 1852, 1(9): 171–173.
2 *Mitāksarā* is a legal commentary on parts of the *Yājñavalkya Smṛti* dealing with the theory of inheritance by birth.

12 Rajshekhar Bose: Rasa and the question of taste

Introduction

A chemist by training and profession, Rajshekhar Bose (1880–1960) worked at the Bengal Chemicals and Pharmaceuticals founded by Acharya Prafulla Chandra Roy. However, he is remembered most as one of the greatest satirists in Bangla literature and as a lexicographer who compiled a dictionary *Chalantika* (1937). His collections of short stories like *Gaddalika* (1922), *Kajjali* (1927), and *Hanumaner Swapna Ityadi Galpa* (1937) written under the pen name of Parasuram threw light on a certain dimension of Bengali society and culture. An ardent enthusiast of Sanskrit literature, he published annotated translations of Kālidāsa's *Meghdut* (1943) and annotated abridged translations of the *Ramayana* (1946) and the *Mahabharata* (1949). The essay presented in this volume, 'Rasa and the Question of Taste' was originally published in 1927 and was later included in his collection of essays *Laghuguru* (1939).

Although Sanskrit poetics and its various schools had received critical attention from scholars since the early 19th century, there remained the persistent question whether anything like literary criticism in the Western sense was ever available in Indian traditions. Scholars working with Sanskrit poetics limited their studies to explication of texts. But, at the same time there were attempts by scholars to take the *rasaśāstra* to the general reading public. The trend continued in the early 20th century. However, another task was at hand – to find a relation between Indian and Western aesthetic theories as also with other realms of knowledge. In this essay, Bose not only takes up the question of rasa, but also relates it to the psychoanalytical school by questioning the primacy of *śṛṅgārarasa* in the aesthetic school and that of the libido in the psychoanalytical. He appeals for an open-ended approach in criticism and argues for a greater vision beyond the temporally limited ideals of good and evil.

*

DOI: 10.4324/9781003224686-13

Rasa and the question of taste[1]

Rajshekhar Bose

'*Kāmastadagre samavartādhi*' – meaning that which came first of all was *kāma* – was what the Rig Veda seers put it in the early stages. Then our rhetoricians came and put together a list of nine *rasas*, assigning the first place to '*ādirasa*'.[2] Along came Freud and his followers, and they firmly stated that most, if not all, of man's beautiful and wonderful creations as well as his soft and tender emotions had their origins in the inspirations of multifaceted kāma.

A few days ago, I was listening to a paper on the psychoanalysis of Tagore's writings in a psychology symposium. The speaker, with great reverence, dissected Tagore's writings, skin, flesh, bones, and all to show where exactly the source of the poet's genius lay. Had Tagore been present at that devilish circle, he would probably have fainted and, having recovered, run to an orthodox pandit for an expiatory measure right away.

What a terrible thought! All that we call desirable, acceptable, and deeply enjoyable have at their root a base desire! Freudians have politely called it 'libido', but it is nothing but an immense aspect of lust. And neither is it straightforward. It has a hundred tongues lolling out in a hundred directions, it wants to lap up an offering to the gods and the leftovers of a vulture at the same time, and the sense of propriety and impropriety, suitability and unsuitability does not affect it at all. Is this vile conduct the source of our sense of rasa? '*Pāpo'haṃ pāpakarmahaṃ pāpātmā pāpasambhava*'[3] – 'Sin am I, sinful is all my deed, sinful is my soul, I am born of sin' – we had thought that this was just an expression of exaggerated humility to placate the gods. Never did we realise that we were indeed so virulently sinful. The creator has condemned us to hell since birth; who are we to bother about good and bad taste?

Why did the first among the six emotions take on so much precedence? It may be true that poetry, literature, the sixty-four arts, devotion, love, affection – all are born of *kāma* (desire). But did *krodha* (anger) generate nothing useful or enjoyable? The author of the *Srimad Bhagavad Gita* has fused kāma and krodha together in '*kāma eṣa, krodha eṣa*', where kāma and krodha are one. He would probably have called the other passions like '*lobha*' (greed) and '*moha*' (attachment) variations of kāma as well. Freud's disciples should seriously consider writing a simple interpretation of the *Srimad Bhagavad Gita.*

Non-experts like me suffer from a different misgiving – what if everyone from the Rig Veda seer to the follower of Freud has made a mistake? Did Eros come first or did hunger? Rasa does mean juice as well. Might not ādirasa mean the gastric juice? Just as the erotic complex grows newer features, might not the hunger complex do so too?

Modern psychologists say that desire undergoes a change when it is repressed or dissatisfied, and that results in the complexities of human nature. Hunger does have its dissatisfaction, but it is not intense enough, so its effect upon the human mind is less strong. Hence 'viraha' or separation has more creative strength than fasting. Of course, one must consider the word 'viraha' in a more expansive sense. All dissatisfaction is viraha, be it just or unjust, normal or abnormal, sacred or profane, and it works without the conscious mind being aware of it.

It is not that the hunger complex has no capacity to create anything. It is said that in more restrictive times, people converted just to have a taste of forbidden meat, though they gave themselves and others various spiritual reasons. Panchkari Bandyopdhyay (1866–1923) had confessed that his craving for bread had led him to forsake the orthodox faith for some time. The refined Hinduism we see nowadays is only too generous – at least where food is concerned. So, greed does not cause the mind to follow the course of religion anymore, though the inhibitions that remain in matters of marriage still cause enough mayhem in life and in novels.

Literature does not honour the gastric juices. Kalidasa's *yaksha*[4] (*Meghadūtam*) was not only lovelorn but starving as well. Still, though he described the pleasures and delights of the city of Alaka, not once did he spare a word about its cookhouses. Tagore too seems a little put off by the idea of food, but even he was not entirely able to shake off its influence. What complex was at the root of the sudden affection towards Kamala that beset the Ghazipur-bound elderly Uncle? Uncle was getting on in years, but he was not one to scoff at his meals. Deeply inhaling the aroma of food being cooked on the steamer, the old man exclaimed, 'Smells good!' Just as a young man dreams of a future conjugal life based on a smile, a sneeze, or a little cough from an unknown young woman, so the old man dreaming about a future array of dishes depending on Kamala's use of seasoning became fond of the orphan girl (*Naukadubi* or *The Boat Wreck* 1906). Of course, Freud's followers will venture a different meaning, but we are not going to listen.

Keeping the gastric juices aside, let us talk about the emotion that is strongest in the human mind. If, thanks to the transformation of kāma, we had love, devotion, art, literature, and all other good things, then why have regrets? The respectable connoisseur wants fruits and flowers and does not bother with what fertilises the roots. The prosaic scientist can dig the roots up and arrange for manure, and our respectable gentleman will not mind. It is true that organic fertiliser helps the trees to grow strong and luxurious. But no one smears manure on the fruit while enjoying it.

However, we must admit to our extreme mortification that we find satisfaction not only in fruit and flower; from time to time, we also crave for a taste of the vital juices feeding the roots as well. When a skilled artist gracefully renders that which society deems hateful or harmful, we appreciate and enjoy it. Or else grief, cruelty, lust, infidelity etcetera would not find a place in poetry, fiction, and painting.

The crux of the matter is – many of our desires have been banished to the deepest corners of our psyche due to different reasons, and quite a few of them have metamorphosed into superior attributes or sentiments. Therein lies their fulfilment. These are beneficial for society and so society cherishes them, and they are considered perfect for use in literature and other arts. But desires which do not have the capacity to metamorphose keep pushing upwards even while they are being suppressed. Society admonishes saying 'Be careful! If you really want to express yourself, do it the way we want'. But repressed desires protest that they do not want to wear a disguise and would rather manifest themselves in their own forms. They could break their prison of stone but not be compassionate towards injured feelings. The watchful artist says to them like a loving father does, 'Come, my children, I'll take you for a stroll in the sun, but you must be dressed properly, and look good. And behave yourselves; no jumping around!' The appreciative connoisseur exclaims 'Whose children are you? How attractive you are! But some of you are perhaps a little restless?' The creator explains, 'Do not worry, they won't make trouble. They have sprung from your heart, but I know how to control them. I'll beat the hell out of the disobedient, I'll make the mischievous one repent, and I'll entangle the uncontrollable in the deepest of mysteries'.

The observer is pleased and notes that 'Yes, this is what art is!' Yet some non-enthusiasts are afraid even after taking such precautions.

Another group of artists are too indulgent to their offspring. They say to their repressed desires 'What is the fear? Where is the shame? There is no need to dress up so much – strip naked, smear on paint and go and dance'. Some lustful aficionados welcome them with open arms saying, 'This is real art, primal and ultimate'. Restrained observers comment 'No, this can never be art. Art is never as impure. If that is art, then why are so many of us filled with disgust at its sight?' The authorities in society say, 'We have no truck with art and all that. But we won't allow ideals of society to decline. We are not saying that all our regulations are for the best but show us a better way of doing things if you can! And if you can't, we won't let you spoil our children in the name of self-expression. We are here and the police are with us'.

No marked boundary exists between these two categories of artists, so the only thing that sets them apart is their own degree of control. We cannot consider the question of capability because an incompetent artist can ruin an image of heaven, while a gifted artist turns a depiction of hell into a pleasurable one. It is difficult to determine where good taste ends and bad taste begins. In a particular age, some people will call a piece of art good, in the next a different group will defame it, and society will always indulge in unwarranted ramblings about art.

The Creator made the world, but man created art. The Creator is one, so we tend to perceive a system in his creation. Men are far too many, and hence there is so much dissent about their creations. The seeds of creation are inherent in the human mind; hence perhaps what the Western psychoanalyst calls libido the eastern seer calls kāma:

> Kāmastadagre samavartādhi manaso retaḥ prathamaṃ yadāsīt
> sato baṃdhumasati nirabiṃdan hṛdi pratīṣyā kavayo manīṣā[5]
>
> Rigveda 10: 129

> Kama emerged first, the first seed of the mind. / Poets and seers probed into their hearts / Discerning through their intellect the bond between the two / How being first emerged from non-being.[6]

The seer is indeed talking about the creation of the world, and we have to consider being and non-being in the spiritual sense. However, in a more expansive sense, this verse is applicable to art as well. According to Freudians, the non-being state of kāma gives rise to the state of being, that is, art. Poets and seers too might have analysed their own hearts and realised the true nature of their own arts within themselves. But the common man is yet to recognise that. Science has not yet been able to ascertain what art is and what it is not, so the disputes on good taste and bad and morality and immorality continue. If someday the parameters of art are determined, one doubts whether polite society will set its mind at rest.

We understand what rasa is but fail to make others comprehend it. Rasa is the main component of art, but there are other elements in it as well which makes it more complex. Sugar might be a pure form of rasa, but sugar by itself is inconsequential when considered as art. It is art only when it is blended skilfully with other objects of rasa. But the ingredients we have at hand are not pure objects of rasa in themselves; they do have a few incidental impurities. A wrong choice or a mistaken sense of proportion brings in an excess of inferior elements, and an unwelcome taste emerges within that which was intended. Additionally, there are the past habits of the consumer, his circumstances, and his personal likes and dislikes. One whose work goes beyond such impediments, builds the consumer's taste, does not pose an obstruction to the greater good, and persists through time is the greatest artist.

Translation: Sudeshna Datta Chaudhuri

Notes

1 Rajshekhar Bose, 'Rasa o Ruchi', in *Laghuguru*, Kolkata: M.C. Sarkar & Sons, 1949, pp. 38–44.
2 'Ādirasa', which is the first rasa, implies *śṛṅgāra* or the erotic rasa.
3 Traditionally, this verse is chanted before chanting the *gayatri mantra* (*Rigveda* 3.62.10), an everyday ritual for religious Brahmins.
4 The protagonist of Kālidāsa's *Meghadūtam*, who is banished from his native land Alaka as well as from his beloved for a year due to negligence of his duties.
5 *Rigveda-samhita*, trans. Rameshchandra Dutta, Kolkata: Bengal Government Press, 1887, pp. 737–738.
6 Re-translated following Sailendrakrishna Laha' s verse translation in Bangla, quoted by the author.

13 Jagadish Bhattacharya: The poetic mind

Introduction

Jagadish Bhattacharya (1912–2007), born in Sylhet, was a professor of Bangla at the Bangabasi College in Kolkata, India, where he later became the Principal. Brought up in the tradition of Nyaya philosophy, his work combined rational acumen and compassionate insight. His principal work was *Kavimanasi* that was serialised in *Sanibarer Chithi* from 1957. The volume, in two parts related to Tagore's life and works, *Jibanbhashya* (1962) and *Kavyabhashya* (1972), was a significant contribution to the history of Tagore studies, where he argued that Tagore's sister-in-law Kadambari Devi had been his muse consistently during the entire course of his poetic life and that his poetic self was truly awakened by her untimely death. His other critical works include *Sonneter Aloke Madhusudan o Rabindranath* (1957) and an unfinished series of commentaries on a hundred selected poems of Rabindranath called *Rabindra-Kavita-Satak* (1974–1983). Jagadish Bhattacharya edited the short stories of Tarasankar Bandyopadhyay and a series of collected poems and stories by noted authors. He also edited *Tarasankarer Galpaguchchha*, the complete short stories of Tarasankar Bandyopadhyay in three volumes from 1975 to 1977, along with a comprehensive biography of the author. However, his fame rests on his works on the study of Tagore. The text presented in this volume was delivered as the first Ramlal Halder and Haripriya Devi Memorial lecture and published as 'Bangla Sahityatattwa' (Literary Theory in Bangla) in *Sahitya-Parishat-Patrika*, Sraban–Poush 1386 BS (1979). It was subsequently included in his collection of essays, *Rabindrachitte Janachetana* (1998).

Rabindranath Tagore's essays 'Sahityer Bicharak', 'Sahityer Samagri', and 'Sahityer Tatparya' (included in this volume) were among the first attempts in Bangla literary history to look at the material sources of literature, the created text, and the reader and locate the place of the creator and reader in the act of creation. Jagadish Bhattacharya, in his essay presented here, takes these three essays as his point of departure in his quest for a contemporary literary aesthetics. However, he does not limit his enquiry to Rabindranath's writings alone but includes those of Michael Madhusudan

DOI: 10.4324/9781003224686-14

Dutt and Bankimchandra Chattopadhyay as well, placing them within a continuity of aesthetic tradition coming down from Sanskrit rhetoricians. Through a critical examination of their works, particularly Rabindranath's idea of the three fundamental constituents of poetic genius, viz. wonder, love and imagination, or empathy, he arrives at his own conclusion that a poet's genius is constituted by the three elements of *Pratibha* or genius, *Vyutpatti* or knowledge, and *Abhyas* or practice.

*

The poetic mind[1]

Jagadish Bhattacharya

*

Literature is a fine art – 'a' fine art because not all fine art is literature. Literature is the fine art with language as its medium. Needless to say, in Bangla the word *silpa* or fine art is used with different meanings. *Silpabiplab* is industrial revolution, and then Abanindranath's paintings or writings are his *Chitrasilpa* or his *Vanisilpa*. In this essay, we will use the word silpa only with reference to art.

Evaluation of art takes three key queries – who, what, and why. First, who is the creator of this art, what is his identifying characteristic, by which attribute is he fit to be deemed an artist. Second, what is art and what are its constituents, genres, and rules – in short, what is a work of art. Third, why is art created; what is its intent; whether art is meant only for the connoisseur; who can be defined as the connoisseur; and even among connoisseurs, what would be the qualities of one who would evaluate and differentiate good art from bad. These three queries may be organised into three stages: the poetic mind, the work of art itself, and the connoisseur. This essay aims to discuss the first.

The creator of verbal art is the poet or the *vākśilpī*. Such art is called 'kāvya' in Sanskrit because its creator, the poet, is the 'kavi'. However, the meaning of the word 'kāvya' does not have the same expansion in Bangla, so that not all masters of words are dubbed 'kavi' anymore. Those who compose prose and dramatic pieces are also masters of the word, but instead of 'kavi' or poet, they are generally called *sahityik* or littérateurs. Kāvya is *sāhitya*, that is, literature in Sanskrit, though the use of the word sāhitya to mean kāvya is a somewhat modern phenomenon. *Kāvyaprakāśa* by Mammaṭa (11th century CE) and *Sāhityadarpaṇa* by Viśvanātha (14th–15th century CE) are both treatises on literary theory.

The word 'sahitya' is derived from the concept of *sahitatva*, literally meaning 'coming together'. When word and meaning come together and become united as one, sahitya comes into being. In human language though, word and meaning go together anyway. So, one cannot just call the togetherness of words and their meanings as sahitya. It can only be called sahitya when this camaraderie is comely and conveys a sense of joy. He who can employ such camaraderie to convey comeliness and enjoyment is the true 'sahityik', the creator of sahitya. This classification may be expanded to call all creators of *rasasahitya* kavi or poet.

The word *kavimanas* did not exist in Sanskrit. It has been compounded later to signify 'the poetic mind'. Literally, it means just that. But the poet here is not just the maker of poetry, but the creator in the sense that every creator of sahitya or literature is a maker or poet. Kavimanas, the poetic mind here, would mean the very nature of the verbal artist's religion of the mind.

*

Is there a way to learn how the poet's mind works? Sanskrit aestheticians have stated that in the boundless world of kāvya, the poet is the only creator. His world of kāvya is created according to his tastes. His creation is exclusive of the rules ordained by fate, independent and *sui generis*. If that is so, the only way to intrude into that realm of mysteries is to know the creator through his creations. The three questions that we posed in the beginning posit the poet at one end and the connoisseur at the other, with poetry in between. According to Rabindranath, the human heart and human nature are the subjects of literature. The poet has refined his words further to state that the external world and human character receive form in the human heart and produce music. Literature is this form and music expressed through language. According to Rabindranath, neither the mind nor literature mirrors nature. The mind turns natural phenomena into an experience of its own – literature in turn transforms them into literary works. The mind, of course, may be the individual mind and the universal mind of which, Rabindranath says, the former is the poet's selfhood and the latter his shared humanity. The world is submitted to the workshop of the individual mind and the individual mind to that of the universal – it is from that higher level that literature is born. Thus, the poet deals with the inner as well as the outer workings of the world. He accepts both first with his individual mind though the shape that it takes then cannot be called literature yet. When he can perceive his experiences through the filter of the universal, the components in his mind turn into literary elements. This is the fundamental mystery of literary creation.

The connoisseur takes a completely different route. He has before him not just the universe but the world of literature created by the poet. As he enters this realm, he gradually submerges himself deeper into the joyous mysteries of the inner and the outer realms of the universe. The diagram of Figure 13.1 may help to clarify the statement.

The first thing we see here is the universe as it is. The universe has within it (1) the human world – human lives, human nature, human thoughts and feelings; (2) the natural world; and (3) the divine world. Together, they may

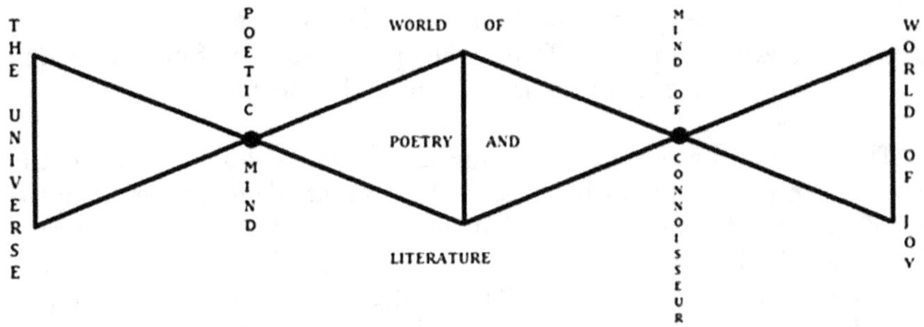

Figure 13.1

be called the truth of the universe. This truth, upon entering the poet's mind, transforms into the truth of the mind, an amalgamation of the truth of the universe and the feeling of the poetic mind. This feeling is bound to be different for every poet, given the unique nature of every poet's psyche. The world of literature lies in the middle, containing the truth of the universe, the feeling of the poetic mind, and the beauty of the verbal art, which are primarily image and music for Rabindranath. Together, they result in the experience which takes place in the connoisseur's mind. The mind of the connoisseur does not directly experience the real world in literature but the world of poetry or the world of letters. The response that it generates in the mind of the connoisseur gives rise to the world of joy. This enjoyment is the final effect of literature.

*

So, the truth of the universe and the feeling of the poetic mind, together with the beauty of the verbal art, create literature. The connoisseur, when he savours the result of this chemistry, does so not in its constituent parts but as a whole. His enjoyment is synthesised and integrated. Yet when the critic goes about his business, he does so in an analytical manner. Depending upon his taste as well as perspective, he accords more significance to the truth of the universe or the feeling of the poetic mind or the finesse of the art. Those who consider the poet's perception more important are naturally drawn more towards the mystery of the poetic mind.

One can look at Bankimchandra as an example. In his discussion of 'Iswar Chandra Gupta: His Life and Poetry', Bankimchandra says:

> No doubt there is much to be appreciated in the poetry of the poet; but it is worth much more to have comprehended the poet himself. Poetry is the mirror which harbours the poet's undistorted reflection. What is the point of appreciating just the mirror? We had better try to understand the person whose reflection it is. We have the poet's creation right in front of us – we may understand that as soon as we read it. More

> important is the question of the power and the means which enabled the poet to achieve this feat. That is the prime objective of biography and criticism, and the lesson to be learnt from the same.[2]

The aforementioned statement, while unambiguous enough, needs a little more clarification. Bankimchandra's analysis is centred on the poet's mind to which he accords more importance than the craft of poetry. The critic must consider (1) with which qualities and (2) with which means the poet has achieved the mastery of his craft. That is 'the prime objective of biography and the criticism'. Bankimchandra has shown how this may be achieved. According to him, poetry is merely the mirror of the poetic mind. That mirror has 'the poet's undistorted reflection'. The critic must identify the poet from the reflection. In other words, according to Bankimchandra, there is no other way to know the creator apart from his creation. This literary theory may be called *srishti-srashta-vada* or one centred on the created and the creator. The creator's identity is in the creation. Bankimchandra has applied this theory while discussing the works of Dinabandhu Mitra and Iswar Chandra Gupta. He has not only disregarded the constituents, genres, and rules of art, but has also stated that 'it is worth much more to have comprehended the poet himself'. Of the three questions – who, why, and what – to be asked of art, he has attached maximum significance to the seeking of the true nature of the poet's mind in literary criticism, albeit through the creation of the poet.

Nevertheless, Bankimchandra has also discussed the lives of Dinabandhu Mitra and Iswar Chandra Gupta. One might argue about the necessity of discussing the personal life of the poet separately, when his poetry apparently is the key to knowing him. Apparently, the necessity lies in seeking out the distinguishing features of the poet's mind in his personal life. This point of view is similar to that of T.S. Eliot's. Eliot is considered as a pioneer of a movement where criticism is based on the craft of poetry. However, even Eliot said in his 1956 speech, 'The Frontiers of Criticism', that those who thought that the biography of a poet should not be written had no real argument. The biographer should know how to select his material, have good taste, and good judgement as well. He should respect the work of the poet whose biography he has undertaken to write. Eliot has also said that even the critic who demonstrates interest in the work of a certain poet is expected to know something about his life as well.

Bankimchandra possesses all of these fine attributes. The introductions that he has written for Dinabandhu Mitra's works and Iswar Chandra Gupta's volume of poetry are divided into two parts – Life and Poetry. The biographical section is short but well selected. In the section on poetry, the discussion of the poetic mind held greater significance than the craft of poetry. The discussion of the biographical elements served as an effective introduction to the knowledge of the poetic mind. While discussing

Dinabandhu, Bankimchandra says, 'Dinabandhu travelled widely and came across many different kinds of people. What he learnt helped him create a multitude of fascinating characters in his books. His plays exhibit a wealth of characters unparalleled in Bangla literature'.[3] Again he states that 'Many of his works are based on incidents and several characters have been inspired by living personalities'.[4] While examining his works, Bankimchandra points out how his extensive and immediate experiences had a distinct bearing on his writing. 'Most of the time, Dinabandhu worked like a trained sculptor or a painter, drawing from a live model. Whenever he spotted a social monkey perched on the social tree, he captured it in his writings, tail and all'.[5]

Speaking of Iswarchandra, Bankimchandra said:

> His greatest characteristic was that he was an admirer of authenticity, and hated the fake. When he was 10 years old, his mother died. His father Harinarayan married a second time after a short while. . . . What Iswar Chandra did then was a testament to his character. . . . His first encounter with the fake occurred with the coming of his stepmother. The true mother had vanished – a counterfeit mother had appeared to take her place. He could not take it anymore, and hurled a wooden rule at the stepmother. Thankfully, the rule chose an even more inane object to strike and wedged itself in a banana plant.
>
> Weapon wasted like the Kirata-defeated Arjuna, Iswar Chandra shut himself up in a room all day. Sadly, no trident-armed Siva appeared to grant him a boon, but his uncle with a slipper in his hand. He broke open the door, beat Iswar Chandra up and left.
>
> And Iswar Chandra discovered his ultimate weapon.[6]

Bankimchandra commented upon the reflection of this incident in Iswar Chandra's writings in one unforgettable sentence: 'He preserved that slipper for the rest of the social order'.[7]

Bankimchandra was a prime example of Eliot's biographer with both good taste and good judgement. Rabindranath, who we may call a neo-humanist, was hesitant about bringing in discussion about the personal life of the poet into the study of his poetry. Tennyson's biography, along with his personal letters, was published in two large volumes after his death by his son. Rabindranath criticised it heavily in the essay 'Kavijibani' ('A Poet's Biography'), saying that

> It may be Tennyson's biography, but it is not the life of a poet. . . . The way he composed his poetry did not match the way he managed his life. His life was not his poetry. His poetry did not take root in his everyday conversations and correspondence, nor in his accomplishments, his activities or appointments.[8]

A month before this essay, Rabindranath wrote a poem called 'Kavicharit' ('A Poet's Life') in *Bangadarsan*. The closing lines run:

> Trapped in a human form,
> Weighed down by each moment,
> Shaken by praise and blame
> You will not find the poet in his life-story.[9]

Needless to say, Rabindranath has tried to show the difference between the poet's biography and the poetic biography. The aforementioned poem begins: 'Watch me not as an outsider/Gaze not at me out there'. This gaze is what results in the poet's biography. But the poetic biography can be divined not from a study of the poet's self, but from his humanity; not from outside, but from within. Again, the same poem says,

> Made of dreams, I walk a hidden path,
> I do not know myself, nor can I make you see,
> Overwhelmed by my own song,
> I am the poet, who can find me.[10]

It is true that in most cases, the personal life and the poetic life of the poet are not the same. The poet Sri Madhusudan is by nature essentially different from Michael M.S. Dutt in Bangla literature. An analysis of the personal life of Madhusudan does not yield a clue to his poetic mind. That, however, is not applicable everywhere. According to Rabindranath, 'if there is a separation in the true poet between his selfhood and his humanity, it is merely the transparent glass-pane of imagination. It is not a barrier to knowing each other'.[11]

When that difference diminishes, the poet's biography and poetic biography become as one. While discussing Tennyson's biography, Rabindranath commented,

> A great man's brilliance may shine through in both his life and his works – both his poetry as well his activities are the result of the same genius. If we look at their poetry through their lives, the significance of that poetry becomes more expansive, more intense. Dante's life is intertwined with his poetry. When we read the two together, the dignity of both is increased.[12]

At the age of fifty, ten years after he wrote 'A Poet's Life', when Rabindranath began writing his autobiography *Jibansmriti*, the same question came up in his mind again. The manuscript says at one point that 'the creation of poetry and the composition of life are parts of a single, greater opus',[13] and 'as the poet's life expresses his poetry, so does his poetry reorganise his life'.[14]

That is why, for a consideration of the poetic life, it is necessary to observe the poet's life from within. Rabindranath has held that the poet is by nature Saiva, an imbiber of poison. He swallows the poison thrown up by the churning of his life and serves the manna of poetry to society at large. Rabindranath's poem 'Kavya' says the same about the poet Kālidāsa:

Did you not suffer the same hurt and cheer,
The same hope and despair just as we do,
O poet immortal! Did you not suffer
The royal court, with all its plots and intrigues?
Were you not ever humiliated,
Mistrusted, judged wrong, neglected,
Deprived cruelly? Did you never
Pass a sleepless night because of a pierced heart?
Yet you have risen untouched, serene,
Your poetry blossoming forth in beauty
Like a lotus towards the sun. That joy
Hints at no pain, no need, nor hardship.
Taking the venom that rose out of life
You bestowed the manna that followed.[15]

One might say after analysing this poem that the chemical workshop of the poet's mind transmutes the poison emerging from his life into the ambrosia of poetry.

*

As we seek the nature of the poet's mind, we may turn to another statement by Rabindranath. He said, 'We have to look into two things while judging literature. First, to what extent does the author's heart have a hold over the world – second, how much of that hold has been disclosed in a permanent form?'[16] The first part of this quote is about the poet's mind. The value of a poetic mind is measured by the extent to which its heart can claim its hold over the world. Rabindranath also states that 'Literature is dependent not primarily on objects of knowledge, but on those of feeling'.[17] We need to note the word 'primarily', which indirectly acknowledges objects of knowledge as having the potential to sustain literature as well. However, in the first statement, Rabindranath talks about the heart of the poet and the claim it may lay upon the world, that is an individual with compassion is a poet. Psychology divides the mind of the human being in three parts – thinking, feeling, and willing. Feeling is the religion of the heart. Both thinking and willing are steeped in feeling to become objects of emotion. In that case, it remains to be considered exactly how far it is practical to call the poet's genius merely intellect or wisdom. Sanskrit has two words for genius – '*aghaṭanaghaṭanapaṭīyasībuddhi*',[18] an intellect skilled in causing unusual occurrences, and '*apūrvavastunirmāṇakṣamāprajñā*',[19] a wisdom capable of shaping unprecedented matter. That particular intellect and that particular wisdom have been together called genius, and that genius may belong to any field. It remains to be considered whether intellect and wisdom may be attributed to the creation of poetry. Sanskrit has a few other terms which may be analysed in this respect – memory, perspicacity, intellect, wisdom, and genius. Memory lets us know the past, perspicacity lets us divine the future, and intellect lets us perceive the present. These are the three worldly functions of knowledge. Wisdom and genius occupy the top level on this circuit of knowledge. Wisdom extends through three ages of past, present, and future and is an assured knowledge principle. It is the very basic condition of a theoretical or doctrinal dispensation. Genius too extends over the three ages, but its distinctive characteristic is to bring in new creations, again and again. If intellect is a worldly function of knowledge, then it cannot be called poetic genius by any hyperbolic embellishment. Similarly, if wisdom is an assured principle of knowledge extending over the three ages, it is better to call it a genius for science or philosophy. Though it might shape unprecedented matter, it cannot be a measure of poetic genius. The main task of poetic genius is to portray an artistic expression of life in a language resounding with joy, meaning, and significance. Poetic genius may be called the power of creating exquisite expressions, richly entwined with life.

Bankimchandra's definitions may also be iterated in this regard. Bankimchandra had segregated human faculties into three categories – the pursuit of knowledge, the pursuit of action, and the pursuit of entertainment, for oneself or for others.[20] The poet's mind is immersed not in the first two but in the last one. The natural tendency of the heart is to bring shades of joy. So it follows that the claim the heart of the poet may make upon the world is the sole yardstick by which one may evaluate poetic genius.

Madhusudan, the first of the modern poets in Bangla, wrote a sonnet[21] on poetic genius:

> Who's a poet – who can tell me? The matchmaker
> Of words, is that what he is? Wielding his pen,
> Does he conquer death? Does the circlet of fame
> Sit on his crown unchanged and undimmed?
> He who the muse Imagination visits,
> Alighting upon the flower of his heart,
> Casts a sunset glow on his world of feelings
> With her many-hued light; I call him a poet.
>
> Joy, regret, anger are his to command,
> His wishes bloom in the flowers of the wild,
> He fetches for all from the garden of the gods
> The sweet fragrance of the Parijat flower.
> Pleased by him, the spirit of the river
> Flows in sweet murmur in an arid land.

The first quartet has a question. Is the matchmaker of words the true poet, the conqueror of death? There might be a couple of reasons behind this query. Clearly, any artist whose talent exhausts itself in putting a few matching words together is merely a manipulator of words, and Madhusudan does not acknowledge such a wordsmith as a true poet. Matchmaking needs effort; it does not hint at the spontaneous concert of form and content. Besides, he might have also been reminded of the rhetoric-laden doggerels written by the kabiwallahs who appeared in Bengal after Bharatchandra.

The next four lines talk about the true poet. 'He who the muse Imagination visits/Alighting upon the flower of his heart,/Casts a sunset glow on his world of feelings/With her many-hued light'. Madhusudan accords the highest position to Imagination in the context of poetic genius. In *Meghnad Badh Kavya* too, he invoked Imagination right after the goddess Saraswati:

> Come, Imagination, my lady honeybee,
> Gather nectar from the poet's thought-garden
> And create a hive from which Gauda people
> Will happily taste ambrosia forever.[22]

Imagination is likened to a honeybee, who gathers the nectar from the flowers of the poet's thoughts and transforms it into honey which is ambrosia for the connoisseur who tastes it. The poet here might be Madhusudan himself or poets in general. We will take this up again when we talk of origins. Imagination has elsewhere been named as Saraswati's dearest friend.[23] This sonnet does not have Saraswati in it, though it is only Lady Imagination who has taken up residence in the poet's mind, and that has resulted in his poetry being illuminated in sunset colours. Madhusudan perhaps knew that the opulence of the human world lasted only as long as the sunset colours of the clouds – *sandhyābhravibhramanibhāvibhavābhave'smin* – but these colours remain forever in the world of imagination created by the poet. Madhusudan's way with words captivated Rabindranath as well. Rabindranath used similar words to discuss Biharilal Chakraborty's (1835–1894) poetry, when he said, 'The golden couplets of *Saradamangal* hint at various splendours like the gold-lined clouds at sunset'.[24]

Thus the octave tries to ascertain the importance of imagination in poetic genius. Madhusudan was the first to accord importance to imagination instead of wit and wisdom in Bangla literary theory. We are not going to talk about classical and romantic literary characteristics here. Madhusudan is proficient in classical literature, yet his own distinctive trait is Romantic. Besides, the differences between classical and romantic literature might be alluring to theorists, but they are not that important to the connoisseur.

The sestet sees the poet looking across the three worlds. First, the human world – 'Joy, regret, anger are his to command'; second, nature – 'His wishes bloom in the flowers of the wild'; third, the world of gods – 'He fetches for all from the garden of the gods/ The sweet fragrance of the Parijat flower'. In all three areas, the poet's imagination not only encompasses the three worlds, but he himself is the creator as well. His wishes make human thoughts appear in poetry and flowers blossom in the forest, and it is he who can bring the fragrance of the Parijat flower from heaven to earth. This last section reminds us of Rabindranath's 'Puraskar':

> From the perilous peak of creation
> The world cascades down
> To the canyon of infinite time,
> Ever in murmuring music.
> The sound waves of stars and planets
> Running directionless in space;
> I'll draw a stream of music
> From these in my humble flute.[25]

Madhusudan wants to spread the perfume of heavenly flowers in the human world, and Rabindranath wants to draw the cosmic music in his modest instrument.

The last two lines of Madhusudan's sonnet depict his final realisation about the poet's achievement – 'Pleased by him, the spirit of the river/Flows in sweet murmur in an arid land'. Madhusudan has used the image of the parched wanderer in the desert land several times in his poetry. In his poem 'Atmabilap', the image appears with a twinge of regret: 'The mirage in the desert/Kills with thirst and craving',[26] and in *Meghnad Badh Kavya*, Sita says to Vibhisana's wife Sarama that 'You are like the brook in the desert to me,/ O wife of the Rakshasa!'[27] Our ancestors used to say that the poison-tree of human life yields two ambrosial fruits – the company of good men and the delight of good poetry. Madhusudan sees human life as the parched traveller, who receives his water of life in the form of poetry. It is a rich and evocative image, true to the poetic life.

*

Rabindranath, the first theorist of Bangla literary theory, has considered three components that make up poetic genius – wonder, love, and empathy.[28] In 'The Significance of Literature', the first essay of *Sahitya*, he says:

> There are also a few fortunate people whose wonder, love and imagination/empathy are ever active – they are always welcome in every corner of nature; various movements in the world of people keep the harp of their heart vibrating in many tunes.
>
> The outside world emerges in their inner beings in various rasas, colours and shapes of the heart's disposition.
>
> This world of the contemplative person is closer than external reality to other people. This world, with the help of the former's heart, becomes easily accessible through feeling in hearts of the people. The unique

> quality that this world gains through the impact of the contemplative heart, becomes most delightful to others.[29]

We will analyse Rabindranath's idea of wonder, love, and empathy later. Let us return to the quote at hand, which makes a few things clear. Since Rabindranath is of the opinion that 'literature is dependent not primarily on objects of knowledge, but on those of feeling', he uses the word 'contemplative'. Needless to say, the creation of poetry necessitates the combination of a gift for contemplation and a flair for activity. According to Rabindranath, poetry is expression itself. Also, poetic genius is neither self-generating nor independent of space and time. Poets are also social beings. That is why every aspect of nature calls to them, and their heart is full of echoes of various movements in the world of people. Third, the inner world of the poet delights the reader more than the outer world. That is because the outer world has reshaped itself in diverse colours, flavours, and forms within the poet's heart, and the poet's empathy makes this world more accessible to others. The distinction it gains because of the contemplative heart makes it utterly gratifying for others.

Discussing that aspect of poetic genius which makes this possible, Rabindranath mentions wonder, love, and empathy. Wonder or 'vismaya' is the sthāyibhāva of adbhuta rasa in Sanskrit rasaśāstra. Viśvanātha Kavirāja[30] has stated in *Sāhityadarpaṇa* that, that which induces an expansion of the consciousness beyond the boundaries of this world is called vismaya. Vismaya is a state of the mind's astonishment. Quoting Dharmadatta, Viśvanātha has also said that this astonishment is the core of all rasas, and it may be felt everywhere. Rabindranath, however, has not kept the meaning of vismaya confined to 'expansion of the consciousness' alone, but has generally brought it within his literary theory as the sense of unfathomable mystery. According to him, the feeling that leads to a new apprehension of the old may be called wonder. In *Jibansmriti*, he talks about a song heard in childhood, 'Tomay bidesini sajiye ke dile' ('Who dressed you up like a lady from a faraway land'), which had a great impact on his song 'Ami chini go chini tomare, ogo bidesini' ('I know you, yes I do, O lady from a faraway land'). In this context, he has stated:

> There is a lady from a faraway land who resides in this world of ours – her home lies beyond an unknown sea – it is she who appears from time to time in autumn mornings and spring nights – she appears sometimes in flashes within the heart, and her voice may be heard in the wind if we listen closely.[31]

Wonder takes the poet 'beyond an unknown sea'. If we go by Sanskrit rasa theory, then the principal rasa of Rabindranath's *Balaka* (1916) is adbhuta, and its sthāyibhāva is vismaya. In the poem 'Balaka' (*Balaka* 36), he talks about the 'awakening of wonder' in the world:

O feathered pageant!
Your wings are drunk with the heady wine of the tempest,
Awakening waves of wonder across the sky
In wild joyous laughter.
That sound of wings,
A sound-nymph flitting by
Rouses silence from its austerities.
The mountains sunk in darkness
Woke up quivering,
And quivered the deodar forest.[32]

Further, this quivering was not just in the rows of deodar trees. The wonder-struck poet felt that

The hill wished to be a summer cloud astray;
The trees wanted to spread their wings,
And cast off the earthly fetters,
Follow that echo and lose themselves in a flash,
To seek the rim of the sky.[33]

He saw,

The teeming grass
Flutter their plumes on the sky of the earth.
Beneath the darkness of the soil, unknown
Seedlings open their wings,
Like a thousand cranes.[34]

And,

Stars flail their wings of light,
Their cry
Startling the dark.[35]

Not just in the natural world, but in the human world too, thoughts and messages fly thick and unseen through the past into the undisclosed, far future. The poet, too, feels his wings unfolding:

With those countless birds
By light of day or night,
This homeless bird flies through shade and sunshine,
From one edge to another.[36]

The same wonder makes the poet marvel at the sight of 'A drop of dew/ Sparkling upon an ear of paddy'.[37]

The poet's oneness with the world commences with the sense of wonder. Love expands this sense. Love here means love for life and the universe. This love unites the individual with the world. In a letter to Lokendranath Palit, Rabindranath says:

> The poet harbours his personal nature within, and sees another, social, human nature outside his being. When these two become as one due to experience, affection and sheer capability, new poetry is generated. Both natures remain entwined in this poetry, otherwise it does not come to life.[38]

In the poem 'Visvanritya,' the poet says:

> My heart aches to merge
> With the spirit of humanity –
> To take the great road of life
> Day and night.[39]

That desire to merge, to be one with humanity, may be termed as love from the point of view of the poet. Rabindranath has considered poetic genius to be 'the universal human heart'. It may be said that this transformation is achieved through love.

The third attribute that Rabindranath speaks about is empathy or imagination, which carries a special implication in Rabindranath's literary theory. Speaking on the significance of literature, he says,

> The power that lets our union with the world become more than just a sensual encounter, lets it turn into a union of hearts, is that of empathy. Empathy turns this union into a way of the heart, and makes us feel at one with all that is disconnected from our beings.[40]

Love is an engagement of the heart, empathy, that of consciousness. Love makes the individual merge into the consciousness of the world; empathy makes the individual enter the hearts of many. It is by virtue of empathy that the poet is able to gain entry into the hearts of the common people. Imagination leads the poet to the truth about human nature and human life and perhaps even the non-human world as well. We can look at an example from Rabindranath in his poem 'Basundhara':

> The fierce forest tiger –
> His immense strength within his immense body,
> Bears effortlessly; – his body flame-bright
> Like a veiled bolt of fire
> Under the forest-cloud, his thundering roar
> As he leaps lightning-swift suddenly

Upon his prey; that simple glory
That joy of intense violence, that splendour bright,
I wish I had a taste of that but once.[41]

It is this imagination which lets the poet experience the mental image of the fierce tiger leaping upon its prey in rapacious joy, like lightning beneath the forest canopy.

The difference in degree of wonder, love, and empathy in poets leads to differences in form and merit in the world of art. All three attributes are present in the poetic mind; but some possess more wonder, some more love while others more empathy, and that makes all the difference as it sets apart and brings out individual qualities in poets and authors.

We have said before that poets too are social creatures. They can rarely avoid being influenced by time and space. However, while they conform to an age, they also transcend it. Their conformity makes them give prime importance to material reality, and their transcendence lets them become one with the universal spirit of humanity of all times. It is not that poets are different only due to differences in country of origin, period, and social system. Poets originating in the same country, in the same age, and within the same social system may show much diversity as well. This occurs because of the distinction of the poetic temperament. The reason for this dissimilarity may either be sought in the combination of wonder, love, and imagination in each poet or in the degree of their conformity and transcendence. We can take three great authors of modern Bangla literature in this context – Bibhutibhushan Bandyopadhyay (1894–1950), Tarasankar Bandyopadhyay (1898–1971), and Manik Bandyopadhyay (1908–1956). All three are from the same country, of the same period, and emerging from almost similar social circumstances. Yet, any connoisseur will consider them to be unique storytellers of disparate categories.

*

In this context, the consideration of vyutpatti or knowledge becomes important. In the past, there has been a debate about the source for poetic capability – genius or knowledge. The majority of critics agree that poetic genius is the main force behind the composition of poetry. But some do say that the original and primary reason for writing poems is one's poetic prowess. The latter is further cultivated by genius and knowledge. There is yet a third opinion which says that poetic prowess and poetic genius are one and the same.

Whether we call it prowess or genius, this attribute is undeniably developed through knowledge. Knowledge has two components – direct experience and erudition. To repeat the quote from 'The Significance of Literature', the poet is invited to experience each aspect of nature, and the many human incidents make the harp of his heart resonate with many melodies. The poet cannot remain unaffected by his time and space nor his community, since he is a social being. Traditions and heritage influence him, as do contemporary issues, changing scenarios, and current thoughts and ideas. Traditions and history are particularly active in the structure of the poetic mind as Rabindranath also accepts:

> I feel you move in the core of my being.
> Your invisible script writes on each page of my life
> The story of my forefathers, mixing them with my blood.[42]

Contemporary queries about human life reverberate within the poetic mind. Besides, experiences of human life and character are indispensable for a life-oriented work of art. This real-life experience is further enhanced by erudition. The poet must be proficient in the literature of the present as well as the past, his own country as well of other lands. As Emerson said about Shakespeare that 'The greatest genius is the most indebted man'.[43] It is true of our literature as well. A poet might borrow a word, a sentence, or even a verse from another, but his ability to awaken new meaning out of it is what makes him an undisputed creditor for ages to come; he subsists on all, while the world subsists on him.

The other aspect of this proficiency is the knowledge of the associated branches of literature. The successful and efficient poet must also be proficient in diction, rhetoric, and prosody. There may be many composers with a natural poetic ability, but, even with their untrained ability in mind, we cannot deny that only a littérateur who has attained sophistication in his writings through study and practice is able to create a perfect piece of literature. Not only that, but the constant polishing of one's own work is also essential. Sanskrit theoreticians have always stated that genius, knowledge, and practice together result in the excellence of literature. Sanskrit theories therefore discuss much about the education of a poet and the ideal way of living as a poet, with an emphasis on a chaste and virtuous lifestyle as well as on artistry in the case of the latter. However, whether a poet needs to lead a virtuous lifestyle must be a matter of debate in all countries, across all ages. This is the issue we hinted at when we were discussing the poet's biography and the poetic biography. Moreover, the ideal way of living as a poet also must be realistically different for each country, era, and society. The connoisseur will agree, if not all others, that genius, knowledge, and practice are three prime constituent attributes in the poetic mind that result in the excellence of literature.

*

We have attempted an analysis of the true nature of the poetic mind in Bangla literary theory. We would like to close this discussion with a poem of mine:

> Tattered robes patched up with vibrant threads,
> Clad in crafted saffron,
> The Baul at dawn.

With an ektara in his hand,
And ankle bells tinkling as he walks
In awe, full of wonder.

As night ends, the solitary field
Lies softened by dew.
Leaning on the annihilating trident
Mahakal
Is mirrored in the crescent moon
As Ardhanariswar.[44]

The poet has been called the Baul at dawn, the minstrel at the ever-renewed commencement of creation. He patches up the worn robe of life with the vibrant threads of his imagination and crafts a unique saffron attire to cover himself. He adores his 'moner manush', his inner being. He is devoted yet dispassionate. So he wears saffron and plays a single-string lute. He sings a song of awakening and brings melodious affability to the wayfarer's journey. His eyes are full of wonder. The solitary field at the end of the night is the emptiness after the *pralaya* or destruction at the end of an epoch. Yet, he sees the hints of a new beginning in the softness of the dewdrops. His gaze is focused on a single image at the end of the poem:

Leaning on the annihilating trident
Mahakal
Is mirrored in the crescent moon
As Ardhanariswar.

He sees the all-destroying trident and the crescent moon at the same time. Mahakal or Eternal Time does not grasp the trident but rests his weary head on it. The moon reflects a different likeness of him as the Ardhanariswar – the composite god, the lord who is half woman – that has suggestions of a new creation. The one who sings the song of awakening on the path of the endless journey of human beings through creation and destruction, the Baul's mind is emblematic of the poet's mind. The dawn that is mentioned here is constantly in the process of arriving – at the end of darkness, it is forever radiant.

Translation: Sudeshna Datta Chaudhuri

Notes

1 Jagadish Bhattacharya, 'Kavimanas', in *Rabindrachitte Janachetana*, Kolkata: Bharabi, 1998, pp. 333–350. The essay was first published in *Sahitya-Parishat-Patrika*, 1979, 86(2–3): 3–20.
2 Bankimchandra Chattopadhyay, 'Jibancharit O Kavitwa', (Introduction to the Collected Poems of *Iswar Chandra Gupta*, 1885), in *Bankim Rachanabali*, Vol. II, Kolkata: Sahitya Samsad, 1954 (Rep. 1998), p. 781.

3 Bankimchandra Chattopadhyay, 'Roy Dinabandhu Mitra Bahadurer Jibani o Granthabalir Samalochana' (A Biography and Criticism of the works of Roy Dinabandhu Mitra Bahadur, 1877), in *Bankim Rachanabali*, Vol. II, op. cit., p. 753.
4 Ibid., p. 755.
5 Ibid., p. 759.
6 Bankimchandra Chattopadhyay, 'Jibancharit O Kavitwa', op. cit., p. 765.
7 Ibid., p. 765.
8 Rabindranath Tagore, 'Kavijibani', *Bangadarsan* (New Series), 1901, 1(3): 124–128, 125.
9 Rabindranath Tagore, 'Kavicharit', *Bangadarsan* (New Series), 1901, 1(2): 105–106. The poem was later incorporated as Poem No. 21 in *Utsarga* (1914).
10 Ibid.
11 Rabindranath Tagore, 'Sahitya Samalochana', *Bangadarsan* (New Series), 1903, 3(6): 284–290, 288. The essay was reissued as 'Sahityer Bicharak' in *Sahitya* (1907). See 'The Judge of Literature', in this volume.
12 Rabindranath Tagore, 'Kavijibani', op. cit., p. 126.
13 RBVBMS 146 (i), p. 1. The manuscript is with Rabindra Bhavana, Visva-Bharati.
14 Ibid.
15 Rabindranath Tagore, 'Kavya', in *Chaitali*, *Kavya Granthabali*, Kolkata: Adi Barhmosamaj Press, 1896, p. 426.
16 Rabindranath Tagore, 'Sahityer Tatparya', *Bangadarsan* (New Series), 1903, 3(8): 358–362. See 'The Meaning of Literature', in this volume.
17 Rabindranath Tagore, 'Sahityer Samagri', *Bangadarsan* (New Series), 1903, 3(7): 317–322. See 'The Material of Literature', in this volume.
18 Attributed to Bhaṭṭa Tauta in *Kāvyakautuka*. See P. V. Kane, *History of Sanskrit Poetics*, Delhi, Varanasi and Patna: Matilal Banarasidass, 1971, p. 349.
19 Abhinavagupta in Dhvanyalokalocana. See P. V. Kane, *History of Sanskrit Poetics*, op. cit., p. 349.
20 Bankimchandra Chattopadhyay, 'Anusilan', in *Dharmmatattva*, *Bankim Rachanabali*, Vol. II, Kolkata: Sahitya Samsad, 1954 (Rep. 1998), p. 535.
21 Michael Madhusudan Dutt, 'Kavi', Sonnet 16, *Chaturdashpadi Kavitabali*', in *Madhusudan Rachanabali*, Kolkata: Sahitya Samsad, 1965 (Rep. 1999), p. 162.
22 Michael Madhusudan Dutt, *Meghnadbadh Kavya* (1861)', in *Madhusudan Rachanabali*, op. cit., p. 35.
23 Michael Madhusudan Dutt, 'Kalpana', Sonnet 38, in *Chaturdashpadi Kavitabali*, op. cit, p. 167.
24 Rabindranath Tagore, 'Biharilal', *Sadhana*, 1894, 3(8): 126–155.
25 Rabindranath Tagore, 'Puraskar', *Sonar Tari*, Kolkata: Kalidas Chakraborty, 1894, p. 172.
26 Michael Madhusudan Dutt, 'Atmabilap', *Madhusudan Rachanabali*, op. cit., p. 186.
27 Michael Madhusudan Dutt, *Meghnadbadh Kavya* (1861), *Madhusudan Rachanabali*, op. cit., p. 72.
28 Translator's note: The Bangla word 'kalpana' in the source text has been translated as 'imagination' in the context of Madhusudan Dutt and 'empathy' in that of Tagore following Bhattacarya's argument.
29 Rabindranath Tagore, 'Sahityer Tatparya'. The essay was later included in the collection *Sahitya*.
30 A Sanskrit rhetorician of the 14th to 15th centuries and author of *Sāhityadarpaṇa*.
31 Rabindranath Tagore, 'An Essay on Music', in *Jibansmriti*, Kolkata: Adi Brahmosamaj Press, 1912, p. 147.
32 Rabindranath Tagore, 'Balaka', *Sabuj Patra*, Vol. II, No. VII, Kartik 1322 (October–November 1915), pp. 418–421.

33 Ibid.
34 Ibid.
35 Ibid.
36 Ibid.
37 Rabindranath Tagore, 'Verse 127, dated 7 Paush 1336 B.S. (December 1929)', in *Sphulinga*, Kolkata: Visvabharati, 1945, p. 130.
38 Rabindranath Tagore, 'Patralap', in Appendix to *Sahitya*, *Rabindra Rachanabali*, Vol. VIII, Kolkata: Visvabharati, 1941, p. 469.
39 Rabindranath Tagore, 'Bishwanritya', in *Sonar Tari*, op. cit., p. 122.
40 Rabindranath Tagore, 'Sahityer Tatparya', *Prabasi*, 1934, 34.1(5): 627–635, 630.
41 Rabindranath Tagore, 'Basundhara', *Sonar Tari*, op. cit., p. 184.
42 Rabindranath Tagore, 'Katha Kao, Katha Kao', in *Katha, Kavya-Grantha*, Vol. V, Mohitchandra Sen (ed.), Kolkata: Majumdar Library, 1903, pp. 97–98.
43 Ralph Waldo Emerson, 'Shakespeare; or, the Poet', in *Representative Men: Seven Lectures*, *Complete Works of Ralph Waldo Emerson*, Vol. IV, Boston and New York: Houghton Mifflin Co., 1904, p. 189. The essay was read as a lecture in Exeter Hall in London in June 1848.
44 Jagadish Bhattacharya, 'Bhorer Baul', *Ekti Alor Pakhi* (1972), in *Jagadish Bhattacharyer Srestha Kavita*, Kolkata: Bharabi, 1992, p. 17.

14 Rabindranath Tagore: Three essays from *Literature*

Introduction

Rabindranath Tagore (1861–1941) was the son of Debendranath Tagore, an eminent religious reformer of the 19th century. The impact of Tagore's genius was felt on every form of literary creation, and he also deeply influenced critical, philosophical, and sociopolitical thought in India. He was the first recipient of the Nobel Prize in literature (1913) from Asia for his collection of poems *Gitanjali* (1910) translated as *Song Offerings* (1912). His literary theory and aesthetics, which had connections between the creative self, the many traditions of India, and several literary cultures of the world, are integrated with his varied activities in the public domain. His major contributions to literary criticism and aesthetics are *Prachin Sahitya* (1907), *Lokasahitya* (1907), *Sahitya* (1907), *Adhunik Sahitya* (1907), *Sahityer Pathe* (1936), and *Sahityer Swarup* (1943). However, his thoughts on such areas are also to be found in numerous essays and lectures related to religion, the human personality and education, and also in letters written throughout his life.

Nearly a decade after *Bangadarsan*, the literary journal founded by Bankimchandra Chattopadhyay, went out of publication, Tagore revived it in a 'New Series' in 1901, as one of his many editorial endeavours. He followed the path set by Chattopadhyay in the section on literature and culture but moved away from some of his prescriptive concerns and set out to look for the fundamentals of literary criticism and thought related to the origin of literature, its nature, and the place of the reader in the creative circuit. Tagore's early ideas on literary theory are consolidated in three essays 'The Judge of Literature', 'The Material of Literature,' and 'The Significance of Literature' published between September and December 1903. Among other details in the essays, he takes up elements constituting the literary universe, namely, the external world, the inner mind, and the universal mind; questions of knowledge and feeling linked with the question of truth and its establishment; the material of literature, chiefly image and music; and the joy in creativity echoing the joy of the creator in the creative act. A central concern in the articles is the attempt to establish a deep, extensive, and

DOI: 10.4324/9781003224686-15

enduring relationship with other human hearts and with external nature. It is possible to read his literary theory from various perspectives today including that of a cultural ecology where literature and the arts bring about complex transformations of energetic processes.

Tagore's prose works were collected in the sixteen-volume *Gadya-granthabali*, published from Majumdar Library, Kolkata, between 1907 and 1909. The fourth volume of the series was entitled *Sahitya* (1907), where some of his essays on literary theory and a few reviews were anthologised. The first three essays from *Sahitya* appear in this volume arranged in a thematic order. Readers may find a further reading of these three pieces in Jagadish Bhattacharya's essay included in this volume.

*

The significance of literature[1]

Rabindranath Tagore

The world outside enters our mind and becomes a separate world. It not only has the external world's colour, sound, and shape, but also contains our likes and dislikes, joys and sorrows, fears and surprises – it gets illuminated in various ways by diverse rasas of our heart's disposition.

We submit the world to the heart's disposition and make the external world particularly our own.

But just as some are unable to convert food from outside to provide nourishment to their body due to insufficient digestive juice, likewise some people cannot sufficiently use the absorbing rasas of their heart for the outside world. They are unable to make the external world their own, a part of their inner world or the world of human beings.

There are some people who are inert and interested in very few things in the world – although born in this world, they are deprived of its largest portion. The windows of their heart are few and narrow, and so they remain as strangers to the world.

There are also a few fortunate people whose wonder, love, and imagination are ever active – they are always welcome in every corner of nature; various movements in the world of people keep their heart's harp vibrating in many tunes.

The outside world takes shape in their mind in various rasas, colours, and shapes of the heart's disposition.

The world of the contemplative person is closer to other people than external reality. His heart makes this world accessible to the people through their feelings. The unique quality of the contemplative heart has an impact on this world that becomes most delightful to others.

Hence, we can see that there is a difference between the external world and the human world. The latter not only brings information about the black and the white, the small and the big, it also speaks in many tunes about the pleasant and the unpleasant, the beautiful and the ugly, the good and the bad.

This human world has been moving like a stream through all our hearts. The stream is both old and forever new. As this ancient stream moves through new hearts and new sensibilities, it gets constantly renewed.

But how do we get hold of this stream and retain it? Unless this exquisite inner world is given form and again manifested before the outside world, it will get created and then destroyed again and again. But it does not want to be destroyed. The heart's world is anxious to express itself, and that is the reason for man's eternal passion for literature.

Two things need to be investigated while judging literature. First, to what extent does the author's heart have a hold over the world – second, how much of that hold has been disclosed in a permanent form?

Often there is no correlation between the two, but when there is, it becomes a rare and great occasion.

The more the heart of the imaginative poet is extended over the world, the more we can derive satisfaction from the depth of his writings. The boundaries of our human world also expand, enlarging the space of our eternal journeys.

But the excellence of craft in writing is also very precious. This is because the force of expression based on a substance, however inconsequential, is never totally destroyed. It gets stored within language and literature. It enhances man's ability to express. Human beings always long for this ability. They try to repay their loans by bringing fame to those who help enhance this ability in them.

How can one externally express the mental world that is unfolding within through feelings?

It needs to be expressed in such a way as to stimulate feelings.

Many elements and tools are required for this.

A man's office-dress is simple – the simpler it is, the more suitable it becomes for work. A woman's attire, her diffidence, modesty, mannerism etcetera are conventions followed in civil society.

A woman's job relates to the heart. Women must give and also attract hearts – hence they cannot afford to be merely simple and direct. Men must be proper – but women have to be beautiful. It is good for men to have clarity in their behaviour, but for women there is the need for many covers, hints, and suggestions.

Literature too needs to take refuge in ornamentation, metaphor, rhythm, hint, and suggestion to fulfil its purpose. It cannot afford to be bereft of ornamentation like philosophy or science.

To express the formless through form, one must preserve the inexpressible within speech. The inexpressible is in literature what grace and novelty are in a woman. It is beyond imitation. It surpasses embellishment and is not overshadowed by ornaments.

In order to establish the inexpressible within language, literature generally blends two elements with language – image and music.

That which cannot be expressed in words needs to be expressed through images. There is no limit to such sketches in literature. Feeling tends to become real through similes, comparisons, and metaphors. Balaram Das said so much in just these words '*Dekhibare ankhi-pakhi dhay*'[2] (literally, 'to behold the eye-bird flies'). How can the restlessness of a restless gaze be conveyed through description alone? The gaze flies like a bird – the many varied desires for expression have gained instant comfort in this image. Apart from this, literature has to take shelter in the music of its words, rhythms, and syntax. Music alone can express what otherwise cannot be expressed. What appears common through analysis of meaning becomes extraordinary through music. It is through this music that pain is generated within words.

Hence, image and music are the basic elements of literature. Image gives shape, and music brings motion to feeling. The image is the body, and music the soul.

But it is not only the human heart that needs to be conserved in literature. Human nature is also a creation that unlike an inanimate substance cannot be explained through our senses. It does not remain static when asked to do so. It evokes great curiosity – it cannot be understood simply by being placed in a cage and subjected to observation like an animal.

Human nature is beyond any such limited perception – literature attempts to bring it out of the internal world and establish it outside. It is a very difficult task. This is because human nature is neither stable nor well harmonised. It has many aspects and many layers. An unrestricted passage between the outside and the inside is not easy. In addition, its playfulness is so subtle, so unpredictable, so sudden that one needs extraordinary talent for its full comprehension. Vyāsa, Vālmikī, Kālidāsa, and other poets accomplished this very task.

Now if we wish to sum up the theme of our discussion in a few words, we must state that the subject of literature is the human heart and human nature.

But even to talk about human nature seems redundant. Actually, external reality and human nature are constantly receiving shape and producing music in the human heart. Literature is this image and music expressed through language. The joy of god manifests itself in nature and in human character. The human heart also endeavours to create and express itself in literature. Such endeavour is limitless and varied. Poets merely serve this persistent effort of the human heart.

The joyful creativity of god emerges from within god himself, and the joyful creativity of the human heart is its echo. The vibration of this joyous song of creation is constantly playing on the strings of our hearts – literature is a manifestation of this music of the mind and of the passion to create in response to god's creation. Literature is trying to express with clarity the tune that the breath of the world is playing on the flute of our hearts.

Literature does not belong to an individual or to a composer – it is a divine message. As the outer creation is eternally trying to express itself in both its good and bad features and in its incompleteness – likewise this divine message is forever trying to emerge from within us in all countries and in all languages.

Translation: Tapan Chakraborty

*

The material of literature[3]

Rabindranath Tagore

Writing merely for one's own pleasure is not literature. Many would say in a poetic manner that just as birds sing out of their own overwhelming joy, likewise the writer writes from his own upsurge of happiness; readers merely overhear his words.

It cannot be said with conviction that in the avian world, birds do not pay attention to the song of other birds. However, whether they do pay attention or not, it does not matter; the writer writes chiefly for his readers.

This does not mean that such writing should be labelled as artificial. A mother breastfeeds only her child and that does not prevent us from calling it spontaneous.

Silent poetry and self-centred effusion of feeling are two idle terms in use in some literary circles. Wood that has not burned cannot be considered for fire or a person merely gazing at the sky with the same silence of the sky cannot be called a poet. Poetry is expression. What a person merely holds in the depths of his heart has no consequence for the outsider. As the saying goes, guessing at the appropriate number of sweets in the storehouse does not bring pleasure to a person, rather it is getting the sweets directly that matters.

Self-centred effusion of feeling in literature is along the same line of thought. One must take for granted that a piece of writing is not for the writer himself, and this has also to be borne in mind while judging a piece.

The natural tendency of our feeling is to make itself felt in other hearts. In nature, we can see a constant effort among living beings to proliferate and to stay alive. Those living beings that occupy the most space through their offspring gain the maximum claim to life and seem to establish their existence in a more real fashion.

Even humans have this tendency. The only difference lies in the fact that the claim to life is a matter of space and time, while the claim to feeling relates to the heart and time. Feeling tries to gain control over many hearts for many years.

In this earnest desire, people have expressed themselves through gestures, various languages and scripts, stone carvings, metal castings, and leather bindings; on the bark of trees, on leaves and paper, with brush and pen, with many attempts – from left to right, right to left, from top to bottom, and from one column to another. Why? To ensure that whatever I have thought and felt should not die but move from one person to another and from one age to the other. My dwelling place, my belongings, my body and mind, the everyday objects of joy and sorrow will all pass away – only whatever I have thought and felt will live forever nurtured by the thought and intellect of people in a living world.

When forgotten ancient manuscripts of a human society appear out of the sand dunes of Central Asia's Gobi Desert, there seems to be a pang of sorrow in the unfamiliar letters of the unknown language. The effort of an energetic soul from some bygone era seems to be making a restless attempt to enter our hearts. The writer is no more nor is the community in which it was written – but its desire to be nurtured within human joys and sorrows travels across ages and is unable to introduce itself – with outstretched arms it looks up with hope and expectation.

The greatest emperor of the world, Ashoka carved the thoughts that he wanted to be associated with for eternity on mountain rocks. These hills would never die nor move but would stand by the never-ending road and call out the same message to passers-by forever. He had entrusted the hills with the burden of speaking.

The hills have carried his words without consideration for the passage of time. Gone are the days of Ashoka, of Pataliputra, and the glory of a *dharma*-inspired India. But the hills still proclaim the messages written in letters long forgotten and in a language that is no more in use. They have cried in the wilderness for long and even the great edicts of Ashoka have beckoned the human heart for centuries through mere gestures. The Rajputs passed by, so did the Moghuls and Pathans, and then the swords of the plundering Bargis with lightning speed caused havoc from one end to the other – no one responded to their gestures. Ashoka would not have thought of the tiny island on the far side of the sea when his artists were inscribing his edicts on rock, and when at that very time the wandering 'druids' of the forest on that island were accumulating the silent astounding emotion of their worship. Many thousand years later, a foreigner would come from that island and decipher those mute gestures of a different time. Emperor Ashoka's desire was fulfilled through this foreigner after centuries. However mighty a king he might have been, his desire was nothing but to inform the passers-by of his likes and dislikes, what he valued, and what he did not. His feelings waited by the side of the road for ages, looking for shelter in the hearts of men. The wayfarers simply passed on, some glancing at the emperor's words and others not at all.

I am not saying that Emperor Ashoka's edicts are literature. All this merely reveals the expectations of a human heart. Our constant endeavours everywhere to build statues, draw pictures, write poems, construct stone temples are nothing but pleas of the human heart to gain immortality in the heart of others.

Whatever tries to make a permanent place in the human heart is generally different from our temporary needs and efforts. We sow seeds for our annual needs of rice, wheat, and millet, but if we desire to grow a forest, we will need to gather seeds for such vegetation.

In literature, it is the pursuit of this permanence that is valued by human beings. This is the reason that despite the outcry of chauvinist critics that there is dearth of meaningful literature, and novels, plays, and poems are fast taking up all the literary space, authors are not really concerned. Immediate needs are met by meaningful literature, but the possibility of permanence is much more in literature that does not serve necessity.

Once a knowledge-bearing message is disseminated, its purpose gets fulfilled and it dies out. New discoveries through human knowledge overshadow the old ones. That which was unfathomable to the wise man yesterday is today no longer new even to an innocent child. The truth that in a new attire brings revolution may not even invoke any surprise in its old attire. What astonishes one is that theories that are accepted by fools today were at one time strongly opposed even by very learned men.

However, feelings do not grow old even after their propagation. A knowledge-bearing message need not be repeated once learned; fire is hot, the sun is round, water exists as a liquid – it is enough if these facts are known once, and it would try one's patience if attempts are made to explain them a second time. But one does not get tired of experiencing feeling again and again. We are not attracted by the knowledge that the sun rises in the east but are drawn to the beauty and joy of sunrise from the beginnings of creation to this day. Feeling, in fact, gains depth and captivates us more easily as it passes through time and tradition.

Hence, if a person wants to keep something of his own in a bright, new, and permanent manner, he must take recourse to the message of feeling. That is why literature is dependent not primarily on objects of knowledge, but also on those of feeling.

Apart from this, matters of knowledge can be transferred from one language to another. When so transformed, they often become more illuminated. Different people can take them up in varied languages and disseminate them in many ways thus truly fulfilling their purpose.

However, this is not the case with feeling. Feeling cannot be separated from the image it occupies.

Messages of knowledge need to be proved, but messages of feeling need to be transmitted. Hints and suggestions, art and artifice are necessary for transmission. It is not enough to merely explain such messages, they need to be created.

This distinctly crafted literary composition is like the body of the feeling. The literary author is known by his ability to establish feeling in this body. It is in accordance with the form and nature of this body that the feeling it harbours receives recognition from people, and in accordance with its strength it gains its extension in human hearts and in time.

The heart's object is entirely dependent on the body. It cannot be poured from one vessel to another like water. The body and soul live as one by glorifying each other. Feelings, subject matter and ideas belong to common people. If someone does not bring them out, another will, in due course. But the literary composition belongs solely to the author. It can never be the same with another author. That is why an author lives veritably in his writings – neither in feeling nor in subject matter. Of course, by literary composition we mean both feeling as well as the means of expression, but it is especially the means that belongs to the author.

A lake implies both water as well as the dug-up trough. But which one is the real creation? Water is not a creation of man, it has always been there. The ways devised to preserve water over a long period of time for the use of people are man's own creation. Feeling is likewise for the public in general, but the artist's achievement lies in finding a suitable form for making it a special joyous object for all.

Thus, we see that gaining ownership over feeling and then making it a property of all form literature, and this is also true of the fine arts. Carbon is all pervasive, commonly existing in water, land, air, and in various elements for everyone; trees and plants absorb it with their inherent strength in special forms, and then it becomes a consumable product for people for a long period of time. Not only does it produce food and heat, but also beauty, shade, and well-being.

Hence, we see that gaining special ownership over an item meant for all and then in the same manner especially making it the property of all form the work of literature.

If this is so, then the substance of knowledge gets automatically separated from literature. That which in English is called 'truth' and that we have named 'satya' or that which can be captured by our intellect should necessarily be free of a person's individuality. Truth is entirely independent of the subject, pure and clear. The theory of gravitation cannot have one meaning for me and something else for another. The varied colours of diverse hearts cannot leave their imprint on it.

The material of literature consists of all those things that call for melody, colour, and suggestiveness from the talented person in order to be transmitted to the heart of others and those that cannot be established in someone else's heart unless they are created in one's own. They can stay alive only by bringing together form and structure, feeling and language, melody and rhythm. The material is one's very own – it is neither invention nor imitation – it is creation. So, once it is expressed, it cannot be transformed or changed – its totality is completely dependent on each of its parts. When there is an exception, the literary quality is compromised.

Translation: Tapan Chakraborty

*

The judge of literature[4]

Rabindranath Tagore

When we sit at home and laugh with joy or cry in sorrow, we never think that it is important to laugh a little more or that the tears are somewhat insufficient. But when it becomes necessary to demonstrate one's joy or sorrow to someone else, however true one's feelings may be, the external expression may fail to convey the full extent of the same.

Even when a mother keeps the entire village awake with her loud wailing, it is not merely to express the sorrow of losing a son, but also to express the glory of sorrow in a son's bereavement. One does not have to prove one's joys and sorrows to oneself but must do so to others. Hence one has to raise one's voice a degree or two louder than what is natural in order to prove one's sorrow.

One cannot simply dismiss this as artificial. Establishing one's sorrow is a natural part of its expression. The bereaved mother continues to be hurt by the fact that her son's worth is acknowledged only by her and that the grievous extent of the loss will not be felt by anyone else in the world and that others will, with a pure conscience, pursue their daily chores like eating, sleeping, and going to work despite the emptiness left by her son. Then she tries to proclaim to the world the immensity of her loss and glorify her son with the intensity of her grief.

There is a natural restraint in that part of the sorrow where it is one's own, but the part that is a declaration often crosses the limits of decorum. A natural desire to stir the unresponsive heart of the other leads to an extreme effort on her part.

Most of our feelings and not just sorrow have these two sides – one for the self and one for others. There is a certain satisfaction and glory in turning my heartfelt feelings into those of all others. We do not like the fact that what disturbs us leaves others untouched.

This is because in order to establish truth, it has to be proved to people. If I alone see the sky as yellow and if others do not, it is my illness that is proved. It is a weakness on my part.

The more people feel the sorrow of my heart, the more its truth will be established. I receive special consolation and pleasure by establishing the truth of my feelings in the hearts of people as well as the fact that what I feel very intimately is not a disease or a weakness or even insanity on my part. It is not difficult to demonstrate to people that a blue object is blue, but it is difficult to make people accept as joy or sorrow what I feel to be my joy and sorrow, what I like or dislike as something to be liked or disliked by them. In such cases, it is not enough to just express one's feelings but to do so in such a manner that they seem real to others.

It is here that there may be exaggerations. What needs to be shown from a distance must be presented in an enlarged manner. That enlargement is in response to the demand for a greater truth. Otherwise, it seems untrue in exact proportion to its smallness. It must be enlarged to make it true.

My joys and sorrows are immediate to me, but they are not so to you. You are far from me. I have to measure that distance and speak of things related to me in a magnified manner.

A creative author is known by his ability to enlarge while keeping the truth intact. Literature is not the exact recording of things as they are.

For what I see in nature is evident to me, and my senses are its witness. What literature shows is natural but not evident. Hence, literature has to fill in that gap of evidence.

This is the starting point of the difference between natural truth and literary truth. The natural mother does not cry the way the mother in literature does. That does not imply that the mother's tears in literature are false. First, natural crying is so apparent in its signs and gestures, in the voice, in the atmosphere around, and in the veracity of its occurrence that it evokes our immediate trust and sympathy. Second, the natural mother cannot fully express her sorrow; she neither has the capacity nor the state of mind.

This is the reason that literature is not really a mirror to nature. And not just literature, no art as such is an exact imitation of nature. In nature, we realise what is evident; in literature and the other arts what is not evident is made manifest. Hence in this case, nothing can be served by making one the mirror of the other.

As a result of this lack of evidence, literature has to take recourse to different kinds of stylistic devices in the use of rhythmic language. It is thus that the subject matter despite being artificial in its external form becomes truer than the natural truth inside.

Here, there is a special reason for the use of the word 'truer'. Natural truth related to feeling is mixed and confused, broken, partial, and transitory. The waves of life go up and down continuously – falling over one another – unmindful of high or low, the trivial and the unique flow together rubbing and pushing against one another. When we see the enactment of human feelings on the grand stage of nature, we naturally select and exclude, fill in by conjectures, and through imagination construct much of it. We do not even know a close relative fully. Our memory like a skilful writer discards a large section of his personality. If all his details, big or small, are retained by our memory without any partiality, his true image will die out in the heap, and if we want to preserve the whole, we will not see our closest relative in his true form. Knowing implies discarding that which is to be discarded and retaining that which is to be retained.

Things also have to be enlarged. We see relatively little of our closest relative. A large section of his life remains invisible to us. We are not his shadows, nor do we know his mind. Our imagination works on that large empty section of his life that is invisible to us. We fill in the gaps and draw up a full mental picture. We do not or hardly know the person who does not stir our imagination, whose gaps remain unfilled, whose appearance alone is present to us, and whose hidden self remains obscure and invisible. Similarly, most people in the world are as shadows to us – almost unreal. We know them as lawyers, doctors, or shopkeepers but not as human beings. In other words, we know that part of them which is externally in contact with us as their greatest aspect – but that which is truly greater in them goes unnoticed by us.

Literature lets us know fully what it wants us to know – that is it makes its presentation by keeping the permanent intact, discarding the irrelevant, keeping the small as small, the big as big, filling in the gaps, and binding together the loose. Literature does what the heart desires within the impartial wealth of nature. The mind is not the mirror of nature nor is literature. The mind converts a natural phenomenon into a mental phenomenon, and literature converts the mental into a literary product.

The method of operation is similar in both. But there are differences because of specific reasons. The mind constructs for its own needs, while literature constructs for the joy of all. It is enough to keep a note for oneself, but for others one has to maintain a proper organised sequence from beginning to end. And that has to be placed in such a perspective and manner that the whole is visible to all. The mind usually collects from nature – literature gathers from the mind. Particular creative strength is required to project what is in the mind to the external world. Hence, what is transferred from nature to the mind and from the mind to literature is far from imitation. In authentic literature, we wish to establish our imagination, our joys and sorrows not just in present time but also in eternity. Hence, its measure has to be balanced with the extensive area of its establishment. One cannot work within the parameters of the transitory when one gathers elements from it and constructs for eternity. It is for this that the measure of great literature differs from contemporary time and the narrow boundaries of the world.

The task of literature is to take objects of the inner world to the external, feelings to language, the personal to the universal and the transitory to the eternal.

The relationship of the world to the mind is similar to that of the mind to the writer's genius. There is no harm in calling this genius the universal human mind. The mind collects its elements from the world, and the universal human mind again selects elements from the mind and constructs them for itself.

I know that what I am saying is getting obscure. But let me try to clarify, although I am not sure if I will succeed.

We experience the existence of two parts within ourselves. One is my selfhood and the other my humanity. If the physical space could be conscious, it would have been able to realise the presence of both the inner partial sky along with the extensive outer space through meditation. Our inner selfhood and humanity are similar. The soul begins to abide in a dark pit if an impenetrable wall is raised between the two.

If there is a dividing line in the authentic writer between his selfhood and his humanity, it is merely the transparent division of the glass pane of imagination. It is not a barrier to knowing each other. In fact, the glass serves both as a microscope and a telescope – it makes the invisible visible and the distant near.

That humanity of the writer is the chief creator. It makes the selfhood of the writer its own, transforms the momentary into the eternal, and bestows wholeness to the partial.

The world is submitted to the workshop of the individual mind and the individual mind to that of the universal – and literature originates from that higher level.

As I stated earlier, it is difficult to judge truth in relation to elements from the mental world. It is easy to prove that black is black as it is definitely so to many – but it is not easy to prove that what is good is truly so, for it is difficult to get a single opinion from most.

Several issues come up at this stage. Which is truly good – one that is so for most or one that is good for a particular community?

If one leaves science aside, it may be stated about natural elements that whatever is black to most is truly black. It has been demonstrated that there is so little scope for a difference of opinion here that it is unnecessary to gather further proof in the matter.

But whether what is good is really good and to what extent are such debatable points that it is difficult to decide what kind of proof is required.

It is particularly difficult because the efforts of writers are not just for the present period. Their target is human society of all times. How can one find witnesses and judges in the present period for something that is written both for the present and the future?

It is often seen that the contemporary and the local occupy the highest place in the minds of most people. One can misjudge if one only considers the opinion of the people of a particular time in evaluating literature. Hence, literature has to look beyond the present and set its goal for all times.

Works that have retained their glory amidst changes in education, feelings, and situations through ages have passed the test of time. Our minds are not easily accessible and, looking at them within the boundaries of a short period, makes it impossible to draw upon the unchanging in the flow of incessant movement. Hence, one has to test elements of the mental world in the inspection hall of a vast expanse of time – there is no other way to arrive at a sure conclusion.

But there has to be working guidelines to judge literature or else there would be anarchy. It is not as if all cases of the Judge's Court get settled in the Court of Appeal. In the case of literature, too, the work of the Judge's Court does not come to a halt. The final resolution takes a long time – some judgement may be available meanwhile, and there is nothing one can do if the judgement is incorrect.

As in independent literature, the extraordinary talent of some becomes representative of all times, and also secures its place in time, so also judgement has its extraordinary talent. The strength to examine is incomparable in some. They cannot be duped by the transitory or the slight; they can at once identify the constant and the eternal. They have been introduced to what is permanent in literature, and they have consciously and imperceptibly merged the signs of permanence with their inner being. Their nature and their education have made them capable of occupying the seat of judgement in all periods.

Then there are also commercial judges. They have bookish knowledge. They sit at the portico of the palace of the goddess of learning and rant and rave, while carrying out commerce in bribery and fisticuffs – they do not know the inner world. They are often enticed by cars, carriages, and watch chains. But there are many relatives from the inner quarters of Saraswati who approach their mother humbly in worn-out clothes, and she draws them close and caresses them. Sometimes they stain her white attire – she smiles and brushes it off. What are the signs by which the doorkeepers of a palace can identify those whom the divine lady picks up as her own despite the dust and grime? They know attires not human beings. They can create trouble, but they have not been given the responsibility to judge. Those who have the responsibility to welcome the *saraswat* or true poets are themselves children of Saraswati – they are one's own people, and they recognise the worth of family members.

Translation: Subha Chakraborty Dasgupta

Notes

1 Rabindranath Tagore, 'Sahityer Tatparya', *Bangadarsan* (New Series), 1903, 3(8): 358–362.
2 Balaram Das was a post-Chaitanya Gaudiya Vaishnav poet from the 16th century, acclaimed for his lyrics of vatsalya and madhura rasa.
3 Rabindranath Tagore, 'Sahityer Samagri', *Bangadarsan* (New Series), 1903, 3(7): 317–322.
4 Rabindranath Tagore, 'Sahitya Samalochana' (Literary Criticism), *Bangadarsan* (New Series), 1903, 3(6): 284–290. The essay was rechristened 'Sahityer Bicharak' ('The Judge of Literature') for the volume *Sahitya* (1907).

15 Alokeranjan Dasgupta: The search for world language and world literature in poetry

Introduction

An eminent poet and critic, Alokeranjan Dasgupta (1933–2020), was a student of Bangla literature, and taught at the Departments of Comparative Literature and Bangla at Jadavpur University, Kolkata, India and Indology at the University of Heidelberg, Germany. A representative poet of the 1950s and the 1960s, Dasgupta explored contemporary issues in innovative forms in his poems. His major volumes of poetry include *Jaubanbaul* (1960), *Raktakta Jharokha* (1969), *Chhau-Kabukir Mukhosh* (1973), *Guillotiney Alpana* (1977), *Debike Snaner Ghare Nagna Dekhe* (1983) *Marami Karat* (1990), *Se Ki Khunje Pelo Iswarkana* (2012) and *Niriswar Pakhider Upasanalaye* (2013). Dasgupta also translated works of Sophocles, Heinrich Heine, Friedrich Ḥölderlin, Goethe and many others. He compiled a volume of translated poems with Sankha Ghosh, entitled *Sapta Sindhu Dash Diganta* (1963). Dasgupta was among the foremost literary critics in Bengal and argued for an inclusive paradigm and an intermedial approach for literary studies. He wrote extensively on literature, arts and culture of many countries, and some of the collections in which they appear are *Silpita Swabhab* (1969), *Sthir Bishayer Dike* (1976), *Dike Digantare* (1986), *Punthipat* (Vol. I 2002, Vol. II 2003), *Je Achhe Antarale* (2010) and *Rabindra Alokbarshe* (2012). The present essay on world literature, first published in 1972, appears in *Dwitiya Bhuban* (1991).

Rabindranath Tagore delivered three lectures at the National Council of Education on 'World Literature' between January and April 1907, titled 'Saundaryabodh' (The Sense of Beauty), Visvasahitya (World Literature) and 'Saundarya o Sahitya' (Beauty and Literature). Tagore was arguing for a unified vision of beauty and truth. He defined the relationship between the self and the phenomenal world through a triad of intellectual, utilitarian and aesthetic connections, where the third was manifest through a realisation of *rasa*. Tagore argued that the aesthetic connection between the self and the world was not limited by space, time or subject, and one had to free oneself from all artificial boundaries of perception and look for the Universal Man through world literature. Tagore's lectures were delivered two years after the

DOI: 10.4324/9781003224686-16

British attempt to divide Bengal, which brought in a high tide of nationalism and which, among other things, led to the establishment of the National Council of Education.

Alokeranjan Dasgupta in this essay relates Tagore's argument with that of Goethe and Gottfried Herder and their successors in the mid-20th century and tries to understand how the praxis of world literature can be realised only through a rootedness in one's own cultural values. Dasgupta also investigates Tagore's writings on rural literature and oral traditions and tries to find an inseparable common core between the 'rustic' lore and the 'elite' art. The author foregrounds this relationship in his approach to the concept of world literature and speaks of the influence of Herder in this context. Later in 1973, Dasgupta writes a monograph entitled *Goethe and Tagore: A Retrospect of East-West Colloquy* where an essay entitled 'The World-Vision and World-Literature' takes up some of his arguments presented in this essay.

*

The search for world language and world literature in poetry[1]

Alokeranjan Dasgupta

It seems surprising that Johann Wolfgang von Goethe could clearly express his understanding of world literature only in the last ten years of his life. It is difficult to concede that this great intellectual, capable of forging bonds among all areas, did not give a clear statement on these grounds earlier. More so, when history makes us acknowledge that the critics August Wilhelm Schlegel and Friedrich Schlegel had identified and defined 'world literature' a long time ago. August Wilhelm Schlegel in his famous lecture series (1802) at the University of Berlin had stated that world literature would not only lead to the realisation of trends in various national literatures, but also inspire a poetic flow through the entire world that would be perennial. Needless to say, this enunciation is not as supplemented by facts as by an enhanced sensibility. Rather, in comparison, the statement made by Friedrich Schlegel six years before is still relevant today: 'The presence of an inner connection is evident in the context of mutual influence. The cooperative nature of modern poetry attests to that fact and this poetry is a part of the larger whole'.[2]

In fact, Goethe was a little late in wholeheartedly accepting the bond of the whole with the part, the essential living core, in world literature. Driven by an endless spirit of investigation, he crossed the boundaries of German literature keeping his compass limited to the exploration of European literature and remaining firm in his dedication to the Athenian source till the end. In between, of course he was closely drawn, at least once quite intensely, to

Indian literature, and then after an initial attempt to learn Sanskrit he suddenly turned to Semitic literature. Although Indian and Semitic literature animated his own writings, the force of the inevitable link between the literatures of the East and the West was never felt in his aesthetic ideas. There is no doubt though that he did extend a warm support to the Schlegel-directed nature of relation between the part and the whole, even if within the limits of European literature.

At the very beginning of 1827, he told his mnemonist pupil Eckermann: 'National literature is now rather an unmeaning term: the epoch of world literature is at hand, and everyone must try to hasten its approach'.[3] In other words, he was drawing the attention of the person or the country to the fact that it was necessary to look around in order to realise that only a madman would dare to think that his own poetry alone was worthwhile and precious. That very year in his journal *Kunst und Altertum* while reviewing a French play, he placed it in the newly emerging perspective of world literature instead of dissecting it from within. Here as well, eager to construct theory, he declared: 'a general world literature should be formed, in which we Germans play an honourable part'.[4]

Critics have reminded us that during this period, Goethe was keen on linking German literature with French and English as a felt need to extend the horizon of German literature. Three years before as well, he had told Eckermann, 'Have not our novels, tragedies, etcetera come from Goldsmith, Fielding and Shakespeare?'[5] The answer is to be found in the question itself. More than a hundred years after this question, in a letter to Hemantabala Devi (1933), we find the same acquiescent large-heartedness in Rabindranath's famous conclusion related to the debt of Bangla literature to the European. Goethe and Rabindranath were both pioneers and chief supporters of the engagement with world literature. Yet, we cannot reject the fact that even while drawing upon Goethe, Rabindranath moved closer to our times. Goethe, in upholding world literature, without completely making the part irrelevant in comparison with the whole, had still reduced its importance. Rabindranath, on the other hand, taught us to view the local or the partial as the foundation of the whole and on this rested his modernity. In the words of Carlyle, Goethe's contemplation, following the path of *Weltbund* or world federation, took the ideological form of a sort of 'commonwealth'.[6] The engagement with the concept of world literature at times might have seemed more desirable to him, as an international ambassador's message of well-being, than an engagement with literature. It was not possible to have any doubt about the beneficial non-partisan bent of the concept, yet one has to agree that writers in later times did not give any more value to this indication apart from taking it as a well-wisher's beneficial thought. Moreover, mapping the ideas of recent Goethe-inspired thinkers starting from Victor Lange to Martin Bodmer, we tend to believe that despite the hard work and dedication of his successors, his concept of world literature has turned into a kind of norm-determining

Eurocentrism. In other words, to put it somewhat harshly, the concept of world literature today implies the preservation of a given European model or framework whose horizon is largely West-oriented. Even the very faithful devotees of one who gave us the divine rationale, 'This Orient is God's own/His own the Occident,'[7] think of the Occident as the world. The report of George Steiner on 'The Uncommon Market' (The Times Literary Review, 14 August 1971) instigated by the self-serving orientation of the 'common market' of the commonwealth, expressed in a playful bantering manner, should not make us forget that there is a grain of truth in every playful banter. Hence, when he reminds us of constructing 'a central triangle with Rome and Weimar on the base and Paris at the apex,' we tremble inside as we cannot wish away the essential fact that the centre here is Europe, even if we leave aside the extent of Goethe's consciousness on the issue. Without going into detailed analysis, it is possible to say that because of this the parameters of colonialism gain precedence in literary criticism or in the literary conscience. In other words, the fact that the literature of the third world in general is not much recognised has at its root the prejudices and conceit of Eurocentrism. This prejudice has become so strong that only if a literature outside Europe is politically or economically advantageous – as Japanese literature is now – it would be considered acceptable to this camp. An indelible stamp of a 'developed' European lineage has cast its shadow over it. The uneasy question of what 'Eurocentrism' is at this moment now has a clue – the tendency to impose a regulative authority on the affairs of the world would be a part of that mentality. Our times are also witnessing a strong inclination for this supercilious authoritarianism in evaluating literary endeavours.

Rabindranath had looked at Europe as the internal driving force in the existence and transformation of a new Indian literature, and the manner of his gaze is a bright example of a praiseworthy acceptance of world literature. Sometimes, there is such obsessive delight in his welcome that he frequently uses the same phrases or similar word-combinations. The following is an apt example:

> A wave of sensibilities has arrived from Europe and is naturally having an impact on our minds. If we deny that our consciousness has awakened as a result of the impact and counter-impact, we would be falsely disparaging our own mental make-up. Something is taking shape in the confluence of sensibilities and after a while a clearer image will be apparent.
>
> As it is true that new sensibilities from Europe are stimulating our hearts, however much we try to remain unadulterated, our literature will never be able to refrain from expressing this truth in some new form or the other. There is no way in which there can be a repetition of the traditional; if there is, I would call it a false and superficial literature.[8]

In this candid welcome there is no sign of any conservatism. It is important to cite another report where, despite his large-heartedness, he does not mince words to talk about Europe's all-consuming colonial perspective in evaluating world literature:

> Literature becomes lifeless when there is an excess of tussle for utility. For utility assaults others and does not attract them. Germany's merchant-boats and battleships did not fill their sails like storm-clouds to cover the world when Lessing, Goethe, Schiller, Heine, Hegel, Kant and Humboldt were creating a literary paradise in Germany. Today in the age of commerce, the more weight that Germany gains, the more the heart of its literature is rendered weak. The English today are also taking up the task of replenishing its coffers, making the weak weaker and aggressively holding up the glory of the Anglo-Saxon alone, like the single horned rhinoceros, as its religion: hence there, on the playground of literature the 'lights go out one by one' and today almost 'silent are the rabab, veena, *muraja* and the flute'.[9]

It is evident that Rabindranath's notions related to world literature were not linked with any predefined notion of geographical expansion. Victor Lange has also reminded us that Goethe's use of the word 'world' (Welt) in world literature does not refer to the geographic – it is expansive and perhaps also has strands of the transcendental. Max Müller too humbly stated, 'Goethe was a complete human being and hence his interest in and attraction for world literature was rooted in his strong human heart'.[10] But Max Müller did not deny that in the course of time, the inheritance of Goethe was transformed into a force that regulated the whole world ('a European power: it has become a force that moves the whole world').[11] This mantra-like enunciation did not emerge out of a tendency towards imperialist expansion. Yet, if we pay attention to the word '*Kulturpolitik*', we must acknowledge that the desire for cultural expansion gets easily linked with the adverse intention of expanding political power. And in this process, many European countries are still engaged, sometimes even collectively. It is obvious that Goethe has been unjustly used as a pretext.

That does not imply that there were seeds of expansionism in his literary theory. We object to the way in which he has been used. This is because it was Rabindranath who told us repeatedly that any contact with the sense of utility in the study of literature or in its creation is a grievous offense. Literature cannot be kept confined to any personal or self-serving interest of the community, and he stated this unambiguously at the end of his essay on 'World Literature': 'Just as the world is not my, nor your field, and knowing the world as such is knowing it in a very rural fashion, so also literature is not my or your construction. We usually look at literature in this rural fashion'.[12]

*

We need to remember that even if Rabindranath did not like looking at 'literature in this rural fashion', he had immersed himself deeply in folk literature during the period of his engagement with different thoughts and projects on world literature. As a common synonym for 'folk literature,' he had chosen 'rural literature' or *gramyasahitya,* and in that choice or practice, there was more respect and love for world literature. The tendency to make oneself free from 'rural narrowness' and to move towards establishing rural literature on a large-scale demand special attention. The statement that follows in our previously quoted section is relevant in this context:

> We will liberate ourselves from that rural narrowness and decide to look at *visvamanab* (Universal Man) in *visvasahitya* (world literature), accept the whole in the work of each writer and in that whole see a connection with all human attempts towards expression. The time has come to take this up as a resolution.[13]

Rabindranath had twelve years before seen this totality and the 'connection with all human attempts towards expression' in folk literature. From then onwards, it was his firm belief that sophisticated literature emerged from folk literature. He wrote to Lokendranath Palit[14] from that perspective that 'Shakespeare's poetic works emerge from nursery rhymes. Now we do not evaluate literature on the basis of ancient parameters, but on that of results'.[15] Despite strongly asserting that an effective expression is the final criterion in modern literature, he had to return to nursery rhymes to look for the source of Shakespeare's creativity in trying to grasp the connection with all human attempts towards expression. In this conclusion, Rabindranath was influenced by Johann Gottfried Herder, the other pioneer in the field of world literature. Herder had seen the archetype of world literature in *Urpoesie*. His famous two-volume collection of folk verses *Volksleide*r (1778/79) is so far the most authentic of such compilations. In trying to determine the nature of German folk poetry, he looked closely at folk poetry all over the world. In fact, he even incited Goethe to take up this work, but Goethe could not devote much time to this. Herder, in support of his notion, included several of Shakespeare's songs in the fifth section of his compilation. Moreover, the seventh section which was the last in this compilation had substantial signs of his horizon encompassing the wealth of folk songs of Brazil, Madagascar, and Peru. Herder's influence in the area of nascent thoughts on world literature was widely felt when, after his death, Johaness von Müller published a second edition of the text 'The Tune of Many Races in Songs' (*Stimenn der Völker in Liedern* 1807). During that period particularly and later, the warmth of response in acknowledging Herder's lived experience of folk life as manifested by people writing, translating, and working with German literature was greater than that accorded to Goethe's ideals. Rabindranath's literary engagement moved along the first direction. The efforts of Bangiya Sahitya Parishad to collect folk literature inspired by

Rabindranath's works are particularly indebted to Herder. Following Herder's line of thought, Rabindranath on more than one occasion had stated:

> At first a few emotions gather together in small dispersed poetic fragments in the common people of the land and float around in clusters. Then a poet takes up the small fragments and in the form of a large poetic work binds them together.[16]

We know that it is as such that folk literature (*Volksliteratur*), the creation of common man, becomes scripted literature (*Autorenliteratur*). There is nothing revolutionary new about the fact that the '*Panchatantra*, *Kathasaritsagara*, *The Arabian Tales*, the legends of Arthur in England and the Scandinavian saga were born in this manner', but the valorisation of folk literature in determining the definition of world literature is historic. We mentioned thinkers from the school of Herder. They also brought a respectful attitude to folk literature. Hans Eppelsheimer in his book on the history of world literature (*Geschichte der europäischen Weltliteratur* 1971) has shown that this open approach on the part of those romantic thinkers led them to spontaneously translate known and little-known works, without engaging with notions of excellence, into their own language: baroque or folk poems, mystic poetry, the *Mahabharata* or *The Last Days of Pompeii*. In Herder's thoughts on literature that drew upon the spontaneity and ease evident in folk literature travelling everywhere, there was sanction and room for movement between *trivialiteratur* and classical literature. A non-rigid perspective on world literature therefore emerged in his reception of literary criticism, and in that of his successors. This direction was also favoured by Rabindranath: it was a sustainable relation of base and structure between the 'rural' and the so-called elite literatures:

> Just as the roots of the tree are connected to the soil and its upper extremities are spread out towards the sky, so also everywhere a large section of the lower portion of literature remains covered and linked with the soil of the country; it is in a particular narrow sense space-bound, local. It is accessible to the people of the country, for their enjoyment, and outsiders are not allowed to enter the space. That which is universal in literature stands on a structure at the base of this lower regional space. In this manner there is always an inner bond at work in our literature.[17]

This fearless study is amazing for us. This strong impulse is also at work today in studies of comparative language and literature regarding the proximity of the popular and the classical. We are of course surprised as we realise that Rabindranath had contributed to this open perspective such a long time back, and at the same time we regret that this novel beginning has not been very well-nurtured to this day. The immediate task of Comparative Literature (whose Tagorean synonym is world literature) is to look for the bonds between the local or the regional with the universal. Here his predecessor is Herder not Goethe. The former puts his conjectures on world literature to test placing them in local or regional environments. Rabindranath also rejected the apparent truth that 'appears separated from the writer, when it wipes out the dust of one's birthplace . . . takes up a disguise'.[18] He has used the notion of integrated truth in the context of European literature. It would be wrong to say that his evaluation was correct in every case. We remain doubtful of the appropriateness of his damaging comments on two works of art like *Anna Karenina* and *Mademoiselle de Maupin*. But if we think of a synchronisation of the whole with the surroundings as a norm accepted by Rabindranath, we must admit that in his own creative writings, this concept has been used.

> The sound of laughter of the girls brings affability to the house; they make tea and serve it, decorate the walls of the house with their handiwork and at the same time read and enjoy English poetry. However inconsequential this may be, Benoy is enchanted with it.[19]

This description is not very ambitious, but it is in this local environment that Moore's poems are appreciated by Rabindranath.

In effect, Rabindranath's objective was a deep bond and a close compatibility with the local and the international, the oriental and the occidental. In this context, he completely rejected the word 'national'. 'There is a belief in our country that India has nothing in common with other countries, and to cling as closely as possible to that uncommonness is the mark of our national literature'. Immediately after this he states unhesitatingly that 'In other words, national literature is the literature of the frog in the well'.[20] Before this, in the period of *Chhinnapatra*, portraying a 'conflict between his mind and the mind outside' he said the same thing giving examples of Goethe, Herder, Schlegel, Humboldt, Kant and other important thinkers.[21]

The elements and nature of world literature worked out by Rabindranath within a very modern frame before the first decade of our century have yet to be realised. But the line of healthy engagement with the connection between the country or the region and the world that he left behind as a legacy proved to be the most potential and vibrant. There was the same harmony of closeness and expansiveness in Friedrich Schlegel's dream of 'Progressive Universalpoesie'. The same urge is evident when Bishnu Dey, writing on Aragon following the line of thought in Goethe, Herder and Rabindranath, asks the Marxist literary critic to look particularly towards the wealth of folk literature. Hans Magnus Ensenzberger in 'The World-Language of Modern Poetry' ('Weltsprache der modernen Poesie' 1960) written almost in the same period as Bishnu Dey's essay 'Sahityer Bhabishyat' (1959) states with the same enthusiasm:

> The process of modern poetry takes us towards a poetic world language . . . it speaks in many tongues. It is not a mechanical affirmation of a standard, but the very opposite that is its aim. This poetic world language frees poetry from all national literatures. That, of course, does not mean that the objective is to create literature uprooted from its native soil or to make it nebulous.[22]

A few years later, on 23 February 1976, a friend of mine was present at a reading session of Indian and European poetry based on Enzensberger's statement in Delhi. He told me that if Enzensberger's name had not been mentioned as the author of the statement, he would have attributed it to Rabindranath. I have not yet differed with my friend on this account. Even today, we perhaps need Rabindranath the most in our engagement with world literature.

Translation: Subha Chakraborty Dasgupta

Notes

1 Alokeranjan Dasgupta, 'Kabitay Visvabhasha o Visvasahityer Sandhan' (1972), in *Dwitiya Bhuban* (1991), *Gadyasamagra*, Vol. II, Kolkata: Pratibhas, 2009, pp. 415–422.
2 See Victor Lange, 'Bezüge sind das Leben – Goethes Weg von der Nationalliteratur zur Weltliteratur', in *Die Zeit*, 18 June 1971, p. 46.
3 Johann Wolfgang von Goethe, Johann Peter Eckermann and Frederic Jacob Soret, *Conversations of Goethe* with Eckermann and Soret, Vol. I, translated from the German by John Oxenford, London: Smith, Elden & Co., 1850, p. 351.
4 Johann Wolfgang von Goethe, *Kunst und Altertum*, 1827, p. 131. Author's translation, cited in Alokeranjan Dasgupta, 'The World-Vision and World-Literature', in *Goethe and Tagore: A Retrospect of East-West Colloquy*, Delhi: South Asia Institute, University of Heidelberg, 1973, p. 58.
5 Johann Wolfgang von Goethe, *Conversations with Eckermann*, Washington and London: M. Walter Dunne, 1901, pp. 80–81.
6 The letter from Thomas Carlyle to Goethe is quoted in William Robertson's *Thomas Carlyle – The Man and His Books*, London: T. Fisher Unwin, 1909, p. 146.
7 Johann Wolfgang von Goethe, *West-Eastern Divan*, Edward Dowden (trans.), London and Toronto: MCHXIV, J.M. DENT & Sons Ltd., 1913, p. 5.
8 Rabindranath Tagore, 'Sahityasrishti', *Bangadarsan* (New Series), 1907, 7(3): 113–126, 124. The essay was anthologised in *Sahitya* (1907).
9 Rabindranath Tagore, 'Sahityasammilan', *Bangadarsan* (New Series), 1907, 6(11): 519–529, 522–523. The essay was anthologised in *Sahitya* (1907).
10 Friedrich Max Müller, *Goethe and Carlyle*, London: David Nutt, 1886, p. 20.
11 Ibid., p. 24.
12 Rabindranath Tagore, 'Visvasahitya', *Bangadarsan* (New Series), 1907, 6(10): 487–489, 499.
13 Ibid., p. 499.

14 Lokendranath Palit (1865–1915), Tagore's friend, was an ICS who served in Bengal and Bihar.
15 Rabindranath Tagore, 'Patralap' (correspondence) with Lokendranath Palit, dated Asharh 1299 (June–July 1892), in appendix to *Sahitya*, *Rabindra-Rachanabali*, Vol. VIII, Kolkata: Visvabharati, 1941, p. 479.
16 Rabindranath Tagore, 'Sahityasrishti', op. cit., p. 118.
17 Rabindranath Tagore, 'Gramyasahitya', in *Lokasahitya* (Gadyagranthabali III), Kolkata: Majumdar Library, 1907, pp. 57–58. The essay was first published in *Bharati* 1899, 22(11): 1006–1045.
18 Rabindranath Tagore, 'Alochana (Patra)', *Sadhana*, 1892, 1(4): 320–337, 325. The letter to Lokendranath Palit was later appended to *Sahitya*, *Rabindra-Rachanabali*, Vol. VIII, Kolkata: Visvabharati, 1941, p. 466.
19 Rabindranath Tagore, *Gora*, *Rabindra-Rachanabali*, Vol. VI, Kolkata: Visvabharati, 1940, p. 173.
20 Rabindranath Tagore, 'Sahityabichar', *Prabasi*, 1920, 19.2(6): 524–526, 525–526. The essay was written in response to the unfavourable and, according to Tagore, irrational critique of his novel *Ghare Baire* (1916).
21 Rabindranath Tagore, 'Letter to Indira Devi Chaudhurani (No. 143, dated 12 August 1894)', in *Chhinnapatrabali*, Kolkata: Visvabharati, 1960, pp. 310–311.
22 Cited in Alokeranjan Dasgupta, *Goethe and Tagore*, New Delhi: Munshiram Manoharlal, 1973, p. 109. Quoted in Lothar Lutze (ed.), *Lesung*, Heidelberg: Südasien Institut, 1967, p. 72.

16 Buddhadeva Bose: Rabindranath and his successors

Introduction

Buddhadeva Bose (1908–1974) was one of the pioneering figures of the modernist movement in Bangla literature. Born in Cumilla, Bose was brought up in Dhaka, where he studied English Literature and then moved to Kolkata in 1931. He taught English Literature at Ripon College and later established the Department of Comparative Literature at Jadavpur University in 1956. Bose was an eminent poet, novelist, and playwright. His collections of poems include *Bandir Bandana* (1930), *Kankabati* (1937), *Damayanti* (1943), *Draupadir Sari* (1948), *Siter Prarthana: Basanter Uttar* (1955), and *Je Andhar Alor Adhik* (1958). Bose was an avid translator, and his major achievements in the field include translations of Kālidāsa, Charles Baudelaire, and Rainer Maria Rilke. Bose was also a committed and influential critic, who wrote extensively on literary history and modernity. His critical works include *Kaler Putul* (1946), *Sahityacharcha* (1954), *Swades o Sanskriti* (1957) *Kavi Rabindranath* (1966), *Mahabharater Katha* (1974); *An Acre of Green Grass* (1948), and *Tagore: Portrait of a Poet* (1962).

Besides being an author and a critic, Bose was also a path-breaking editor. While in Dhaka, he published several issues of journal *Pragati* from 1927 to 1929. *Pragati*, along with *Kallol* and *Kali o Kalam*, published the earliest examples of avant-garde literature of the time. From 1935, Bose started publishing a quarterly called *Kavita* which soon became one of the leading literary journals of its time and brought a number of poets, authors, and critics together. He also started a publication house named 'Kavita Bhavan' which, along with the journal *Kavita*, welcomed a host of young poets into the Bangla literary scene.

What is now called the 'post-Tagore period' in Bangla poetry witnessed two major shifts during Tagore's lifetime. While a host of poets were trying to come to terms with the fundamental shifts in Bangla poetic form brought about by Tagore right from his early literary career, a demand for a radical change was being felt by other creative writers during the period of Tagore's maturity. This second phase found its finest proponents in the likes of Jibanananda Das, Sudhindranath Datta, Amiya Chakravarty, Bishnu

DOI: 10.4324/9781003224686-17

Dey, Samar Sen, and Bose himself, who, gradually but firmly, attempted – through their own works – a thorough revaluation of the poetic ethos of their predecessors. There was a deep engagement with Tagore, but their relationship with their immediate predecessors remained distant.

While Bose's assumption that Tagore's immediate successors had very little influence on the future course of Bangla poetry might have had a hint of truth, whether all of the poets he mentions were so obviously similar and merely imitated Tagore remains a questionable proposition, although this perspective seems to have dominated the critical understanding of this period of Bangla poetry for a very long time. It is important to remember that Bose's argument, despite his being one of the finest critics of Bangla poetry, is a partisan one and probably received best as emerging from an anxiety of influence.

The essay presented in this volume, written in 1952, appears in his anthology *Sahityacharcha* (1954).

*

Rabindranath and his successors[1]

Buddhadeva Bose

The term '*swabhabkavi*' ('natural poet') was probably first used to describe the poet Gobindachandra Das (1855–1918). I cannot quite recall now who used the term, but it must have been a knowledgeable person, for the term suited Gobindachandra perfectly. Besides, the unstated division that this term of description makes between poets is not without substance. Rabindranath did a good thing by getting rid of the concept of the '*nirab kavi*' ('silent poet') which laid to rest the superstitious idea of that 'mute inglorious Milton', but there is a very real and definite reason why the notion of the swabhabkavi is still with us. Of course, in the usual sense, every poet is a swabhabkavi, for there can be no creation without a kind of natural inner creative power, but, there are those who are quite the opposite of the swabhabkavi, even though there is no such simple convenient term to describe them. The term swabhabkavi is not just used to describe a person who is by nature a poet, that is something that need not be stressed, but it is also used to describe a poet who relies entirely on emotion, believes in inspiration, that is to say, someone who writes whenever the fancy takes him, but who never really *thinks* about his writing – in whose consciousness, the relationship between the head and the heart is that of a wife and a mistress. It is true that nothing remains in poetry if the heat of emotion is absent from it, but in order to convey that emotion to the reader, one cannot be its slave, rather, one must overcome the emotion and master it. It is possible to use the term swabhabkavi in this sense, where this mastery, this ability to control, is not present in a poet. This trait (of poetic naturalness) may be present either due to individual or historical factors; some are naturally swabhabkavi, but there may be times when the state of literature itself produces such swabhabkavi. Gobindachandra Das may well be called a swabhabkavi by nature in the purest sense, because he seems to be quite untroubled by the fact that the excess of emotion in his verses is under no form or kind of poetic control; moreover, we find the rather surprising declaration in his writing that, despite being his contemporary, he seems never to have felt the need to acknowledge the existence of Rabindranath Tagore. But one cannot assert that his flaws would have vanished had he only received tutelage from Rabindranath, for despite such tutelage mishaps have occurred – for there have been many historical swabhabkavis in Bengal, from Satyendranath Datta (1882–1922) to Nazrul Islam (1899–1976), who have appeared in the first phase of Rabindranath's poetic dominance.

Will it be wrong to assert that the young Bengali poets of the early 20th century were swabhabkavi in a historical sense; that it was, for them, a way of being? Why? Of course, because of Rabindranath. This was the high noon of Rabindranath's genius, and even though there was no lack of effort to run him down in various quarters across the country, the younger poets were irresistibly drawn to his magnetic presence. But Rabindranath is not the kind of poet who may be enjoyed at leisure; his influence is like a turbulence which destroys peace, and the fear of losing balance and being swept away is present everywhere. That he is a very great poet is something we have known for a very long time, but something that we perhaps do not quite fully understand or recognise even today is that Rabindranath is perhaps too great for Bengal, we cannot contain him in our limited hearts and minds; he exceeds the limits of our tolerance. But perhaps today we have earned the courage to confront him, for many things have taken place in Bangla literature since then. But what was the situation like in the first, or the second, decade of the 20th century? Could the narrow, timid Bangla literature of the time have withstood such flaming seeds and such a fiery personality? No. Since there was nothing more then, than the mere cleverness of a Dasarathi Roy (1806–1857), the well-wrought devotion of a Ramprasad, the clean-cut journalese of a Iswar Chandra Gupta (1812–1859), or, at best, the trumpet-blast of a Madhusudan Dutt (1824–1873), it was quite easy to be amazed, astonished, agitated, disturbed, angry, and overcome at the advent of Rabindranath Tagore, but it was not at all easy to tolerate him; in fact, at the time of the first encounter, it was not even possible to simply accept him as he was. Proof of this can be found from both sides: at the unceasing denunciation among the critics and, in the case of poetry, at the unprotesting way in which his successors succumbed to his influence. Moreover, there are other proofs available, if we pay heed to the responses of readers. Rabindranath's readership is still fairly small, even today, when compared to his fame or, for that matter, to the vast, multifarious quantity of his output; and the ordinary readers of Bengal, those whom we may call *the public*, have so far taken their taste of Rabindranath not in his works but in the emergence of two pleasurably watered-down versions – Saratchandra Chattopadhyay, the novelist, when it comes to prose and Satyendranath Datta for poetry.

The first two decades of the 20th century were difficult times for the Bangla poet. The poets of this era, who came up during Rabindranath's middle phase and faded away with the rise of Nazrul Islam, such as Jatindramohun Bagchi (1878–1948), Karunanidhan Bandyopadhyay (1877–1955), Kirandhan Chattopadhyay (1887–1931), and many others, whose leading light was Satyendranath Datta, were writers whose compositions were so undistinguishable from each other, so tiresome, so colourless, and so vapid, that it is difficult to separate one poet from another, with only Satyendranath Datta having some distinctive characteristics of his own (and even then he will be remembered only for the felicity of his rhyming); and I would like to suggest that the reasons for this were not individual but largely historical. The logical conclusion one comes to from all this is not that these were poor poets, for many of them wrote some individual poems of merit, but rather that they were the inhabitants of, or migrants to, a place that was both unbearable and inescapable. That is, it was both imperative for them to imitate Rabindranath as well as impossible for them to do so. As immediate successors, they were too close to Rabindranath to understand that Gurudev's poetry was dangerously deceptive, and if one did not know this and allowed oneself to be seduced by its sweet siren-song, one was bound to sink in the quicksand. Those who witnessed the publication of *Sonar Tari* (1894), followed by *Chitra* (1896), followed by *Katha O Kahini* (1900), then *Kalpana* (1900), *Kshanika* (1900), and *Gitanjali* (1910), when they were still in their youth, they had no choice but to be seduced by the maya contained in these works; instead of being awakened from their dream on hearing Rabindranath's melodies, they remained in slumber, their self-awareness succumbed to the pleasure of the dream, and this gave birth to the deluded notion that merely imitating Rabindranath's mellifluous rhymes could make their poetry beat to the same rhythm; that by being as fluid as water, their verses would gain the flow of the river. They swore an oath on Rabindranath but failed to comprehend him; in making the effect their sole aim, they neglected to observe its formal structure; they failed to grasp that the simplicity in Rabindranath that so entranced them had the character of water; that is, Rabindranath is simple only on the surface, only in appearance; go deeper and you discover unresolvable complexity, with streams and counter-streams, whirlpools constantly in churn; go even deeper, and storms are born, with nightmares where reptilian creatures clash with bloodied crocodile fangs. They failed to notice the dynamism of the great poet in whom they took shelter; they took no advice from him on how they ought to travel and kept circling him, satisfied at having dropped anchor in his shadow. That is to say, in trying to imitate Rabindranath they did precisely that which Rabindranath had never done himself. For this error, for this failure to understand, their writing displayed that frothiness, a helpless unchecked enthusiasm, which is the hallmark of the swabhabkavi; they mistook laxity for spontaneity and drowsiness for concentration and became noted in history for this reason: that by sacrificing themselves in the flaming heat of Rabindranath, they left ample warning for future generations.

*

Let me repeat, there was no alternative to this at the time, at least, not for poetry. This may sound excessive, but when we consider the range and nature of Rabindranath's genius, then it should be quite evident. It is our great good fortune that we had a Rabindranath among us, but we had to pay a price for this gift, and we are still paying for it. The price is this that he has made the task of composing poetry in Bangla a far more difficult task than before. There cannot be more than one Rabindranath, and, in order to write poetry after him, it becomes necessary to choose something which he has not already done and even if it is comparatively trivial, and it is almost certain to be trivial, we must be content with it. And this is where Satyendranath and others got it completely wrong. To them, writing poetry after Rabindranath, far from becoming more difficult, became infinitely easier; rhythm, rhyme, language, metaphor, the use of various stanzaic forms were now all ready-made, and there was no need to look elsewhere; their poetry began and ended with just such a sense of having things smoothly handed over to them. For them, the things that Rabindranath had not done in poetry were not worth doing or did not even exist; they would continue to do precisely that which Rabindranath had done or was doing – such was their vaulting ambition. And the reason why they did not take three steps back after taking one step forward in this endeavour can also be found in Rabindranath. There are no limits in Rabindranath – he is always inviting everyone close to him with both arms open, never saying that 'Be careful! Go away!' Most unfortunately for his successors, there is no sign in him that will awaken a sense of fear, leading to good sense, along with the devotion he naturally inspires. There is no overarching universal conception spanning heaven–earth–hell in Rabindranath as may be found in Dante or Goethe; neither is there that gallery of eternal portraits one finds in Shakespeare; even Milton's impenetrable maze of language is absent in him. The experience of reading him is without thorns; there seems to be not even a fine line separating us from him; nowhere is he inaccessible, hidden from view, or at least so it seems when seen from the outside; he never sends us rushing to fetch the dictionary, never tires us out with thought, never makes us toil in search of sense. Even his subject-matter is not exotic or hard-to-get nor is there any wondrous excess in it; he has written about what he has seen and taken in with both eyes wide open from this Bengal, here and now; he has not looted the streams of history or geography for his subject-matter; and he has not traversed the rivers that separate the human realm from the demonic or the divine. It is precisely for this reason that emulating him is as impossible as it is tempting. His writings everywhere seem to encourage the fatal belief among his successors, which is 'I think I too can write basketsful of the same thing' where, apparently, there is no need for scholarship, not even for any kind of preparation, so easily does it flow, so smoothly do things happen, that it seems as though one can write 'like that' as easily as one wishes, the only thing needed being a pinch of 'feeling'. At least the poets under discussion here were of this kind: in trying to emulate Rabindranath they lost themselves completely in him or, at best, produced childish imitations.

Rabindranath's poetry needs no other help to express or manifest itself; this lightness, this clarity makes him a dangerous example to follow. Because the reader does not have to labour over his writing, it becomes quite easy to fall into the error of believing that it is possible to see all of him at a single glance; and because there is no visible grandeur in his subject-matter, it is equally possible to fall into the error of believing that even lesser poets can easily follow his path. 'What we call childish can be very apt as subject-matter for poetry, but is not worthy of consideration as a mode of composition'[2] – this sentence from Rabindranath says a great deal about himself and other poets. He had said this in the introduction to the first volume of his *Rachanabali* (Collected Works) about his poems from before *Manasi* (1890), whose faults he said were due not to the paucity of ingredients but rather because of the incompleteness of composition. When considered in terms of ingredients or subject-matter, many of the poems from his mature stage are similar to *Sandhya Sangeet* (1882) and *Prabhat Sangeet* (1883) – in fact, his entire poetic oeuvre is of similar nature; from the centre to the periphery of his poetry this 'childishness' is spread out, which he had stated as being very apt as subject-matter. This 'childishness' clearly indicates that his poetry is not a combination of elements gathered from the outside; it is something that is created from within, the spontaneous expression of his innermost thoughts. The way in which the perceptible world outside has appeared before his eyes from day to day has shaken his soul and is something he has spoken of over and over again; the joys and sorrows of everyday existence and the momentary blossoming of evanescent multihued feelings – he has captured them in his poems and, even more than in his poems, in his songs. It is for this that his poetry is bodiless, opposed to interpretation, whose 'substance' cannot be separated out, which cannot be unfolded and displayed, where no difference remains between the poem and the reader's experience of it; which does its work on our minds but we cannot quite fathom how it does so; whose mystery we cannot capture through all the complicated apparatus of critical analysis; where, finally, we have to admit defeat and say that it is enough that this has come to pass, it is good that this exists, there is no more to be said.

Such poetry makes life worth living, but if its ideal remains constantly in front of us, other poets are in danger. Let me try to explain where this danger lies. Every person has feelings, has joys and sorrows; when it is seen that the expression of these is magically transformed into poetry, and such expression is 'quite simple and direct', where there does not seem to be any design behind it, then other poets are tempted to surrender to just about any kind of feeling or, in the absence of the real thing, to provoke their own minds themselves. And Satyendranath Dutta stands as a salutary example of just what happens as a consequence. I have selected him from among many others for very clear reasons; he is the most accomplished composer from among his similarly aged contemporaries, a true representative of his age, and recognisable even when placed beside Rabindranath. Yes, recognisable, possessing a different shape, but if we consider the nature of this shape, we will understand why, if we have read Rabindranath, there is no need for Satyendranath today. Needless to add, this difference is not one of a kind, nor is it that which exists between a senior and junior poet who are participants in the same movement; nor can we say that this is the difference between a major and a minor poet. Whether so-and-so is a major or a minor poet or just how major so-and-so is – at some juncture of critical analysis such questions become redundant; is such-and-such a genuine poet is the main question. It is this genuineness that cannot be found in Satyendranath. There is no shame in being a small retailer after Rabindranath's grand wholesale efforts; it is, so to speak, inevitable; but because Satyendranath's merchandise is apparently identical, his place in Bangla poetry is so clouded by uncertainty. He has used Rabindranath's props and costumes, the same play of seasons, the same pictures of rural life, of patriotism; but the force of emotion and the warmth of faith that we find behind every word or object – flower, bird, moon, cloud, dewdrop – used by Rabindranath, because of which even the hundredth reiteration of the 'sigh of the jasmine woods'[3] can evoke afresh in us the melancholic longing for heaven, is wholly lacking in Satyendranath; when we read his poetry we often feel that his 'feelings' are artificial, churned up merely for the sake of composing poetry. That dream which according to Rabindranath is a vision, that dream which according to Rabindranath is also an awakening, becomes, according to Satyendranath, a mere daydream; that flower which was the symbol of the world-spirit is transformed into a fancy plaything; thoughtfulness becomes superficial brooding; a serious quest turns into luxuriousness; and the beauteous spirit of humanity *manassundari*[4] manifests itself as a trivial game of fairies.[5] At the same time, there is a degeneration in terms of style as well; the writing that emerges, after Satyendranath dispenses with the inner wisdom, control, and taste that is present in the intoxicating sweetness that pervades Rabindranath's rhythm, contains only a thin tune, a hollow sound, and a quick, rapid beat that can be perceived even by the untutored reader of poetry. This is what made Satyendranath so popular in his time, he adulterated Rabindranath's poetry to just that extent that would appeal to the mass. Satyendranath, thus, became the embodiment of just what the common mass of readers expected, or received, from Rabindranath. He demanded nothing from his readers except the ability to listen, so his poetry became a kind of playing at writing, a species of metrical exercise. This thing we call 'play' is permissible in the composition of literature only as long as there is some kind of intention behind it, if there isn't, it becomes mere childishness.[6]

And this directionless effort of composing rhyme merely for the sake of rhyme, this childish procedure, had once appeared in a major way in Bangla verse; the huge number of innocent, easy-listening, and insubstantial verses that had flooded monthly magazines in the name of poetry at the time Satyendranath's fame was at its height, when his influence had exceeded that of even Rabindranath, has been wholly swept away by the benevolent passage of time. As Rabindranath's poetry was transformed seven-fold into mere rhyming trinkets and lozenges at the hands of Satyendranath and his disciples, it became apparent that there was nowhere else to go in that direction, and it was time to return.

*

It is not my intention to criticise Satyendranath and his band, I have merely been trying to explain the historical situation. I know whatever there is to say in their support; and this has been implicitly stated in the first part of this essay. Their time was unfavourable, and it was unfavourable precisely because it was favourable; there was no conception of a poet's task other than adding to Rabindranath's lustre. In the case of prose, we have the appearance of two followers of Rabindranath who came soon after him, yet who, nevertheless, were wholly original – Pramatha Chaudhuri (1868–1946) and Abanindranath Tagore (1871–1951); but in poetry, the rise of Rabindranath was so all encompassing that it took two to three decades for Bengal to overcome its awestruck astonishment. This was the time of Satyendranath and his group, and they withstood Rabindranath's first tremendous blow, that is to say, they helped those who followed to withstand it; and for this we are indebted to them. This is not something I say from abstract analysis, I have earned the right to say it in the light of my own experience. In my youth, I too have experienced the spell of Rabindranath, the desire to escape from which seemed to be wrong – like being engaged in treason; and I have known, too, the drowsy intoxication of Satyendranath, the magic of his fragile sound. And Bangla poetry spent year after year on this; no one wanted anything else, no one could imagine that anything else was even possible – until such time as Nazrul Islam appeared triumphantly with the flag of his *bidrohi*[7] (revolutionary) poetry.[8] That was the first time that Rabindranath's spell was broken.

I have called Nazrul Islam a swabhabkavi in the historical sense, which is undeniable. His writing is intimately bound with our previously mentioned 'childishness' in terms of formal technique; I cannot see in Satyendranath the literal echoes of Rabindranath that can be found in the love poems Nazrul composed in *Balaka*-metre;[9] and traces of Satyendranath, too, can be found in Nazrul's verse. Nazrul's poetry is unrestrained, unstructured, loud; there is no tendency towards maturity there, as he has written throughout like a talented child, with no change taking place in his poetry – one cannot find any difference between his writings from the age of twenty and when aged forty. Nazrul's faults are manifestly clear, but his individuality shines through all his faults; despite everything, it is undeniably true that he is the first original poet after Rabindranath. Satyendranath is at least his equal in terms of skill, and his diversity is somewhat greater, but the difference between these two poets lies in the fact that Satyendranath seems to be tied to or contained within Rabindranath while Nazrul Islam appears as a separate poet who succeeds Rabindranath – minor, of course, but new. The way in which Nazrul broke free from the extreme heat of Rabindranath, achieving the impossible, so to say, happened quite easily; there was no history of concentrated effort behind this; rather this became possible because of some fortuitous circumstances. Nazrul composed poetry with the same ideals as Satyendranath, but his distinctiveness derived from the stark difference in his background. He was a Muslim, born into a different tradition, but at the same time one who embraced the Hindu ethos, not through effort, but spontaneously. His childhood and youth were spent not in a city, not in the effort to become a *bhadralok* in school and college, but in sessions of *jatragan* and *letogan*,[10] running away from home to work in a bakery and then becoming a soldier. These things, which were disadvantages in societal terms, became distinct advantages when he set his hand to writing poetry. Because his circumstances were different and somewhat wild, and because, instead of troubling him, these circumstances only served to strengthen his inborn faculties, he was able to escape Rabindranath without any kind of literary preparation, solely on the strength of his own nature, infusing Bangla poetry with fresh blood. Though there was not the same amount of nourishment as there was excitement in his poetry, even then he at least awakened a desire for the new; and though his direct influence was not very permanent or useful, he was at least able to show that it was possible for Bangla poetry to follow a path that was different from Rabindranath's. The desire that he awakened sought its fulfilment in many ways: along came Mohitlal Majumder (1888–1952) with his muscular strength, after throwing off the Satyendranath-induced stupor that had infused his *Swapan Pasari* (1921); came Jatindranath Sengupta's (1887–1954) shallow, but for those times useful, anti-religiosity; and after these experiments appeared the latest effort of the *Kallol* group,[11] and the bell was rung for Bangla literature to take a new turn.

*

Nazrul Islam did not himself know that he was bringing forth a new era: there is social and political revolt in his compositions but no literary revolt. If he had not been a lyricist and composer, and if he had not embraced the novelty of the Persian *ghazal*, as fortunately he did, then he would have remained content with following the ideals of Rabindranath–Satyendranath. But he was able to spread the discontent that was not present in his own mind in the minds of others; it did not take long for the process that arose unconsciously in him to rise to the surface. The primary characteristic of what is called the *Kallol-yug* is revolt, and the target of that revolt is Rabindranath.

For the first time, there arose among new poets a sense that Rabindranath was inadequate – not as criticism of the barren past, but with respect to their own creations. It was felt that in Rabindranath's poetry, there was no intimacy with the real, no depth of passion, no sign of the trouble and strife of life; it was felt that his vision of life had unjustly neglected the unavoidable corporeality of human beings. It is undeniable that there was excess in this revolt, and there was some mudslinging too, but the truth that was also there has been realised with the passage of time. The main thing was nothing more than this: an attempt to wake up from an idle fancy and an effort to endure and resist Rabindranath. There was need for this revolt – for not only the liberation of Bangla poetry, of course, but also in order to truly receive Rabindranath. It must be noticed that those young writers who had been the most ardent admirers of Rabindranath were at the forefront of this revolution; I know of at least one young man who would recite *Purabi* like a madman lying in bed by night and write opinion pieces attacking Rabindranath by day. This cannot be dismissed as the loss of appetite brought about by an excess of drink, for the treatment was also present within, because the desire for balance and the quest for a path to self-expression were both there. 'What I have to say I shall say in my own words' – this desire had become overwhelming that day, and thus Rabindranath had to be placed at a distance, at least for then. When the season for *fazli* mangoes is over, I shall not ask for even more *fazli*-like mangoes, I shall ask for custard apple instead – this witticism from *Sesher Kabita* (1929) was true for this time.[12] The fact that one becomes a mere fragment of Rabindranath if one tries to become a better Rabindranath finally became clear – the Kallol group thus aspired to become different from Rabindranath.

Obviously, saying it like this makes the whole thing appear kind of mechanical and also somewhat forced. It is not as though there was no element of force here; in fact, some rubbish was also brought in by the stream of this revolt, but the clear contours of this revolt became apparent when the turbulent waters of Kallol had subsided, and Sudhindranath Datta's journal, *Parichay* (1931) appeared, displaying signs of intellectual stability and maturity, and the signatures of the newest poets began appearing one by one in *Kavita* (1935). Sudhindranath's criticism helped clear the air; and, on the other hand, after the high pitch of Nazrul, after the mellow tones of Premendra Mitra (1904–1988), there appeared in Bangla poetry a compactness, an intellectual density, a presence of hitherto-neglected elements in the selection of subject-matter and diction, and a blurring of the boundaries between verse and prose. Needless to say, such transformation comes about in literature as a result of the spirit of the age, but the solutions to its practical problems need the specific individual talents possessed by different poets. And for the Bengali poet in the third and fourth decades of the 20th century, the biggest problem was, of course, Rabindranath. The mutual dissimilarities between our modern poets are many and in some cases irreconcilable; the palpable and sensuous Jibanananda and the cerebral, decadence-conscious Sudhindranath stand at two opposite ends, and then again Amiya Chakravarty (1901–1986) has not the slightest thing in common with either of them. Yet the reason why these poets are all participants in the same movement is because they have brought in the taste of the new in various ways, the common feature that is noticeable in each lies in the fact that instead of merely enjoying the wealth of their predecessors, they have been actively engaged in increasing its returns, with interest; whatever be the kinds of things that can be found in their writings cannot quite be found in Rabindranath. How may I avoid [the influence of] Rabindranath? – this thought has worked, unconsciously, and sometimes even consciously, in their minds; some poets, like Jibanananda, have simply stepped away from Rabindranath, while others have found the strength to confront him by assimilating him fully. In this battle, and this can well be called a battle, they found sustenance from the storehouse of Western literature and their arsenal in the uncertainty, tiredness, and ennui of modern life. If one pursues the thread of their relationship with Rabindranath, one finds intriguing results: it will be seen that Bishnu Dey bears the burden of Rabindranath in a sarcastically oblique manner; Sudhindranath openly uses Rabindranath's phrasing and diction in his description of the life-consuming monstrous spirit; whereas Amiya Chakravarty, despite being a denizen of Rabindranath's world, brings wonder into this world through his technical diversity and by introducing much matter from the realm of prose into his poetry. That is to say, they did not remain content with Rabindranath's hypnotic forms, and they learned how to put him to use, thus making meaningful his influence on the subsequent development of Bangla poetry. It became possible for Subhas Mukhopadhyay to write original poetry of the highest order by transforming '*bela je porey elo jalkey chal*' ('the day wanes, let us go to the water') (Rabindranath Tagore, 'Badhu', *Manasi*, 1890) to '*galir morey bela je parey elo*' ('on the bend of the lane the day wanes') (Subhas Mukhopadhyay, 'Badhu', *Padatik*, 1940) and '*kalsi kankey laye path sey banka*' ('with pitcher on hip she takes the turn of the path') to '*kalsi kankey chalchi mridu taley*' ('with pitcher on hip, I move in slow rhythm') through a process of literal imitation, because the example of these poets was before him; such a thing would not have been possible ten years earlier. Satyendranath and his peers would echo Rabindranath without being aware of it – this proved fatal for them; but these poets are fully aware of just how indebted they are to Rabindranath and have no hesitation in letting their readers know this fact, sometimes they will put in entire lines [from Rabindranath], mixing them in with their own conceptions. This lack of hesitation, this staunch courage, is proof of their self-sufficiency and their self-confidence. Irrespective of how their poetry perishes in the future, they will be honoured by history because of this reason: that at a time of crisis for Bangla poetry, they restated the fundamental truth that *satya-siva-sundar* cannot be received unchanged from the hands of the guru; it must be sought with one's own life, and the art of poetry is not inherited but must be earned through one's own labour.

Bangla poetry grew out of its state of Rabindranath-dependent infancy in the two decades between the two World Wars from the time of Nazrul Islam to that of Subhas Mukhopadhyay. Those who emerged after this period and those who would arrive even later had nothing to fear from Rabindranath – that obstacle had been overcome by the poets mentioned earlier. Of course, a few other dangers were becoming apparent, such as getting sucked into the maze of Jibanananda's diction or the whirlpools of Bishnu Dey and other poets, from which today's young poets seem unable to escape, despite their best efforts. There is nothing to be surprised or saddened by this – as this has always been the case; the pressure of repetition leads to the cracking of the shell of the old, and new seeds are scattered from within. I see that those new poets who are writing nowadays are far too busy with technique right from the start; I know where this has come from, and I have supported it at the appropriate time, but now I cannot but see it as an aberration. The techniques which were necessary during the writing of *Chorabali* (Bishnu Dey 1937) or *Khasra* (Amiya Chakravarty 1938) have now become clichés, and besides, when there is an excessive concern with style, as is the case with contemporary English and American poetry, one understands that intellectual bankruptcy is not far behind. I do not want to reduce the importance of formal achievement by saying this, but, after all debts have been paid to form and technique, it still needs to be said that poetry is not written in order to display virtuosity in the use of vowels and consonants, but in order to say something, and, the greater the thing that needs to be said, the more lucid its expression, the greater is the formal achievement that is found there. It seems to be the case that the time has come for Bangla poetry to cultivate lucidity anew, and the need has arisen to recover its spontaneity. And here Rabindranath may be of assistance – I hesitated even while saying this because one does not need to give any advice about the primal source of a thing. That it is no longer necessary to discuss the matter of Rabindranath's influence is a sign of the maturity of Bangla poetry and also a proof of Rabindranath's freedom from the shackles of devotion. He stretches across the entire horizon of Bangla literature, and he is part of the very flesh and blood of the Bangla language; in order to be indebted to him, it is no longer all that necessary even to study him, for it can be taken for granted that the debt is universally acknowledged, not just today, but for any writer in Bangla for the ages to come. And even where an intimate relationship is directly established, even there, it is a matter of joy that there is no longer a possibility of being bewitched; Rabindranath's appropriateness and usefulness will gradually permeate and find expression in multifarious ways in Bangla literature. The Bengali poet of the coming days will have to rise on his foundation; an indication of the next steps of the evolution of Bangla poetry may also be found here.

Translation: Samantak Das

Notes

1 Buddhadeva Bose, 'Rabindranath O Uttarsadhak', in *Sahityacharcha*, Kolkata: Signet Press, 1954, pp. 135–152.

2 Rabindranath Tagore, 'Introduction' to *Rabindra-rachanabali*, Vol. I, Kolkata: Visvabharati, 1939, p. xv.

3 Although the theme is recurrent in Tagore's writing, the exact phrase '*juthibaner dirghaswase*' may be found in his song '*Amar kantha hate gan ke nilo bhulaye*', *Gitabitan*, Kolkata: Visvabharati, 1974, p. 275.

4 The idea of *Manassundari* is found in Tagore's eponymous poem in *Sonar Tari* (1894). Tagore had developed an idea of *jivandevata* (lit. god of [my] life) in the course of his poetic maturity, often understood as the fountainhead of his creativity. Scholars have tried to understand manassundari as the jivandevata in her '*preyasi*' (beloved) form.

5 '*Lal Pari Nil Pari*' in original also refers to two of Satyendranath Dutta's poems collected in *Abhra-Abir* (1916).

6 Author's note: 'This 'intention' is not necessarily some kind of definite object; an emotion can often provide the necessary direction, the consolidation necessary for success, to a composition. For example, let us compare Satyendranath's '*tultul tuktuk/tuktuk tultul/kon phul tar tul/tar tul kon phul/tuktuk rangan/kingshuk phullo/noy noy nischoy/noy tar tullo*' ('Piyanor Gan', lit. The Piano Song, *Abhra-Abir*, Calcutta: R.H. Srimani & Sons, 1916, pp. 21–24) to '*ogo bodhu sundori/tumi modhu manjari/pulokito champar loho abhinandan/swarner patrey/phalguno raatrey/mukulito mollika mallyer bondhon*' (*Gitabitan*, Calcutta: Visvabharati, 1974, p. 505). These are both written in the same metre, composed in the same playful way, and neither has any tangible message to convey. But just why the latter is incomparably better even as a specimen of verse cannot be explained merely through the distribution of alliteration and sound-combinations – its poetic value is the real thing here. The first example has no emotion behind it, and it has been created wholly mechanically, and so its rhythm is so immature and so childish. The mastery of rhythm in '*ogo bodhu sundori*' must be sought in the touch of emotion that is present, which has also enabled it to become poetry. The thing is, unless one is a good poet, one cannot compose decent rhymes; the greater the poet the greater the mastery of poetic devices; and the mere rhymester who receives the title 'king of rhyme' has, ultimately, nothing to teach us, even about rhyme'.

7 'Bidrohi' is also the name of one of Nazrul's most famous poems, published in 1922.

8 Author's note: 'Of course, there was a kind of opposed current present then, but this was wholly in the realm of criticism, and this criticism, too, was not particularly intelligent, but more interested in picking holes. What was necessary for literature was not 'opposing' Rabindranath but rather revealing the real nature of Rabindranath. And because Suresh Chandra Samajpati or Bipin Chandra Pal was of no help here, they had absolutely nothing to do with the breaking and remaking of Bangla poetry'.

9 Rabindranath Tagore experimented with Bangla verse forms and metrical patterns throughout his poetic career. He used a free verse form in *Balaka* (1916), for the first time in Bangla poetry, which was immediately hailed by the larger poetic community.

10 Jatragan is a theatrical form found in Bengal and Odisha. Letogan is another performing art tradition common in the Rahr region of Bengal. While the first depends on a set script and a formal stage, the second is more improvisatory in nature.

11 Dineshranjan Das and Gokulchandra Nag brought out a monthly journal called *Kallol* in 1923. Starting with Suniti Devi and Manindralal Basu besides the two editors, who also constituted the 'Four Arts Club', a number of young and upcoming poets, novelists, and writers of short stories gathered around the periodical, which helped bring about a modernist revolution in Bangla literature. Such authors included Nazrul Islam, Premendra Mitra, Achintyakumar Sengupta, Balaichand Mukhopadhyay, Jibanananda Das, and Buddhadeva Bose himself. Although the journal published poems by Tagore at times, it is largely credited for the avant-garde movement in post-Tagore Bangla literature, and the contributors are often referred to as the *Kallol group* and the period as the *Kallol-jug* or the '*Kallol*-era'. It may be mentioned in this context that the publication of *Kallol*, which came out for seven years, was closely followed by the publication of three major periodicals of the time: *Sanibarer Chithi* (1924) and *Kali o Kalam* (1927) from Kolkata, and *Pragati* (1927) from Dhaka.

12 Author's note: 'In the line immediately preceding this, Amit Roy had said, "I will not say that we want something better from successors, rather I will say that we want something different." This is perfectly true. If one compares a poem to a poem, the difference between good and better is not that important, it becomes applicable only if one compares a poet to another poet, in totality. That is to say, though the difference between Rabindranath and other Bengali poets is immeasurable, a good poem by a minor poet may be as good as a poem by Rabindranath, if there is something unique to it, if it displays character. And there can be no doubt that after all the *fazli* mangoes have been consumed, the seasonal custard apple is infinitely superior to mangoes imported from Madras or mango-scented syrup, just as infinitely superior is *Sandhya Sangeet*, as compared to *Britrasamhar*, after Michael. In *Sesher Kabita*, Rabindranath uses Amit Roy's lecture on literature to describe the literary revolution of *Kallol*, even though in a satirical vein, but in doing so he is also writing down a general principle of literary history. This defence of Nibaran Chakraborty was done well, but the poem that followed this lecture was not sufficiently un-Tagorean to win Amit Roy the case'.

17 Sudhindranath Datta: The liberation of poetry

Introduction

Like Janus, Buddhadeva Bose wrote in an obituary, Sudhindranath Datta (1801–1960) and Jibanananda Das embody Bangla modernist poetry in its entirety. Beginning his poetic career as a close successor of Tagore in his first anthology of poems *Tanvi* (1930), Sudhindranath found his own diction in *Orchestra* (1935). His later works include the collections of poems *Krandasi* (1937), *Uttarphalguni* (1940), *Samvarta* (1953), and *Dasami* (1956); an anthology of translated verses titled *Pratidhwani* (1955) and two volumes of critical essays called *Swagata* (1938) and *Kulay o Kalpurush* (1957). Datta also published a journal called *Parichay* (1931) and edited it until 1943. Datta studied English Literature from Scottish Church College and enrolled simultaneously for post-graduate programmes in English Literature and Law, both of which he left unfinished. He worked for *The Statesman* as an editor and also served the Damodar Valley Corporation and the Air Raid Precautions programme during the Second World War. His unfinished autobiographical sketch *The World of Twilight* was published posthumously. The essay presented here, 'The Liberation of Poetry,' was read at a gathering in 1928, and it first appeared in print in the first volume of *Parichay* in July 1931. A significantly different version in the 1938 collection of essays, *Swagata*, has been translated for this volume.

The primary urge of the modernists was, as Buddhadeva Bose suggests in his essay *Rabindranath and his Successors*, to move out of the literary aura of Tagore and to find a new diction as well as a novel approach towards art and the world. Datta in his essay states that 'thc poet is not the progenitor of poetry, but its descendant' and tries to trace the emergence of modernism primarily through the English lyric tradition. He looks deeply into the thoughts of T.S. Eliot in this context and strongly argues for an 'impersonal' art of poetry, adhering to 'authenticity' and 'honesty'.

It may be mentioned in this context that *Parichay* successfully created a lively interest in the question of modernity among poets of his time. Tagore himself was a regular contributor to *Parichay*, and he took up the question of modernity in his essay 'Adhunik Kavya' (*Parichay*, April 1932) and

DOI: 10.4324/9781003224686-18

translated Eliot's 'Journey of the Magi' as 'Tirthayatri' in *Parichay*, in January 1933. Datta incorporated this translation by Tagore at the end of his essay when it was published in *Swagata* in 1938.

However, this was not the only change that he made in the 1938 edition of the essay. It is possible to trace a growing interest in Buddhist philosophy on the one hand and phenomenology on the other in Datta's thoughts. Through a few subtle but critical changes, he shifts from his earlier position regarding what constitutes poesis. While in 1931, he mentions extraordinary intellect and intuition (*swajna*) and a resonant empathy (*anukampan*) with the external subject as the fundamental elements of poetic genius, in 1938 he calls for an enlightened knowledge (*bodhi*) as well as universal empathy (*anukampa*).

*

The liberation of poetry[1]

Sudhindranath Datta

Poetry is primordial. Or, if this adjective offends our scientific sensibility, we may say that poetry was born when primitive man first wove various stretches of rhythmical sound with various objects and feelings in an indissoluble colligation. That happened thousands of years ago. After that point, human language gradually evolved; and man realised that sentences that locate the caesura at a consistent point are the easiest to remember. The development of poetry from such beginnings is easy to surmise: individuals would have emerged here and there whose imagination was quicker, whose memory was sharper, who were capable, with the silent approval and occasionally active participation of the community, of re-narrating memorable events at designated auspicious moments. As communities turned into ethnicities, as men started placing regular activities under the specialised control of professions, the previously unspecified role of managing narration ended up being assigned to the bards. Those bards can count the modern poet as their successor.

We need not go into the genealogy of poetry; that is the anthropologist's business. It suffices for us to understand that the poet is not the progenitor of poetry, but its descendant. The first poem appeared not in the mind of a particular individual but in that of a human collectivity; what the first poem represented was not one man alone, but life as a whole; the intent of early poetry was not analysis but synthesis. Between then and now, the manifest universality of poetry has suffered steady attrition; the stellar scope of its creativity stands confined today to the meteoric fragment called the poet. This has prompted the question: has poetry reached the end of the road? I believe it has. It is my view that this particular journey has reached its natural conclusion. If after this moment any major effulgence does emerge from poetry, I will construe it as the crematorial fire of some meteor rushing to an untypical doom.

From the foregoing, it does not follow that this inevitable decline can be laid at the door of the modern poet. On the contrary, I would suggest that never before in the history of literature has the poet merited the respect we owe him today. There is perhaps evidence at last in favour of the declarations of his superhumanity that had been heard from time to time. Even as he faces the steamroller of civilisation which, having made short work of the greatest achievements of the past, is about to flatten him, the poet has the audacity to stand guard at the gate of beauty. He has no hope left. He is aware that defeat is certain. He realises that he is alone: the people he is fighting for perceive his promethean defiance as some sort of madness; the world he cherishes will survive only fortuitously, if at all. And yet his efforts are of the highest order, he does not stop singing. His songs perhaps do not convey joy and gladness. Anger and frustration have perhaps made his voice strident. He is perhaps screaming to wish away his anxiety. Nevertheless, only his words can be heard over the cacophony that heralds the impending catastrophe. He thus deserves our homage; howsoever eclipsed he may be, he deserves our homage.

It will be said that I exaggerate; and that, if poetry is truly an art, then it need have no fear on account of an antagonistic environment. This view is not easy to dismiss as irrelevant. It is indeed its ability to bring about congruity between man and his environment that makes art so indispensable to life; and while hostile social surroundings can indeed make art impossible, nonetheless art must finally transcend its environment or admit total failure. The force of this argument becomes clear from the evidence of modern painting and music; whatever may have befallen the other fine arts, it cannot be gainsaid that even the grotesque atrocities of contemporary civilisation have received spectacular aesthetic representation in the painting and music of our times.

There is one matter that I must clarify at this juncture. The position I am addressing has nothing to do with the fuss that was made in the ninth decade of the 19th century under the rubric of art for art's sake. On the contrary, that position is best viewed as a protest against the unfounded hubris of Wilde and his blasé friends. Whatever else we may have lost over the last fifty years or so, considerable interest has accrued to our experiential capital. The abundance of conflict has driven home the lesson that serious independence is not only rare in the human world but even unavailable in the most secluded corners of the universe; and given that art is no alien monster but inhabits the same world we all do, it follows that the criterion for artistic achievement is situated at its encounter with contemporary lived reality. This is not to say that every poet is a slave of time. However, one can assert that it is only unanchored poetry that is not amenable to contextual assessment; and, while such poems may successfully seek a pyramid's shelter and cheat death and may satisfy the curiosity of a few, nonetheless they fail to address the tacit questions of the soul.

If we apply these criteria, several problems of literature lend themselves to resolution. It is here, perhaps, that one discovers the key to the otherwise puzzling fact that Tennyson was unable to write great poetry although he had all the qualities of a great poet. The poet's duty is to gather the disorderly experiences of every day into a garland of definitive perceptions. The poet's purpose is to build an equation that brings the fragments of life around him into alignment with life's continuum. The poet's task is to distil pure consciousness through the chemistry of his own consciousness. This cannot be accomplished by withdrawing from the world or through renunciation or within the constraints of aristocratic prescriptions – poetry finds its freedom in acceptance; a poet who seeks a portion of eternity cannot afford to be a chooser but must walk the streets of the city as a beggar living on leftovers that come his way. For the path of poetry offers no shortcuts: every ravine must be crossed on foot, every mote of dust must be welcomed into one's tangled hair, every thorn must be allowed to draw blood; escape is not an option there, to pause is to perish, to try to turn back is to be kicked by one's successor. Anyone unwilling to acknowledge this truth will do well to recall the dismal end-game of 19th-century poetry. When Cézanne was looking for beauty on whitewashed walls, mist-draped Swinburne rushed from grove to grove hoping for a tryst with a forest nymph – laying bare the ultimate vacuity of supraterrestrial art.

It was surely because Tennyson and Swinburne's great enterprise went bankrupt that poets suddenly took to critical evaluation on such a scale; and it soon became clear to all that a vain endeavour to preserve the old way was what had led poetry in its complacency to lose everything it had. The auditors found it easy to demonstrate that the entire 19th century, apart from a few poets at its outset, had seen a line of spendthrifts, that the thought of contributing to the capital never once occurred to them; that they did not realise that even a prodigious estate must keep expanding to meet the needs of new scions and to offset the effects of depreciation, on pain of destruction, a destruction that no gold mine can protect the estate from. At the inception of the 20th century, it became obvious that endless abuse had dried the very marrow in poetry's bones – that all that was left, bereft of meaning or emotion, was a skeleton – in a desert populated by echoes lay an exhausted, drained, characterless skeleton.

> What are the roots that clutch, what branches grow
> Out of this stony rubbish? Son of man,
> You cannot say, or guess, for you know only
> A heap of broken images, where the sun beats,
> And the dead tree gives no shelter, the cricket no relief,
> And the dry stone no sound of water . . .[2]

It may not be readily admitted that this passage accurately characterises the 19th century. Some will definitely invoke Browning and claim that at least that poet does not answer to this description. I more than agree that even in the poetic desert of the 19th century, Browning did not confine himself to nostalgia but was creative. It was he alone, apart from Wordsworth and Coleridge, who realised that poetry, if it is to survive, cannot afford to sit in the comfort of the decadent mansion it has inherited and dream of fairy tale princes; it must shed its faded crown, its rusty armour, its threadbare garland of victory, and walk right into the marketplace, where virtue and vice, good and evil, god and demon are busy vocalising their disunity. Among his contemporaries, Browning alone – if only hesitantly – acknowledged that the dance of the gods is not always eurhythmic and that the cry of a mother in labour does occasionally interrupt the melody of the spheres; only he recognised that the procession called life may sometimes suffer a slight diminution of splendour when the haves stay away, but that it turns into a wake when the have-nots are excluded.

This is why Browning was the first to try to situate poetry in its temporal context. While he made an effort, he did not, however, succeed; and a search for the factors that led to this great failure leads us to two characteristics of his writing. First, apart from a few rare counterexamples, Browning's protagonists were all tourists from the afterworld; and second, all the fallen that he spoke for had gone astray either under coercion or owing to circumstances. The former represents, not acceptance of reality, but escapism; and the latter counts not as insight, but as sophistry, the conceited sophistry of a self-righteous advocate making a plausible case on his client's behalf and deceiving the judge. For Browning – however harsh this may sound – is a Christian, not Christ, which is why he makes it a point to show that the fallen, though unworthy of sitting in the ranks of the virtuous in this world, will receive grace in the afterworld; that the circle broken in life will be made whole in death; that meanwhile the infinite circuit of the conventional world will proceed without a hitch, its unruffled onward march will reaffirm the ubiquitous goodness of the order of things, silencing the concrete questions that the sceptic keeps raising. Unfortunately, even this omnibenevolent world displays such perversities that I find myself unable to assent to Browning's emphatic optimism; even the morbid fascination with filth that one finds in pornography strikes me as somewhat healthier than his flight from reality.

Be that as it may, the 20th century dawned amidst these exaggerated affirmations of virtue. Consequently, no serious poet could fail to perceive that a return from self-deception to reality would involve a ruthless abandonment of all that is decorative, of all contentless portraiture. For the mere construction of a new tower accomplishes very little; one has to render the structure fit for human habitation and in tune with the times; one must let the sunshine come in and dry its damp walls; the wind's twelve quarters should not knock on its bolted doors in vain. Therefore, placing brick on brick with a tawdry external beauty in mind will not do: one must keep in view those who are going to live here. One must remember that they are human beings; one must remember that they are creatures of flesh and blood, subject to joy and suffering, prone to change, and eager to flourish. If this means jettisoning conventional architecture, so be it; if such a move invites unjust charges of nihilism and materialism, they must be accepted. The first imperative is authenticity, the second imperative is authenticity, the third imperative is authenticity, and the last imperative is authenticity. The 20th century is all about authenticity and honesty.

We tend to be suspicious about the word 'honest' nowadays. For it has served as cover for a disproportionately large number of deceptions. Nonetheless, this notion has become indispensable. Authenticity in literature means direct perception wedded to non-apparent revelations. In other words, when a poet intends to speak for a thing seen or an emotion felt, his verses shall cleave to that object or that feeling and shall have no truck with its high or low value in the socially recognised scheme of things.

At this point, some readers are likely to object that a poet who devalues what is socially recognised cannot claim to embrace the world. My response is to recall that 'society' is not synonymous with 'world'. If it makes sense to love India as one's own land without acknowledging the validity of the Indian Penal Code, then devaluing the socially recognised scheme of things does not involve asking the world to go to hell; just as the government administering India does not represent the authentic being of India, likewise the comportment and beliefs of certain persons do not betoken the universal reality of the humans. It follows that one who would view death as irrelevant would indeed be turning his back on the world; but one who has lost faith in the notion of female chastity is hardly devoid of insight into life – on the contrary, it is he who can be seen as truly believing in life. For death is indeed the core fact of life: to set it aside is to insult life itself; but the human body, or for that matter human society, is so trivial when viewed in the context of life as a cosmic process that a decision not to sanctify the fidelity of women does not devalue life but on the contrary affirms it all the more.

Those who might find this approach to honesty excessively abstract may need to be reminded that without access to the transcendent dimension, even ordinary, unsubtle mortals can hardly survive, let alone poets. Even if there is no goodness at the core of the cosmos, the poet must establish an imaginary order in terms of which our quotidian segments of experience can be collected into meaningful arrangements; and bringing any kind of order to the nothingness surrounding us presupposes two rare desiderata: consciousness, a pure consciousness, and resolve, a self-effacing resolve. It would, however, be seriously unfair to imagine that only the poet has a need for, or a right to, these two pole stars. When it grows dark, both of these beacons become indispensable; one who is not given to aimless wandering and fervently wishes to reach his goal will need these two pole stars to navigate by. The poet is distinguished only to the extent that his words lend voice to the infinite quest of man; this is also the limit to his capacity for distinction.

For any poet whose personal itinerary diverges from this universal quest is on his way to the neglected shelves of the library. It is perhaps in this sense that E.M. Forster has said that all great art is impersonal; personal experience becomes significant only when it moves onto the fourth temporal axis and merges with universal experience. This is why the poet cannot afford to reject and why he must have a sense of his time.

Perhaps an image will help drive the point home. The poet is like a matchmaker; his utility ends with the union of the bride and the groom; it would be absurd to try to remember his name after that moment. The task of bringing effective unions about, however, calls for extraordinary intelligence and tact and perhaps for illumination as well. It is not enough for a matchmaker to memorise the names of all prospective suitors of both sexes; he must also attain a universal empathy that enables him to spot the right matches at once. The way to such an attainment does not go through his own marital experience – that experience is a hindrance, not an aid; to even have preferences is a luxury he can ill afford. If the exigencies of his taste dissuade him from finding a match for a woman just because her face launches no ships, then the job no longer suits him, and it is time for him to retire. In the other direction, any attempt to apply his match-making expertise to his own home life is just as perilous. Therefore, he has no alternative but to be independent, scrupulously fair, and neutral; if matches made by him lead to dysfunctional marriages, general faith in the future of marriage as an institution is bound to suffer. It must have been considerations of this sort that led Eliot to characterise the poet as a '*catalytic* agent' – a term so clearly akin to the Bengali word *ghatak* 'match-maker' that Bengali chemists use *anughatak* (a derivative of the word *ghatak*) for the notion of 'catalyst'.

The conclusion that art has no business being purely personal may alarm many readers. They may well say, or at least think, that at a time when the overmechanisation of civilisation has reduced nearly everybody to the interchangeability of dust particles, when only the poet stood apart as a reminder of the human capacity to be different, it is now the poet's turn, alas, to be industrialised; the project of cutting human trees down and making matchsticks of them all will now proceed unimpeded, now that its last opponent has been removed. Such fear, however, would be misplaced; for it is precisely the complete immersion of the personal in the universal that sets the shackled personality free at last. The truth of this proposition has been demonstrated again and again in history; even today, at the moment of tradition's inexorable decline, the names of Buddha, Christ, or St Francis of Assisi are neither meaningless nor impotent, they can still inspire people to accomplish the impossible. But I do not mean to emphatically invoke the ideals of religion in the context of poetry; my point is not that they are memorable on account of their piety; it is their self-immersion in the universal that is of concern to my argument. In other words, just as spiritual greatness can only be attained by abandoning one's isolated ego, likewise great poetry begins where personal joy and sorrow end. This is not to say that every poet is identical to every other poet; despite their shared spiritual greatness, Christ is hardly to be equated with Buddha; likewise, for all that they are both great poets, Shakespeare is quite distinct from Goethe.

If there is an air of paradox to this conclusion, perhaps a metaphor might help dispel it. Poetry is like a sea, while the poet is only a river. He may, if he so pleases, dive into the sand of a desert. If he wants to merge into the sea, however, he must flow in a particular direction. Although he shares with other rivers this directional imperative, nevertheless he retains the right to choose whatever depth, whatever speed, whatever chemical composition may best suit his individual trajectory. As for the sea of poetry, we find considerable variation there as well. Some of its coasts are mountainous, some spots are muddy; the waves are stormy in one area and unruffled in another. Even its overall contour is not fixed once for all: underneath its surface, the magma of human consciousness does its invisible work all the time, alternately augmenting and diminishing its superficial size. Furthermore, evidently its reception varies, depending as it does on time, place, and circumstance. There is one constant, however, that characterises it through all this variation; in the absence of a better term, we may use the word 'texture' for this unchanging quality of poetry. One finds texture to some degree, however, in every animate or inanimate inhabitant of creation; it therefore follows that poetry is by its very nature intimately connected to the universe.

Those of us who are still tinged by the afterglow of the 19th century's individualism will perhaps inveigh against impersonal poetry's claim to sovereignty; their objection to granting poetry the right to set its own standards may take the form of asserting that to allow this would remove from literature all that is melodious, leaving but a grotesque medley of screams in its stead. If the point of such an argument is to demonstrate the superiority of traditional literature over modern writing, I have no retort to offer; the vagaries of taste lie beyond all reasoning. Whatever else 19th-century poetry may have been about, however, it had little truck with individuality; to establish this, all one needs to do is recall the lessons of one's student days. I cannot say whether candidates for examinations today are obliged to quote 'appropriate passages' in order to demonstrate Wordsworth's influence on later authors: in my time, however, only those endowed with a photographic memory would top the class; had I acquired that rare skill in my youth, it would have been easy for me to reproduce abundant evidence that poets in the 18th and 19th centuries did not seek uniqueness of signature either – that in order to conquer the hearts and minds of their readers they merely conformed to contemporary canons of taste. In other words, as circumstances changed, the goddess of poetry exchanged her garlands and flowery crowns for ornaments of solid gold, and on every tryst with the poet she would always insist on wearing these paraphernalia of conventional beauty to mask her incipient decay. At the inception of the 19th century, Wordsworth revitalised literature by putting it back in touch with popular speech, thus terminating the career of that overdressed and promiscuous society lady known as classical poetry; this is why he deserves our homage – this is why literature shall remember him for ever.

Wordsworth tried to unify prose and poetry, but he failed: the language of daily speaking is distinct from that of poetry, and this is as it should be; prose and poetry are differently constituted. If prose rests its case on reason, poetry's quest is for passion. Hence, prose keeps pace with the steps of an argument, whereas poetry dances to the tune of feelings; where prose elicits our informed assent, poetry would rather have our devotion; prose indefatigably adds line to line until a complete picture emerges, while poetry makes no effort at all, but just places a few dots on the canvas of our imagination, from which the very same portrait magically springs forth. This mystical enterprise of the poet is brought to fruition with the help of imagery and symbolism. A word has two sides to it: a semantic denotation and an aesthetic connotation. Prose deploys words by dint of their first aspect: words in prose convey elements of thought. But poetry resorts to words under the spell of their second aspect: the poetic word is a vehicle of feeling. It now becomes clear why poetry has forsaken aristocratic commiseration and taken to such fellow feeling as is felt by all men. On this basis one easily sees why the following passages are memorable poetry, so memorable that even lazy minds like mine find them easy to recall:

> . . . immemorial elms
> And murmuring of innumerable bees.[3]
> (Tennyson)

> I am late; the cherry blossoms gone;
> the day, my darling, was doomed.
> And yet, bearing your forgiveness,
> a smiling azalea blooms.[4]
> (Tagore)

> As cool as the pale wet leaves
> of lily-of-the-valley
> She lay beside me in the dawn.[5]
> (Ezra Pound)

> 'Grey sky surface, quivery, suffering. Where are you, cloud? Do come forth.
> Show your evening visage of languor, speak in words of measured pace.
> Soften the sun's eyes with your ointments, lull, oh lull him into sleep;
> Shower your raindrop kisses on everyone, bring your flush to every face.[6]
> (Satyendranath Datta)

Among twenty snowy mountains
The only moving thing
Was the eye of the blackbird.[7]
(Wallace Stevens)

It takes only a moment's reflection to realise that no dictionary can bring out the associative connotations of these passages. That these vehicles carry these connotations uniquely has to do not just with what the words mean, but also with the emotions underlying them, their arrangement, their sound qualities, and the appropriate use of metre. The aggregate of these characteristics is known as form; every constituent of form is indispensable. It is the complete union of form with content that gives birth to the poetic. Hence the untranslatability of poetry; hence the constitutive separateness of poetic diction from the way one speaks; hence the predominance of form in modern poetry. Wordsworth had imagined that abandoning classical artifice would be enough to eliminate the artificiality of poetry. But we have come to realise that language is only one of the foundations on which form rests. Thus the poet today is no longer satisfied with Wordsworth's advice. He maintains that pure poetry cannot afford to take form more seriously than content, for the bond between form and content is essential and constitutive.

The point is that poetry cannot escape the rule-governed character of language. A word that belongs to no language, one that merely strings sounds together to evoke some meaning-free resonance, can only find an appropriate niche in some religious chant, not in a poem. If the goal of poetry is to connect the poet's capacity for empathy with that of the reader, then poems will always have to source their words from the dictionary. This argument does not negate the poet's long-established right to coin the occasional new word but merely affirms the greater agility of adult words compared to toddlers and notes that the connotative power of alchemy exceeds that of chemistry. However, the agility of words is circumscribed by obvious limits, just as human efficiency also has limits to it. A word is like a coin; excessive use frays its edges; exposure to countless hands leaves it too dirty to count as currency; banished from the current of daily viability, it finds a new home in the glass case of a museum. Going obsolete must not be confused with oblivion; an archaic word has its uses in certain contexts. When the use value of an obsolete coin plummets, its exchange value as a numismatic rarity rises steeply.

It follows that, in sensitive hands, even archaic words do not diminish the literary worth of a poem; to see this, consider the Anglo-Saxon words in Doughty's writings. What goes for words of high lineage goes for swear words as well; in the right context, to convey this or that connotation, all words are pressed into service in modern poetry – words high or low, young or ancient, domestic or foreign. As far as language is concerned, the modern poet's only criterion is pertinence, for language is but one ingredient of form. This is why he has no choice but to reject Wordsworth's misplaced revolutionary zeal in matters of language. Note, however, that even the extremist Wordsworth, when moved by a need for perceptive and authentic diction, could bring himself to write:

And now the same strong voice more near
Said cordially, 'My friend, what cheer?
Rough doing these! as God's my judge,
The sky owes somebody a grudge!
We have had in half an hour or less
A twelve months' terror and distress!'[8]

And that our period's conservative Rupert Brooke, in a diction all his own, makes choices that are not so differently configured:

The damned ship lurched and slithered. Quiet and quick,
  My cold gorge rose; the long sea rolled; I knew
I must think hard of something or be sick
  And could think hard of only one thing – you! . . .

Do I forget you? Retchings twist and tie me,
  Old meat, good meals, brown gobbets, up I throw,
Do I remember? Acrid return and slimy,
  The sobs and slobber of a last year's woe.[9]

Language, feeling, and rhythm are the three elements that combine to constitute poetry. No a priori dictates should govern our handling of language or feeling; these two, like young men and women in our times, ignore the counsel of their elders and insist that the priority of passion requires the reinstatement of personal choice where partnerships are concerned. For good or ill, language and feeling have blackmailed us into submission with the threat of inauthenticity. It is now rhythm's turn. Will the anxious avoidance of the inauthentic even force us to stop counting the syllables? If this comes to pass, what remains of poetry? The question needs to be taken seriously.

A full examination of the issue, however, lies beyond our scope here. The point to be stressed is that rhythm and rhyme are very different indeed: rhyme is a relatively new poetic device, whereas rhythm has been with us since time immemorial. In our discussion of the origins of poetry, we suggested that poetry begins when rhythm and emotion meet. Our account may have been mistaken; we chose to put rhythm first, perhaps a privilege it does not deserve. Rhythm and emotion are surely twins, connected in every fibre; and one must note that the words 'emotion' and 'motion' are not synonymous – that emotion gives primacy to pauses rather than to motions. In other words, at the highest level of eloquence, no emotion chooses to run; it walks at an unhurried pace that distributes its movements and stops judiciously. Conceivably, sounds and pauses configured in this circumspect way are what constitute rhythm; if this is the right approach, then the frontier between prose and poetry is up for renegotiation. In this connection, consider Tagore's *Lipika*; one look at the following passage quoted from it should convince any reader that emotion-laden prose falls under the rubric of poetry.

> Here evening descends. Sun-god, in which land, on which seashore does your morning begin?
>
> Here the *rajanigandha* trembles in the darkness, like a veiled bride at the bridal chamber door: where does the dawn's *kanakchampa* blossom?
>
> Who wakes up? Puts out the lamp lit at dusk, throws away the garland of white roses woven at night?
>
> Here the doors shut one by one, there a window opens. Here the boat is tied to the shore, the boatman sleeps: there the wind has filled the sail.[10]

If we are able to break free of our habits when we listen to these lines, we detect the resonances of some rhythm beneath the surface. This sense of an underlying rhythmic order, however, has nothing mysterious to it; the symmetries in question are exclusively rooted in the alternating configuration of feelings and metaphors. The moment the evening on one of the scales is weighed down by the rajanigandha flowers, the counterweight of a kanakchampa flower blooms at dawn on the other scale. No sooner does our doubt manage to ask, 'Who just now woke?' than the sacrament and the garland conjure the question away. With the winds of dream on imagination's unfurled sails, the boat with the sleepy helmsman takes off on its journey to nowhere in particular.

If this text can be validly classified as poetry, we must acknowledge the possibility of writing poems without conforming to the metrical demands for which experts in poetics have been devising mathematical schemata over thousands of years. In fact, what metrics calls metre is nothing but a mechanical device; under that whirling Ferris wheel's undue influence, we sometimes miss the fact that a particular poem has no significant affective content to offer. Poets who wrote in Sanskrit had perfected the mechanics of metre, attaining superb heights that have successfully masked the egregious poverty of Sanskrit literature to this day. It is by such means that the following well-known verses from the *Ajavilāpa*, without the slightest touch of actual effect, are able to produce a perfect sense of profound grief in my mind:

> Sragiyaṃ yadi jīvitāpahā hṛdaye kiṃ nihitā na hanti mām.
> Viṣamapyamṛtaṃ kvacidbhavet amṛtaṃ vā viṣamīśvarecchayā.[11]

> If this wreath has the power to take away life, why does it not kill me, (when) placed on my breast? By the will of the almighty even poison sometimes becomes (is changed to) nectar, and nectar poison.[12]

But as soon as the spell is broken, I realise that Kālidāsa was forced to enlist the aid of poetry's pet nymph because the stream of spontaneous emotion had run dry.

Even modern poets who may not approve of my view in every detail will admit that, when poetry crosses the threshold of true greatness, the counting of syllables and other enumerables disappears, all that one sees is a magnificent simplicity. Where the language of poetry is the voice of authenticity, the rhythm of poetry is nothing but the footsteps of authenticity. It will be said that this is hardly a fresh discovery, that all great poets were always aware of this principle, and that the rhythm of living poetry is consistently selfless, consistently spontaneous. Indeed, a serious poet would never claim to be an innovator – he knows that what is merely novel can only invite ridicule; he therefore eschews invention and clings to discovery. His goal is to liberate tradition from the oppressive stranglehold of convention; he intends to restore the natural rights that poetry is entitled to. Since the inner nature of poetry is a concrete reality that he sees with full clarity, it is easy for him to grasp that Shakespeare's blank verse does not need the mediation of scholarly exegesis and that the following passage is such a direct transcription of the wild emotions of Lear that the reader would do well to meet the passage face to face, instructing the industrious annotator to keep his pedantic ideas to himself:

> Blow, winds, and crack your cheeks! rage! blow!
> You cataracts and hurricanes, spout
> Till you have drench'd our steeples, drown'd the cocks!
> You sulphurous and thought-executing fires,
> Vaunt-couriers of oak-cleaving thunderbolts,
> Singe my white head! And thou, all-shaking thunder,
> Strike flat the thick rotundity o' the world!
> Crack nature's moulds, all germens spill at once,
> That make ungrateful man![13]

The same capacity for supra-sensory listening that enables us to perceive tacit symmetries and intimations of equilibrium under the surface of even such incoherent raving also makes the following passage by D.H. Lawrence sound like a rhythmical poem to our ear:

> I wish that whatever props up the walls of light
> would fall, and darkness would come hurling heavily down,
> and it would be thick black dark for ever.
> Not sleep, which is grey with dreams,

nor death, which quivers with birth,
but heavy sealing darkness, silence, all immovable.
What is sleep?[14]

If the intimacy I postulate between feeling and rhythm is not just a figment of my imagination, then our a priori assumptions regarding metre are just as inexcusable as our usual inanities about language. It is best to let feeling find its own rhythm. Here, again, contextual appropriateness is the only criterion that matters; and even if it declines all counsel from the mathematics of metre, rhythm in *vers libre* invariably conforms to the standards of its own inner rigour, as in the examples we have just seen. But autonomy has nothing at all in common with unruliness; and if all rhythm manifests the footsteps of feeling, it follows that just as spikes on the emotional curve may lead to breaches of metrical regularity, likewise particular feelings as they cast about for an appropriate rhythm contour sometimes arrive at a solution that attracts no censure at all from the metrician. Consider an example of the latter:

When lovely woman stoops to folly and
Paces about her room again, alone,
She smoothes her hair with automatic hand
And puts a record on the gramophone.[15]

Interrupting *The Waste Land*'s convention-free, non-ornamental, speech-like handling of metre, T.S. Eliot abruptly resorts to this classical quartet in order to showcase an opprobrious love affair of our day. A moment's reflection will make it clear to us what makes the use of such a form apposite here. The first line is a quote from *The Vicar of Wakefield*, where Goldsmith characterises his frivolous heroine's departure from the norm in these terms. Now, the circulation of this passage over two hundred years has quite used up all the effect it once genuinely carried; what this dried-up husk of a line now conveys is a schmalzy, affectatious reference to feelings once felt. Thus, the moment I read this line, I, for one, am overwhelmed at the contentless sentimentality of the overtures of love that have become standard in our times; in the verses that follow, the way this grand and canonical beginning gives way to a cruelly nonchalant follow-through devastates me. The convention-bound narrowness of this passage displays for us the vacuity of an unperturbed, perceptually challenged woman pacing about the ruins of a nuptial room; and the word 'gramophone', highlighted by the rhyme, cheekily informs us that this trivial little farce plays out as mechanically and as stridently as any device of automatic, mechanical reproduction.

If this illustration of autonomous rhythm is placed alongside Pope's Homer, one sees immediately why the modern poet refuses to submit poetry to the established conventions. He maintains that a poem is like a crystal as science describes it: given an opportunity, it will assume the shape it is destined for; but external interference contributes nothing but pathological distortions. This view implies absolutely no trans-natural status for poetry; while the modern poet does admit the existence of inspiration, he construes it only as recompense for unending perspiration. It is natural to ask, at this point, why the poet has the audacity to demand recompense of any sort if poetry is so very autonomous and impersonal. The answer is that a poem's autonomy is comparable to that of a tree. Once upon a time it reached out for the sky, conceivably, impelled by the unalloyed joy of spontaneous growing. But the soil of earth's childhood was abundantly fertile, which is no longer the case. Today, the entire world has to be turned upside down in a frantic search for seeds for the bounteous tree of a poem to begin its earthly career. Perhaps, after days of arduous labour, a bud appears on the plant, but this leaves the poet with no time to even breathe; he must spend sleepless nights tending the plant so that this fortuitous emergence can blossom; and in return for this extraordinary devotion all that the poet asks is that the robust tree of poetry should not reserve the comfort of its shade for him alone but should extend this generosity to all visitors.

The description I have offered of the modern poet's disenchantment is of course an absurdly oversimplified summary – I am obviously obliged to save space. In reality, his progress has followed as straggling a path as that of the Israelites of old. The way to his promised land repeatedly disappeared in the sands of the desert, was forgotten where fleshpots beckoned, and was betrayed when he forsook his God to kneel before false idols. As he emerged from the excitement-filled tavern of the Symbolists, he was so enthralled by them that his eyes could not tell a molehill from a mountain. This inebriation dispelled, he promptly exchanged Symbolism's morbid sentimentality for Imagism's egregiously explicit vividness, expecting it to deliver. However, while images have clearly perceptible outlines, they remain lifeless, for they have nothing directly to do with flesh and blood; this is why the innovation-studded architecture of idolaters such as H.D.[16] gave way to the faux folksiness of the Georgian pastoral. Meanwhile, history unleashed the Great War on us all; the turmoil drowned those ruralising efforts; even those who would rather have toed the line were compelled to turn their gaze away from the yeoman's idyllic acre and look at the fields on the western front, where the plough is nowhere to be seen, where instead it is the guns that draw vivid lines of death. The ultimate expression of this realisation is perhaps to be found in the following poem by Owen:

> Move him into the sun –
>
> . . . .
>
> Think how it wakes the seeds, –
> Woke, once, the clays of a cold star.
> Are limbs so dear-achieved, are sides,
> Full-nerved – still warm – too hard to stir?

Was it for this the clay grew tall?
– O what made fatuous sunbeams toil
To break earth's sleep at all?[17]

The naturalness one had sought did begin here. But the trial by fire of the modern poet was far from over; he did not yet understand that peace would bring even more despair, more solitude, more terror than war itself. Only recently has his error been corrected; not a trace of his hubris and swagger remains; his completely unpretentious pen finds it easy today to write:

These fought in any case,
and some believing,
   pro domo, in any case . . .
. . . .

Died some, pro patria,
   non 'dolce', non 'et decor' . . .
walked eye-deep in hell
believing in old men's lies, then unbelieving
came home, home to a lie,
home to many deceits,
home to old lies and new infamy;
usury age-old and age-thick
and liars in public places.[18]

Was this his promised land, though?

I have been speaking of the modern poet's efforts; it is time now to evaluate his accomplishments. I am absolutely convinced that he has written great poetry. He will not rank with Shakespeare, perhaps; but this is a matter not of lesser excellence but of a difference of category. It is indubitable, of course, that most of the poets now writing are not modern but merely of recent vintage. But this demerit is hardly confined to our period of history; throughout the literature of ages past, too, the heat of the sand exceeded that of the sun. One serious charge against much of the best poetry of our times, however, must be accepted as partly valid: the charge that today's poetry is opaque. But obscurity has two sides to it – the reader's side and the author's. The type of obscurity that stems from the reader's laziness should not be laid at the author's door. Even if philosophy, science, and mathematics are set aside, consider the degree of enthusiasm, attention, and rigorous labour accepted as a precondition for entry into other fields of the humanities; if the poet requires at least that degree of respect and concentration, surely his demand is valid. In contrast, the type of obscurity that stems from a lack of imagination and reflects the poet's own irresolutions is only partly to be excused as a side-effect of our transitional times; it is on the whole something the poet must be held responsible for.

I have argued earlier that poetry attains immortality only when its quest moves beyond deliberations and arrives at insight. This dénouement is seldom, if ever, seen in modern poetry; and I, for one, do not expect to see the modern poet triumph on this front. For the elements of human living, once readily intelligible, have over five thousand years grown complex and contorted, a far cry from their early straightforwardness; and, given the continuous growth of our knowledge, we are no longer able even to naively grasp the old worldview. The intellect of our times is prone to scepticism; its scrutiny has subjected the once uncontested foundations of human achievements to such ruthless empirically based criticism that we tend to feel no serious respect any longer for the so-called eternal verities. Thus, the tree of poetry today is no longer like a banyan, securely rooted in the earth; it is more of a rhododendron in the hills, reaching out to the winds and the sky; its body is thus overarticulated and its stature stunted; its canopy gives no shade, its branches bear no fruit; all that it has to offer is a random restlessness and flowers – cruel, blood-drenched flowers.

Even after one admits the inevitable narrowness of scope in modern poetry, however, one cannot possibly ignore the great self-sacrifice of the modern poet. May we never forget that he once set out on his pilgrimage with everybody playing triumphal music to cheer him on, and with a clear goal ahead, guaranteed to be attainable and to bring him glorious fulfilment. His fellow travellers, unable to overcome the temptations of the wayside inns, have abandoned the quest; where he sets his head, the dark night denies him all stellar guidance. And yet he has plodded on, without pausing to breathe, not trembling at the dangers that lurk, not heeding the gradual dimming of all hope of a safe return. He has not once mistaken sentimentality for feeling; in his anxiety to experience every bit of the drama of life, he has even peeled off his skin; imagining that nostalgia might hold him back, he has gone so far as to uproot all attachments to the valley he came from. It is possible that he has been going round in one big circle, and that this realisation is about to dawn on him, destroying all thought of progress towards any shrine; perhaps he will soon perish. And yet his march does not slow down; his efforts do not flag, his feet show no signs of fatigue. It is as if, in recompense for this absurd self-sacrifice, all that he wants to know for certain – amidst this universe constituted of sound and fury signifying nothing – is that his own creation signifies even less.[19]

Translation: Probal Dasgupta

Notes

1 Sudhindranath Datta, 'Kavyer Mukti', in *Swagata*, Kolkata: Bharati Bhavan, 1938, pp. 19–39. The essay was first published in *Parichay*, 1931, 1(1): 24–42.
2 T. S. Eliot, 'The Waste Land', *Complete Poems and Plays: 1909–1950*, New York: Harcourt, Brace & World, Inc., 1971, pp. 37–50. A section after the first verse has been omitted.

3 Alfred Tennyson, 'The Princess: A Medley' (1847), in *Poems of Tennyson*, T. Herbert Warren (ed.), London: Oxford University Press, 1910, p. 307.
4 Rabindranath Tagore, 'No. 47', in *Likhan*, Calcutta: Visvabharati, 1926. The poem, in original and in the poet's own translation is as follows: '*Pathe ho'lo deri, jho're gelo Cherry/ Din britha gelo, priya./ Tobuo tomar kshama-hasi bohi / Dekha dilo Azalea*'. 'I lingered on my way/ till the Cherry tree lost its blossoms, / but the azalea brings to me, my love, / thy forgiveness'.
5 Ezra Pound, 'Alba', in *Lustra*, London: Elkin Mathews, 1916, p 45.
6 Satyendranath Dutta, 'Jaksher Nibedan', in *Kuhu-o-Keka* (1912), Calcutta: R. H. Srimani & Sons, 1937, p. 48.
7 Wallace Stevens, 'Thirteen Ways of Looking at a Blackbird', Harmonium (1923), in *The Collected Poems of Wallace Stevens*, New York: Alfred A. Knopf, 1954, p. 92.
8 William Wordsworth, 'The Wagonner', in *The Poetical Works of William Wordsworth*, London: Edward Moxon, 1858, p. 134.
9 Rupert Brooke, 'A Channel Passage', *The Collected Poems of Rupert Brooke: With a Memoir*, London: Sidgwick & Jackson, 1918, p. 109.
10 Rabindranath Tagore, 'Sandhya o Prabhat', in *Lipika*, Allahabad: Indian Press Ltd., 1922, p. 17.
11 *The Raghuvamsa of Kalidasa*, M. R. Kale (ed. & trans.), Bombay: Gopal Narayen & Co., 1922, p. 183.
12 Ibid., p. 65.
13 William Shakespeare, *King Lear* (The Arden Shakespeare), Act III, Sc.ii, D. Nichol Smith (ed.), Boston etc.: D.C. Heath & Co., 1917, pp. 63–64.
14 D. H. Lawrence, 'And Oh – That the Man I am Might Cease to be – ,' in *The Complete Poems of D.H. Lawrence*, Hertfordshire: Wordsworth Editions Ltd., 1994, p. 154. A part of the original quotation has been omitted.
15 T. S. Eliot, 'The Waste Land', *Complete Poems and Plays: 1909–1950*, op. cit., p. 44.
16 Hilda Doolittle (1886–1961), American poet and novelist.
17 Wilfred Owen, 'Futility', in *The Poems of Wilfred Owen*, Edmund Blunden (ed.), London: Chatto and Windus, 1933, p. 73. A part of the original quotation has been omitted.
18 Ezra Pound, *Hugh Selwyn Mauberly*, Part I, London: The Ovid Press, 1920, p. 12. A part of the original quotation has been omitted.
19 The author here had reproduced Tagore's Bangla translation of T.S. Eliot's 'The Journey of the Magi' (1927) titled 'Tirthayatri', originally published in *Parichay*, 1933, 2(3): 454–455.

18 Jibanananda Das: On poetry

Introduction

Jibananada Das (1899–1954) is the most influential Bengali poet of the post-Tagore era. A student of English Literature, he taught in several colleges in Kolkata and Delhi. Sometimes referred to as the loneliest of poets, Das's volumes of poetry include *Jhara Palak* (1927), *Dhusar Pandulipi* (1936), *Banalata Sen* (1942), *Satti Tarar Timir* (1948), and two posthumous volumes *Rupasi Bangla* (1957) and *Bela Abela Kalbela* (1961). He also wrote a number of novels including *Malyaban*, *Sutirtha*, and *Karubasana*, which were published posthumously. His critical essays were collected in an anthology entitled *Kabitar Katha*. The essay 'On Poetry' presented in this volume appears in that collection.

Jibanananda Das's poems embody the poet's unique experience of his time, which was marked by colonial rule, a terrible famine, the struggle for independence and its achievement through a history of communal hatred, bloodshed and partition, an aggressive emergence of industrialisation and urbanisation, and finally the apathetic discontent of modernity that crept into the details of everyday life. The trauma of the period left an unmistakable mark on his poetic diction that perhaps sought redemption outside the realm of the rational – through the medium of synaesthetic imagery. Jibanananda Das brought a new kind of experience in language that was made to portray a sensual modern spectrum of feelings.

If Tagore's poetics, emerging out of a romantic tradition, was looking for an integral relation between the poet, the text, and the reader, it was up to the new generation of poets to find a different aesthetics of its own. It may not be a coincidence that all the major poets of this period such as Jibanananda Das, Sudhindranath Datta, Amiya Chakravarty, Bishnu Dey, and Samar Sen also displayed their critical concern about a poetics of their time based on historical understanding and philosophical analysis. In the present essay, Das begins with a very crucial question about the necessity of poetry, about its *locus standi* vis-à-vis other forms of knowledge and expression, like that of religion or philosophy. He moves on to an understanding of the nature of poetic genius and its relevance. Finally, taking a decisive stand

DOI: 10.4324/9781003224686-19

against a utilitarian approach to poetry, he wonders whether a dialogic relation between poetry and society where both would mutually sensitise and purify each other is possible and then advocates going back to the heart of nature again in a modern context.

*

On poetry[1]

Jibanananda Das

Not everyone is a poet. Some are poets; poets – because in their hearts reside imagination and within imagination, intellect and experience, and they are nourished by centuries of poetic traditions and all the light that emanates from contemporary ones. Yes, they are helped. But not everyone can be helped. Only those within whom there is imagination and within imagination the essence of intellect and experience are the ones who can be helped; it is through a contact with many realms of being and becoming that one creates poetry.

Can anyone really say where this radiant glow of imagination comes from? Some say it comes from God. If I accept that then it is like cutting a beautiful knot with a diamond knife. Maybe that diamond knife is something that belongs to fairyland or maybe it is as real as flesh and blood. Within the limits of my own understanding this is what I think – using all the developments in human knowledge and poetic theory, theorists will labour their utmost to try and unravel this marvellous knot. What I believe about this at a personal level, or whether I have found enough basis for a firm conviction or not, I will no longer discuss in this essay. But unfortunately, I cannot subscribe to the opinion of those who say that it is necessary to acquire competence in world literature and the past and present of their own literature and then write poetry. Because I have felt the intense fragmentation of this world where even a whisper of supplication at the clash of the human being and the environment is stilled – in the darkness and quietness of the world, a heart suddenly lights up like a candle, and we slowly realise the presence of genius and the pleasure of poetic creation. When this incredible experience leaves us, poetry is not written anymore. What is written is verse, and it is filled with ideals of social living, didactic principles, several exercises of the intellect and profuse ideologies which aim principally at provoking the reader. The effect of such verse is short lived, it does not impart any joy to the reader, or only provides a low level of satisfaction as the reader looks in vain for the form of true poetry.

I do not wish to say that poetry will not be inscribed by the complexities of society or race or human beings and embody the beauty of their manifestation. There is no bar against that. There is a lot of that in some of the greatest poetry. But if in a premediated manner, the poet wishes to dress the skeletal frame of poetry with an intellectual apparatus and ideology, and also hope for a poetic glow, poetry will not be created – there will only be verse – with theory, ideology, and processes of intellection. I have already said that the nature of poetry is different in that there is no deliberate ideology or philosophy that waits in the wings of the poet's mind to take shape into poetry – and even if they are there, they are kept in abeyance by the magical aura and urgency of the imagination; therefore intellection and ideology, question and opinion are in a true poem like the veins, capillaries, and blood corpuscles that lie hidden behind the coy glance of a beautiful woman. They remain hidden. A discerning reader will be able to sense their presence and realise that they are contained within the aesthetic economy of the poem and are not disturbing it at all; from a poem one derives deep joy; in it the problems of existence do not seem like turgid waters in which the Indian myna bathes but seem like the white afternoon sunlight in the emerging river – in beauty and freedom.

Else, why should we not go to Patāñjali or to Vedānta or to the six schools of philosophy instead of going to Māgha and Bhāravi for our questions and thoughts? When we need to know something about life, society, or people, why should we not go to Professor Radhakrishnan, Mahatma Gandhi, or Pandit Jawaharlal Nehru, instead of going to the works of Rabindranath? We should then go to Bergson and the social and economic theorists and activists of Russia – instead of going to Yeats or to the poetic efforts of Eliot.

Now I wish to say something that will seem like an overstatement but is not really one – to me it is intensely true. The power of poetry to teach is not indissolubly woven into it the way the Ardhanarishwar is, both clearly man and woman at the same time; it is not as obvious as is grass, flowers, or a woman's beauty. It contributes towards the emphatic appeal of the beauty of the grass and the woman but is itself not present as the inner radiance of this beauty – however, its power or presence is realised later and appreciated. Those who do not acknowledge this and those who wish to say that the main thing in poetry or just as important as the beauty quotient is the lesson or philosophy or social content, I would like to tell such people that human beings – in whichever undetermined century – created a taste that was not the taste for philosophy or religion or science – but the taste for poetry (art) – which is determined by its own laws and principles of expression and tasting and from which we get a distinct pleasure that we do not get from science, philosophy, or religion – and it is also true that the particular taste or enjoyment that we get in religion or philosophy we do not exactly get in poetry; if in the flow of time, human beings have created this unique kind of pleasure or taste (or may be some non-human created it for human beings) – how can we approach that distinct kind of pleasure and ask it to provide other kinds of tastes and pleasures? And if poetry is able to provide all those other demands made from it then it does not deserve to exist as a distinct kind of pleasure-entity. What it can provide, philosophy and religion can also provide along with reformers, intellectuals, and activists.

Then there is no need for poetry's particular consummation. But I know that poetry requires its own integrity. I will once again reiterate what I have said before: 'Not everyone is a poet. Some are poets because in their heart there is imagination and within imagination intellect and experience, and they are nourished by centuries of poetic traditions and all the light that emanates from contemporary ones.' In philosophy, social reform and the wide range of human activities and intellection, the magical fusion of thought, experience, and imagination that one gets in poetry is not there.

It is possible that poetry throws light on the problems of human life. But it does not do it the way philosophy does; irrespective of whatever is highlighted or focused and wherever its creative origin lies, it will come back to me in the form of beauty, and it will delight my imagination; if it does not do that then the poetic resolution that the poem offers is simply a new avatar of an old resolution or idea or may be it is a new idea (although the possibilities for that are very slim), but it is still not poetry – only intellection. But the illumination that the poetry offers, whether it is the new in the old, or the entirely fresh and new – only if it nourishes my imagination and enriches my sense of beauty does it fulfil the objective of poetry; it may have other kinds of values – some of which I have already mentioned – it may sow seeds of knowledge in me; it may enhance the range of my emotions; it may draw me from crassness to elevated refinement; transformed by the magical light of the imagination, the more this poetry will bring all these back to me in a vast and deep manner the more the original light of poetry will blaze like a star creating new orbits and nodes of passionate response.

All persons of genius have one distinct ability – and there they have consummate excellence. The poet too has consummate excellence in his particular sphere – the creation of poetry. We may think that because he is a genius, he will have consummate knowledge about economics, sociology, political science, and various other fields. We have to realise that this cannot be the truth. The pseudo-poet may have real expertise in all such fields as would perhaps have those who are pseudo-philosophers. However, that person who has been powered by his own genius to become a poet or a singer or painter, and is not simply powered by intelligence, is consummately present in the world of art only and not anywhere else. If we look for the best and not the second-best gift that a talented person or person of genius can give us then we have to look where his power operates and expresses itself in so consummate a manner that it is beyond all questioning.

Let us for instance take the example of Shakespeare. As one reads his plays, one encounters the truest, most compelling and richly diverse forms of meanings and truths regarding human character in the world, not as one would get them from a psychoanalyst, but from a poet in his own element. They are like pearls from the deepest recesses of the waves of an ocean or from the savoured or unsavoured stars from skies that range beyond the skies of poetry. However, if Shakespeare had to give a lecture on Elizabethan society in a large gathering of people, I doubt it would have been in any way more remarkable than what a sociologist would have had to say (maybe he would have factored in excessive laughter, joking, and unusually flamboyant praise of the administrators of England). Or, say for instance, if he had to give a lecture on the current politics of England, I doubt that it would have a real eloquence and it would have lacked even the minimum relevance that political analysts of the time would have had. Besides, there would not even be a tinge of reflection of the startling wonder of Shakespeare's poetry which overwhelms us with its wide and profound reaches in his speech. Starting from the Vaishnav period, Rabindranath is the greatest poet of our language. What I said about Shakespeare applies equally to Rabindranath, and to all poets, actually. As in all other cases of genius or exceptional talent, one will have to look where the poet is most himself in order to find the greatest treasures of poetry. Therein, there is no philosophy, political science, sociology, and religion or, perhaps, they are all there, but they are not really themselves anymore; their discursive application has to be left in the hands of other people – they are not naturally the poet's.

No one should now therefore think that I am requesting the poet to not do anything other than the creation of poetry. I am certainly not doing that. The poet is perfectly capable of confronting and fighting all that is wrong or dissonant in his everyday life and work, and at the very outset of this essay I have said that in the poet's world of imagination, intellect and experience will be present. I am simply speaking here of the fundamental nature of his genius that cannot contribute anything extraordinary to everyday life, even by destroying his poetic ability. If the person is a true poet, then he will not be able to give to the method and expression of everyday life any greater gift than the gift of his poetry. However, like any other intelligent, everyday person, he may still contribute effectively to this world both in terms of doing and thinking. The enlightened imagination of the poetic world will not find expression there – nor will it be needed.

Those who have read my essay up to this point will have understood that my point is not to say that poetry bears no relationship to life. There is relationship, but not in ways that are conventional. Poetry and life are both born of the same source; when we use the term 'life,' we understand that immediate reality is an integral part of it. As the poet or even the ordinary, everyday person views this jumbled, chaotic thing that we call life, he may not be able to fulfil the demands or craving of his imagination through it. However, with the creation of poetry, the poet gains both moral and aesthetic satisfaction, and the imagination of the reader is also satisfied. What we understand as reality is not fully reconstructed, however, in poetry. Here, we enter, as it were, a new world. If we could imagine a kind of water that was different from the water we know; or if we could imagine a lamp that was different from all the lamps we know – then we could leave the day and night of this world, human beings, and their aspirations and all the dust, skeletons, and stars of this our life and enter a new order that would be poetry. Yet, all this has an integral, subterranean connection with life, that which is both ambivalent and new. Within this created world one sometimes gets to hear such things, see such colours, smell such things, come across such incredible people, or face unimaginable conflicts – or face such incredible pain that one feels that all this was somewhere reflected all this time. And it will remain somewhere not in a fragmented form but completely and wholly self-contained to the last ray of saffron yellow sunlight in the world. It is within these emanations that feeling is born in our hearts, and as the nebula leads to the formation of stars so also the harmony of things is engendered in our hearts, and then this reflected, unspoken world slowly starts speaking and melodies are born; it is not only that these realities or melodies remain just that. In fact, they fuse with the intellect and imagination of some people – and that is how poetry is born.

Poetry is essentially not utilitarian or geared towards providing moral education for the masses. It does not even serve such lessons by aestheticising them – the poet has no intention of doing anything of the sort. In the poetry of *King Lear* or *Balaka* – in the best poetry of the world and in its radiance of the poetic imagination, there does not seem to be any particular goal that the poem is directed towards. Reading poetry is geared towards a unique and independent kind of aesthetic fulfilment; I have spoken of this before. However, poetry is linked to society and the individual in two significant ways. First, there is an indication in all great poetry that it is calling into question all existing cultural and social norms and non-human forms as well and trying to create them anew. This creative upsurge is, as it were, removing all tangled irrelevancies and taking one towards infinite joy. Mighty as the white rain clouds, yet delicate and subtle at the same time, this indication in poetry even if it has been ignored by individuals, society, and civilisation (though it has not been ignored at all times) has helped humankind in the past, and it will also do so in future. That is why the more the great poetry of the past and the present occupies the consciousness of people, the more benefitted will human society be. However, great poetry is not something that can be distributed by the millions like the Bible.

It is in this context now that I will raise the question of the second integral relationship between poetry and human society. What I say may be unpalatable, but I believe it to be true. Poetry is not for everyone, and till that point when the hearts and minds of the general populace have not attained a new horizon, only poets of an inferior degree will enjoy popularity in marketplaces and dockyards. Great poetry will have no place in the totality of human society and civilisation. In fact, in the hands of the opinion makers of this section of people, great poetry will have to bear the ill reputation of being too luxurious, idly imaginative, and useless – although we know that it is not idly imaginative, but, with the help of the great power of poetic imagination, it asks questions to a great primeval Mother – to Aditi, the mother of the gods – and the pain and triviality of the questions are repeated; and again and again at all levels of each age, there is the pain and joy of new creations to find at last the beauty of harmony within the universe for all.

Is poetry truly necessary for us? If so, then why is it necessary? Is it a law of Nature that such few people like poetry, or does this trend reflect their uninformed and lowly education? If more people learn to love and appreciate poetry, will that make them lead better lives, and will that then lead to greater social good in a proportional manner? The question is, within the overall struggle and effort to achieve higher and better states of social existence, what role does poetry play? These are perhaps questions that the well-meaning members of social improvement groups may ask, but the questions are genuine and sincere, and, although not in great detail but very briefly or perhaps in the form of just an indication, the answers to these questions have been provided by me in the earlier paragraphs.

But the key issue here is that the masses need a change of heart. But who is going to bring about that change? Is this transformation ever going to take place? Is it ever going to happen that the character of the masses that existed three thousand years back, and the same character that exists now in the restless crowd, will suddenly undergo radical transformation? It is hard to imagine the general reader to become real connoisseurs of the best poems written in Elizabethan England or in 19th- and 20th-century Bengal. Such a possibility is enough to make one laugh. Yet, maybe we cannot just dismiss it like that. When I see that not only third-grade artists from the worlds of music and painting, but also their first-grade ones are earning recognition, I wonder why it is that first-grade poets live in banished worlds. Yet, when I see that civilisation seems to be like some giant she-elephant giving birth and populating the large open spaces and sidewalks of cities with foolish, tusked offspring, then I feel that anything that is fine is directed against these old layers of grossness and insensitivity, and it is that invisible hand which has the power to place the old lamp within the new structure and transform the lamp itself; its profound use of the contemporary and the timeless is for only a few initiated ones, not for all.

However, will there be a change in everyone? When? Who is going to bring it about? Will the poet have to transform himself into an educational leader? Will he have to build a university founded on the principles of aesthetics and beauty? Will he have to play the role of a dictator in creating a university that resonates to idioms of beauty? Does he have to engage in propaganda? Once again, does he have to turn dictator in order to pursue the principles of beauty and harmony in his life? But if some magic of the evening hour should suddenly transform the current rhythms of human society, the poet will not have to do anything; he will just have to remain true to the imperatives of his own poetical genius and leave his art in the hands of only a few; it is possible that this few number will increase because human beings wish to break free of their world of eternal compromise and adjustment. And if the currents of civilisation do not change, then let us believe that our comrades and the hobgoblins of poetry will certainly do something for poetry. Leaving aside the question of true connoisseurs of poetry such as Goethe or Lamb, or Pater in his own way, or Rabindranath or Yeats or even

Eliot within the norms of his own aesthetic world, there are countless individuals who are committed to beauty and its appreciation in the bourgeois world of the West. Not even a small fraction of such genuine connoisseurs is to be found in the middle classes of our society. In our country, a painful lack of true appreciation of art is shocking and causes a poet in his spare moments, some amount of bitterness.

But unless civilisation can be born anew by shedding its layers of accumulated grossness and loss of sensibility, what can a poet who is not a third-rate poet, who does not have the sympathy of the literary workers confined to the pit they have dug themselves, do? He is going to look for solace in nature, wander around in cities and ports, lose himself in crowds, attack anomalies and inconsistencies which stand in the way of true creativity with the power of imaginative thought; again, he will re-enter the embrace of nature with some similarly fragmented and beleaguered persons, go back to Aditi, the primal mother in the quiet of the sunlight and the deep blue silence of the sky.

The poet will have to remain faithful to his genius: perhaps one day his oeuvre will be needed along with the best poems of the world to be sown in the deathless golden-wombed croplands in the heart of the universe and all its beings.

Translation: Sreemati Mukherjee

Note

1 Jibanananda Das, 'Kabitar Katha', *Kavita*, 1939, 3(3): 8–17.

19 Bishnu Dey: Progressiveness in Bangla literature

Introduction

A pioneer of literary modernism in Bangla, Bishnu Dey (1909–1982) was a professor of English Literature. His first book of poems *Urvasi o Artemis* (1933) received immediate acclaim. His collections of poems include *Chorabali* (1937), *Anvishta* (1950), *Nam Rekhechhi Komal Gandhar* (1953), and *Smriti Satta Bhabishyat* (1963). Dey translated extensively, particularly from European modernist poets. Dey also wrote on literature and culture regularly, and his volumes of critical essays include *Ruchi o Pragati* (1946), *Sahityer Bhabishyat* (1952), *Elomelo Jiban o Silpasahitya* (1958), and *Michael, Rabindranath o Anyanya Jijnasa* (1967). An ardent Marxist, Dey worked relentlessly for several cultural organisations like Progressive Writers' Association, Anti-Fascist Writers' and Artists' Association, and Indian People's Theatre Association. The essay presented in this volume was published in *Arani* (1945) and later appeared in three of his collections of essays, *Ruchi o Pragati*, *Sahityer Bhabishyat*, and *Janasadharaner Ruchi* (1975).

The idea of 'progress' was one of the most immediate questions in the cultural scenario of the 1930s and 1940s as mentioned in the introduction to Manik Bandyopadhyay in this volume. The goal of the Progressive Writers' Association, as it appears from various articles and reminiscences, was threefold: (1) to have a platform for the cultural activists who had an internationalist perspective; (2) to break away from 'the supine and escapist literature' and look for something that would make 'art full-blooded and virile', and (3) to form a united cultural front in colonial India. Bengal played an active role in the Association in its early days, and at the time of its third conference in Kolkata in 1938, many literary figures in Bengal were with the Association. The Progressive Writers' Movement, however, spread beyond the Association and the field of literature, and other like-minded progressive organisations were also established, notably the Anti-Fascist Writers' and Artists' Association and the Indian People's Theatre Association.

Bishnu Dey addresses the question of progress in literature from this background and also shows how this idea of progress, despite its internationalist

DOI: 10.4324/9781003224686-20

approach, is not merely a foreign import, but also a natural culmination of a series of developments in the field of literature and culture in Bengal from the earliest time to the contemporary period.

*

Progressiveness in Bangla literature[1]

Bishnu Dey

Progressiveness is a frequently discussed word in Bangla literature. But now it has acquired a specific meaning. The extension of the historical perspective accompanying growing scientific approaches towards reality in the intellectual environment of the last few years seems to have contributed to it. Besides, the tendency of contemporary writers for experimentation has brought in a conscious approach towards writing. We may say that our literature has left behind its infancy, and contemporary writers have no doubt about the identical nature of theme and technique, subject and form. The progress of technique depends on the mind's expansion or transformation, and how can there be creative passion on the map of the mind if it does not look towards life? The lake of creativity actually finds its source in common life although its blue water reflects the image of the firmament. Some discover this source in the everyday life of common men, while others find the leaders of the people in the dialectic progression of history.

The problem arises from the imbalance between knowledge and creative acts because very often the focus is shifted from the life one experiences to the indirectness of derivative knowledge. A somewhat unchanging conceptualisation of art and literature is the outcome of vested interests of human consciousness or its inclination to maintain a stable property. The natural tendency of language for stability brings in hesitation in the act of writing. Once the writer decides to set himself afloat, he will not encounter the doubts of a mind that is tied to the anchor. In a living piece of writing, the artist and the art-object, the subject and technique are strung tightly together like a bow and arrow. It may run the risk of not finding the target, or the bow may even break under tension, but the eternal feature of any progressive literature lies in such a tension. Habitual art may be a delightful commodity or an excellent cottage industry, and in this mechanised system of production any progressive question would be redundant.

The progressive kind of mentality may begin from acts of negation. Then it comes down from its ivory tower to the ground of reality. The chief element here is that consciousness or that sensibility. It is the muscular stamp of that sensibility that comes forward in the rock of habitual stasis, in colours and lines, in use of words, in the orthodox style of language, and in the stubbornness of syntax. The conflict between the directness of life and the indirectness of all cultures often takes the form of gross muscle-flexing.

It shows the necessity for artists to remain impartial so that they can take impersonal decisions, as Picasso did, to keep the conflict under control. The great subjective style is easy in practice, but even if it is not strung like a bow, the arrow too is not released. The anguish of personal loneliness, though, may still come with pathetic sensational songs without caring much about changes in the outer world. One must admit the passing success of useless activities. The continual chanting of negation does just the contrary; it proves the undeniable presence of reality. It is like *Hiranyakashipu*[2] proving the presence of his God.

The dedicated pursuit of technique could ultimately take an artist to the origin of technique. That the modes of composing literature are contrary to the ways of consciousness or belief is an idea produced only in the unusual mind of an ultra-leftist. Because, just like the truth derived from scientific procedure, truth gained from artistic procedure is also a classless acquisition. So, the final destination of Mayakovsky's symbolism was revolution. This was the only justified destination; otherwise there remained Rimbaud's death in a desert. Another example in this regard is Louis Aragon's play with the subconscious turning ultimately into songs for the USSR. So, nobody is asking the writer to give up writing – he is only being reminded of the preparation he must take as a writer. This preparation includes an understanding of one's own personal crisis not as something originating from some dark recesses of the mind but as part of a larger historical crisis. This understanding again extends the scope of the theme and the form and provides a polyphonic completeness to life processes. It is in the infinite possibilities for an all-inclusive development that the artist spontaneously becomes an artist. There is little profit in the obsessed search for theme or some elusive personal distinct style. Even in pure artistic consideration, it is difficult to bring completeness and balance to individual style when society is breaking up. Because the sensibility of individual freedom cannot survive when society loses its equilibrium, and the complete expansion of the mind is not possible without a sense of this freedom. So, freedom exists only in the recognition of limits and in accepting mutual relationships. Where is that freedom in the abstraction of loneliness – in a disengaged analysis?

The origin of poetry may be mysterious, but poetry itself is not a secret magic. Poetry is a form of address that recognises its relationship with the addressee. There is little scope for address in the philosophy of *So'ham* or 'I am He'. Our writers know that the perceived and the known get metamorphosed by the knowledge of the perceiver, and any change in that knowledge also brings forth change in their dispositions. Interpretation finds its completion only in that change. That is why these writers never enter mechanically in a new systemised habit nor do they want to patch up fragments gathered from a particular philosophy. Marxist philosophy, especially, discards all such once-for-ever acquired mechanical habits. The basis of Marxist philosophy lies in the living culmination of the ever-dynamic relation between the dual and the non-dual, and there is hardly any space here for the stasis of customary philosophy. The inquisitive attachment to the subject is always more meaningful than the parasitic guile of conventional philosophy.

The love for the object or material identity ushers the way for an objective outlook, and this outlook enables man to have glimpses of manifold and extensive comprehensiveness of life. One then understands that the artistic object and the artistic form are just two sides of a process. Eliot in English Literature almost achieved this immersion in the object, and its amazing consequence today has been left unfulfilled with the interference of an unreal socio-religious philosophy. Yet, we must admit that Eliot's veneration for the object made him the greatest English poet, and his objective engagement made his influence emancipatory. I must reiterate that there is no emancipation in slavish adherence to a particular political ideology. The selective application of philosophy brings distortion to the minds of the leftists, and Auden, Spender, Lewis et al bear witness to that. Caudwell's *Illusion and Reality*, or Jack Lindsay's *Short History of Culture*, and *The Anatomy of Spirit* have taught us that even when an ideology is supported by deep knowledge, it still takes a long time to disseminate itself at the very source of art and literature. The poems of Caudwell and Lindsay bear evidence of the ordinariness of proto-Marxism. Despite that, Caudwell gave his life for this ideology. But the counter revolutionary urge to break away from a self-imposed structure was not unusual for those who did not follow a singular ideology in life and thought and wanted to administer bits of Marxism like a vial of medicine or an annual forecast of the almanac for some glamorous effect. In comparison, Eliot's intense endeavour for objectivity is rather more progressive. In his case, one saw that personal indiscipline in selecting a subject could crystallise into the control of the object in a concrete way. Such thought, notwithstanding its intrinsic anarchy, could still widen the vision of history, and the vision, nonetheless, becomes graspable. But mere cleverness does not serve any great purpose, and the stubbornness of a fragmented mind leads to the resultant quicksand and not to the emancipation of the individual self. Our writers are aware that the true treasure lies not with Valéry's self-devouring serpent but in *visvarupdarsan* or the vision of the cosmic form.

It is, nevertheless, far from being a simple assignment. Moreover, there is an intense though narrow stress of tradition on Bangla literature. Economic structure alone cannot determine the creation of cultural texts ignoring other conspicuous monuments. Our writers, of course, tried to bridge realities of lived experiences with consciousness (Tarasankar Bandyopadhyay's use of 'local colour', for example). But consciousness is a stream deep and strong, and this deep interior world is the playground of all art and literature. If there comes an overwhelming movement to change the collective consciousness of the country, such indecisiveness about consciousness and lived reality may be put to rest very quickly. Recent historical incidents have enhanced the self-consciousness of the people, and their imagination too could not escape the impact of such events. So, while our writers are becoming increasingly interested in the lives and movements of common people, they are also paying more attention to questions of literary tradition and technique.

Though the tradition of Bangla literature is as old as that of post-Saxon English Literature, its feeble flow only dazzled intermittently. Bangla literature is very close to the Sanskrit tradition, but it has its own distinct Prakrit heritage. Even in old and immature compositions like *Srikrishnakirtan*, we may find a clear yet fair opposition of indigenous folk consciousness to the courtly tradition of Sanskrit. Such distinctness of folk consciousness cannot be dismissed as rustic coarseness; on the contrary, it springs from the mind which is passionately attached to life, understands it directly, and is a mark of the liveliness of the people's culture. It is a way of accepting life and the philosophy of the quotidian. Hence we find in it a pragmatic dwelling in reality amidst joys and sorrows, and at times, hints of a happy revelation of the invincible energy of life. As oppositions here can coexist amicably, gods and goddesses become ordinary people while mortal man becomes the source of all wonder. To look for obscenity in this emerges from orthodox whims because its system of value was embedded in society's temporal unity in a life-encompassing emotional framework within a hierarchical religious system. Within that framework, people could move freely in different mythological domains and there was a relationship between the above and the below. Often the downtrodden people pulled down the powerful from their high citadel as a secret act of revenge. This was how the non-Aryan deity Siva entered the prestigious Aryan circle like the Greek god Dionysus. But when this neo-Aryan Siva became a luxurious godhead in the Brahminical system, he was brought down from his newly assumed throne to the ground as an intoxicated and worthless husband exposed to all befitting chastisements. The rich trader who once boastfully announced his allegiance only to the Brahminical system had to submit ultimately to the power of Manasa, a folk deity. Of course, it is also true that we did accept the scholarship of Sanskrit literature and used its style and rhetoric indiscriminately in our general literary practices. Yet, the pseudo-classical garb of the post-Mahabharat and post-Upanishad literature could not bring stagnation to the flow of Bangla literature because the indigenous poets remained rooted to their soil. The conventions thus appeared a little different in our protesting Prakrit literatures as they had to negotiate with the faith and perspectives of the common people and their everyday lives.

This is no denying that the limit of our freedom at that time was not under our control, nor was there any opportunity or necessity for self-consciousness. There were two gross ways left for some exercise of freedom: first, the making and unmaking of gods and goddesses, and second, scholarly discussions about man–woman relationships. The sophistication of the latter can still be traced in amorous conversations of the common rural people.

In the restrictive domain of the medieval period, people could find compensations and resolutions in the path of humanity, as is apparent in various mangalkavyas, Chandikavya, panchali of Siva–Durga, and jatra. The same spirit also worked in the visual arts of *pata*,[3] *pātā*,[4] dolls in fairs, in *alpana*,[5] and bratakatha, and in rhymes and rural songs. (In this respect, Abanindranath's book *Banglar Brata*[6] is an eye-opener for us.) The ballads of Eastern Bengal are a direct reflection of this life. The all-pervasive folk mind made its presence felt even in the Bangla *Ramayana* and *Mahabharata* and enlivened Vaishnavite theological scriptures with narratives of romantic love. I admit that the conventions of *Padakalpataru*[7] are lifeless, because the Vaishnavite poets had their interests in subjects that appealed to the common people, and not in mere exercise of conventions, unlike the Sanskrit theoreticians. Yet, at times, the intensity of their subtle realism strikes us in the midst of our middle-class conventions. We suddenly confront lines which could only be found in the best of world poetry and that take us to the innermost recesses of human experiences. They expand the domain of our insight and emotion. The Vaishnav poet amazingly communicates to us the fact that the pangs of love are the pain and joy of the ambivalent dynamic relation of two dynamic beings. This consciousness is, however, somewhat indistinct, but it continued unabated till our European age.

Then there came the storm of change. Iswar Chandra Gupta may be considered as the last of the people's poets. He wrote in a great anarchical period in history, casting pitiful glances towards the past amidst the uncertainties of contemporary life. In a sense, Vidyasagar is our purest and greatest European, and that is why Bengali culture found its shape in his humanism and compassion. He tried to find a general balance from his own inclusive world and expressed it in a Sanskritised language. He chose this kind of language probably because Sanskrit had a long history, and, second, there was the attraction of the great distance of Sanskritic heritage from the anarchy of contemporary regionalism. Madhusudan's delayed and romantic exuberance, though devoid of proper theme, brought him back to contemporary Bengal. His great genius created a luminous language, and this was what he learned from Europe and contributed to Bengali culture. His rebellious innovations, notwithstanding their European origin, created gods and goddesses, even in their grandiose appearances, very much in the spirit of traditional Bengali imagination. Madhusudan was enriched by European traditions, yet his understanding of Bengali common life was surprisingly wonderful. His vision helped the new civilisation to have its own language, and he held it against the testing ground of reality. That is precisely the reason for our delight in the lively and indigenously powerful language of his two plays, which we never find in Bankimchandra's successful amalgamation of Hindutva and British governance.

We rather find similar delight in the writings of some lesser writers like Kaliprasanna Sinha (1841?–1870), Tekchand Thakur (Peary Chand

Mitra, 1814–1883), and in some poems of Hemchandra Bandyopadhyay (1838–1903) addressing the contemporary period. They lead us to imagine a temporary balance between two contemporary worlds. That is why we have to accept Dinabandhu Mitra as a writer of the first order, especially for his healthy sense of reality and satire in *Sadhabar Ekadasi* (1866). His constant, non-escapist, people-oriented mind and creativity did not rush blindly to the past in the bewilderment of the attempt to link the stream to a source, acts to the cause. The compassion of his humanity and the humour-tinged good sense have placed him at the pinnacle of our dramatic literature.

Yet, the equilibrium was undoubtedly incomplete and temporary. Otherwise, why did our leading novelist Bankimchandra get confused in spite of his serious self-esteem? However, the prescription for European civilisation, Brahminism, and middle-class grossness was not Bankimchandra's responsibility alone. His genius merely tried to resolve the conflict, and it will be unfortunate for the country if the reactionaries start drawing him to their side in today's literature and politics.

The large appearance of Rabindranath in the small tradition of Bengal was indeed an event ordained by nature. It would not be an offence if we get excited like Galileo with such a tremendous discovery. It is impossible to give any idea of his genius in this brief introduction, though there is hardly any comparable figure available in other literatures. An approximate historical comparison may be made if on the one hand, Chaucer from English Literature, and on the other, Goethe from German literature, were brought together. Rabindranath brought new orientations to Bangla culture. Each book of his was a step forward in terms of technique and an expansion of subject-matter. Besides, Rabindranath taught us the lesson of decency, and the future generation would never be able to deny this inheritance even in orthodox opposition. Rabindranath brought the refreshing expanse of the world to a Bengal entrapped in narrow regionalism. He gave us the romantic yearning for the new, and the subtle and delicate beauty of love. Most importantly, we found in him a consciousness of beauty as a primary imperative for aesthetics. The strong sense of honesty and responsibility of the Victorian character entered Bangla literature through him.

A sense of individuality and privacy may also be found only in the Bengali consciousness of a post-Tagorean society. Tagore was not only the greatest of poets, but also the first and the finest example of a responsible professional author. His contributions will enrich our many-sided self-consciousness, though the completeness that is there in him is a part of his individual personality. Bangla literature and its ever-changing traditions constituted his extensive field of work; yet, his personality resembled the reticence and stasis of the great Himalayas and not an individual effusive flowing river. A mere mechanical reading of Rabindranath, from a leftist perspective, will not do justice to his greatness. Describing him in terms of his aristocratic family background or as one appearing at the juncture of a dying feudal system and the rise of bourgeois culture would only be a partial explanation of his irresistible and lonely genius engaged passionately in acts of creation. The influence of Maharshi Debendranath Tagore (1817–1905) and the Brahmo mentality definitely played their roles in his firm conviction in beauty and goodness not as a distant theory but as a liberal truth of life. Yet, the myriad mysteries of life remained unending for him:

> Yet, the void is not void,
> but filled with fiery vapour,
> woeful. There I am, lonely,
> and with that fire create a dream world
> in my radiant songs.[8]

How wonderful was his eighty-year long completeness, vigorous yet ever unsatisfied! He went on developing new techniques and literary subjects in such innovative ways that he left his time behind to become the greatest poet of modern time. Yet, although his star-trekking genius found its sustenance in the romantic soil of Bengal and was part of its everyday reality, it remained in a faraway realm in its completeness. In comparison, Madhusudan Dutt and Dinabandhu Mitra are our near neighbours.

It is heartening that the writers of our time now stand at a great juncture of history and are anxious to realise the true nature of literature. In this quest, the influence of Yeats' 'Great Mother' is conspicuous. She is the Universal Mother; the long memory of mortal man; the Unconscious of Freud – who goes about creating frenzied conflict between yearning and separation, and an anxiety of losing her once she enters the realm of the public and becomes theirs. That is why when we have reached the present phase of the development of human consciousness, we have started to realise that the subject evolving out of life and the technique are just two sides of the same creative act. The writers are not mere craftsmen, nor inspired souls, but are complete human beings, both socially and individually. We have also learnt that in the history of art, form and matter have remained integral to each other ever since primordial time when men started living collectively. Today, we see that after many centuries of engagement with form, symbols that are given shape become easily decipherable, but only if there is harmony in society. Hence, the overt appeal of highbrowed formal engagement and convention is not in imitation of the earlier writer's bourgeois wealth of detailed object analysis. Surely there is no call to return to the first ages of commodity revolution in the basic religion of socialism.

Translation: Parthasarathi Bhaumik

Notes

1 Bishnu Dey, 'Banglasahitye Pragati', in *Sahityer Bhabishyat*, Kolkata: Signet Press, 1952, pp. 9–15.

2 A mythological *asura* slain by Vishnu in his Narsimha avatar.
3 Paintings, usually narrative scrolls, accompanied by songs.
4 Wooden covers for manuscripts, often with decorative engravings or paintings.
5 Decorative paintings on floor, often with ritualistic significance.
6 Abanindranath Tagore, *Banglar Brata* (*Visvavidyasamgraha* 4), Kolkata: Visva-bharati, 1943.
7 A collection of Vaishnav lyrics compiled by Vaishnavadas, later edited by Satish Chandra Roy and published by the Bangiya Sahitya Parishat in 1915.
8 Rabindranath Tagore, 'Purnata', *Purabi* (1925). The poem was first published in *Prabasi*, 1924, 24.2(2): 198–199.

20 Rezaul Karim: Bangla literature and Muslims

Introduction

Rezaul Karim (1902–1993) was a polymath whose works encompassed the disciplines of literature, history, politics and culture. However, he is primarily remembered as an eminent Gandhian nationalist, who devoted his life to spread the message of communal harmony and a pluralistic idea of India. Born in Birbhum district, Rezaul Karim studied English Literature and Law, and the major part of his life as a public intellectual was centred in Berhampore, Murshidabad, India, where he practised as an advocate and taught literature at the Berhampore Girls' College. He was a prolific author who wrote regularly for several leading journals of his time including *Saogat*, *Desh* and *Muhammadi*, as well as various local journals and magazines. His works include *Farasi Biplab* (1933), *Naya Bharater Bhitti* (1935), *Bankimchandra o Musalman Samaj* (1944), *Sampradayik Samasya o Gandhiji* (1969), *Samskriti Samanway: Kichhu Bhabna* (1983) and sketches on the lives and works of Kamal Pasha (1941), Maulana Abul Kalam Azad (1942), Dara Shikoh (1944) and Muhammad Iqbal (2003). Karim also edited journals like *Saurabh*, *Durbin* and *Murshidabad Patrika*. The essay 'Bangla Literature and Muslims' presented in this volume was written as a preface to *Kavya-Malancha* (1945), a compendium of Bangla poetry by Muslim poets from the medieval times to the early 20th century, which Karim jointly edited with Abdul Kadir (1906–1984).

From the early 19th century, as the Bengali literate community came in contact with the 'Western' system of education, the Hindu communities reaped its benefit more than the Islamic communities. However, a new wave of change in temperament towards the 'Western' mode was perceived within the Islamic communities in the last few decades of the 19th century. Also, Bangla literature predominantly portrayed as a Brahminical corpus of texts was often enriched through external influences like Islam, and here again a new appraisal was necessary. In the meantime, the political situation became volatile with the emergence of the Muslim League and the Hindu Mahasabha in the early decades of the 20th century, creating a communal rift that was further instigated by the colonial powers. The editor notes

DOI: 10.4324/9781003224686-21

that an anthology of works by Muslim poets through the ages could not be compiled until 1945, two years before independence. He also points to the availability of several such collections in Urdu. Rezaul Karim makes a claim in his essay for a proper appreciation of the significant role played by Muslim poets in shaping the history of Bangla literature.

*

Bangla literature and Muslims[1]

Rezaul Karim

The contribution of Bengali Muslims to the gradual development of Bangla language and literature is not insignificant. Of all contributions of his forefathers, the modern Bengali Muslim would be first and foremost proud of those made to Bangla language and literature. Muslim rulers were attracted to Bangla literature soon after having established their authority over the land. They became its patron in many ways. Many poets, writers and artists left their mark through their genuine service to Bangla language, and traces of their unfading contributions have not disappeared till date. Many records of work by Muslim poets have to a large extent been destroyed because of an absence of any scientific method for preserving them. There is very little hope of their being retrieved. But not all works have been completely destroyed. Our archaeologists do have their responsibility and duty towards this. Many a lost treasure could see the light of day with their efforts. In this regard, it is worth mentioning the intense pursuit and labour of the greatly respected literary scholar Munshi Abdul Karim (1871–1953). In fact, there is no other way but to fall back on his work to receive a comprehensive outlook of the immense contribution of Muslims to ancient Bangla literature. This is a universally accepted truth.

A few authentic books on Bangla language and literature have been written in modern times; for example Dr Dinesh Chandra Sen's *Bangabhasha o Sahitya* and Dr Sukumar Sen's *Bangala Sahityer Itihas*. Further, many writers have discovered a glorious era of Bangla literature by collecting ancient manuscripts and publishing them in the form of books. However, no representative compilation of poems by Muslim poets has been published till now. The entire manuscript literature is an enormous matter. Many people may not have the inclination or the time to read them extensively. But it is the duty of every lover of literature to read at least a few of these poems. Many had felt the need for a compilation of selected works of those poets and artists who served Bangla literature from ancient times till today. This book is being published to fulfil their needs. Our friend Abdul Kadir Sahib is very well versed in Bangla literature and especially in ancient literature. The difficult work of compilation of this volume would not have been possible without his help.

There is no dearth of this type of selected works in Arabic, French and Urdu. *Kitab al-Aghani* is an invaluable voluminous compilation of Arabic literature. Recently, a renowned professor of Calcutta University, Dr Mohammad Ishaque, has published a compilation of Persian poems entitled *Sukhanwaran Iran*. There are several similar compilations in Urdu also. But there is no compilation of works by Bengali Muslim poets. So today, we gift this volume to readers of Bangla literature. Our friend Abdul Kadir has already introduced the poets mentioned in this volume.

Keats had said that 'A thing of beauty is a joy forever'. The truth of these immortal words of Keats will be comprehended by paying attention to the poems in the compilation. A true poet is a constant worshipper of beauty. Wherever he finds beauty, he gathers it with great care. The world of a poet is one of constant beauty. He sees the playful variants of the beautiful everywhere and is ever engrossed in it. It is this expression of the beautiful that receives various forms in his work. Readers will be enthralled by the bringing together of the beautiful in selections from early as well as modern verses in this volume. They would find here the unprecedented knowledge of the beautiful as in the poems of Shelley, Keats and Wordsworth.

Going deeper into the poems, the reader will understand that Muslim poets follow the principle of 'art for art's sake' to a great extent. They are constantly inspired by a fascinating sense of beauty and poetic consciousness, and this enables them to describe things with such perfection. Just as birds sing deliriously with joy, flowers blossom and rivers flow swiftly, likewise in this compilation there are poems which in their own joy and vitality have come up very naturally. There is no artificiality, no stressful imagination and no hindrance to the smooth rhythmic flow. It is as if the poems have blossomed out of natural emotions. In many of the poems, there is a special quality of sweetness in the beauty and craftmanship of expression. Conceptual issues are also taken up in many of the poems. They may be classified as spiritual poems. We find deep spirituality expressed in the poems of Sheikh Madan Baul. 'You are tied up and I too am tied up, there is no salvation'. How many others have been able to give expression to such a profound thought on salvation?

Poets have generously gathered beauty from the unlimited treasures of the beautiful in nature and woven them into garlands of poetry. In places, the beauty described by them has crossed the limits of the finite and moved into the infinite. One cannot deny that sensuousness is an essential part of the worship of beauty. The poet's mind will surely bear traces of external nature. But there is bound to be a cover of modesty over the sensuousness that is almost absent in Keats and Swinburne.

The poems in the compilation are a token of the immortal contributions of Islamic culture in Bengal. These poems amply prove that Muslim poets, beginning from the Middle Ages up to the present, have been able to leave a permanent mark of Muslim consciousness on Bangla literature and language. We expect that those in pursuit of Hindu–Muslim cultural harmony will not reject these immortal contributions of Muslim poets and littérateurs but take them to be the chief elements of such unity.

It has been proved beyond doubt that the contributions of Muslims to Bangla language and literature are immense. Muslims in the Middle Ages never thought that living in this country and singing songs of Arabian dates or of Afghanistan nuts and pistachios alone would make Islam remain pure and untainted. They established a deep connection with the soil of this country accepting its traditions, and, engrossed with feelings for the country, they wrote on subjects linked with the land in its language and with its metaphors. They did not think of the deserts of Arabia, the vineyards of Iran or of the roses of Basra. They did not hear the bulbul sing. They heard the *shyama*, *koel*, *finge* and *doel* sing by the banks of rivers and rivulets and under the creeper shrubs of this land. And they wrote of them. Instead of the narratives of Sohrab–Rustam, Jamshed, Afrasiab, Darius, Kaikhusru, Laila–Majnu, Shirin–Farhad, they knew better the narratives of Ram–Lakshman, Sita–Draupadi and Radha–Krishna. Hence, they gathered the material for their poems from these stories. That is why they derived great pleasure in preaching Islamic spirituality mediated by the love-play of Radha and Krishna. The thought that this practice might convert them to '*Kafirs*' did not occur to them. It is for this reason that the Muslim poets of Bengal did not ignore the Vaishnav songs. They gave a new form and flavour to these songs by integrating them with the Islamic traditions. Nowhere else would there be found such synthesis of Islamic and Hindu traditions. The reader will be amazed to see the suggestions of synthesis in the poems of ancient poets published in this volume. Despite the adoption of Christianity in Europe, its artists and poets were not able to discard pagan feelings, traditions and metaphors. The puritans tried hard to abolish pagan feelings from literature but failed. And not just in the Middle Ages, famous poets of the 19th century (like Shelley, Keats, Scott) also were totally immersed in the literature of the pagan era. With their genius, they created marvellous expressions from the gems that they retrieved from the works of the pagan era. It is doubtful whether the unique beauty of the verses would have remained if the pagan era had been rejected.

The Muslim poets of Bengal did not completely do away with Hindu metaphors, similes and stories. For this, they cannot now be condemned. They will always be revered for their legacy of such rich, mellifluous and vibrant poems. Today, we feel glorified in their honour.

In the early stage of the British rule, Bengali Muslims did not engage with Bangla literature with much eagerness. But after a temporary period of inertia, they turned their attention to literature again and started creating new literary works. During the period of the Nawabs, Muslims had engaged with Bangla literature on a large scale. Today, due to the hard work of researchers, these works have been partially retrieved. Dr Dinesh Chandra Sen has openly acknowledged the invaluable contributions made by Muslim poets to Bangla literature. We know particularly about Chandidas, Vidyapati,

Krittibas and Kasiram Das. During the same time, there were many poets and littérateurs among Muslims who were writing with the same ability. They were no less inferior to Chandidas, Vidyapati, Krittibas and Kasiram Das. The best ingredients of poetry such as rasa, poetic form, feelings and exact rhythm were present in poems by Muslim poets as well.

A large body of literary manuscripts were lying in neglect for a long time. Today, as a ray of hope, they have caught the attention of the lovers of literature. These manuscripts are treasure troves. One cannot say that they do not contain any undesirable material. But if one knows how to go deep into them, one is sure to find gems. Many Muslim poets have emerged in recent times. Their gifts to Bangla literature, especially by Kazi Nazrul Islam, have resulted in enhancing the wealth and glory of Bengal. In this volume, a few representative poems of modern Muslim poets have also been included. My last submission is that, had our good friend Abdul Kadir not taken the pains to collect the poems, this volume would not have seen the light of day. For this, he deserves great appreciation from us all.

Translation: Tapan Chakraborty

Note

1 Rezaul Karim, 'Bangala Sahitya o Musalman', in *Kavya-Malancha*, Abdul Kadir and Rezaul Karim (eds.), Kolkata: Nur Library, 1945, pp. i–vi.

21 Manik Bandyopadhyay: Why I Write

Introduction

Prabodh Kumar Bandyopadhyay or Manik Bandyopadhyay (1908–1956) as he came to be known was born in the Santal Parganas and spent his childhood in various towns of the then undivided Bengal. He studied Mathematics in Presidency College, Calcutta, and opted for an impoverished and difficult life of a professional writer, uncompromising in his philosophy and convictions. Though he began his literary career with poetry, his first published work was a short story called 'Atasimami' (*Bichitra* 1928), which brought him immediate critical acclaim. He published a series of novels including *Padmanadir Majhi* (1936), *Putulnacher Itikatha* (1936), *Ahimsa* (1941), *Chatushkon* (1942), *Darpan* (1945), *Chinha* (1947), and *Swadhinatar Swad* (1951) and collections of short stories including *Pragoitihasik* (1937), *Sarisrip* (1939), *Bou* (1940), *Holud Pora* (1945), *Aj Kal Parsur Galpo* (1946), *Khatiyan* (1947), and *Chhotobakulpurer Jatri* (1949). He was associated with the 'Kallol' movement, and some critics considered him as the brightest of the group. A staunch realist, Bandyopadhyay was deeply involved in psychoanalytical perspectives in the earlier part of his career. Though he never lost interest in the area, his later works show a strong influence of Marxist philosophy. The brief essay presented in this volume entitled 'Why I Write' is taken from an eponymous collection published by the Anti-Fascist Writers' and Artists' Association in 1944.

In 1936, the Progressive Writers' Association came into being at the initiative of authors like Sajjad Zahir, Jyotirmay Ghosh, and Mulk Raj Anand and received patronage from stalwarts like Munshi Premchand and Tarasankar Bandyopadhyay. Its annual conferences brought together a host of young authors and intellectuals on a common platform and aspired for a general understanding of literature and its relationship with the masses. It also inspired a number of artists from different parts of Bengal. During the period, a group of Marxist intellectuals started a 'Friends of the Soviet Association' in Calcutta. At the same time, the left-leaning and progressive writers' movements also had to face hostile attacks from right-wing political affiliations. Somen Chanda, an acclaimed young author,

DOI: 10.4324/9781003224686-22

was murdered in Dhaka by unknown goons on 8 March 1942. Hundreds of intellectuals condemned the killing, and an Anti-Fascist Writers' and Artists' Association was formed, which had its first conference later that month under the leadership of Ramananda Chattopadhyay, Bishnu De, and Subhas Mukhopadhyay. In 1944, the Association published an anthology of essays by a number of authors in response to the question 'Why does one write?'

In this precise and distinct essay, Manik Bandyopadhyay speaks about a common ground for the author and the reader, namely the language. He initiates a debate between knowledge and experience, perceiving the author as an enabler of experiences, and not a mere transmitter. He also calls the profession of writing as being one of a pen-pushing labourer and that the labour becomes fruitful only with its proper reception.

*

Why I Write[1]

Manik Bandyopadhyay

I write to speak on things that cannot be made known by any other means. Whatever other writers may say, I have no doubt that their answer to the question why they write is the same.

Mental experiences shelter thought. My experiences from my very childhood have been greater than those of many. The notion that some are born with talent is not at all true. Intellectuals lacking self-knowledge and with the desire for a cover of mystery and security believe in the statement. The intense desire, enthusiasm, or addiction for gaining mental experience and the ability to bear its pressure emerge, get enhanced or diminished because of several logical and understandable reasons. I have more or less known the history of my perspectives ever since I was two-and-a-half years old.

The zeal for writing is like any other fascination. It is similar to the desire for learning mathematics, developing mechanical tools, looking for the ultimate meaning, learning to play games, singing, or making money. The ability to write depends on the intensity of the desire to write and the single-minded concentration on learning to write. Needless to add that one has to have a valuable resource of things to say – what else other than the compulsive desire to give can lead to the impassioned urge to write?

I write to share with others only a minute portion of the many ways and manners in which I have experienced life. No one else would have known what I have known in this life, (not the kind of knowing as in the Bangla rhyme '*jal pare, pata nare*', literally, meaning 'the water falls, the leaf trembles'). However, there is an extensive, common semantic core between my knowledge and that of others. Based on that, I share some of my realisations with them.

It would be incorrect to say that I give or share – I facilitate reception. I make one realise. My reader acquires mental experience through my writing – the poor person would have never received such experience without my facilitation. But I think it is ridiculous if this makes a writer arrogant. A writer's ardent desire to make his readers receive is much greater than the latter's desire for receiving. His success is greater than his reader's if he can make him receive. A writer is a mere pen-pushing labourer. If all his pen-pushing is of no use to him, his life is meaningless and of less worth even than that of the labourer crushing stone by the wayside.

I am not unhappy that I obtain pleasure from the praise that I receive as a professional pen-pusher. Even now at times, I rue my weaker moments of inattentiveness when pride sets in, and I wonder when I will be a true writer.

Translation: Tapan Chakraborty

Note

1 Manik Bandyopadhyay, 'Keno Likhi', in *Lekhaker Katha*, Kolkata: New Age Publishaers, 1957, pp. 11–12.

22 Ashapurna Devi: My thoughts on literature

Introduction

Ashapurna Devi (1909–1995) was one of the most prominent Bangla writers of the 20th century. She was chiefly known for her short stories, novels and children's literature.

Ashapurna Devi was born in a large, traditional family in North Calcutta. At that time in her family, girls were not allowed to go to school nor were private tutors employed for them. She taught herself to read and write. She discreetly sent a poem entitled 'Bairer Dak' to *Sisusathi*, a children's magazine, when she was thirteen, and that was the beginning of a very rich literary career for her.

Ashapurna was married off at fifteen, and for a long time at the beginning of her literary career she wrote only for children. From 1936, she began to write fiction for adults. Her first novel *Prem o Prayojan* was published in 1944. As a housewife and mother, she hardly had any time of her own, and the large body of writing that she produced stands as a testimony to her tenacity and her undaunted spirit.

In her writings, Ashapurna brought a comprehensive, detailed view of life in the urban middle-class family, focusing on everyday activities, material objects and the inner lives of common people. The small drama of everyday lives and a different layered human reality underlying the quotidian continued to fascinate her throughout her life and provided her with an incentive to write. She was not rebellious in any outward sense, accepting life and upholding some of the core values of middle-class existence. Yet, her world of fiction was also full of strong, courageous women, struggling for equal opportunities. Her writings therefore were also a fervent appeal for justice and a new social order, for a change in the status of women. Her trilogy *Pratham Pratisruti* (1964), *Subarnalata* (1967) and *Bakul Katha* (1974) portraying the lives and struggles of three generations of women constituted a landmark in the history of women's literature in Bangla. *Agnipariksha* (1952), *Sashi Babur Sansar* (1956), *Unmochon* (1957), *Uttaran* (1964), *Baluchari* (1967), *Jaha Chai Taha* (1968), *Harano Khata* (1974), *Uttar*

DOI: 10.4324/9781003224686-23

Purush (1976), *Ahalya Uddhar* (1981), *Nilay-Nibas* (1987) and *Path Janahin* (1992) are among some of her well-known novels.

The essay 'My Thoughts on Literature' anthologised in this volume presents a short and succinct statement on her purpose in writing.

*

My thoughts on literature[1]

Ashapurna Devi

Whenever there is a conversation on the ideals of literature, I say that I do not subscribe to the view that literature should have any fixed goal. The earth is vast, the world is full of variety and the incessant flow of life is still more varied, and literature speaks of that endless life. Hence it cannot be caught within a rigid frame. The devotion, the beliefs and the values that are supremely true to one could be trivial and worthless to another. And perhaps within the same life, values change, and the supreme truth of one age becomes a shadow in a later one.

An author deals with life that is constantly moving forward. She cannot remain still at a particular central point. Times and periods change, social consciousness changes and so do the questions that an author asks of life. It is in accordance with these changes that transformations occur in language, form and technique. Only her dharma of literature and her sense of truth do not change. I am the most inconspicuous of authors trying to write. Yet, I have been an inhabitant of this literary world for half a century and that has given me the right to express a few of my thoughts on literature. An artist chooses her artistic elements in accordance with her disposition. My choice has been ordinary homely people living in society. They are very ordinary human beings struggling hard in their day-to-day existence. These human beings break, crush, bend and twist opposing circumstances. At every step, they get wounded and pierced by unattainable desires, and behind the wrecked identity there is an *amrita*-coveting soul crying in tortured pain.

No dramatic event takes place in their lives except disease, sorrow, poverty and sudden accidents, and hence the sound of their soul's cries never goes up in resounding peals. It can only be heard if one is attentive. My dharma of literature is to convey that barely audible sound, and sincerity and love are essential to do that. This is the rule that I have been trying to follow in my literary life. I just talk about what I feel, and I do not strive to say things in order to surprise. I never step out of my known world.

But I have realised that there is an endless stream of hidden mystery in this known world. I have felt that there is a lot more to a human being than what is visible on the surface, and that invisible part consists of the incessant conflict between his life and its questions. This is because he does not know that he is not only helpless before his circumstances, but even before his inner disposition. He does not know how his unconscious drives his conscious self, and how like a spider he constantly weaves a web that imprisons him.

I write of these people. Right from my childhood, it was as if a window to a mysterious world had opened to my inexperienced wondrous gaze – the picture of the unknown inner world of human beings. I was surprised to see that a person was more than I took him to be. I saw noble thoughts and ideals in seemingly ordinary people and sometimes great poverty of heart in well-established members of society. I tried to recount this realisation in numerous short stories. My restlessness emerging from these experiences even in my childhood made me think and suffer and triggered the compulsion to write. I started writing novels later when I was moved towards it by certain observations and questions that occurred to me.

Right from my childhood, my questioning temperament would strongly protest against the prevailing unjust social conditions. Why should there be so much disparity among people? Why should there be such inequality? Several such questions made me sorrowful. I was particularly pained by the condition of women. Why should they be without any rights whatsoever? Why do they spend their lives in confining darkness? These questions did not allow me to be at peace and perhaps resulted in *Pratham Pratisruti* (*The First Promise* 1964) whose protagonist is the symbol of protest. She tried to break rigid customs and wanted to see women as well established with human dignity. Of course, now those times are over. Legal measures have ensured the abolition of unbearable helplessness of women. They have come out of darkness and gained the right 'to win over [their] destiny'.[2] Our gratification lies in witnessing this change. Yet, a lot remains to be achieved. A society where each human being can be counted as a member with equal dignity has not yet emerged.

In my life's long engagement with literature, despair might have gripped me at times; yet I never believed that decay would have the last word. I know that dissatisfaction is there, but there is fulfilment as well.

The world is eternally full of life and waits with its unending store of love for everyone. Such love assures that 'No one is insignificant, no one is without value, no one is dispensable'.

To me, the religion of literature is to carry forward that message of hope. It is literature that will declare that human beings are not merely creatures of flesh and blood; in them is manifested a divine identity, and it is the duty of literature to bring back faith in human beings.

Translation: Subha Chakraborty Dasgupta

Notes

1 Ashapurna Devi, 'Amar Sahitya Chinta' (1978.), in *Ar ek Ashapurna*, Kolkata: Mitra o Ghosh, 1994, pp. 21–23.

2 Rabindranath Tagore, 'Sabala', in *Mahua*, Kolkata: Visvabharati, 1929, pp. 60–62.

23 Mahasweta Devi: I/My Writings

Introduction

Mahasweta Devi (1926–2016) was born in Dhaka. Her father, Manish Ghatak, was a well-known poet and novelist, and her mother, Dharitri Devi, was also a writer and social worker. She did her Masters in English from the University of Calcutta, India. Early in her life, Mahasweta Devi took up various jobs, worked as a journalist, and later taught at Vijaygarh Jyotish Ray College in Kolkata. Mahasweta Devi has to her credit twenty volumes of short stories and more than a hundred novels. However, she was known as much for her creative writings as for her deep involvement as an activist working for the rights and empowerment of marginalised people and tribal communities in India. Her work as activist involved negotiating with the government, organising events to showcase the craft of marginalised communities, forming of groups and bodies for the empowerment of such communities, editing a journal that served as their mouthpiece, and, perhaps most important of all, focussing on a long and sustained effort to fight on behalf of the de-notified tribes and to sensitise people to their plight.

In the piece selected for this volume 'I/My Writings', Mahasweta Devi speaks of the responsibility of the writer to her people and acknowledges that her commitment to the people is the driving force of all her writings. The demands of literature are those of life, and the author asks for uncompromising commitment and honesty from the writer in view of the dark period in history in the 1970s when she is writing. She looks upon writing as a form of grounded protest that has the capacity to hold out images of transformation. The themes are lessons learnt from history. The raw material of history, however, has to be transformed into art, and the author elaborates on her ways of choosing words and syntax, constantly moving back to the lives of common people. Writing for her is a painful activity, but she wants to retain her pain, because forgetting, she states, is 'akin to dying'.

Mahasweta Devi's first novel was *Jhansir Rani* (*The Rani of Jhansi*) published in 1956. She carried out an extensive research work for the piece from many sources, and, although the novel received considerable attention, she had to wait till the publication of *Kavi Bandyaghati Gayinr Jeeban o*

DOI: 10.4324/9781003224686-24

Mrityu (*The Life and Death of Kavi Bandyaghati* 1967), *Hajar Churasir Ma* (*Mother of 1084* 1974), and *Aranyer Adhikar* (*The Right of the Forest* 1977) to mark her distinctive place in Bangla literature. Her other significant novels are *Titu Mir* (1984), *Chotti Munda O tar Teer* (*Chotti Munda and his Arrow* 1980), *Pterodactyl, Puron Sahay o Pirtha* (1989) while 'Draupadi', 'Sikar', 'Sisu', 'Bichan', 'Stanyadayini', 'Sanjhsakaler Ma', 'Daulati', 'Ajeer', 'Romtha', 'Daini', 'Rudali' etc. are some of her outstanding short stories.

Many writers today engaged in grappling with the situation of the marginalised in history, and with the role of the middle class in the context of that history, acknowledge Devi as a pathbreaker in the field.

*

I/My Writings[1]

Mahasweta Devi

I write with hesitation as I am not adequately prepared. It is easy to write stories and novels but difficult to talk about them. For writing is not a pleasurable task for me. Writing brings sadness, pain and suffering, and many questions torment me. It is true that I eventually find solace in writing, but it is also true that I suffer. Yet, I write, for I can do nothing else. I do not think there will be any change in the form of my relationship with writing in my life.

Desh: Literary Edition has wanted to know from me 'my particular viewpoints, my mind-set and a few words on my purpose of writing, if I have any', and I think the answers are evident in my writing. I will come to the purpose of writing later. I can talk about one such purpose just now. I love to think that there is a reader who reads my work and immediately understands what I wish to say. I love to think she has read *Amrita Sanchay* (1964), *Andharmanik* (1966), *Sandhyar Kuasa* (1962), *Bayoscoper Baksa* (1964), *Subhaga Basanta* (1968), *Kavi Bandyaghati Gainr Jiban o Mrityu*, *Hajar Churasir Ma*; my novels not published as books *Aranyer Adhikar* and *Ghare Fera* (1979); my long and short stories 'Ajeer', 'Urvasi o Johnny', Bayen', 'Jalasatra', 'Jal', 'Surjyasantras', 'Wrong Number', 'Sanjhsakaler Ma', 'Kanai Bairagir Ma', and 'Epar Bangla Opar Bangla'; and my two novellas *Dharmabat o Kanchana* and *Nrisingha Durabatar*. (I don't have a copy of the latter published in *Chatushparna*.) These represent my mental being, which probably means nothing, and perhaps the reader knows that these writings constitute my self. These writings answer all questions related to the literature I have created so far.

To talk about my thoughts on literature twenty years after the publication of my first book *Jhansir Rani* today is to enter into a discourse on my literary works. A very positive fact is that, with a few exceptions, I have not been able to draw the attention of serious literary critics. It is a matter of hope and joy. For a long time now, ominous clouds have been gathering in the national and social space, but one does not hear the bells of the fire-engine in Bangla narrative literature; in this situation, it would have been surprising and appalling if critics were also drawn to an individual political writer who did not belong to any party. My minor writings have found place in a voluminous history of narrative literature. That has further reduced the chance of people comprehending me. Probably I am to be blamed for that. For once upon a time, I was a popular writer. I believe I am known to the larger reading public to some extent for my works during that period. Many of my writings during the period are not literature. It is better to forget those books while considering my literary career today. But I am not ashamed of writing the way I did. I was learning to write. And then one day I was not satisfied. The demands of literature got linked with those of life and have remained so to this day. A question that left its mark in the deep graphite of my mind with a ceaseless vibration was this that if I believed in honesty, commitment, and protest, how could I speak differently in literature and look the other way? Today, I know that the mind is deeply layered, like the womb of the earth. There was a ceaseless upheaval in some subterranean layer. The prime attitude towards writing was becoming crystallised, diamond-sharp. Gradually, I began writing in a different manner. I realised I was becoming less popular and that sales were going down. Writing was my sole occupation then. Depending on one's writing for a livelihood was not a hopeful proposition, but I had no other option. In a very conscious manner, accepting loss, I turned the direction of my literary endeavours towards the solitary path. The path has become more and more solitary over the years. My greatest, though not the lone, joy has been that I have always been able to stand face to face with myself in solitude. My shadow in the mirror does not ask me why I did not do what I could have done; why I did not keep my commitment; why I denied my society, people, place, and time. This is a big reward for me. In comparison with this, the temptation of superficial gain from literature is like a dispensable cellophane paper. I am infinitely and eternally indebted to each chapter of my life for having been able to do this. The ceaseless vibration, changes in layers, and transformations continue deep within my mind. The sedimentary rocks keep hardening. My writing represents the seismograph.

This is me, the self that writes. I have probably clarified my stand on my attitude, perspective, and purpose of writing. With my limited popularity, my role as a writer has probably become clear and comprehensible to West Bengal. My expectation is predominantly from the creator of literature. She would be honest, with a conscience and a sense of commitment to the people, her time, and her country. Her pen would be uncompromising and fearless. It is the mind that writes and not the hands. If the creator betrays her faith, how can her literature be an attempt to uphold her commitment? There is no other way but to repeat what I have said many times before. I saw the worst form of mental bankruptcy and the darkest degeneration in the intellectuals and writers of the seventies. When people were being torn apart daily in blood-drenched experiences, literature denied the lessons learnt from the deep agony and remained preoccupied with the vain suicidal game of making false flowers blossom in unreal dream-filled gardens of fairy lands. No one did a full analysis of this, and very few texts remained as documents of the period. We forgot that we live in our children and in our descendants. Will our descendants forgive this lack of honesty and courage? What if a science-fiction like episode takes over? If our descendants walk backwards from a yet-to-arrive future and hold us responsible or blame us, what shall we say? That we were afraid? That we believed provisional security was of utmost importance? I hear the sound of the accuser knocking on my door all the time, and I do not know why. Yes, I remain pained, angered, torn apart, agonised, and full of questions. And I feel as frightened as Sujata when I think I will forget Brati (*Hajar Churasir Ma*). I do not want to be relieved of this pain as long as I live. Because for me, forgetting is akin to dying. That day would be my death. Will I live just because my body lives?

I believe in analysing, judging, and documenting contemporary time in my writings. Because I believe that it will lead us to move to a larger, more open and free space. I believe in a people and society-oriented historiography. I think it is absolutely necessary on the part of the creative writer to make history her chief and core area of learning. That transformation to a higher plane occurred in the case of Bhabanisankar in *Amrita Sanchay*, and an entire society received a new birth from the darkness of the 18th century to the aspirations of an enlightened society in the 19th century in *Andharmanik*. The poet in *Kavi Bandyaghati* embraced death to bring about the realisation that death was a lie, for he himself was the future. Even if the future was murdered by the present, truth could not be turned into a lie. The courtesan Kanchana who assisted the revolting fishermen in the Kaivarta Revolt placed her agonised query before the future while dying in *Dharmabat o Kanchana*. The social order in Lakshman Sen's Bengal turns Saran into a *romtha*, a branded criminal in *Subhaga Basanta* (*Romtha* in English translation) who would later be killed, and before his death Saran asks why a romtha should not be allowed to live. He takes the entire society to task, protests against the dark system that brands him a romtha with a triangle marked by a hot iron rod on his chest, and then delivers him to be boiled alive in a cauldron of ghee by an Ayurveda practitioner. Sujata in *Hajar Churasir Ma* is quite apolitical. Yet, while looking for an explanation of her son's death in the 1970s, she finds the entire social system as dishonest, and she does not see any justification for the murder of her son. The same theme related to people occupying different levels of society has recurred in my stories – in 'Kanai Bairagir Ma', 'Jalsatra', 'Jal', 'Pindadan', 'Epar Bangla Opar Bangla', 'Wrong Number,' and others. Again, in 'Surjasantras', as the blacksmith forges shackles and begins putting them around the protagonist's waist, wrist, and ankles, he (the protagonist) begins to grow like Vaman Avatar. The earth cannot contain him, and so he lifts his feet up on the sun's stomach. The sun is startled by the defiant act. I have always believed in transformation to a higher plane. Thus, Sadhan in 'Sanjhsakaler Ma' finds his mother in the aroma of rice. Chandidasi in 'Bayen' dies under the train's wheels to save the very people and society that had banished her and returns from the underworld of dark superstitions to a human identity in the eyes of society and of her children. The nuances of the story 'Ajeer' are deep-rooted. Patan, the descendant of a slave who sold himself and his descendants for a paltry sum, kills his landlord's wife in vain for not giving him the *ajeerpatta* or the slave bond. He was, in fact, always free and never a slave. No one can bring freedom to a slave who does not know that he is free. The novel *Ghare Fera* written last autumn reveals the character of all fifty- to sixty-year-old authors and the horror of the denial of their commitment to human beings and to the country. The denial brings not only immense wealth and fame to the protagonist Asesh but also simultaneously the final death of his literary identity, leaving just the parasitic body. The love story in 'Urvasi o Johnny'[2] is an extrinsic matter. Johnny loses his voice and that implies that the public can no more be in good form. Johnny has lost his voice to an invisible cancer's dictate. Johnny's tears are a protest. I had to talk about the subject matter of some of my representative novels and stories to clarify what I have to say. Birsa Munda, the protagonist of *Aranyer Adhikar* and the leader of the Mundari Revolt, is poisoned to death by arsenic by the British rulers while in custody with his case still pending. That was because he had called for total rebellion – had raised the cry of Ulgulan.[3] Bibek or Batu, the protagonist of the unfinished novel *Bibek Biday Pala* (1983), is born at the same time as Chaitanya in the Sultanate of Bengal. He is a dwarf. His height does not allow him to see the sky, but he sees the ground. The exploited, naked, terrifying image of society during Hosain Shah's regime is revealed to him in his experiences. His only consolation is that a boy from Nabadwip, not known to him, has become a true human being and is dedicating his life in search of salvation for man. Chaitanya is totally absent in this novel. Bibek feels that the respect accorded to Chaitanya by people compensates for all the loss that he has experienced in his deprived life. He loses all desire for life the day he hears that Chaitanya is being worshipped as a god in his lifetime itself. He goes back to the *adivasi* society that had cast him out as 'inauspicious' on the day of their harvest festival. He throws out the straw ghost, symbolic of the inauspicious, that is on the stage and takes its place. The adivasis are dancing in a drunken frenzy with spears in hand and will pierce the image of the ghost when it is time. Batu says:

> My name is Bibek. I am very small and weak. I cannot live without depending on you. You did not give me shelter, nor will you ever, you will kill me again and again, I know that. But I will definitely come back. If you bury me in your fields, I will come back as seed, paddy, marriage, childbirth, as all that I will keep coming back. When you give me total shelter I will forget my deficiency and become a complete human being.

The adivasis pierce him ritualistically with their spears. 'Batu, while dying, is surprised to see that like other human beings in the world, his blood too is red'. *Bibek Biday Pala* is a protest against deification.

I think it is through my writings that I have been able to uphold my ideals, goals, and beliefs. I do not have faith in protests that scream out. In all my writings, I make protest my theme when, from the premise of protest, I can initiate a transformation towards a more pure and useful ground.

So, I do not use direct experience in a raw fashion in literature. I have to consult maps, documents, manuscripts, and history to write. To write *Jhansir Rani*, I have to know Bundelkhandi, Marathi, and old Marathi in the 'Modi' script. I have to roam around Bundelkhand when Mansingh is at the height of his power. Actual experiences, familiar people, known lives rarely leave their imprint on my literature, important books, and writings. Experience, theme, statements, language, and style have to be processed incessantly. Then they become artistic, and then I write. I believe in this processing and the transformation into the artistic. Even the first sentence appears to my mind fully formed, and then I write. Before that how much I should write and how much I should leave out have to be determined by mathematical laws of addition and subtraction and taken to a firm point. That central point has to be extended into writing. Since this transformation into the artistic becomes necessary in each writing, experiments with words, language, and prose style have to be carried out constantly. I have a long-standing interest in the repository of Bangla words and in new orderings of prose forms through experiments with grammatical structures. I benefitted from using the medieval Bangla-prose style while writing *Kavi Bandyaghati Gainer Jiban o Mrityu*. It is evident from the texts of Kavikankan or Krishnadas Kaviraj that the Bangla language was already well-developed at that time. I thought that their writing had enough hints on the grammatical structure of the period's colloquial prose style. It was then that my interest in what I elsewhere called the living language, or the spoken language of the common people (not dialect), had emerged. Gradually, I began to be more convinced that we use a limited number of words while writing, and an overuse of such words have taken away the power of expression from Bangla words, making them anaemic and powerless today. The same perspective is true of grammatical structures in dialogue. From then on, I began to incorporate terms from geography, geology, chemistry, and other subjects along with words that common people use particularly in the context of their work and profession, the way they speak, and I mixed them all with *tatsama* words (Sanskrit loan words) in my writing. I also experimented a lot with sentence structures. The best examples are *Kavi Bandyaghati Gainer Jiban o Mrityu*, *Bayascoper Baksa*, and 'Urvasi o Johnny'. These three pieces have examples of what I have been saying. In the first text, I used many words, verbs, verbal-adjectives, and adjectives from medieval Bangla. In *Bibek Biday Pala*, apart from the dialogue, I often used popular words in descriptions as well. I drew up a list of a few thousand widely used words and verbs while working on *Anandapath* with my co-editor (Ganesh Bagchi) about five years back. The wonderful expanse of the field for the application of Bangla verbs is really amazing. That increased my fascination with words and led me to the astoundingly meaningful and potential word 'ajeer'. Ajeer means a slave who has sold himself for a very low price. This particular word seemed like a symbol of the dark side of our social structure. The word had been used by Nazrul and others, and probably many use it even now in their conversations. When popular words are rarely being used in our daily urban lives, I find words even in dictionaries and use them. I write down those that attract me and make use of them when necessary. I have used *raktotsab* (festival of blood) and *asipatraban* (a sugarcane field, also a stratum of hell for those who destroy trees and disobey the scriptures) in *Ghare Fera*. I still have with me certain words such as *parnanar* (a male figure made of leaves, sometimes used to represent a person for ritual purposes), *subhiksha* (time of plenty when one may expect to receive alms), *pappurush* (evil incarnate), *chorat* (a corner, especially the two ends of a boat), *daksankranti* (last day of Aswin, which usually falls in mid-October), *thakurikalai* (black gram that is as black as the Thakur or Krishna), *garbhadas* (one who is a slave even in the mother's womb, son of a slave), and *jãyatipatra* (horoscope). I do not use words for the sake of using them. A rose is a rose is a rose is a rose is something I do not understand. Because I am absorbed with local myths, sayings, popular beliefs, religious beliefs, etc., I feel that popular words are stronger and more nuanced, and I profit from using them.

This is me, and this is my writing. My engagement with literature involves all this commotion and labour. I do not know about others. I am the only writer whom I know intimately. Talking about myself I wish to say that it is exactly like this that I want to go on writing. I do not believe in any other way. Don't I want popularity? I will respond by saying that when the writer is reading a hundred books and writing a text, the common readers should also engage with what they want from literature and make a few windows on their walls. As I write this, I feel that when there is the darkness of Mausala Parva's Dwarakapuri in the country's mental world, I am perhaps building castles in the air. But if I need to ask, I will ask for the impossible, that which is out of reach. Who can say that what is impossible today may not become possible tomorrow? What else do I want? I want, in all humility, that words that are generally used for me be withdrawn. Like:

> Mahasweta Devi among women writers . . .
> She writes like a man . . .

These words are not true. We can do away with old, ancient words like woman and man, the author or authoress. The senior women writers whom I felicitated were individual littérateurs, who wanted to be known as women writers. We don't want that. Doctors, clerks, scientists are not described in a similar manner. One who writes is a writer. The word 'writer' can be used for all, I think. In language, the dictates of grammar do not have the last word, and linguistics also accepts common practice.

Do I write like a man?

No. I am myself. I write like myself. I cannot write in any other way. An engagement with literature is not a continuous pleasurable activity. It is one of pain and suffering, of questions and longings. Let this pattern imposed by me regarding myself be the ultimate and final one this time. I do not want to be free from it.

Translation: Subha Chakraborty Dasgupta

Notes

1 Mahasweta Devi, 'Ami/ Amar Lekha', in *Mahasweta Devi Rachanasamagra*, Vol. XI, Ajay Gupta (ed.), Kolkata: Dey's Publishing, 2003, pp. 517–521. The essay was originally published in *Desh, Sahitya Sankhya*, 1383 (1976).

2 'Urvasi o Johnny' narrates the story of Johnny, a ventriloquist who loses his voice to cancer, and that portends the end to his career. Unable to grasp the turn of events, he experiences transference of his own trauma to his partner, a talking doll called Urvasi, whom he idolises as a living associate. The story ends with Johnny's violent attack on Urvasi, as she bursts out crying during a performance.

3 'Ulgulan' literally means a great tumult. It also refers to the Mundari revolution against the British Raj at the turn of the century under the leadership of Birsa Munda (1875–1900).

24 Debes Ray: In search of a new form of the novel

Introduction

Debes Ray (1936–2020) was born in the district of Pabna and was one of the most important writers of contemporary Bengal. A Marxist in his political conviction, Ray's novels and short stories often depicted the lives of marginalised people from the northern parts of Bengal. His major literary works include *Jajati* (1973), *Manush Khun Kore Keno* (1976), *Tistaparer Brittanta* (1988), *Samay Asamayer Brittanta* (1993), *Lagan Gandhar* (1995), *Tistapuran* (2000), and *Barisaler Jogen Mandal* (2010). Ray was the editor of *Parichay* between 1979 and 1998. His novels and short stories bear testimony to his keen interest in experimenting with narrative forms and regional variations of language. He has also written extensively on Bangla narratives, particularly the novel. His critical works include texts on Rabindranath Tagore, Tarasankar Bandyopadhyay, and Manik Bandyopadhyay and collections of essays such as *Upanibesher Kal o Bangla Sambadik Gadya* (1990), *Upanyas Niye* (1991), and *Silper Pratyahe* (1991). He also edited a volume of Dalit short stories in Bangla translation. The present essay is taken from *Upanyaser Natun Dharaner Khonje* (1994).

The necessity of a new study of novelistic practices after independence was increasingly becoming important because of two different factors. First, the legacy of a successful struggle for political independence and the formation of nationhood led to a strong post-colonial thrust towards the understanding of narratives. And second, translations of narrative literature from all over the world, including those from Latin America and Africa, gradually became available in Bangla leading to a dialogue within literary discourse itself, and it became necessary to rethink the history of narrative genres.

The following essay by Debes Ray 'In Search of a New Form of the Novel' exemplifies the post-colonial perspective on narrative forms. Ray, as a novelist, begins his essay with a quest for a locus standi for the author within a complex perspective of narrators working across time and across forms. He then moves into the area of the history of the novel and shows how colonisation led to the rupture of the intrinsic relations between speech and meaning, which were then again reformulated. Finally, he looks into the form of the

DOI: 10.4324/9781003224686-25

novel and its relation to colonial technologies of dissemination, articulates a positive discontent with the 'European' notion of the novel, and argues for a distinct discourse deeply rooted in its traditions and not inhibited by a sense of foreignness in its own space.

*

In search of a new form of the novel[1]

Debes Ray

There is this word in English called 'sane' which in Bangla we call 'sat'. The concept of 'sadasat', however, is in no way connected to this word, being more a word that signifies an agreement with some civilised practices of social living. What can a novelist have to say about the possibilities or the crises of a sane society? In Charlie Chaplin's film *The Kid*, we find the boy Jackie Coogan throwing stones at the glass panes of numerous windows so that Chaplin can get a chance to replace them once they break. This was Chaplin's strategy to gain success in his profession as one who repaired glass panes. But a novelist in an entirely sane society is called upon to write not when a glass pane shatters, but when the entire house or, indeed, entire multi-storied buildings come crashing to the ground. It is a good time for the novelist who wants to write when time falls apart.

But why? Is it that the novelists like fishing in cloudy waters? Or they want to make Cassandra-like prophecies? Cassandra herself is, in fact, a character far too 'artificial' for a novel. She needs the stage, the backdrop of the epic war, the balcony, and the stairways of the castle, with its darkness and its open window. All this is too difficult to rustle up in a novel. If a novelist is ever in need of a Cassandra-like character, he will want a softer Cassandra.

The question therefore remains: why does a novelist require, or choose, a troubled time for the context of his novel? Or why does he want to turn time around? Or is it that characters and events cannot be moved from their centres unless time is made chaotic. An individual's unreasoned desire draws the novelist and so does his impending catastrophe. That does not mean that situations of catastrophe attract the novelist. Rather, it indicates that in that impending catastrophe and unreasoned desire, the novelist sees a human truth, not usually acknowledged as such in the rational frame of things. But a truth does not rest upon good or evil for its validity. Somewhere, rationality may be in jeopardy and the possible truth may have been destroyed, and in its place may have been born another truth, which despite its fearsome aspect and undesirability, is nevertheless the truth. The novelist has perceived this dark other side of truth.

Yet, the tale of chaos and destruction of time will not become the truth of humanity unless one remembers that which was a possibility, a desire, and an intention and was also logical. In the novel, one always remembers and is also always reminded of that desire and possibility, of the intended and the probable. If the novel does not remind one of that, it becomes a superficial tale. The novelist ascends the steep meeting point of these two truths of humanity – the truth of reason and the truth of destruction. And it is for this reason that the novelist is a co-worker of those who, in their respective workspaces, are in quest of rationality and common sense in the human world. That common sense is the rarest quality and has been repeatedly highlighted in moments of extreme crises.

As a Bangla novelist then, what is my identity and which area of art do I profess? In a very loose way, the answer to this question may be that I am a writer of stories and novels, or I am a novelist. But am I free of all hesitation when I claim this to be my identity? I say that I am a writer of stories and novels, or that I am a novelist, to give a description of what constitutes my job. I say this because this is how it is said and this is how it can be easily said and I can get by with saying this. The easy acceptability and functionality of these words and sentences have a three-hundred years' old history, and possibly one can go back another hundred years too. With this long legacy that these words have, one therefore feels safe to explain one's identity in this way.

We learnt these words from the colonisers who came to our land from Europe. They went to other lands too, in Africa and in Asia, and it is in these lands and from them that we learned to identify ourselves in this way – 'I am a writer of stories and novels'/'I am a novelist'. Before that, we did not know what was called the novel, or the lyric, or the tragedy and comedy. The makers of colonies taught us that a country's economics was in its industry; its government meant democracy; and a country's arts and literatures were invested in these many sections and subsections: the lyric, the tragedy–comedy, the novel. Now, after about three or four hundred years, these have become common knowledge to us all. These universal truths 'discovered' by the European Enlightenment have spread the Age of Reason and the Age of Science all over the world. In that chapter on the expanse and spread of ideas and knowledge, it is industrialisation, government, and definitions of culture that have become the primary sentence, rendering 'colonisation' a mere subclause. The curious turn of Cartesian logic is such that questions related to the medium in which these concepts attained universality have been rendered irrelevant, irrational, and unscientific. Now, if any Indian raises a question as to why the interpretations of our languages in accordance with the Sahib's or the Westerner's comparative linguistics or our religions in accordance with his comparative theology or our literatures in accordance with his comparative literatures need to be accepted by us, he will be told that languages, religions, and literatures have been thus from time eternal. The universal judgements regarding these are not to be underestimated because of concepts regarding colonialism and the appearance or disappearance of the Westerner. In other words, what the Westerner taught us in the colonies became general truths, untainted by colonialism. We will be taught that it is the consequence that is of primary importance, not the process. We will be taught that in the spread of civilisation, the exchange between two civilisations is always beneficial. Now we could of course accept these conclusions if only we could keep our ears somewhat closed to words such as 'civilisation' or 'progress' or kept ourselves somewhat open to the use of words such as 'the progress of civilisation'. But it is not possible for all to bear in mind these convenient closures of listening and writing. And thus, it is also being said these days that the arithmetic that the Westerner taught us was 'imperialistic arithmetic'. In *Race and Class*, Issue No. 32 (2), 1990, Professor Alan J. Bishop, Faculty of Education, at the Cambridge University, authored an article entitled 'Western Mathematics: the Secret Weapon of Cultural Imperialism', explicitly challenging the myth of culturally neutral knowledge and placed 'what many now call "western mathematics" in its rightful position in the arguments – namely, as one of the most powerful weapons in the imposition of western culture'.

Similarly, we have been taught the meaning of a 'novel' by the European and, though the heritage of the Anglo-Saxon novel is not particularly rich, we have learnt from Scott. And since we have learnt of the novel from Scott, we have endeavoured to introduce the barons and the highlands in keeping with Scott's novels into ours, though these are absent in our realities. In 1865,[2] we too learnt to read and write novels. What cruel irony was hidden in this learning of the 'educated subjects' in the colonies! Only thirty years before this, the entire Bengali community had been unequally divided over the question of whether the widow should be burnt alive with her dead husband on his pyre or not. That the Company had been able to frame a law against this practice of sati[3] was on the strength of support from a numerically smaller group of Bengali Hindus. Only a decade before 1865, the Company, supporting Vidyasagar (1820–1891), had been able to pass a law legalising the remarriage of Hindu widows.[4] And in 1865, the heroine of the first Bengali novel announced to the world that 'This prisoner is the lord of my heart'. But this was a false proclamation – similar to the falsity of similar proclamations made in other colonies and continents of the world. But, despite the falsity of the content, the language of the proclamation was true. In that language, this false proclamation appeared to indicate the truth. The power of the coloniser, having inserted itself between the word and its meaning, had done away with the distance between the two. It is from that time that we have begun to lose our identity of being our own storytellers. We took it for granted that that language and that proclamation was the novel. The signification slipped through the gap between the language and the proclamation. This is the novel that the English taught us. We lost our own stories.

We had a certain style for our stories in the bratakatha, the *panchali*,[5] the *kirtan*[6], and the *kathakata*.[7] The framework for these genres was in accordance with a convention; yet, this convention repeatedly recreated itself anew with the retellings of the many narrators of kirtan, bratakatha, panchali, and kathakata. In the voice of these different narrators, the story changed to become many distinct stories. The same story being moulded by the different personalities of its many tellers became new, different stories, like the unchanging masks of the Chhau dance, recreating themselves in constantly changing forms – the stories so familiar, so often-heard, so well-known; yet the ritual would remain incomplete without its repetition one more time. The brata, the panchali, the kathakata, and the kirtan would remain incomplete. Within the predetermined form of the bratakatha or the panchali, the storyteller would introduce his own tales. There would be humorous anecdotes involving the gods and goddesses; Siva and Krishna's stories would be narrated with an air approximating that of reporting scandals; and in this process, the pre-fixed, unchanging formats would be touched with the contemporary, lending them an added dimension. These oral cultures were successful in evading the invasive attacks of the English and in retaining their originality. In the city of Calcutta, there were present diverse forms of the *kirtan*, the *kavigan*, the *kheur*, the *khemta*, each with its own visual–aural form in those days.[8] But the English were unfamiliar with these cultural idioms, and we, accordingly, began to forget our identities. It was around the middle of the 19th century, when the Derozians came forward to take up the responsibility of the Bengali-Indian culture, that these indigenous cultural forms began to fall into disuse and were consigned to oblivion.

The same has happened in Latin America and in Africa. Despite the many varied ways in which colonialism spread, the colonisation of the mind appears the same everywhere. Colonial India, despite colonisation, remained India. But the attack of Western education was so pervasive that the foundation of the many thousand-year-old languages, literatures, philosophies, and theoretical studies was shaken. The *kaviraj* or ayurvedic doctor could no longer study his Ayurveda to diagnose illnesses, and the *smarta*[9] could no longer go to the ancient scriptures and give his verdict. Perhaps the example of the smarta pundit should be left out, for the social system in which he functioned was the one that was fast disappearing. But what about the Ayurveda? Our lives and deaths had been linked to that science for years. The philosophies, the aesthetics, and other areas of theoretical study that had been around for centuries were rendered irrelevant within a few years of the Hindu School's functioning – such was the power of imperialism.

Yet, India, because it is colossal, and China, because it is insular, have been able to retain their languages, and the literatures in the many languages have remained their own literatures. This is despite the many direct and indirect ventures of colonisation they have encountered and the insertion of imperialism's agenda into their own civilisations. And we may, from around this point, locate a new beginning of these cultures.

Perhaps it has not been an identical process in Africa. There the Europeans have permitted the Africans to live with their tribes and their languages in the forests, bringing them to the cities when labour was required, or the United States of America have put them on ships and have taken them away purely as labourers. A certain class of 'elite' Africans has been formed by the Europeans, who learnt the European languages and socialising processes and received their education. This 'elite' class of Africans has henceforth become the model for the other Africans and their lifestyles the country's lifestyle.

As a result of this, the question of language grew increasingly intense in Africa – would the European's language be Africa's language? Would Africa's significant novelists – Achebe, Soyinka, Aluko, Ngugi wa Thiong'o, La Guma continue to write in English as they were writing? Or would an African tribe's language find a universal form, if not now, then sometime in the future?

A symbolic incident comes to my mind. James Ngugi was beginning his lecture for the Fifth General Assembly at East Africa's Presbyterian Church in March 1970. He said, 'I am not a man of the church. In fact, I am not even a Christian'. His near-atheist lecture provoked an old man in the audience to come rushing at him with his stick held high. 'You've kept a nice Christian name for yourself! And here you go lecturing against religion!' shouted the man. This self-contradiction had not struck Ngugi before this. He discarded his first name 'James' and gave himself the African name Ngugi wa Thiong'o. He changed his name, though he had to continue using the English language to establish the truths of Africa: *The River Between*, *Weep not, Child*, *A Grain of Wheat*.

The spread of imperialism did not allow any of the local practices or languages to keep themselves alive on the Caribbean or the West Indies islands. The native societies with their native languages have all been lost, and English is now both their mother-tongue and father-tongue. Yet they are not inhabitants of the mainland of either Europe or America. In spite of this, however, they have been taught, over many generations, by their colonial masters that their relationship with Africa is one of disgust and contempt. After independence, they have had to live a life torn by the conflicting pulls of hatred and proximity, living as aliens on their native land. Or at least, it is this exiled life that has recurred repeatedly in their novels. Naipaul, Lamming, Wynter, Patterson – all these writers may be seen to be in quest of an African Asian past, with their novels bearing great similarity with the Jewish myth.

Even today, Spanish, Portuguese, and French are the languages spoken and written in Brazil, Surinam, and the French Guinea. In country after country, in continent after continent, for centuries after centuries, mother tongues have been destroyed. One wonders whether a literary revival of those languages would ever be possible.

Yet, in all these countries, indeed in ours too, literature has played a significant role in re-establishing the legacy of the national cultures through our own languages and through that of the coloniser's.

> For in the struggle to achieve decolonisation and independence from European control, literature has played a crucial role in the re-establishment of a national cultural heritage, in the reinstatement of native idioms, in the re-imagining and re-figuring of local histories, geographies, communities. As such, then, literature not only mobilised active resistance to incursions from the outside, but also contributed massively as the shaper, creator and agent of illumination, the source of the fire, within the realm of the colonised.
>
> (Said 1990: 1)

But this is a complex process. Many of the Latin American writers like Carpentier, Asturias, Juan Rulfo, García Márquez, Cortázar, Fuentes, and others; Ngũgĩ wa Thiong'o, Amos Tutuola, Achebe, Soyinka, and many other writers of Africa have attempted to discover the pre-colonial forms of narratives and literatures of their native lands and their native languages and are continuing to do so. They have visited the Negro, the Indian, and the Mestizo heritages in this endeavour. Carpentier, one of Latin America's most important writers of the postcolonial age, has a novel entitled *The Lost Steps*. Just as Thomas Mann's *Tonio Kröger* had at one time become the iconic symbol of Europe's crisis of culture, Carpentier's *The Lost Steps* too is a novel that represents the inner conflict of the Latin American writers. The Latin American writer's search for subject had been the subject of Carpentier's novel.

A well-known music director of cinema arrives in the forests of Orinoco, drawn there both for professional reasons as well as by his dedication to music. There, in the depths of the forests, he chances across a primitive tribe who sings songs and plays instruments that hark back to the pre-Columbian age. He discovers the lost track but, as a denizen of the modern world, returns to the city where he hopes to find an appreciative audience. The track is again lost. He could not retrace his steps back to the forests as he finds that, consequent to floods and landslides, the path to Orinoco is lost. What Carpentier had tried to say is this – that if a novelist wishes to say anything, he has to first rediscover a connection to his pre-colonial past, a connection that he will lose subsequently. Just as there is no nostalgia or sentimentality associated with this re-discovery, there is no fresh pain or sense of desolation in the renewed loss. For us, both of these are equally true – the rediscovery and the renewed loss. Without the rediscovery, we will not be able to find the roots of our existence and will remain as parasites on metropolitan culture. And without the renewed loss, we will be unable to establish an accord with our modern-day existence and will forever harbour a nostalgia for the past.

In the Arab world, the literature that is the 'illumination within the realm of the colonised' has moved forward along a meandering path. Writers like Naguib Mahfouz, Mahmoud Darwish, and others have been banned in their own countries. The award of the Nobel Prize to Mahfouz had considerably embarrassed the Egyptian government because his books were banned in Egypt. Mahmoud Darwish, the poet of the Palestinian Resistance, is surely an old man today. Yet, these were the writers who, through their critique of Islam and imperialism, discovered the new truth of the Arab world. And non-Arab writers like Salman Rushdie are living off the pre-colonial Arabia. It is necessary to remember that Rushdie writes only in English and that the English-reading world supports him from their anti-Islamic standpoint.

Those who have written in support of Rushdie have never written or spoken in support of those Arab writers who have been murdered, imprisoned, or attacked in the pro-American Israel or in the anti-American Libya, Iran, and Syria. Writers like Mahfouz and Darwish, however, have placed themselves within the realities of their Arabian land and both supported and opposed Rushdie. There lies the nobility of the rootedness of Mahfouz and Darwish.

Amidst the thoughts and ideas of these literatures authored in once-colonised, or semi-colonised, lands, where can we place ourselves, we who write stories and novels in India in one Indian provincial language which is, yet, the sixth-largest language community in the world?

Like the Arab writers, we have to know and recognise our own land and our society – the unity of our land and the diversity of our society. And yet, it is this attempt to understand that pushes us into an insurmountable conflict. The European model of the novel gives a certain structure to the unity of our land and at the same time destroys the perceptions gathered through experience of our social diversity. The European model therefore serves as an obstacle to the writer's endeavour to understand his fellow countrymen and their lives. When we write a novel on the lives of the adivasis, it becomes an anthropological novel modelled on the European and taught to us in a certain way by the Westerners. The adivasi consequently does not come across as the core of India's flow of humanity.

What will be the model or the form of my novel? Surely that which renders the novelist's experience and wisdom into a narrative? This, possibly, has been the obstacle that I have repeatedly encountered for the past forty years in my attempts to write short stories and novels. Not that I have always recognised that there was this obstacle that was thwarting me. It is only now, as I try to climb uphill so as to see at a stretch the trajectory of the Bangla novel, that I am filled with a helpless frustration. For I can understand that there is no relief for us in the European form. As I have said earlier, we had our own way of telling a tale – in the forms of panchali, the kathakata, the kirtan, and the kavigan. The exact nature of these forms can scarce be identified today, so completely have these forms been relegated to oblivion by the Hindus and Brahmins nurtured on the arrogance of the anglicised renaissance on the pretext of these being low culture. We have been taught that the public taste discovered these forms in the depraved desire for auto-eroticism in the bylanes of the capital city. But it is now time to approach these forms from the other side and to recognise that, born clandestinely in the native alleys of the new capital of Calcutta, these forms were a form of public resistance, born out of the defencelessness of the indigenous public. They were fostered by the elite households of the emerging city, sung in their courtyards, and they would spend their money to keep these forms alive. In fact, even the women of their households could be the audience for these songs and tales. And then, after they had partaken as much as they needed, these elites threw these forms onto the rubbish heap. By then, the English had given us the printing press, and we were reading Bangla stories in print.

Here is where my theories, or the theories that I derive through my explorations in history, end. I do not know any more than this. I have, in fact, no way of knowing. Even had I wanted to, I would not have been able to author a *mangalkavya*[10] today or a kathakata. All the connections between modernity and the mangalkavya and kathakata have been sundered. The ties of love that had bound Carpentier's natives to their land were not present in the lives of the late 18th- or the early 19th-century middle-class Bengalis of the city of Calcutta. They were exiled in their land from the beginning, their very courtyards and their homes being a foreign land. In the shelter of imperialism, the greed for that parasitic life was so great, and its power so limited, that even the folk forms were devoured by that urban existence. But in a land like India, folk life is so diverse, complex, and expansive that even the imperialism-sheltered middle class has been unable to annihilate it. Just the other day, Meera Mukhopadhyay (1923–1998) revitalised the *dokra*[11] art form as the foundation for a new form of sculpture.

I have no conclusion to draw here. I am only a novelist concerned about a novelist's crisis of art; a novelist of tomorrow who will demand to lay claim to a language in which her words will seem true and not fabricated. I am only concerned about that novelist of tomorrow who will demand to construct a sentence that she, and only she, will create. Between the sentence and the meaning that she desires to place into that sentence, it is only she who will be present as its author and its narrator; as a colonial subject, she will not insert any colonial teaching into her sentence. It is that novelist of today, or tomorrow, that I am thinking of, who will so desire – who will be free, and whose writing will be free, and the meaning that she will embed into her words will also be free.[12]

Translation: Sipra Mukherjee

Notes

1 Debes Ray, 'Upanyaser Natun Dharaner Khonje', in *Upanyaser Natun Dharaner Khonje*, Kolkata: Pratikshan, 1994, pp. 11–18.

2 The year of publication of Bankimchandra Chattopadhyay's *Durgeshnandini*, often identified as the first novel in Bengal.
3 Regulation XVII of 1829, banning the practice of 'Suttee' for the first time, was issued by William Bentinck, Governor-General of India.
4 Hindu Widow Remarriage Act, 1856.
5 An oral narrative form with rhyming couplets.
6 Kirtan literally means chanting. However, since the post-Chaitanya period, it has developed as one of the richest performative traditions of Bengal in the Vaishnavite and Shakta communities.
7 A performative oral form that narrates and explicates religious stories.
8 *kabigan, kheur* and *khemta* are urban, popular forms of music, having their roots in rural traditions, which emerged in the late 18th and early 19th centuries. Kheur and khemta were often looked down upon as degenerate forms popular among the decadent section of the urban gentry.
9 A learned person well-versed in *Smriti* or the branch of authoritative texts dealing with social regulations.
10 A long narrative poem establishing the cult of a folk deity.
11 A lost-wax metal casting technique used by traditional artisans of Bengal and other parts of India.
12 The author mentions these works in a note following the essay:

Alan J. Bishop, 'Western Mathematics: The Secret Weapon of Cultural Imperialism', *Race and Class*, 1990, 32(2): 51–65.

Edward W. Said, 'Figures, Configurations, Transfigurations', *Race and Class*, 1990, 32(1): 1–16.

25 Sisir Kumar Bhaduri: Form in theatre

Introduction

Sisir Kumar Bhaduri (1889–1959), often known as *Natyacharya*, was one of the greatest personalities in the history of Bangla theatre. After completing his studies in English Literature from the University of Calcutta, he joined as a professor in Metropolitan Institution established by Vidyasagar. During his term as a professor, he took part in a number of amateur productions of Bangla and English plays, before he joined Bengali Theatrical Co. as a professional artist in 1921. However, his association with the Company was a short-lived one owing to some differences with the management. He was able to bring together a host of theatre artists and formed his own theatre in March 1924. In August 1924, he staged Jogesh Chaudhuri's *Sita* in Manomohan Natyamandir. The production received immediate acclaim and introduced a new age in Bangla Theatre. For the next three decades, Bhaduri went on to produce many plays based on the works of Rabindranath Tagore and Saratchandra Chattopadhyay. He established 'Srirangam' theatre in 1941, which also hosted a series of remarkable productions by other stalwarts and young dramatists, the most notable of them being Bijan Bhattacharya's *Nabanna* (1944) that paved the way for a revolutionary transformation of Bangla Theatre. Bhaduri was honoured with 'Padmabhusan' in 1959, which he refused to accept stating that the Government should try to establish a national theatre, instead of bestowing individual honours upon theatre artists.

Sisir Kumar Bhaduri's emergence as a dramatist coincided with a very crucial phase in the Indian Freedom Movement. A quest for Indian roots in different areas of culture was being sought by many. After an initial struggle with the professional theatre scenario, Bhaduri was able to establish his own theatre in 1924. In his immensely successful production of *Sita*, he introduced a series of changes in keeping with a nationalist perspective, such as the remodelling of the auditorium and the introduction of stage-directions in Bangla, bringing in signs of the 'auspicious' in theatre with traditional decoration and incense, using Shehnai for the interludes instead of English concerts, and a thorough renovation of production design and acting style

DOI: 10.4324/9781003224686-26

reminiscent of traditional theatre forms. He realised that his contemporary theatre, primarily inspired by the English stage, was not an adequate medium for the demands of his time. At the same time, the tradition of relying to a great extent on Sanskrit texts was not sufficient, since indigenous theatre had lost its connection with ancient forms. Therefore, it was only appropriate to search for a national form of theatre in traditions that were alive for several centuries. In the essay 'Form in Theatre', Bhaduri sketches the transition from the traditional theatre to the Western stage and argues for a movement that would bring in certain indigenous elements.

*

Form in theatre[1]

Sisir Kumar Bhaduri

There are plenty of discussions about a national theatre but hardly any about what should be the nature of the national drama. Different communities have different lifestyles. As drama is the reflection of life, it is only natural that each community would have its own dramatic presentation. The variety of vegetation depends on the nature of the soil. Similarly, the nature of the community will decide the nature of its national theatre. There is a wide difference between the natures of the drama in ancient India and in ancient Greece and Rome. In our own times, the nature and modes of performance of Chinese and Japanese drama are very different from the dramatic practices of modern Europe.

In our own Bengal, the dramatic performance called the *jatra*, which was in existence for five to six hundred years, was completely different in shape from modern Bangla theatre. It did not have either a stage or a backdrop or the grandeur of lighting. It was extremely popular with all sections of society. It was based on our Hindu religion and myths. Our plays and dramaturgy analysed the philosophy and myths which grew out of the Vedas. The task of our drama was to educate even the uneducated through the enactment of the mythological stories which carried serious philosophical messages.

Mahaprabhu Sri Chaitanya belonged to the 16th century. The biographical narratives about him give the information that among the innumerable festivals that Bengal had all the year round, plays were much performed. In the courtyards of the wealthy, during *durgapuja, raslila*, and *dol*,[2] different kinds of *palas*[3] used to be performed with joy. Mahaprabhu himself used to enthusiastically participate in these performances. His followers joined in these dramatic festivals happily, which added to his enthusiasm. In those days, the jatra was an extension of the worship of God. The most performed, however, was the devotional Krishna-jatra. Mahaprabhu himself used to play the part of Rukmini which added to the flow of Krishna-devotion in the minds of the people. Even the aged pandit Advaita[4] did not feel any shame in taking part in this *natya-leela*. Nityananda's[5] enthusiasm is a matter of legend. We observe that in the 16th century, the jatra was an important part of the social life of Bengal. Moreover, the extensive prevalence of it during that period seems to indicate that the jatra had been performed for the previous two to three centuries without interruption. The popularity of the jatra continued till the end of the 19th century. Even a few years ago, village landlords used to organise drama festivals during the occasions of durgapuja, dol, and raslila. Not that the jatra has become extinct in our day, but the form of jatra has changed. Even few years back, the jatra was a part of the worship of the divine. Literacy was not regarded as the only mode of education. Despite a lack of acquaintance with the alphabet, even the illiterate farmer would be able to acquaint himself with the basic tenets of Hindu religion and philosophy through the jatra, the performances of which were based on mythological narratives. The high ideals of life – love for truth, altruism, sacrifice of the self for the good of the greater community, chastity, filial piety, fellow-feeling, and devotion to the divine power – used to be transmitted into the minds of the people, but later the over-dependence on mythological themes cut the jatra off from contemporary issues. The ordinary life of people and the problems of it found no place in the jatra.

Extreme lack of realism does not lead to popularity – it does not do any service to the people. Consequently, jatra started losing its popularity, and inevitably that led to its decadence. After the tiresome repetition of the mythological themes, the need for a secular drama was felt. From the end of the 18th century, that is, from the beginning of the British colonial rule, the English theatre started in Kolkata. This theatre attained its fullness in the 19th century. It had encouragement and financial patronage from some rich and famous native gentlemen. It was not possible to make a success of the English stage merely by a handful of Englishmen. The English theatre would not have been successful without the help of the leaders of the contemporary Bengali society like Dwarakanath Tagore[6] and others. When the theatre known as Sans Souci[7] was destroyed in fire, Dwarakanath Tagore found another place for its Western directors. The English-educated natives were primarily interested in the English theatre. Baishnabcharan Adhya[8] played the main protagonist in a Shakespeare play in which the other roles were played by English actors. Around this time, Shakespeare plays also started being performed in schools and colleges. This English tradition of acting is not yet extinct. This way, the desire to establish a Bangla theatre for Bengalis after the model of the English theatre became stronger.

Over a number of years, in the city, a Bangla amateur theatre had grown in imitation of the English theatre. In different parts of the city, wealthy and educated gentlemen had plays performed in either their own homes or leisure houses with zeal and help. However in these performances, the common people were not allowed entry. Despite their eagerness, the populace could not watch these plays. For some time, these amateur theatre groups came up and gave grand performances. Then as the interest of the organisers waned, the establishments also died untimely deaths. The notable examples are the plays *Vidyasundar, Sakuntala, Kulin Kul Sarbaswa* by Nabin Basu and *Ratnabali* and *Sarmishtha* at the theatre at Belgachia. From the beginning of the 19th century till the December of 1872, the amateur theatre groups were coming up and dying. The first professional theatre group was created by the actors of such an amateur group. This group contained some extraordinarily talented young men. Among them the names of Ardhendu Shekhar Mustafi, Girish Chandra Ghosh, and Amrita Lal Basu are to be etched forever in the history of the Bengali stage. We ought to remember that the description of the stage that we get from the ancient Indian treatises on drama bears a marked resemblance with the stage and drama of the 'Elizabethan' age. For that reason, when these actors did away with the pure tradition of the Bengali jatra to set up a proscenium theatre, it did not seem a European innovation to anyone. In those days, an imitation of the European tradition was a matter of special pride. The psychology behind this was 'what they can do, we can do even better'. Even the traditionalists accepted this theatre with eagerness, and not only did not object to the westernised shape of the theatre, but also gave wholehearted support to its performance.

With the establishment of the professional theatre, the English theatre of the 16th century was set up permanently in Bengal. We get the history of the first years of professional public stage in the memoir of Amrita Lal Basu.

The first actor to demonstrate the intricacies of the acting of the English stage was an Englishman named G.W. Lewis.[9] According to Amrita Lal, the kind of spirit and power that Girishbabu introduced to his acting on the Bengali stage was inspired by his observation of the acting at the Lewis Theatre. In addition, the inspiration of the Lewis Theatre led to the establishment of the Bengal Theatre[10] and the National Theatre[11] in 1873 on Beadon Street. In fact, drama of this kind still continues to be performed, which means that the jatra has given way to theatre in our country. However, it is true that (even now) more people watch the jatra compared to the (westernised) theatre, though the jatra resembles the European theatre to a certain extent and is unsophisticated.

From the end of the 19th century and the beginning of the 20th there has been a trend in Europe towards the avoidance of the (proscenium) stage. The attempt is to include the viewers in the world of the actors instead of continuing with the backdrop-adorned, brilliantly lit world of fantasy played on the raised platform which separates the viewers completely from the action. This is known as the Arena Theatre or Theatre in the Round, but this concept has been present in our country for centuries. Ours is a poor country. The ordinary viewer does not have the means to buy expensive tickets. It takes a lot of money to set up a pleasing backdrop on a floodlit stage. The other negative side of this is that the grandeur of the backdrop distracts the attention of the viewer from the acting, which is the life of a play, and this affects the play badly. The elimination of the backdrop or the fascinating lighting does not affect the aesthetic effect of a play. If we can do away with the expensive stage décor and re-establish the open-air jatra, it will not have any negative impact on the aesthetic pleasure and, in fact, will lengthen the life-spans of the theatre groups and provide the producer as well as the actors relief from a lot of unnecessary labour. It is not going to be indicative of national pride if we let the jatra, which has been a provider of emotional satisfaction to people for over four to five centuries, die out. It will be the loss of an achievement.

However excellent the acting is, if we adopt the techniques behind the brilliant lighting and the various tricks for the backdrop following the Western fashion, we will never have a national theatre. In the name of a 'national theatre', if we build one in imitation of the west, it is merely going to be a space for a display of expensive pomp. Today, when the west is making a move towards discarding the Picture Frame Stage, why should we not bring our theatre to the open-air arena of the jatra? Why can't we rebuild our jatra and make it relevant to our own time?

Translation: Sucheta Bhattacharya

Notes

1 Sisir Kumar Bhaduri, 'Natyer Rup', in *Natyacharya Sisir Kumar Rachana-samgraha*, Debkumar Basu (ed.), Kolkata: Sisir Kumar Bhaduri Institute of Dramatic Research and Culture, 1987, pp. 55–64.

2 Raslila is a folk dance-drama popular in Northern parts of India. Dol, or doljatra, is a festival popular among the Vaishnavites of Bengal, Odisha and Assam. Both raslila and doljatra are related to the life of Krishna.

3 Pala is a narrative folk ballad.

4 Advaita Acharya (1434–?) was a famous scholar who served to spread Vaishnavism and announced Sri Chaitanya as one of the 'avatars' of Lord Vishnu.

5 Nityananda Prabhu (1477/78–1532?) was the chief follower of Sri Chaitanya; Nityananda left home at the age of twelve, and, after his travels over twenty years to different places of pilgrimage, arrived at Nabadwip. He remained with Sri Chaitanya during the latter's stay in Puri.

6 Dwarkanath Tagore (1794–1846) was a distinguished industrialist, philanthropist, and social reformer.

7 When the British Theatre burned down in 1838, Esther Leach, the popular actress, suggested that a new theatre be built as replacement. With support from J.H. Stocqueler and others such as Prince Dwarkanath Tagore and Lord Auckland, the Sans Souci Theatre (Calcutta) came into being in 1839. The last play was performed in 1849.

8 An actor in the Sans Souci Theatre in Kolkata, he is remembered as the first Indian to act in an English language theatre founded by the British. He played the role of Othello in Shakespeare's play in 1848.

9 Henry George Lewis (1817–1978) was a drama critic, playwright, and philosopher remembered for his book *On Actors and the Art of Acting* (1873).

10 Founded in 1872 by Sarat Chandra Ghosh, Bengal Theatre had the first permanent stage in the history of professional Bangla theatre. It was inaugurated with the staging of Madhusudan Dutt's *Sarmishtha*. It was also the first playhouse to introduce female actresses on stage.

11 The first Bangla public theatre with a temporary stage opened on 7 December 1872 with Dinabandhu Mitra's *Nil Darpan*.

26 Sankha Ghosh: Theatre moments and the search for language

Introduction

Chittapriya Ghosh (1932–2021), commonly known by his pen name Sankha Ghosh, was among the principal literary figures of his time. A student of Bangla language and literature, he taught in various colleges and universities, including Jadavpur University with which he was associated for nearly three decades. An erudite scholar of Tagore studies and modernist literature in Bengal, his critical works include *Kaler Matra o Rabindra-natak* (1969), *Urvasir Hasi* (1981), *Nirman ar Srishti* (1982); *Chhander Baranda* (1971), *Nihsabder Tarjani* (1971), *Sabda ar Satya* (1982) and *Aitihyer Bistar* (1989), *Samasta Kshater Mukhe Pali* (2007) and *Prati Prashne Kenpe Othe Bhite* (2012). He also served as the Director of Rabindra Bhavan, Santiniketan.

Ghosh was primarily known as one of the foremost poets of the second half of the 20th century. His collections of poems include *Dinguli Ratguli* (1956), *Adim Lata-gulmomay* (1972), *Murkha Baro, Samajik Nay* (1974), *Babarer Prarthana* (1976), *Panjore Danrer Sabdo* (1980) and *Mukh Dheke Jay Bigyapane* (1984). His memoir related to his poetic works is entitled *Kabitar Muhurta* (1987).

As is well known today, Rabindranath Tagore, essentially a lyric poet, experimented with poetic diction and gave a whole new lease of life to the Bangla language. He also experimented with dramatic language. Throughout his life, he addressed the question of lyricism in dramatic dialogue in various ways, writing plays in verse forms, introducing many songs in his plays and then composing a series of song-plays and dance dramas. In the essay presented here, 'Theatre Moments and the Search for Language', Ghosh takes up this very question of language in Tagore's drama and relates it to the core of Tagore's thoughts on drama.

Ghosh takes a historical approach and evaluates the dramatic corpus of Tagore in terms of the elements that bind the plot, the characters and the form of the play. Beginning from his early experiments with songs in plays like *Valmiki Pratibha*, *Mayar Khela* or *Bisarjan*, composed in the last two decades of the 19th century, Ghosh arrives at *Saradotsab*, *Dakghar*, *Muktadhara* and *Raktakarabi* in the second and the third decades of the

DOI: 10.4324/9781003224686-27

20th century, when the dramatic dialogues in prose become very lyrical. He goes on to examine his later plays which raise questions about the efficacy of the form itself, like *Bansari*, and then he again moves from prose-plays to a new form of dance-drama like *Chandalika* and *Shyama* during the later years of his life. By juxtaposing Tagore's ideas and language to those of Maeterlinck and Eliot, Ghosh arrives at the conclusion that Tagore's quest for an integration of the 'dramatic' and the 'lyrical' found realisation in his late dance-dramas where the plays were no longer bound by their language and acquired many different layers of signification.

*

Theatre moments and the search for language[1]

Sankha Ghosh

'I have developed doubts about the formation of sentences'[2] – we know that the one who said this was a master of words. It may be worth pondering if some impact of this apprehension was the cause behind his turning to painting in his later life. Yet, when we remember that Rabindranath used the line given before while composing his dance dramas, another question comes up. What is the significance of his questioning the power of words and turning to composing plays in a song-centric form? Was he thinking that prose or verse was not enough for theatre anymore? Did Rabindranath notice some incoherence in so many years of his practice? How did the search for words for his plays influence him all his life, why was his theatre spread across three periods of prose, poetry and songs and what were his barriers in terms of language to capture theatrical moments – these questions then come to our minds.

*

The massive influence of Ibsen finally led to the firm establishment of prose in Western theatre. Shaw and Synge possibly held contrasting theatrical ideologies but both took refuge in prose-based dialogues. Synge had stated that to touch reality, his plays may contain a couple of words that he never found in public usage in Ireland or had never heard in his childhood. Again, this search for prose cannot be taken as an exploration of realism, when we find Maeterlinck trying to depict distant surreal worlds in his static drama by the same means. Yet, in similar quasi-contemporary theatrical dialogue, Rabindranath chose to use a verse form. Why?

Perhaps a major reason for this is a short-term refuge in Shakespeare's ideology. At that time, though we find him interested in a few contemporary European writings, there is not much eagerness. In the context of Ibsen particularly, like Synge, he too seemed rather apprehensive. That is the reason why in order to break out of poetic plays, he chose to resort to traditional dramatic techniques, to Shakespeare or sometimes even to the poets of the Romantic era. Some effects of the depth of his preoccupation with Shelley and Keats in his poetry spread to his drama as well. An effect similar to that of the romantic poets who had used drama in a leisurely manner, or later that of Tennyson or Browning as they composed plays, was evident in the diffused expanse of his works like *Raja O Rani* (1889) or *Bisarjan* (1890).

In general, he was still doubtful about the use of prose. The fluidity of his *Prachin Sahitya* (Ancient Literature) on the one hand and, on the other, the mild influence of Bankim did not give him the prose that could unite both functional reality and the graceful inner world. It is evident why the language of *Hutom Pyanchar Naksa* (Kaliprasanna Sinha 1862) or *Prafulla* (Girish Chandra Ghosh 1889) did not find Rabindranath's acceptance. He was attracted by the prose of fairy tales of Bengal instead. We also find that even in the dialogues of his novels like *Naukadubi* (*The Boatwreck* 1906), formal language was being used. Contexts of *Baikunther Khata* (1897) or *Hasyakautuk* (1907) are relevant here as well, but we feel that Rabindranath's prose still could not come to terms with abandoning the safe ground of jest and touch the depth of theatrical necessity.

Rabindranath used poetic language at the time, but today we do not understand any imperative need of the same in the inner context. We are often reminded of the observation of Eliot that what could be said in prose should be said in prose in the context of *Raja O Rani* or *Bisarjan*. It seems that the linking of some other nuances with dialogue in the two plays is not always the intention of the playwright nor is the opening of any unexposed levels by the forceful imposition of poetry. There was an indirect proof of this when *Raja O Rani* evolved into *Tapati* (1929) in his later years. And if one reads *Bisarjan* and *Rajarshi* (1887) together, *Rajarshi* is more impactful in certain situations, I believe. In the middle of a secluded forest when Gobindamanikya asks Nakshatra Roy 'Why will you kill me brother, for the sake of the kingdom?' How much of the resonance that the long and deep comment creates in the entire storyline and in the periphery of characters can be brought forward in this dialogue of *Bisarjan*?

> Will you kill me? Speak, say the truth,
> You wish to kill me, these words are playing
> In your mind day and night? With these words
> In your mind you smile at me as you
> Speak . . .[3]

However, side by side with this relatively prosaic environment comes a type of poetry, which did not fulfil the playwright's purpose. Dhurjatiprasad had said at one time that Rabindranath's poetic dialogues were never a result of unnecessary poetic urges, but this inference requires reconsideration. On the contrary, it seems that poetic concern was the biggest challenge of his plays of this era. Here, poetic concern does not mean that the compositions are inclined towards abstraction, not even when Rabindranath himself talks about the 'excessive use of lyrics'. The thought of the writer that Ila and Kumar make an out-of-context entry in *Raja O Rani* for the sake of lyrics does not seem appropriate either. Their 'entry' is not just for the sake of lyrics, and it is also not a hindrance. For that matter, we find as well that the modified version of *Tapati* could not be without Kumar either, and a new set of lovers were brought in through Naresh–Bipasha. Actually, the problem of *Raja O Rani* is that the story of Ila and Kumar enters the narrative cycle almost like Abhimanyu – it finds no way of getting out.

Thus, the problem of such writings lies not merely in the content nor in a few different characters either. It seems that the lyric takes advantage of the verse form of the play and expresses itself forcibly through most of the characters of that period. A little analysis reveals that most of the people in these plays are eager to establish their importance, and the need to turn around the face of the characters towards the inner circle is not realised appropriately in these cases. To elaborate this statement, I wish to use the diagrams of Figures 26.1 and 26.2.

If A, B and C are characters of a play in Rabindranath's verse-plays, they mostly touch the main storyline as in Figure 26.1 and touch each other – but they seem outside the core circle of events. As a result, chances of the dramatic conflict between events and character and between characters that could often be created become minimal. In the second diagram, we find only a portion of the characters inside the circles, the remaining is viewed in perspective, and since their build-up is centripetal, even before reaching the climactic moment, they create waves many a times within the dispersing inner circle. It seems that in *Raja O Rani*, Rabindranath cannot appropriately create adequate vibes through conflicts.

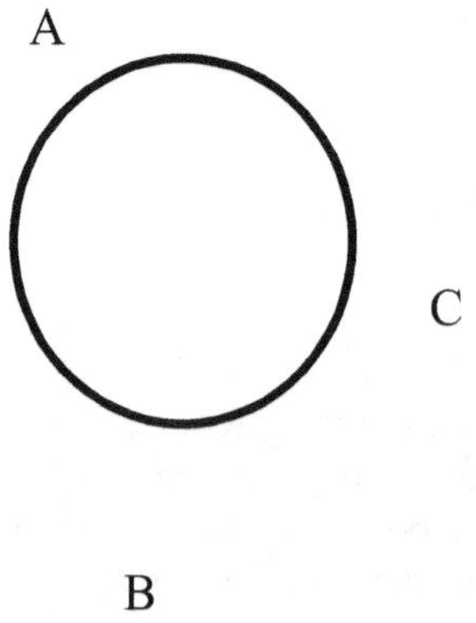

Figure 26.1

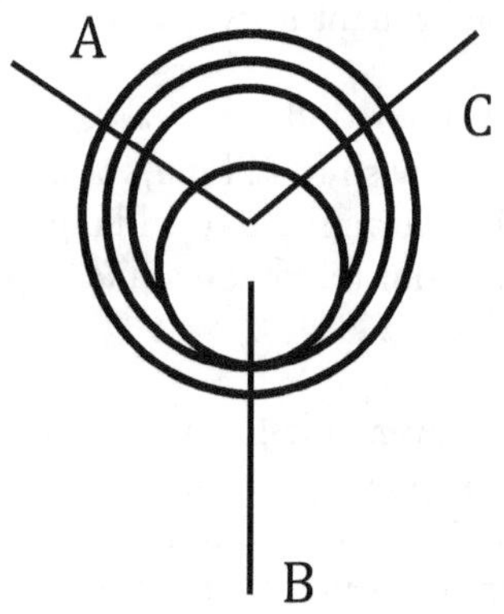

Figure 26.2

The thought arises then, why was it so? The often-heard comment that he is not adept enough in developing plots does not seem acceptable enough. Was there any dearth of storyline in *Raja O Rani* or *Bisarjan* at least? Here the problem does not lie with the story but in that the characters, in order to establish themselves on their own, get somewhat decentred which is largely because of the appearance of poetry.

How do we interpret this appearance of poetry? If we notice carefully, we can see that many characters of these plays of a particular period are busy talking about themselves, and reminiscence is a characteristic of such plays. Not just Bikram–Sumitra, but also Shankar or even Debdatta do not easily miss an opportunity to give a passionate expression to memories. The individual perception of memory of each of the characters and the unbridled freedom of projecting oneself must be an advantage of the lyric form, but how appropriate is it for theatre? In this sense, the appearance of lyrics has a negative effect in Rabindranath's poetic plays.

That these projections of oneself, extensive descriptions and monologues were not always very pleasant for the playwright is evident from the English translations of the plays and from subsequent critical discourse on plays. In English, *Bisarjan* is almost half the size of the original, and *Raja O Rani* or even *Malini* (1912) are much shortened. And if we try to get to the root of this editing, we find that they are those poetic descriptions, prolonged reminiscences and individual outbursts that are specifically rejected.

It is not unfair to assume that it is this unease in Rabindranath's consciousness that gradually made him write shorter plays. The shorter length of *Chitrangada* (1892) or *Malini* as compared to *Raja O Rani* or *Bisarjan* is noticeable, but even reducing the complexities of the storylines did not address the core problem of language, and so the compositions became shorter still in his writings in *Kahini* (1900). Poetic plays took respite in the form of dramatic poetry, similar to Browning taking recourse to dramatic monologue.

After a long gap when Rabindranath focused on playwriting once again, we see prose as his exclusive language. The first play *Saradotsav* (1908) of this period is contemporary to *Gora* (1910). We must remember that *Gora* was the first Bangla novel to use common dialogue in a melodious and robust form.

*

The surprising factor is that when Rabindranath found prose trustworthy, a renaissance of poetic plays was taking place in Europe, and by then there was a change in his own thought process as well. In the history of his poetry that was his 'musical' era, and even in his plays he was not considering direct realities of life as his focus but was rather interested in deciphering the intrinsic mysteries of life. Whatever the nature of this mystery, the conscious desire to penetrate it moves towards bringing about a musicality in his writings, and the use of poetic language would probably not have surprised us at this stage. Instead, just at this time, not only did he befriend prose, but he even made an audacious statement on poetry based on his earlier experiences while writing *Tapati*, clearly stating that it was not possible to create various types of moods in verse.

How did this newfound friend behave with the playwright? Not that it was impossible to find a suitable intonation of that period through prose. Writers abroad like Maeterlinck or Synge had already demonstrated such formats. But how much of the kind of vibrant prose that they used, the splendour of hidden clouds that emanated from such writings, did Rabindranath discover in his new endeavours? Dramatic moments now were distinctly different from the traditional ones; concepts of conflict had also changed a lot, but an intrinsic drama prevailed even there. Soft clouds clash against one another and create thunder. Yet the poet is unable to capture the kind of prose that could be compared to such clouds easily. Even by somewhat inappropriately taking this analogy further, one may say that the language of *Saradotsav* is like autumnal clouds, pleasing to the eye, where there is no excess of agitation. This is a world spread out like a fairy tale, and *Prayaschitta* (1909) is of worldly sawdust. Some moments in *Raja* or *Achalayatan* (1912) are stimulating – specially in *Raja* (1910) – but generally, even here, a large section of the prose is not vibrant and lacks depth, which is why these plays distinctly have an excess of songs. In drama production, some directors may find it intimidating to bring their separate rhythmic style into balance, and at times this even leads to a requirement for editing. In *Raja O Rani* and *Bisarjan*, poetry and prose had their distinct angles, but a kind of release from that evolved in the form of the poetic language of *Chitrangada* and *Malini*. Now, however, arose the problem of two distinctly different types of dialogues – commonplace, on one hand, and simultaneously that of unbridled passion on the other. Going to and fro between the two was not so easy, and a new kind of complexity arose. This conflict was larger than the kind that was prevalent from the use of poetry in earlier times. The reason was that if prose was necessary to touch the inner world of poetry, then its mélange was to be set so finely that descending from it would destroy the ambience; yet ascending a bit would also throw it out of pivot from its well-designed construction.

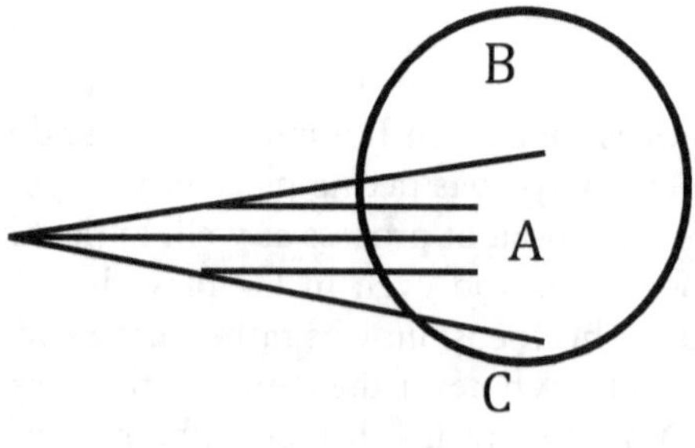

Figure 26.3

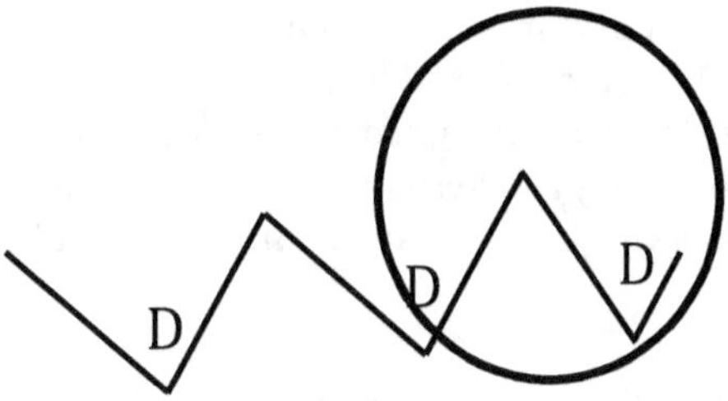

Figure 26.4

The responsibility of language now is not just to touch the dramatic circle; it has to reach the core. It is worth pondering what kind of syntax is required for this. An overtly ornamental language rises and moves out like B, and in contrast the use of unforceful slack prose may fall like C; this apprehension is always there in drama. At times, possibly due to this dichotomy, the language oscillates between the crescendo and the diminuendo, creating angles like the lines of D. By this calculation, one may say that the prose of *Prayaschitta* follows the C line, and *Raja* and *Achalayatan* are like D – at times there arises 'Taffeta phrases, silken terms precise, Three-piled hyperboles'[4] like one of the Lord's descriptions in *Love's Labour Lost*, but in the next moment they fall rapidly into downright lifelessness.

For this reason, without being able to make every-day common language deep in meaning and resonant, it was not possible for Rabindranath to synergise his dramatic language with the dramatic moments of the time. And the key to such success was hidden in the construction of multilayered prose, like the A lines – mere ornamental style was not the right path for the purpose. Maeterlinck gives words to his blind characters in *The Blind* (1890) like this:

> 'I think there is a storm rising'.
> 'I think it is the sea'.
> 'The sea? Is it the sea? But it is hardly two steps from us!'
> 'It is at our feet! I hear it all about me! It must be something else!'
> 'I hear the noise of breakers at my feet'.
> 'I think it is the wind in the dead leaves'.[5]

There the natural flow of the unornamented prose also contains several layers hidden in each of the words, which create a hazy impact in the minds of the connoisseurs. Ajitkumar Chakravarty stated that the meaning he found in reading this play was not seconded in the criticism of Henry Rose. Was it that Ajitkumar's interpretation was futile? I do not think so, since here too the characters become multidimensional like poetry. This prose is in no way 'poetic', but for the same reason it is so close to it.

Rabindranath's search for suitable language for drama finally found gratification in his play *Dakghar* (*The Post Office* 1912). In *Dakghar*, the language is not different or alienated from natural everyday usage, yet it is far reaching. Observing it externally too gives a sort of satisfaction, yet for perceptive readers, this flow can open up layer after layer with new interpretations:

1 I wake up on my bed to find that the oil lamp in the room has gone out and gong-bells ring from what far-off darkness – dong, dong, dong.[6]
2 I should rather close this half-door of yours.[7]
3 It is not time yet. Some say time runs out, some say it is not the time. I think it will be time if you strike the bell.[8]

Only once in between 'Autumn Messenger' and 'Rain Messenger' it makes us pause; we resist a little in our minds thinking that such distinct metaphors were not necessary. Have we already not understood the happy dualities of the seasons? Why were then Autumn and Rain mentioned as characters? In the play, the entry of the likes of the royal doctor seems to express the inexpressible to a somewhat large extent. Yet, how easily beautiful this calm statement is 'Say that Sudha has not forgotten you'.[9] It feels good to think that this was the last line of the play.

The use of such language is found in the period of *Muktadhara* (1922) and *Raktakarabi* (1926) as well but with a slightly different implication. The prose used in *Dakghar* creates a sad distant environment, creating a magical form in the conflict of desire and reality. But the dramatic objective of *Muktadhara* or *Raktakarabi* is a little different. Here, especially in *Muktadhara*, one can frequently hear the thunder. The cloud of a destructive dusk that is mentioned in *Raktakarabi* spreads all its hue in the fiery dialogues of *Muktadhara*. There may be some resistance stating that the preoccupation with language is greater here, though we have to remember that there is a comparative elevation in the setting itself. 'What is it that has been raised in the sky? It is scary indeed'.[10] It is expected that the play that starts with such a dialogue will be strung at the same pitch all along. In fact, for a little while we find that citizens take entry and set the tone down a little in traditional fashion, and we simultaneously see that a kind of banter in the style of *Achalayatan* merges quite well with the speech style of Uttarkut.

One more thing has to be considered in context of the robust conception of *Muktadhara–Raktakarabi*. We know for a fact that on reaching the *Gitanjali* era, Rabindranath had achieved a kind of bliss in his mind, and a sort of musical compatibility had developed in his character. For this reason, his interest in characters or storylines with diverse and complex purpose was getting relatively subsided. The overbearing importance of Amal in *Dakghar* and the projection of his own voice even in Amal give the composition an ease, but the complexities woven in *Raja* or *Achalayatan* did not allow such ease. However, it seemed that within a few years, the outside world and his personal life started getting distraught with the conflict of several thoughts and concerns. So far, he had been creating his inner self, and now that structured character stood at the juncture of a critical historical period. In 'The Three Voices of Poetry', Eliot explained how the playwright plants a seed of his identity in each of his characters; the characters grow by finding form through those seeds. Several complexities had now been created in Rabindranath's mind, which is why fragments of those thoughts could find form in his characters, the possibilities of conflicts were intensifying and the language was finding appropriate strength as well. Had no new concern arisen in this era, then more such plays could have been expected. But the habit of overtly illustrating now caused a new concern.

Meanwhile the appearance of Pramatha Chaudhuri, the pressure of realism and the voice of the youth in this new age were creating an unintentional lustre in prosaic language at the time. In the history of theatre just a few traits of this tendency, and not its beginning, are evident in *Raktakarabi*. When Bishu speaks in a roundabout language, we do not disapprove of it considering that through his words he is trying to draw a veil on his character as his agony arising out of lost love must be kept hidden. The Professor's language is restrained due to his grooming, and love, power and agony in the King's dialogues create a volcano out of language. It seems that the dialogues do not conflict with the characters as Nandini can speak individually with each of them. Only perhaps we hear the King a little in excess as a new beginning of the verbose.

We find another noteworthy technique of dramatic impact in *Muktadhara* and *Raktakarabi*, one that allows incomplete, fleeting interpersonal expressions to create a rhythm, like this portion from *Muktadhara:*

> This is clearly the sound of a waterfall.
> First tabor sounds of the starting of a dance.
> The sound seems to be growing, it is growing –
> As if –
> It seems as if –
> Yes, yes, no doubt. It is the free flow. Who broke the barrier?
> Who broke? – He will not be spared.[11]

Dramatic conflict reaches its peak here, and the last rapid expressions of Bibhuti, after several incomplete expressions, suddenly come up like a great free-flowing wave, and we can visualise its growing excitement just from the words.

This slender, balanced flow is not so much there in *Raktakarabi*, though there were many opportunities. However, in the next stage in *Tapati-Bansari*

(1933), there is an expansion within language somewhat like the B line in the third diagram, and this does not seem unnatural at all if we consider the writer's mentality at that time. In *Sesher Kabita* (1929), Rabindranath puts forth his own conflicts with himself through Amit's words, and it really helps us to understand the conflict in his personality irrespective of its importance in the novel. At times, it even seems that to come to terms with the contemporary, Rabindranath was getting ready to don the mask mentioned by Amit. We find *Sesher Kabita* almost at the same time as *Jogajog* (1929). The two were being published almost simultaneously in two journals – we need to remember this as also their polarised extrinsic differences.

This difference, so to say, is indicative of that very conflict – conflict between the face and the mask. For the last ten years of his life looking back from now, Rabindranath was in distress from inner conflicts. From these conflicts, while we got several powerful writings like fire sparks, we also found him at times circling around emptiness. Would it be wrong to think that his excessively conscious preoccupation with language emerged out of this very struggle? This consciousness could lead to a sudden unnecessary play of words as in *Taser Des* (1933):

> Culture, culture, culture.
> Do you have an editor's column in your paper?
> Two large columns. . . .
> We need a mandatory law.
> What do you mean? Mandatory law!
> The new word for ear-boxing law. This too is a new contribution.[12]

Subsequently, after mildly mocking at contemporary journalism, having said 'Okay, we will see to it later', when the King asks 'Foreigner, do you have any request?', we understand then that the drama is set to leave behind the interim inconsequentialities and take off again.

As in the novel *Sesher Kabita*, and likewise in *Bansari*, the earlier struggle is visible almost literally. One of the important characters of *Bansari* is Khitish, but how important is he? He is used by Bansari at best, and we find these sharp dialogues from *Bansari* in the perspective of modern literature:

> You are the meteor of new fashion in literature . . . wiping away old styles from the sky.
>
> There is no convention of making words sticky by applying sticky jaggery.
>
> Write, write, do not hesitate, write in a language that comes from tearing arterial veins . . . like the angry rays of sunset attacking the breast of the storm-clouds.[13]

Since Khitish has been established as a representative of 'modern' poets, we readily comprehend the significance of these words. Again, at the other end, from this dialogue of *Bansari*, we immediately understand the earnestness of the poet to find synergy between pursuit and fruition:

> Why did the Almighty not give me the power to write like this, where a blood-red fountain of fire would be bursting out with every word.[14]

We have witnessed this fire fountain or angry light of sunset in many of his last writings and not just in his paintings, but still we find the image of a Rabindranath struggling with language issues in such fiery expressions.

Moreover, *Bansari* was published in 1933 and his dance drama *Chitrangada* in 1936. Later, as a kind of an explanation for his dance drama and facing a dilemma related to the crafting of sentences at the very end of a long journey, he wrote to Amiya Chakravarty about many people having many views about the ideal of language: 'Its value is decided by so many fleeting moods. I cannot figure out the ideology behind its value'.[15] But when the watchmen of realism in literature chase him, he 'can hide in my [his] songs', which is why he included his third language in his theatre dialogues – music.

*

Discovering the music of words to integrate the message had been Rabindranath's pursuit for long, but we find that extrinsic concerns of language diverted him from that objective time after time. But now he had reached a state of unhesitating confidence of expressing himself through songs. Hence, he was able to portray the internal complexities of the characters in his dance-dramas as he was also able to take us to the deep meaning of the subjects of the plays of his last era through music. That he was finding more satisfaction through these compositions and that he was again gaining ground in his last stage is proved by the progress in *Chandalika* (1938) and *Shyama* (1939) after *Chitrangada*. The primary difference that was evident in these dance dramas in contrast to the ones of his first era was that songs were not merely connectors in this case. *Valmiki Pratibha* (1881) or *Mayar Khela* (1888) were either 'a dramatic garland through music' or 'a musical garland through drama', but the new composition went further. Here the language was not only limited to songs, but there was a complete mastery over an adequate language of dance as well. The mix of song and dance was able to conquer words, so the dramatic opportunities became stronger, and Rabindranath could consider it as 'more dramatic than lyrical'; now he was far more his own self in the world of theatre.

In his article on 'Dialogue on Poetic Drama', Eliot had made one of his characters say that the future of drama, especially poetic drama, lay in the route determined by the ballet. However, he had some apprehension about ballet as well, since the art form contained everything that was expected in a play, except 'poetry'. Did Rabindranath too reach the same destination as Eliot with his plays? Perhaps Rabindranath's dance drama would satisfy

Eliot, as, while it was true that 'it had a form', it was also true that it had 'poetry'. His intended dramatic completeness was fulfilled.

Translation: Anirban Datta

Notes

1 Sankha Ghosh, 'Natyamuhurta o Bhashar Sandhan', in *Kaler Matra o Rabindra Natak*, Kolkata: Dey's Publishing, 2009 (6th ed.), pp. 37–50. The essay was originally published in 1961.
2 Rabindranath Tagore, Letter to Amiya Chakravarty dated 14 February 1939, in *Chithipatra*, Vol. XI, Kolkata: Visvabharati, 1974, p. 224.
3 Rabindranath Tagore, '*Bisarjan*, Act III, Sc. ii', in *Rabindra-Rachanabali*, Vol. II, Kolkata: Visvabharati, 1940, p. 342.
4 William Shakespeare, '*Love's Labour Lost*, Act V, Sc. ii', in *William Shakespeare: The Complete Works*, London and Glasgow: The English Language Book Society and Collins, 1964, p. 191.
5 Maurice Maeterlinck, *The Blind*, *The Intruder and Other Plays*, Richard Hovey (trans.), New York: Dodd, Mead and Co., 1914, p. 95.
6 Rabindranath Tagore, '*Dakghar*, Sc. ii', in *Rabindra-Rachanabali*, Vol. XI, Kolkata: Visvabharati, 1942, p. 390.
7 Ibid., p. 392.
8 Ibid., p. 388.
9 Ibid., Sc. iii, p. 406.
10 Rabindranath Tagore, *Muktadhara*, *Rabindra-Rachanabali*, Vol. XIV, Kolkata: Visvabharati, 1943, p. 187.
11 Ibid., p. 238.
12 Rabindranath Tagore, '*Taser Des*, Sc. ii.', in *Rabindra-Rachanabali*, Vol. XXIII, Kolkata: Visvabharati, 1947, p. 176.
13 Rabindranath Tagore, '*Bansari*, Act I, Sc. i', in *Rabindra-Rachanabali*, Vol. XXIV, Kolkata: Visvabharati, 1948, p. 147–148.
14 Ibid., Act II, Sc. i, p. 173.
15 Rabindranath Tagore, Letter to Amiya Chakravarty dated 14 February 1939, in *Chithipatra* Vol. XI, op. cit., p. 224.

27 Badal Sircar: The language of theatre

Introduction

Sudhindra Sircar, better known as Badal Sircar (1925–2011), was one of the foremost theatre personalities in India. He studied civil engineering and then later in life did his Master's in Comparative Literature from Jadavpur University. As a town planner, he also spent some time working in England and Nigeria. He also toured several European countries and the United States where he had a varied experience of different genres of theatre. His meeting with Jerzy Grotowski among others was of particular significance in his dramatic career. He left his job in 1975 to devote himself fully to theatre. Sircar became engaged with theatre as actor, director and playwright and the major breakthrough came after *Evam Indrajit* which was written in 1963 and published and performed in 1965. He established his own theatre group 'Satabdi' in 1967. In 1972, he produced *Spartacus* which was the beginning of a new era of theatre culminating in the emergence of what he called the 'Third Theatre'.

The Third Theatre was defined as one where the distance between the actors and the audience was removed, where minimum props were used, and which was animated by a passionate commitment to social justice. It was also a theatre that could be easily accessed, that was supple, and that could be taken to people in distant villages and to city streets, but underlying it all was an intense passion and a physical expression of that passion. Theatre was not simply enactment but the attainment of 'a state of being,' and numerous workshops were held to achieve this end. The aim was to touch the audience, make her or him react. Workshops were also held to explore what was called 'sound and movement mirroring' to suggest, for instance, the devastating storm in the Sunderbans merely through bodily movements in *Michil* (1974). *Bhoma* (1975), *Gandi* (1977), and *Basi Khabar* (1978) were some of the plays from this stage of the group's journey.

The text included in this volume has been taken from *The Language of Theatre*. The play *Bhoma* that appears in the text was first performed on 21st March 1976 in Rangabelia in the Sunderbans after a period of very close interaction with the community.

DOI: 10.4324/9781003224686-28

Some of Badal Sircar's critical writings on theatre are *The Third Theatre* (1978), *The Changing Language of Theatre* (1982), *Theaterer Bhasha* (1983), and *Voyages in the Theatre* (1992).

*

The language of theatre[1]

Badal Sircar

What our country needs today is an alternative theatre or a 'Third Theatre,' and what form that alternative theatre needs to take is something that I have discussed earlier. What I wish to discuss today is the language of the theatre and, in particular, the language of the Third Theatre.

It is language that links one human being with another. A language is a set of signs or symbols. All who live in a community internalise this system of symbols in early childhood; that is why they are able to use the signs indicated by a language to communicate with one another. Another society or community will use a different set of signs, that is, another language, for communication. For them to communicate with the members of the first community, it would be necessary to acquire their language.

Within a speech-community, people may communicate with each other through the medium of language – through speech and through listening. There is yet another way in which communication may be established – through reading and writing. This in fact is how the major languages allow expression. What one person has written may be read by another, and this allows us to dispense at times with the whole system of speech and hearing. Now, written language needs to be separately learned, as another set of symbols; where literacy is not widespread, a writer will not be able to establish contact with all the members of his speech-community. However, if someone were to read out his works, he would still be in communication with others in spite of his physical absence.

Even within written language, only a small portion of whatever is set down – or whatever *may* be set down – may be termed 'literature'. Short stories, novels, poetry are all forms of literature. What the writer inscribes is transformed through the alchemy of print into innumerable copies which reach innumerable readers. The reader reads in solitude at his or her own pace. The reader and the writer need never meet in person.

What the playwright writes is called a play. A play too is a part of what we call literature, and it may be read, through its script, the same way as a poem, novel, or story. But there is a vital difference – a play can be easily extended beyond the boundaries of literature through acting, which is its performative aspect. Acting is a wholly different craft, and one may not include it within the boundaries of literature. Here, the connection is direct and tangible between the actors and the audience, even if not always between the audience and the author. If the playwright neglects this particular skill and fails to take cognizance of it in his writing, what he writes may be acceptable as literature but not as drama.

When the playwright is done with his work, the director steps in. He is from another artistic world; and his medium is different. He reads the play over and applies some thought to it. His imagination transforms the words of the script into vivid visual images. These are realised with the help of the actors and actresses, as well as the paraphernalia of the stage, such as costumes, music, and lighting. This process of transformation of the written script into an enactable play may be called *dramatisation*.[2] It is on the basis of the director's dramatisation or theatrical conceptualisation that the actors and actresses bring the play to life. Their acting is the medium which brings them in touch with both the written text of the playwright and the director's dramatisation thereof. This triad of play–dramatisation–enactment is succeeded by a fourth and final stage, namely, performance, which is realised only when a troupe of actors brings the play to life through the enactment of its dramatic form before a live audience.

Theatre is therefore the sum total of the written play, its dramatic *form*, its dramatic *enactment*, and its performance. I am aware that these terms may not please everyone, but let us use them for the time being. In different places, at different times, and in different forms of the theatre, one or the other of these four components may have been underemphasised or dropped entirely. It may even have happened that one of these constituent components was subsumed into another.

Theatre has its roots in 'ritual' – this is something I have said earlier. Ritual prioritises performance. This implies active audience participation, and therefore enactment and performance can hardly be distinguished here. The dramatic troupe in this case needs to focus on drawing the audience into the world of the play. For in the case of ritual drama, the dramatic form has usually been settled for generations past, with slight changes being made from time to time. In fact, the *play* may be said to be non-existent, and even the dramatic form does not require a director for its presentation.

In direct contrast are the world of Greek and Sanskrit theatre and the drama of Shakespeare, Molière, Chekov, Ibsen, and Brecht, where the written word is of profound and paramount importance. It is possible for different groups at different times and in different places to enact their plays in their own individual styles while still remaining faithful to the original text. Their particular skill at enactment – their interpretation of the written word – has enabled these plays to transcend time. These dramatic texts serve as foundations for different interpretations. We need to remember that these playwrights transcended the boundaries of pure literature and demonstrated an instinctive understanding of all aspects of theatrical performance. Many of these dramatists were directors themselves, and their writing would have been shaped by their vivid dramatic imagination.

Within our folk traditions, the strongest dramatic form has probably been that of the *jatra*. Other dramatic forms have been weaker in comparison, and in many cases written scripts have been dispensed with altogether. Folk legends and Puranic tales have often been directly dramatised from the source material, and sometimes the actors have improvised impromptu on stage in the course of performance. Here, dramatisation and acting merge into performance and cannot be distinguished from it. This happens mainly because of the presence of the audience with its modes of participation and response. The role of the audience in the performance of folk drama is generally very strong, for its most important aim is the recognition of this presence. The performance is supreme. The exact opposite is the situation in the city playhouses, to which we have given the name 'Second Theatre'. Here, the viewer is kept at a distance, shrouded in darkness, encouraged to be utterly passive, utterly solitary. Here, too, the distance between acting and performance is minimal but for reasons quite the opposite of those that prevail in folk theatre. The audience being virtually absent as a factor even when physically present, the performance hardly deviates from the set dramatisation. In this kind of theatre, there is therefore the play, its dramatisation, and its enactment, but in the absence of audience involvement, there is no special value inherent in the performance.

The intrinsic value of performance is reduced to its lowest level in the naturalistic drama. Here, the entire apparatus of the theatre is geared towards sustaining the illusion that whatever the viewer sees or hears is reality, not stagecraft. The characters and their actions belong to an autonomous world, which is the world of real life. The presence of the audience does not have the remotest effect on them. To say this is to disregard the audience entirely; therefore, the performative aspect of drama, which so strongly needs audience presence, loses its innate importance.

Then again there is the modern ritualistic drama in which performance and audience response are both equally important; yet, even here, it is the dramatisation that is the most significant factor. For this is unlike pure ritual, which is ancestrally inherited; this dramatic form is not present in our blood and bones and must be created anew. If this task is undertaken by the director, the resultant dramatic form is his own creation, and if it is undertaken by the group, the form and the enactment blur into each other. The *play* as a factor may cease to exist. It is not the play that gives rise to the drama, but the drama – the enactment – that breathes life into the play.

Ritual predates writing. The spoken language too lacked in those times the breadth and complexity it possesses today. Communication was achieved not merely through words but also through symbolic sounds and gestures. This combination of sounds, words, and gestures nevertheless constituted a more universal language than any today. Its intelligibility extended beyond the boundaries of clan, community, or language.

The greatest strength of the theatre is the presence of a live audience. This is something the Third Theatre seeks to draw upon directly. This is why it lays great stress on the symbolism of intonation and gestures. This is not to disparage language; the power of language is priceless. But one need not depend on language entirely. Intonation and gestures may be used to supplement language, to make it stronger, more all-encompassing, and more universal. This is something that the Third Theatre seeks to do, something that is a major part of its mode of instruction.

We generally use the word 'language' in a very limited sense. We tie it down to a sect or a speech-community. However, language in an all-encompassing sense will include the language of the eyes, the face, and the gestures. It will include the meanings conveyed by intonation, touch, and even by pictures, musical tunes, and heart-rending screams. All of this is contained in the language of the theatre. Yet, when we use the word 'language' in connection with the theatre, particularly naturalistic theatre, we refer only to its verbal component. The over-arching dimensions of language are lost in the practice of confining it only to verbal communication. The reason for this is not far to seek. In the routine of our daily lives, which is what the naturalistic drama seeks to convey, we witness the same prioritisation of verbal communication and the use of gestures, touch, and intonation to add strength to the actual spoken words. It is as though these paralinguistic elements have no life of their own. And they are in fact used very sparingly in our materialistic civilisation, which, as it advances, leads to a simultaneous downgrading of the use of our physical faculties – those related to speech and touch. Keeping the face inexpressive, smiling genteel smiles, exercising restraint in the movements of the head and the gestures of the hands, all count as markers of urbanity; in our competitive society, they serve as hallmarks of class and superiority.

As long as society does not change, all this can very well be a part of its code of manners. But why should this be carried into the theatre? The theatre makes available an escape from this stifling bondage, which in fact no other sphere can offer. Are we so taken up with naturalism that we accept everything in its name? Or are we now so used to servitude that we fear freedom and worship the very chains which bind us?

Our folk drama is so popular because it has never paid much heed to the cult of naturalism that prevails in the theatre. And while our *jatra* is, in comparison with other forms of folk theatre, dependent on continuity and co-ordination as factors in the narrative, it is nevertheless free of naturalistic influence in its modes of execution. The style of enunciation, the intonation, and the gesticulation are all pitched at a much higher level than in real life. Besides, the absence of stage scenery, the employment of live music, and the use of a choric character – the *bibek*[3] – all indicate the employment and strengthening of a particular theatrical idiom, and all mitigate against the naturalistic tradition.

The Third Theatre is not a mere imitation of folk theatre, but it does have much to learn from it. The *message* is the main theme of the Third Theatre. Presenting this message to the audience in the clearest, strongest terms possible, so that the viewer may undergo a change of consciousness or arrive at some stage of action, is the aim of the Third Theatre. It is in accordance with this need that the language of the Third Theatre needs to be shaped. It may draw, for this purpose, on the different idioms of the text, the dramatisation, and the performance. To use one of these and to neglect the others is to fall short of the aim.

Let us take, as a hypothetical example, an actor, a man from the city, whose knowledge of village life is minimal. He knows, at the most, that peasants live in villages and that they are poor and oppressed. He may have some slight awareness of the divisions and categories that exist – *jotedars*,[4] peasants, sharecroppers, landless labourers. It may so happen that this man finds himself one day in a position where he obtains, through his reading or through discussions with others, a deeper knowledge of village life – certain facts regarding its situation, certain statistics, and certain analyses. Imagine his amazement and embarrassment, amounting almost to guilt, when he realises how little he has known, all his life, about his countrymen. And mingled with that newfound guilt will be a new awareness – namely, that so many of his countrymen are in the same position that was his until very recently – that of not knowing, not having known. He might then resolve to create, out of the mingled amazement, embarrassment, and guilt that he feels, a new theatre, a new play. This might well be its beginning:

'I know.'
'What do you know?'
'What I did not know earlier.'
'What did you not know earlier?'
'So many years I spent not knowing. Now I know.'
'And what do you know now?'
'Many things. Many, many things.'
'What kind of things?'
'The kind of thing which no one knows. Just as I did not know earlier.'
'And what did you not know?'
'I want to speak out. I want to speak out to those who still do not know.'
'What is it that you want to say?'[5]

And one has to stop here. Really, what *does* he want to say?

Perhaps our man from the theatrical troupe had seen a remote village in the Sunderbans – a village called Sardarpara. He had met the inhabitants. *Adivasis* is what they were called, but they were not indigenous to the land. Maybe they had been sent there by others to wrest the land from the jungle and to create settlements in the wilderness. Or they may possibly have come on their own driven by hunger and with the dream of a tiny parcel of land. Here they lived in constant danger from the forest, fighting its snakes, tigers, and crocodiles; fighting perennial hunger; drinking tamarind-mixed salt water from the river and destroying their bodies. Through inexhaustible toil, they pushed back the jungle and built their homes. But then they found the land was not theirs, and someone, sitting somewhere in the city, owned that land on the strength of a piece of paper inherited from an ancestor. So they were landless labourers, breaking their backs for three rupees a day, and that perhaps only half the days of the year. And then our man may have heard from the village schoolmaster the story of Bhoma, who was now dead, but who in fact was more than an individual; Bhoma was a group. There are Bhomas, and hundreds of groups of Bhomas, all over India. In fact, they are not Bhomas at all, but *Bhomras*.[6] They can sting, like bees. How little our theatre-person knew about them, yet he knew enough to know that only further questioning would give him the answers he sought. And that is why, in those lines of the play, the answer to the question, 'What is it that you want to say?' came out thus:

> 'A lot. About Bhoma.'
> 'Who is this Bhoma?'
> 'I really can't say. I've heard something about him. But I've never seen him.'
> 'You've only heard about him?'
> 'Yes.'
> 'And yet you say you know him?'
> 'Yes, I know something – now. I know Bhoma exists. Even this I did not know earlier.'[7]

Once again there is a pause – a hesitation. Will the listeners listen? They may have heard this earlier, from someone else, but did they *listen*? So the next line is like an admonishment:

> 'Shut up; stop this nonsense!'

And it seemed to the theatre-worker, thinking about himself as a test case, that people as a whole had become hard and indifferent, concerned with their own happiness. We have sacrificed long-term good to short-term pleasures. There is nothing which tugs at the heartstrings anymore. It is not about lack of knowledge; it is about lack of feeling. We are aware of everything around us – hunger, injustice, oppression and torture, war, killing, and atomic destruction – but we have awareness without empathy. Our blood has turned cold inside our veins. And so he wrote, deliberately, wrecking the mood of the previous lines:

> Fish are cold-blooded creatures

And the reply –

> Humans, too, are cold-blooded.[8]

And that is how his play took shape. No story. No characters. Just so many words, a language, the words of the Bangla language – symbols once again. The very allotment of the lines is made without rhyme or reason. Such language will never do in contemporary theatre. Perhaps this is the language of the Third Theatre. Just like our theatre-person, there is someone in search of a character like Bhoma in the world of the play. Only the Bhomas of this world can give him the release that he seeks, that he requires for his own self. And so he sets out in search of them, acquiring on the way experiences which give him knowledge, feeling, and a capacity for thought. Somewhere in Howrah, a factory which is mortgaged to a bank fails to repay its loan; the factory is shut down; 28 workers are ruined. A person who has sold his country down the drain opens an account in a Swiss bank. A nuclear test results in the birth of two million deformed babies. All of them make their way into the world of his drama, heedless of the requirements of plot, continuity, or even internal coordination. The one abiding note is the search for the Bhomas of this world; the keynote is like the line of a song, which, slender as a wisp of smoke, insists – 'Human beings are cold-blooded.'

So much for the plot. What about the dramatisation? What will be the language of the theatrical dramatisation?

The Bhomas are at work, cutting down the jungle. A forest – a woodsman – trees. From the trees, the seed; from the seed, the trees. The actors are bunched up on the ground, tight, like seeds. Soft music. The seed rises out of the soil, grows, grows into giant trees, banyans. The actors are standing now, straight or in a triangle pose, their outstretched arms branching towards the sky. Two of them are transformed into men, woodcutters. Their song is heard as they swing their arms in rhythmic arcs:

Move those arms – Heigh- ho
Cut the trees – Heigh-ho
The tiger's paw – Heigh- ho
Serpent-charmer – Heigh-ho
Kill that croc – Heigh-ho
The jungle's gone – Heigh-ho
The harvest's ours – Heigh-ho.[9]

The men-who-are-trees are falling, the woodcutters stack them neatly. Then happens ploughing; after this, the sowing of seeds – harvesting. Then all the actors come together to make a factory. They are implements and sections of implements. The actors are stiff, ramrod straight, powerful but with lifeless movement. Suddenly, one of the parts – he is Actor Number One – cries out 'I know.' Another says – 'What do you know?' One by one, Numbers Two, Three, Four, Five, and Six all put this question to Number One. And then they all cry in unison – 'Why did you say you knew?' The machinery has stopped, it is over. 'Rot and nonsense,' cry all the sections as they spread out over the stage, seated or supine, in attitudes of indifference. Underlying it all is that indifferent statement – 'Fish are cold-blooded creatures.' Number One's response has a stern despair: 'Men, too, are cold-blooded.'

Six men are all you need to stage this play. But you can also employ ten or fifteen or twenty. Men or women, both will do. Any age and any cast of features.

Who will do the dramatisation? A director? Yes, perhaps. But will indifferent actors manage to convey this play to an audience? If the actors do not feel in their blood and bones the shame, the bafflement, the guilt, the embarrassment, the awareness – and the passionate desire to know – that drive both the writer and the director, their enactment will be useless. Every actor must share the same passion and shoulder his or her share of the burden, otherwise it will not work as Third Theatre.

All actions in the naturalistic drama are modelled on actions in the real world. How the characters speak, what pitch they adopt, and whether they should be sitting, standing, or reclining in an easy chair are all indicated by the actions of our daily lives. But the alternative drama imposes no such restrictions. The actors are allowed full freedom in their gestures, gait, and intonation. Consequently, they can concentrate on finding the best method of releasing the full meaning of every word to the audience and on driving the same into their consciousness. Doing this through dramatic form and dramatic enactment is a foundational aim of the Third Theatre.

Let us look at lines in that same play for an example –

- An old man passes away in front of the Enquiry counter at Sealdah station.
- A child is born behind the bookstalls at Sealdah station.
- Leave Sealdah and get onto V.I.P. Road. Move to Dum Dum airport. See India!
- Darjeeling in summer, Kashmir in the Pujas, Waltair in winter.
- It is spring, season of flowers, time for the vaccine.
- Drink only boiled water. Or drink Coca-Cola. See India! See India! See India![10]

Of course, one wants to travel, and one needs to travel. But travel is a luxury to those who are born and die in a station like Sealdah. Yes, Sealdah is a station and so is Dum Dum – one for trains and the other for aircraft. But the street names surrounding Dum Dum airport come with the sound of whiplashes to the homeless, unfed unfortunates who encounter them in a play staged at Sealdah. V.I.P. Road is not for commoners, neither is Kashmir and Darjeeling, especially if one is exhorted to drink Coca-Cola as an alternative to water (and this does remind us of that notorious phrase connected with the French Revolution – 'If they don't have bread, let them eat cake'). And the switch in language from Bangla to English ('See India!') tells us that it is all geared towards foreign tourists.

'Leave Sealdah and get onto V.I.P. road'. If the actors mouthing these lines begin spinning in circles as they spell out the words; if they spin and gesticulate and hold up their hands turning the announcement of Kashmir-Coca-Cola into colourful signboards; if they move frenziedly like circus horses as they mouth the phrase 'See India'; if an actor, standing at the centre, lashes out with the whip like a ringmaster, then perhaps one mode of dramatisation could be said to have been attained, a mode that will allow them to convey their point. Given the time and opportunity and the freedom that they have, they will be able to think of some other dramatic mode which will be even more effective.

If one forgets that the prime aim of this kind of play is to load the lines with meaning and effectiveness, and if one takes for granted the freedom that comes with the form, one runs the danger of the dramatisation becoming somehow untruthful. The gestures of the body would then become lifeless and merely ornamental. Their superfluity would make the message weak and vague. The dramatist, the director, and the actors all need to remember this. Their artistic planes are different; they meet only on the ground of absolute fidelity to their own art. Perhaps, I need not have made a separate mention of this, but we do live in a commercialised society where art is sold in the market like other goods and therefore this statement.

The art of the theatre should be directly shaped by its matter – in this lies its truth. Form should come out of content. To say this clearly is not in any way to denigrate the form.

Let us consider one instance of this relation between form and content. Let us imagine that this theatre-person of ours has read a couple of books which are neither plays nor novels. Now, India was for long years a British colony. Our country was governed by British imperial power, governed and oppressed and looted, and we were subjected to humiliation, oppression, and injustice. We know all this, we discuss it, and in discussion we use the terms 'British' and 'English' as shorthand for 'British imperialism'. But we do not know, and do not consider it necessary to know, the details thereof: how their system of exploitative governance led to changes in India's political and economic systems or how it led to changes in Britain itself. And so, even 35 to 36 years after independence, we are at a loss to estimate the poisonous effects of imperialism on either our politico-economic framework or on our mentality and consciousness. So we learn in our school histories that Lord Cornwallis implemented the Permanent Settlement; yet, we do not make the connection between this and the perpetuation of divisions between the upper and lower classes which we hold dear even now, divisions which lead us to despise manual labour in field and factory even today.

The subject here is a mix of history, economics, and politics; dry facts and statistics are its blood and bones and marrow. There is no story or no room for the creation of characters. It is such a subject as properly belongs to schools; yet, it must be made to reach a wider audience through that art form we call the theatre.

Fine, then, let's create a school for our play. Let the spectators sit in three 'classes' which face the centre from three sides. In each class sit two actors playing the role of students. An actor dressed as a teacher faces each class. On the fourth side, where there are no actors, is a stage. This is occupied at different moments by actors representing the headmaster or Lord Clive or Warren Hastings or Lord Cornwallis or the East India Company or the British government. Let there be an actress clad in the Union Jack. She represents a mother figure, Britannia. Another actress is an Indian woman, a mother who has just lost her child. Let the 'students' come up onstage from time to time. Let them join hands with the teachers to represent, through speeches and songs, words and gestures and cries, the agony of taxation, famine, and war. Let the dramatic theme arise from the conjunction of opposites – the biting satire of the lines and the ingrown pain of the oppressed.

The dramatic form is engendered by the demands of the subject. Content generates form. Another point is this – such a play cannot even be written without adequate thought regarding the style of the play. The playwright must have ample notion of the requisite dramatic form. Such a form is only possible in the Third Theatre; in your contemporary theatre-hall, one can hardly convert the members of the audience into make-believe students, that, too, in three different classes, nor can one get the real actors to blend into the audience.

I have said this earlier, and I say it again – the hallmark of the Third Theatre is the supreme importance it gives to the audience; it seeks to bring the audience within the ambit of touch. This meeting point of actors and audience offers unparalleled opportunities. It needs to be properly utilised at every stage – from play to dramatisation to enactment to performative event.

Two thousand years ago, the Slave Rebellion led by Spartacus kept the mighty Roman Empire in turmoil for four years. When the rebellion was finally vanquished, some 6,500 slaves were given exemplary punishment by being crucified along the Appian Way. One of the leaders of the revolt, dying in agony after four days on the cross, had cried out just before his passing: 'We will return, we will return, and we will be a million.'

If this Slave Rebellion becomes the subject of a play in the Third Theatre, it will be entirely possible for the actor speaking these lines to descend from the cross, move over to the spectators, and whisper these words to one of them. The other actors might follow suit, each one speaking in similarly hushed tones. Then their voices might mingle, rise into a hum, into a mighty crescendo that proclaims –

> 'We will return, we will return, and we will be a million.'

Or it may be that the audience sees a number of processions onstage and a person who seems to have lost his way in the crowd, who is now looking for the right procession that will take him to his new home, his real home. If at the end of this play, someone sees in that procession of authentic human beings the truth of the dream he had once dreamt, if it comes with melody in its voice, its hands outstretched, and if the members of the audience respond by shedding their inhibitions, come onstage, hold the hands of the actors, and join the procession then and only then the strength of the Third Theatre will be realised – the ability of the stage to bring together actors and audience.

The theatre is something which must be both seen and heard, and all theatrical devices are geared to helping the audience see and hear everything at all times. But this is not everything! We forget that all this must lead to a theatrical experience. What is required is not mere seeing and hearing but the actual drawing in of the spectator into the theatrical experience. What about the dramatic incidents of everyday life? Say, when a man is run over and crushed by a passing vehicle – this is a completely dramatic event, and it leaves a strong mark on the mind. But does anyone see and hear everything the way it happened? One man sees the accident from the window of his house but then loses sight of both victim and vehicle in the milling crowd. Another sees nothing but hearing the sudden sound of brakes pushes his way through the crowd and sees the blood-drenched body. And so there are many who see or hear only in relation to their location and range of vision at that moment, but all of them undoubtedly undergo a dramatic experience. Keeping this salient fact in mind the practitioners of the Third Theatre may choose not to remain fixed in front of the spectators; they may move to the flanks or the rear; they may virtually encircle the audience and bring its members into the enactment. But this should only be done in order to enhance the dramatic experience, in order to make it more meaningful and effective, and never as a novelty or a flashy device. In this honesty lies the essence of the play.

I wish to discuss one last item today. All the instances I have given today relate to one form of the Third Theatre. This is staged in an intimate setting, with a comparatively small audience seated on the same level as the actors and illuminated by the same light. The actors are free to move at the front, or the sides, or the back. They are free to engage directly with the audience through eye contact as also through touch. To this particular form, one may give the name 'Anganmancha'.[11] But the Third Theatre has yet another form. As it is supple, and may be transported and accessed easily, it may be staged in villages and marketplaces, in slums, schools, and gardens. It is not unusual for it to be staged in front of an audience numbering a thousand or five thousand. The relations between the physical space occupied by the actors and the audience cannot be definitely established, nor can the greater part of the audience be brought within the ambit of a physical proximity as in intimate theatre. Does that mean that this is not part of the Third Theatre?

Of course, this is also Third Theatre; to this variety, we may give the name 'Muktamancha' (indicating an Open Stage); it is not less necessary than the Anganmancha theatre. It may lack the intensity and depth of the Anganmancha form, but it makes up for that by the sheer numbers it reaches, for it is not restricted by the necessity of issuing limited invitations on the basis of the available seats. The troupe does not need to wait for people to evolve into viewers; rather, it seeks out people in their own homes, amidst the routine of their daily lives, and through theatre transforms them into an audience. This implies a fundamental expansion of the range of the theatre, an exponential increase in its ability to touch people.

My argument is that both these forms are required in the Third Theatre. Their idioms are different; the language they employ in stagecraft, enactment, and dramatisation is different. Therefore, the different registers of language required for these two forms need to be independently mastered. A particular troupe may not be able to make parallel use of both forms. But the Third Theatre is after all a movement, with many groups, and it is to be hoped that they will, in their different ways, employ both forms to strengthen the movement.

Translation: Paromita Chaudhuri

Notes

1 Badal Sircar, *Theaterer Bhasha*, Kolkata: Raktakarabi, 1983, pp. 35–49. It was first delivered as the third of the four Dwijendralal Roy Memorial Lectures, 1981, organised by the University of Calcutta.
2 The term used is *Natyarupayan* (literally, giving a dramatic form), shortened thereafter to *Natyayan*. The other key terms are *Natak* (play), *Natyabhinaya* (enactment), and *Natyanusthan* (performance).
3 The *Bibek* (lit. conscience) is of paramount importance in folk drama. He not only links the scenes but also sings the soul of a character through his songs.
4 Landlords. However, the word *jotdar* powerfully suggests oppression.
5 Badal Sircar, *Bhoma*, Kolkata: Naba Grantha Kutir, 1980, pp. 5–6.
6 The word used is *Bhomra*, referring to a bumblebee and clearly indicating its capacity to sting.
7 Badal Sircar, *Bhoma*, op. cit., p. 6.
8 Ibid., pp. 6–7.
9 Ibid., p. 63.
10 Ibid., pp. 8–9.
11 'Anganmancha' has been translated by Sircar as 'Space Theatre' and has been described as 'theatre-in-the-round.' Later, Badal Sircar moved towards the 'Muktamancha', the open theatre or theatre in public spaces.

28 Syed Mustafa Siraj: The Alkap theatre tradition and Third Theatre

Introduction

Syed Mustafa Siraj (1930–2012) was born in a village called Khosbaspur in Murshidabad. He took part in Leftist student movements in the pre-independence era from a very early age and then joined an Alkap group. He gradually became a master or *ustad* in the group and received critical acclaim from the audience. Siraj moved on to become an author and won fame as one of the principal novelists of his time. His novel *Mayamridanga* (1972) emerged out of his experience in Alkap. He received the Sahitya Akademi award (1994) and many other accolades for his novel *Aleek Manush* (1988). A prolific and versatile author, Siraj also wrote short stories, detective fiction, and poems and authored more than two hundred and fifty books. He was also a member of the *Gananatya Sangha* (IPTA) and worked for the preservation of the traditional performing art practices. The essay presented in this volume, 'The Alkap Theatre Tradition and Third Theatre,' published in a journal in the 1970s, demonstrates his understanding of the form and its relation to urban popular culture, which gradually started to capture the rural entertainment scenario.

A number of traditional performative practices came out of rural societies as an integral part of the daily lives of the people. Of these, several theatrical traditions like *Alkap, Gambhira, Leto, Palatiya, Kushan*, and *Khan*, prevalent in various parts of Bengal, gained popularity. Alkap is popular in the Murshidabad–Birbhum region and its adjacent areas. It is also a complex form combining acting, singing, and dancing and relying heavily upon narrative improvisations in metrical forms. The play is usually performed in open spaces, sometimes also on stage, and revolves around a central narrative. It often refers to local issues and problems and encourages active participation of the audience in the course of the performance.

Siraj in his essay critically assesses the emergence and decline of the Alkap form and its role in society during the days of its glory. A celebrated artist himself, he draws upon his own experience of the tradition, including its various internal dynamics, and talks about the potentials inherent in the form. He also narrates how certain historical forces started imposing limitations to

DOI: 10.4324/9781003224686-29

the form and often resulted in the breaking up of the groups. He also brings into the picture the style of Jhanksa, the greatest performer of Alkap, and concludes with a brief note about when and how the form failed to realise its possibilities and aspirations and gradually faded away.

*

The Alkap theatre tradition and Third Theatre[1]

Syed Mustafa Siraj

Theatre for the audience

In the last few decades, modern Bangla theatre has witnessed varied experimentation with drama and dramatic convention. Following Bijan Bhattacharya's *Nabanna*'s (1944) enormous success in the 1940s, one could hear slogans heralding the Nabanatya Andolan, or a New Theatre Movement. For the most part, what theatre needed at the time was fresh inspiration from Marxist politics. A number of dramatic techniques began to be employed as staging conventions were broken. Actors would emerge from the audience; realistic sets were abandoned in favour of symbolic ones. As acting methods changed and actors started communicating with the audience, the playwright could appear within a play to destabilise the boundary between the 'real' and the 'illusory.' Classical Greek or Sanskrit techniques were revitalised. We witnessed Poster Drama, staged during meetings and in the streets, as part of electoral politics, and we started hearing of the Theatre of the Masses. Eventually, Brechtian theatre arrived on the scene. Of late, we have seen the rise of Living Theatre, Third Theatre, and so on.

There is no reason why this long and continuing performance tradition cannot be regarded as an expression of the vibrant sociocultural life of urban modernity, as they are primarily articulations of social resistance. Much of this theatre is, in fact, theatre of protest, carrying implicitly or overtly the influence of Marxist philosophy. Of course, some plays deal with different 'bourgeois or petit-bourgeois' themes, such as our so-called alienation, individual existential crises, the disappearance of a system of values, dissolution of social ties, and renegotiations in the relationships between woman and man.

Revolution was the final aim of this theatre of protest, and this was perhaps the reason why their slogans called for inclusion of the audience within their drama and dramatic conventions. I believe Brechtian theatre and the more recent Third Theatre are also very clear on this point; or shall we say they are not hesitant to announce their purpose unequivocally.

Some methods of communicating with audiences – by blending them in with the performance or allowing exchanges with characters – were in use even in the 1940s in the productions of the Gananatya Sangha. Third Theatre started doing something even more revolutionary. The actors do not dress according to character. They play their parts in whatever they wear to the theatre. On occasion, they might make use of a hat or a towel; a single *dhol*, or a kind of drum, might provide the soundscape. A lot is expressed through physical postures. The actors sometimes perform amidst the audience. Third Theatre traces the origins of its methods back to proscenium theatre which came from England, as well as to two indigenous folk forms, which could then be called 'First' and 'Second' Theatre. Different forms are practised in different parts of the country: in West Bengal, we have *tarja*, *jatra*, *gambhira*; in Maharashtra, *tamasha*; in Uttar Pradesh, *nautanki* or *Ramlila*; and in Karnataka, we have *Yakshagana*. Outside these two traditions we can posit Third Theatre, where two actors can stand for a door, and its opening can be indicated by making a creaking sound with the mouth. This is a new form of theatre in the metropolis.

If tarja can find a place among indigenous folk art, why exclude Baul traditions? Bauls also perform vocal duels with one another, much like a *kabir larai*, or a contest between bards, and engage in dialogue with the audience. Perhaps the name tarja (duel) was given by some Englishman, and it evokes pity and humour in us.

Among our own countrymen, Hari-Bagdis, Doms, Charals, and Bauris in rural areas wore their hair long. They maintained impressive moustaches and beards. Among Muslim farmers, some sported chin-tufts of various shapes, while others following the Shariat had their moustaches shaved but kept long beards. When similar Western fashions are introduced to us, we identify them as modern trends. The same goes for *ganja* (cannabis) and alcohol and many other things besides. The lifestyle of the poor, when represented as Western fashion, appears modern. Theatrical practices of the West arrived through similar channels, and it can hardly be doubted that our practices over the last few decades are a result of over-eager imitation of Western theatre's refuse.

My ire is not unfounded. *Sang*, or skits and impromptu plays, which have been handed down through generations in rural traditions such as *Gajan* (year-end rituals), *Nabanna* (harvest festival), and others, take up contemporary issues that are relevant to village life and are no different from poster-drama. A fried egg is what we have in the village. It becomes an omelette when brought to the cities by Westerners.

Was there nothing that the 'Progressive and Revolutionary' movements in theatre in Bengal, spanning over a few decades, could have learnt from our local, indigenous tradition of Alkap?

I have not yet had the opportunity to watch Third Theatre, but I have read a few reviews and reports. Its similarities with Alkap are remarkable. In the 1950s, Alkap's popularity spread like a tumultuous tide through Birbhum, Murshidabad, areas in northern Bengal along the river Padma, in Bangla-speaking regions of Bihar, such as Purnia, Dumka, and Santal Parganas. You could catch a performance anywhere in the villages, in market places and rural fairgrounds. Although the stream has become feeble and narrow, it has not completely dried out. Alkap has given birth to its own distributaries – break-off traditions, such as *Pancharas*. The latter has been contaminated by the saline waters of Kolkata's jatra and Hindi cinema. The infusion of urban waste brings its own stench.

Alkap was for and of its audiences. It brought forth seeds of the theatre from society itself and sowed them among its audience. Saplings sprouted there. The fruits of collaborative labour and nurturing were then shared equally. Both parties remained engrossed in the abundant overflowing of these vital spirits. This is the ultimate aim of all theatre – the passionate unison of performer and audience. It is much like the physical union of lovers.

But to be convinced that the Alkap tradition is the most revolutionary and progressive form of theatre, one has to turn to one's own country. Urban theatre has never tried to do so. Had they done so, perhaps they would not have had to turn to foreign traditions.

The form and nature of Alkap

What, then, is Alkap?

Let me speak from personal experience. Between 1950 and the autumn of 1956, I was part of an Alkap group. By a modest estimate, I must have spent some sixty thousand hours in that world. Even after twenty-five years, bits and pieces of those sixty thousand hours suddenly appear out of my unconscious in the form of dreams and leave me feeling vulnerable. But let me not speak of my personal feelings anymore. At least ten people need to come together to form an Alkap group. I am speaking here of the standard model, which comprises an *ustad* or master, a comedian or *sangal*, an assistant clown, two boys who dance and sing and play the female parts, a harmonium player, a *tabalchi* or percussionist, and about four members of chorus. The form demands that the harmonium player, the percussionist, and the chorus all take part in the acting too. Similarly, everyone has to join in the singing when the songs reach a rhythmic crescendo or during the chorus.

The performance space is defined by the audience who sits on all four sides. Like in jatra, there is no entry or exit. Often the performance takes the form of a duel, which is called a *pallar asar* or a Battle of the Bards. The two teams sit at the extreme ends of the performing area, leaving ample space in between. The first team performs for close to three hours, after which the other team takes the stage. They continue to perform in tandem through the night and into the next morning. The day rolls on. If the two sides are evenly matched and the rivalry fierce, a single performance can go on for thirty-six hours. (To make the rivalry even more bitter medals and bananas are kept on display.) The teams take their meals and showers in brief intervals before rejoining the contest.

These duels are doubly expensive. Most performances are, therefore, single-group shows. But this means more intense work for that one group. Typically, a performance must continue for twelve hours at least if the group hopes to draw in the audience. That is why most groups favour the duels. Besides, the groups have much to gain from duels. If the opponent is a worthy one, there may even be a lot to learn from them.

The main pillars of the Alkap group are the dancing boys and the clown or jester. They are essential to the performance. For the dancing boys, the formula says: Between twelve and twenty is the perfect age/For the dancing boys to take the stage. The basic criteria are that he must have good facial features and a melodious voice. The lower age for recruiting new talent is twelve. Their training begins right away. The boys must wear their hair long like girls, and they must at all times wear a frock and silver bangles. They must shed their male identity and assume a feminine body language. They must learn feminine gestures by looking at women. During performance, they wear sarees and blouses. Over time, this practice impacts their physique and mentality as well. The Alkap ustads compare this process to the making and worshipping of the divine idol, which is moulded out of clay, straw, and wood, decorated and given painted eyes. A female dancer awaits in hiding inside even though the external form is that of a man. If the clay is not soft, an idol cannot be made from it. Unless a dancer is transformed at a tender age, the body becomes rigid and stiff. The idol must then be immersed in water, discarded. The same applies to this doll: age between twelve and twenty is perfect. Beyond that, they must leave. The voice breaks, and the tenderness is gone. They must trim their hair, putting aside their silver bangles. The skeletal framework of wood and straw begins to surface. The play of *maya* is over.

It is nothing short of maya – because under that tent, before the eyes of an engrossed audience, he is like a fabled village fairy – woman, and yet not a woman; a man, yet not man – not even a gendered being – a character – a radiant point of convergence in the theatrical process – like a nose-pin.

Some groups do, however, have older dancing boys. They are not immersed in the waters after adolescence. What is one to do if no new talent shows up? Besides, there is always a longing, a sense of belonging that is hard to leave behind. He, who was for nights on end the very form of female dance on stage, finds it difficult to trim his hair, take off his bangles, and return to the usual male ways of being. But for how long? Sometimes, if they are skilled, they can take on in their male guise the role of comedians. Some even go on to become the ustad. Some become actors. They do find something or the other to do. Many a *chhokra* (young lad) from Alkap groups have gone on to become renowned ustads and sangals in later life.

But instead of all this, why not take women for these parts?

At the time, there were several problems with allowing women into these groups. For Alkap groups, it was impossible to find women – it was unthinkable. There were social taboos. Besides, there was the risk of disputes within the group. The ustads were of the opinion that it was impossible for women to evoke the same maya in the performance. The actors in Alkap have to move among the audiences. You see, there is always the chance that some member of the audience will grab at a woman, pull her by her hand. We recognised the danger.

In the 1960s, as the Alkap form began to ebb, women started joining the groups. Pancharas entered many of the groups. Our village had a group with a woman member. They have now disbanded.

Let us now describe a typical performance. Usually, by way of musical instruments, there would be a harmonium, a pair of percussions (*dugi-tabla*), and cymbals (*kattal* or *khanjani*). On the eleventh key of the harmonium, that is to say on the fourth note of the standard, mid-range scale, the whole group would raise a celebratory cry. The Goddess Saraswati would be invoked first, followed by some others of the pantheon, the local presiding deities and *pir*-s, Ustad Tansen, the first teacher of that particular group, and all subsequent masters. Finally, the current ustad would be praised and his name announced.

Then comes the choral hymn. The boys sing the main tune while the others take on the refrain at a higher tempo. The riff plays for two or three minutes. There are no fixed riffs. This is to allow the dancing lads to prepare themselves before they stand up on stage with the song at their lips. These are usually folk tunes such as *khemta*, *tappa*, or *jhumur*. The manner of performing is unique to Alkap. A choral refrain is usually sung for all songs as the chhokra starts to dance. The sangal comes in after the dance. He plays around with the audience and with the chhokra, before starting a duet with him. Then the ustad takes the stage, moving to the rhythms. He sings in the *payar* form, impromptu like a *kabiyal* or a bard, of some contemporary event and holds forth for almost twenty minutes – he speaks of the performance perhaps or of the village or of problems across the country. The actual *Kap* begins after this. Alkap is, after all, a theatre group. Once the Kap is enacted, someone in the group, or a chhokra, performs a verse or two, and with that one phase comes to an end. The next phases will repeat the same sequence of events.

The form of the Kap

The main component of the performance is the Kap or the play. It is sometimes referred to as Sang, because in essence Alkap theatre is satirical with a heavy dose of humour. The pinch must be executed delicately with humour and wit.

But these plays have no written form, which is to say, Alkap is not to be found in written or printed texts. There is no playwright either. The actors are not required to remember lines. They are all aware of a basic framework for each play – that is usually a structured plot. Depending on the rhythm and pace of the play, it proceeds, taking the audience with it. Each play goes through many performances, and, on the way, it is improved upon, modified, until it reaches perfection. When it gets a definite form, it assumes a distinct structure as well. But even that is no guarantee that it will not change further. To suit the demands of a particular performance, a play might have to undergo significant changes.

Let me offer an example. There was a play called *Sampatti Bantan* [property division]. It was a very old play and had proved its popularity time and again. It is regarded as one of the representative pieces of Alkap theatre. The story goes: Two brothers are separated. The property they will inherit consists of a two-roomed house, a palm tree, a cow, and a blanket. The younger brother is assertive, excitable. Calling the village elder over he starts to sing his lines enthusiastically:

> Brother, that umbrella is mine
> I'll take whatever is my share, including that grain crusher.
> Brother, that hookah is mine
> I'll take whatever is my share, including that cattle-peg.

This went on for some time. The clever village leader divided the things: it was easy to distribute the two rooms. Each got one. Then he gave the upper part of the palm tree to one and the lower half to the other. As for the cow, one got the front portion and the other, the back. The blanket was divided by day and night.

The younger brother took the lower half of the tree. He would rest against it and smoke his hookah, as was his wont. He would tell people he was resting on his father's riches, and there was nothing quite like it. He took the front portion of the cow, because he would be able to tell people that he was getting grass to feed his cow. (For a villager these are sentimental matters.) He took the blanket during the day, so he could go around showing it off. If someone asked, he would proudly tell them it was his share of his father's property. People would see the blanket around him and think well of him.

Then came the climax. The older sibling ate delicacies made from the palm fruit during the rains, because the upper part of the tree was his. The younger was left with his regret. He got fodder for the cow. The older one got the milk. During the winter, the older brother slept wrapped in the comfort of the blanket. The younger brother and his wife shivered in the cold.

The younger brother hatched a plan. Since the base of the tree was his, what prevented him from chopping it down? The older had climbed the tree to cut the leaves so he could plug a hole in the roof of his house. (The one playing the tree would be of a tall stature.) The younger took an axe to the tree. The older brother realised he was in danger. Then he went to milk the cow. (The cow was played by a member of the chorus, who bent down, hands on his knees.) The younger started wrestling with the cow's head. The cow started to kick and thrash about. The milking was spoiled! As for the blanket, the younger brother kept it in a tub of water in the morning. He was its rightful owner then and could do what he liked with it. He claimed that his children had defecated and urinated on it and so it had to be cleaned. The older brother was shocked to see a wet blanket at night.

It is clear that the play ends in reconciliation. Every Alkap play had a strong message, as is usual for folk theatre. This old and time-tested Kap took a few hours in all. There were plenty of details – I merely narrated the basic plot. But depending on the performance, there is nothing to prevent the performers from going beyond the existing plot. Events such as the partition or Hindu–Muslim communal conflicts can easily find their ways into this plot, and I have seen it happen. The old Kap, then, is imbued with new significance. Thousands of audience members clapped and cheered enthusiastically. On another occasion, the Kap could as well include the conflict between a poor farmer and the greedy mahajan or moneylender. This could increase the length to one and half or even two hours. Usually Alkap plays last from half-an-hour to two and a half hours, not more than that. That said, I have seen an Alkap group that hailed from Rahimpur in Malda district, across the Padma River, to hold forth for over four to five hours. Although they performed within the tradition, I must add that their plots were more like those plays on social issues produced by the jatra groups of Chitpur. The Rahimpur group was famous, but they had moved away significantly from the basic style of Alkap theatre.

Let me explain how Alkap is performed. In the staging area, the actors merely stand up in whatever costume they are wearing and assume their roles. Take for instance a play called *Pathshala* or *The School*. A member of the group stands up and says that 'I am a postman. My bag seems to be filling up with letters. Let me go and deliver them.'

He starts walking purposefully. He has a notebook in one hand and a postcard too. An up-tempo music starts to play. To indicate a change of place or time, there are musical interludes like a radio filler. Film techniques are employed as well: fade ins, fade outs, cuts, jump-cuts, and dissolves. The fading in and out happen when the speaker is about to sit down, and the next actor has already stood up. The effect of a cut can be achieved when the first speaker sits down after delivering his lines, and the next one stands up immediately to assume his part. This requires a particular kind of sequencing. Such techniques are Alkap's very own – not derived from cinema. If we have to show two situations parallelly, there is no alternative to the jump-cut. In terms of the techniques employed to propel the plot forward, Alkap has much in common with cinema, not traditional theatre with its painted scenes.

Let us return to the postman. He comes to a halt. The music stops, and his rhythmic walk stops with it. He wipes his forehead. He has walked a long way. When he ventures into the audience, it is inevitable that some member will say that 'Uncle, do you have a letter for me?' A funny dialogue will ensue between actor and audience. Then the postman will ask, 'Is this so-and-so village? Does so-and-so live here? Can you point his house to me?' Someone in the audience is bound to point at the staging area. The postman will, accordingly, make his return. He will stand in front of the harmonium calling out a name. A peasant will respond and stand up.

The postman delivers the letter and leaves. The music starts playing. The postman sits down to that tune, marking his exit. The peasant keeps standing. He cannot read. He decides, 'Let me go and see if the Gomasta (tax-collector) can read it out for me. The Gomasta has no time and scolds the peasant. He decides that he must educate his son and goes looking for a teacher. He asks the audience, 'Sir, can you tell me where to find a good teacher?' A local, village teacher's name is mentioned. He is a real person from real life. The man asks 'Is he here now?' Inevitably, he is among the audience. He now finds himself in trouble! The actor goes to him and pretends to plead. (The Bangla word for 'pretension' is 'kapat,' which gives us the 'Kap' of Alkap.) The whole audience has started laughing. The ustad, who is a master at dictating the rhythms of the performance, takes over at this point. He stands up and remarks 'You, idiot! I am the teacher. Come, tell me what it is you want.' And with that, the play returns to its original storyline. Maintaining this fluidity between the boundaries is at the heart of Alkap theatre.

This is the performance tradition of Alkap. The plot develops through cinematic techniques, and it takes the audience along. The actors have to improvise on the spot when it comes to dialogue. They may have to resort to singing their dialogue at times, which may also be formed on the spot. In a way, Alkap is both ballet and opera.

Because there is no written play text, the dialogue keeps changing in Alkap. Episodes change too. In the play titled *Selling the Son*, we see a father taking his hungry son down the street. The boy is inquisitive and asks 'What is that?' whenever he sees something. Sometimes the father answers 'That is a man.' The boy says 'I want to eat a man, father.' He even wants to eat the burning Hasag-lamp he sees in the performance area. People laugh. Once the character of the son was played by a renowned actor from the Buro-Turigram of Birbhum, Sangal Latu. I was playing the father. It was at the time of the autumn festivals, taking place inside a pandal. On one side, beside the idol of the deity, the drummers sat with their *dhak* or drums. Latu pointed at the dhaks and said 'What are those, Baba?' I said 'dhak.' Before I knew it, Latu was making his way through the audience, saying 'I shall eat that dhak.' The drummers saw him approaching and clung on to their dhaks, shouting 'No, no, no!' The audience was in splits.

I did not understand it then. I later realised that this, then, was an instance of audience participation! The drummers know that the dhaks are the means to their livelihood. The dhaks are their lives. The sudden intrusion of this actor into a potentially real aspect of their lives brought out their true, natural selves: they had to save their means of survival, and so they shouted, 'No, no, no!'

Alkap confronts its audience directly in this way. The same play had a dream sequence. The father and son are resting by the wayside, tired from all the walking. They rest by a tree, whose roots are formed by the shoulders of two audience members. No one seemed to mind. The hungry boy dreams, his now-deceased mother stands in front of him with a plate full of rice. A cymbal serves as the plate. He tries to move towards her, and as he does so, he trips and wakes from his dream. The mother disappears (the actor has taken his seat). And the son, his voice hoarse, screams, 'Baba!'

Until this moment, the audience was finding it funny. With this cry, they all fall silent, blue with anguish and sorrow. They hold their breath. Alkap is a peddler of dreams. Anything can happen in that world. The boundaries between the real and the fictive are blurred. The legendary King Vikramaditya and his wife, Bhanumati, can speak to each other over the telephone, and the princess, instead of riding a bewitched tree, can fly in a rocket. No one questions them. The audience knows it is a dreamworld. That is what art does – gives us wings to dream.

Place and time become confused in Alkap theatre. Often, there is no clear distinction between the past, present, and future. Has Einstein himself not told us that time is ever present? Psychologists also tell us that in dreams one loses the sense of place and time. Alkap is a dream world. This is what ustads refer to as the realm of maya.

But then, all of a sudden, Alkap can take these dreams and shatter them against the harsh, familiar, and mundane experience of our reality. Its tradition sanctions – even demands – this of Alkap. There is no dramatist behind it all, not even the notion of a single author. There is no shackle that ties the play to an author. The actor does not have to memorise someone else's words and repeat them like a parrot. The dialogue must be composed during performance.

This is why the artist's persona and the character's persona can come together in a moment of spontaneity. However, a functional restraint also evolves from experience. The artist learns, also about the limits, transgressing which might create a rupture between the two. The drama will be poorer for that. Once we went to the Gananatya Sangha's festival in Berhampore. The performance was to take place inside the Grant Hall. It was unconventional to perform in a proscenium theatre, and I realised my mistake immediately. On the way, I had introduced the group to Shakespeare's play, *The Merchant of Venice*. They had anticipated that this would be a Kap for the urban crowd, and that is exactly what it turned out to be. We remembered only the basic outline of the story. I played a Mahajan or money-lender. Comedian Kassem Chashi played the borrower. It was going well. The relationship between the borrower and the Mahajan is a familiar tale in villages. Suddenly without any prior warning, I see the chhokra Dhara stand up. With a mischievous smile, he announced in a dialect that was a cross between his *Khottai* (from Bihar) and broken Bangla: 'Ahoy there, Miss Monkey-trainer! My monkey is called Bhaglu. Ahoy, Bhaglu, where did you go? Are you on the roof? Where are you! Come, come. Show them your tricks.' Kalu, who was part of the chorus, entered the fray. Bare bodied, he tied up his dhoti and rolled up a thin towel to make it look like he had a tail. He started playing the monkey going down on all fours, throwing things into confusion. I was stunned and filled with anxiety. There is a separate, short Kap which deals with a Monkey-trainer, but how could the two possibly mesh?

During the court scene, Kinu, another member of the chorus, was playing the tabla. He had bent low, placing his hands on his knees. On his back, resting on his elbows, was the second comedian (*pash kepe*), Maru. He was a trainee then. Maru wore a grave expression. He is the Judge after all, listening to the pleas. Everything went along fine, until, once again, the Monkey-trainer made her reappearance. The monkey ran amok in the court. The Judge was furious and ordered 'Go! Get a pound of flesh off him!'

The monkey-trainer started shouting – 'Hey Judge-man! I have one thing to say. You asked me to chop some meat off. So here you go. But there's no talk of shedding blood. Take the meat all you want, you animal, but you can't shed blood, yes!'

The communists in the audience, expectedly, applauded loudly. I felt happy. Not because of the claps we received, but because I realised the power of Alkap theatre. We were able to transcend the reality and context of *The Merchant of Venice*. I was happy seeing the added layers of meaning that were added on to reality by a folk theatre form. The real became magical. Dhana, or Dhananjay, the ustad, was from a family of illiterate Doms.

Present in the audience that day was the labour leader, Mohammad Ismail. He smiled and said 'Take them to the village and plant them among the bamboo bushes. You'll see how they flower there!'

He was right. We were later invited by the Gananatya Sangha in Calcutta to perform at the national festival. Our group was advertised in the newspapers. We did not go. We knew that it would be impossible to communicate with the Calcutta crowd. Their reality is different from ours. Besides, the audience is an indivisible element of the performance. Without audience participation, Alkap is like fish out of water. It will die.

Theatre on a palm tree top

We speak of theatre in streets and public spaces in cities. Once we took theatre to palm tree tops. That is the beauty of Alkap theatre.

This happened in Salar, a village of some prosperity. It was a single-group performance. As the night went on, people started dozing. Sangal Latu said 'Ustad-ji, let's stage a cracker of a Kap – the one about Kallu Fakir.' Kallu was a poor man. His wife had run away to the city with a salesman. Poor Kallu decided that begging was his only option. He took on the guise of a visually and physically challenged person. A Muslim spectator was coming towards him after his morning namaz. He allowed the spectator to adjust his cap. He even actually collected some money. He went to the city to beg and, sure enough, spotted his wife. Having decided to set his wife's house on fire, he waited for an opportunity. Suddenly he heard his wife say to her new husband, 'Oh no! I completely forgot. I had kept some silver coins hidden in the taro-bushes behind the man's house!'

Kallu Fakir ran to get the coins. When he reached the taro bush behind his house, he found the village chief performing his daily rituals. Realising his trouble, the chief let out a growl. Kallu thought it was a tiger. 'Dear god, a tiger!' he cried and ran for life.

Dawn was breaking. A little behind where the spectators were seated, I spied a palm tree. Its tentacle-like roots went up to almost four feet, after which the trunk was bent a little. After this bend, it grew straight, lifting its head above. It was evident from its smoothened trunk at the base that the kids had long been using it in their games.

Latu ran and started climbing the tree. He heard the alarmed cries: 'Tiger! Tiger!' and quickly latched onto the trunk. A crowd gathered there. They played along with him. 'No no, that's no tiger. It's the village chief.' Some continued to scare him by growling like a tiger. Latu was wearing a cap. He put his feet around the tree and sat there. People tried to reassure him so he would come down. All of it was play-acting, of course. I watched this unfold, stunned. I had to start playing the music to keep the show going. The chhokra started his act. The dispersed audience members began to return to their places.

Then I see Latu speaking to someone from where he was hanging on to the tree. He was jesting. Even then I didn't catch his drift. After a while, he climbed down. He rejoined the performance and, smiling, said that 'I have earned my reward, Ustad-ji. I spoke to the entire village back there.' That is where the performance came to a natural close.

The field where we performed was surrounded by huts standing close to one another. Trees were sparse. That morning, Latu Sangal had succeeded in involving in the theatrical performance even those who were absent from the audience. The women were tending to their housework. Some were sweeping the courtyards, some washing utensils – some with their kids on their backs, sleep dust in their eyes. A woman was being bullied by her mother-in-law somewhere, and another, brushing her teeth with ash in the pond nearby, was performing her morning rituals. Each one turned around to hear Latu's voice – a voice that came from a dark figure in a cap atop a palm tree. The voice took the woman in the pond by surprise. She then started giggling helplessly. She was aware that it was theatre night. The sleepy child made faces at Latu. The domineering mother-in-law took a moment's break and acknowledged Latu's humour with 'There is no peace even in death, do you hear?'

Latu gave us a detailed description and then remarked in his Birbhum dialect, 'So? You saw how far I took our theatre? Up to the tree-top! I got a rare glimpse of the dawning world from that height.'

His words were nothing short of philosophical. But are the finest jesters not the finest philosophers too?

Ustad Jhanksa

'Alkap is a rare maya' – he used to say. It took me a while before I finally understood why he called it rare. One autumn afternoon, we had sat down to rest by the banks of the Bhagirathi, a little way off Karnasubarna, when he said:

> There is such a thing as maya, Master-ji. Let me tell you all about it. Yesterday at the performance they had hung fourteen lamps, no less. I counted. There were no fewer than five thousand people. It was a big event. There you could see that thing – maya. Finally, once the performance was over people went their own ways. The lamps were dimmed and the tent was dismantled. The dancing boy took off his costume. But do you not think it strange that the celebration of art in our minds and hearts wasn't over yet? The tent was still over our heads, the fourteen lamps continued to glow. Mohini's dance went on . . . You have gotten on a train, Master-ji. You will carry the momentum with you even after you disembark. I don't think we are getting out of it in this lifetime. Some power carries us along on its magical journey, and we, Alkap artists, live and breathe by that.

He used to speak with his eyes shut. His voice was gentle. He was a Harijan by caste. A group of people had migrated from Bihar to Bengal and settled on both sides of the Bhagirathi. By profession they were farmers, earning their living by selling their produce. They are of the Chai caste, sometimes called 'Diyari.' Their mother tongue is called Khottai Chaiboli – Diyari Hindustani (language of the Khotta Chai community, or a dialect of Hindustani spoken by the Diyari community). That's where he came from.

In the world of Alkap theatre, he was known as Ustad Jhanksa or Jhanksu. His real name was Dhananjay Sarkar. He hailed originally from Dhanapatnagar, a village of Chayis situated beyond Jangipur on that side of the Bhagirathi.

Through Birbhum and Murshidabad, through the Santal Parganas, and the Bangla-speaking parts of Dumka and Purniya and in villages, fairs, and bazaars all across the land that is drained by the five rivers, Padma, Ganga, Dwarka, Ajay, and Mayurakshi, he held absolute sway. People called him the King of Alkap. An art form that had fallen into disrepute was transformed by him to something respectable. It was owing to his efforts that the tiny kerosene lamps that used to light up Alkap performances were replaced by grand tents, carpets, and gorgeous lanterns. People were no longer shocked to hear that the group's fees were one hundred rupees. In the 1950s, one hundred rupees in a village went a long way.

Jhanksa had recovered Alkap from its humble, dusty state and helped it evolve. He was a large, bronze-complexioned man, tall and broad. His nose was proud and sharp, his cheek bones high. At the performances, he used to stoop a little, his hands folded. People would clap from all corners to show their regard for him. He would say that 'Alkap is a form of folk theatre. It is for the education of the people. A reflection of our lives. It is like a mirror. You may see your faces in this mirror.'

Ustad Jhanksa spoke in finely chiselled Bangla at the performance. He took care to infuse his stories with a societal consciousness. I went on several performance tours with him, and I learnt much. He used to string stories and verses together on the way to performances or even during a performance. He could carry a plot forward with great skill. If the performance flagged at any point, he would infuse it with new spirit and recapture the rhythms.

Ustad Jhanksa had a major role to play in the rise of Alkap in the 1950s. Right from the beginning, Alkap was a very powerful critical form. In Jhanksaji's hands, its lashes fell hard on the back of rural society. His voice could be heard far and wide.

And how its popularity grew! The fan following that the comedians and dancers enjoyed was comparable to that of film stars. Ustad was respected as the director of the group. People would rush to watch performances leaving their daily labour in fields. The village roads would be filled with people. Just as young men and women are driven by a crazed passion to try their luck at Bollywood even at the cost of the family savings, the finest of the Alkap groups started attracting not just men but young women too. They wanted to be a part of it.

Behind this raging popularity was the work of that man from Dhanpatnagar, Chai Pally. He passed away in silence about a couple of years back. An obituary appeared in *Jangipur Samvad*, the journal founded by Dadathakur. That was it.

Had Ustad Jhanksa been born in the land of the sahibs, he would have had a folk-art academy in his name by now. There would be research centres and museums to honour him. And yet, his passing came so unceremoniously here!

In search of origins

What are the origins of Alkap? Ustad Jhanksa used to speak of a barber from Rahimpur in Malda. His name was Banamali. After he lost his vision, Banamali is said to have been inspired by the sound of squabbling between the two wives of a neighbouring village chief. He was known as Ustad Bona Kana.

Through experience, I learnt that Alkap's origins lie elsewhere. The tradition has its roots in years of community practices in rural areas. If one has to point to a specific point of origin, it must be the Gajan festival that marks Chaitra Sankranti or the end of the Bengali year. The festival celebrates Lord

Siva. Songs to Siva were an essential part of Alkap performance in its early days – gambhira is an offshoot. To this day, the association with the deity continues. But as Alkap developed, somewhere it left behind its religious associations.

In the Rurh plains in Bengal, around Birbhum and Murshidabad districts, Alkap theatre is often referred to as 'Chhyanchor.' It is used in a derogatory sense, as it is used also to refer to petty thieves. In the local dialect, however, 'Chhyanchra' also refers to a vegetable mishmash. It is likely that the miscellaneous nature of these rural performances gave it that name.

The name 'Alkap' has its origins in North Bengal. (Alkap in North Bengal is the subject of Narayan Gangopadhyay's novel *Chaitalik.*) 'Al' is an ancient word. It means jovial festivity. 'Kap' is also of ancient origin, referring to comic skits. Taken together, 'Alkap' means a comic play. Such fusion between synonymous words (like *ghar-bari* for house, *khat-palanka* for bed, *saj-posak* for dress) is not uncommon in Bangla. That said, even though the literal meaning of Alkap is 'comic drama,' its social meaning is somewhat different. Usually it stands for plays that are comic satires.

During the performances, however, Jhanksaji used to offer yet another explanation. 'Al' means a bee's poisonous sting. The Kap which is laced by a bee's poison, that is Alkap,' he would say.

In a way. his explanation makes perfect sense. Alkap is a form of satirical, comic theatre. It was born among the humblest rural folk. The high castes saw it as something despicable, lowly. There is no denying that vulgarity and obscenity were part of Alkap and Chhyanchor in its early days, even if that was but a minute fraction of what we see in the commercial theatres in Calcutta today. In its older form and aesthetics. Alkap was not all that outrageous. Rural society was rife with taboos. Theatre would often try and uncover these taboos, strip society naked. The wealthy landlords, religious leaders, zamindars, and moneylenders were often exposed through art. Naturally, this was not to their liking. Besides, the form was born in the humble homes of people who were looked down upon: *chhotolok*, and hence was considered of low-birth and untouchable, something to be mocked.

Rural society began to change post-independence. The first major movement ensured adult enfranchisement. In the hope of securing a vote bank, political parties tried to develop rural roads and a transport network. The chhotolok grew in confidence. Primary education spread, and other social and economic changes started to disrupt the rural hierarchies in culture and society. The everyday life of the villages was undergoing transformation. The man who considered it perfectly natural to go around bare-bodied started wearing a shirt. Social scientists and economists are aware of these changes. But as the changes hit established rural sociocultural hierarchies, Alkap theatre found ways to spread rapidly. Even those from the upper echelons started to accept Alkap as an art form. During religious festivities, Alkap groups were invited to perform. Performances were to be seen in the courtyards of zamindar families even before the zamindari system was dismantled. I was part of the group until 1956. By then, Alkap had found its way to the suburban townships. The educated and those who considered themselves high-brow started appearing in the audience. We performed several times in Behrampore. There were many groups that took part. We performed twice on invitation from the Gananatya Sangha. This continued even after I left. The Alkap performances in villages and towns were ticketed like the jatra shows in Calcutta. In 1964, I came to Calcutta. In the seven or eight years leading up to that, Ustad Jhanksa and several other young ustads had successfully taken Alkap to great heights.

But from the 1960s, the cultural rejects of urban societies began to enter Alkap. The artists are to blame for this, of course. Just as audiences in the cities were overwhelmed by cinema and jatra, Alkap artists too felt their attraction strongly.

The king of Alkap, Ustad Jhanksa, was ageing. Right before the old king's eyes, an urban demon was tightening its grip on the form. It changed its name from Alkap to 'Pancharas,' or the five rasas, but it was like a possessed village girl, dressed in an urban prostitute's clothing.

Pancharas is performed even today on high, make-shift stages like in jatra. Like in jatra, actors wear make-up and wigs before coming on to the stage. They put on fake moustaches and beards and costumes – shirts, trousers, coats and ties, boots – like rejects from the Bombay film industry. We can safely say that even before Alkap lost its nurturing father, the form itself had died. The man spent his last days in great pain.

Long hair, moustache, beard, and sideburns

While researching for his book, *Primitive Man and His Ways*, the Danish anthropologist, Birket-Smith, spent several years among the Tuareg, Lap, and Maories in the Sahara, in Lapland, and in New Zealand. Similarly, the British explorer, Wilfred Thesiger, spent a considerable period of time in the six thousand-square mile marshland which forms the Tigris–Euphrates river basin in Iraq. *The Marsh Arabs* was a result of these experiences. And let us not forget Bertrand Flornoy's time among the Jivaros of the Amazon basin, known for their expertise in the grizzly art of tsatsa or head-shrinking. The French ethnologist spent nine months in their midst, which enabled him to paint the first accurate portrait of the community in his book *Jivaro*. Colin Turnbull, a disciple of Ma Anandamayi, spent years with the Pygmies. He recorded his observations in *Forest People*. This is hard work – often life-threatening. The research itself is like a struggle. Here, I have mentioned as precedents only those works I can see from my desk.

Once – this was back in the 1950s – Mrinal Gupta, a school teacher at Karnasubarna, sent for me when a Kolkata-based researcher of folk cultures came calling. My village was about four miles from his school. The gentleman wanted to know about Alkap.

Mrinal was a folk culture enthusiast. He had even made a documentary on ivory crafts. He is now working at Writer's Building. I wrote to him: 'You cannot learn about something from a distance. Why don't you send him? I can show him around. He must witness several performances. Needless to say, it will be hard work.'

I never heard from him again. Years later in Kolkata, I found myself flipping through a book on folk cultures. It defined Alkap: 'Alkap is performed by Muslim peasants.' It was accompanied by a few examples of Alkap songs.

I was at a total loss. I encountered the same definition once again in one of Tarasankar Bandyopadhyay's novels. I was rather surprised. He was from Labhpur, a village that is home to many an Alkap troop. Many performances have taken place over the years. We have performed a number of times in Labhpur and its neighbouring village of Pushuliya. My partner Latu would come with us. How can the author of *Hansuli Banker Upakatha* make such a mistake?

There is a profound sense of alienation here, a distance. It gives rise to indifference, even disregard. Where does this come from? Can we trace it to our caste system, which has left an indelible mark on the collective unconscious? Or is it the internalised sense of being colonised? Or perhaps it stems from an apathy that plagues us as a people, which rejoices only in picking up the leftovers of foreign cultures.

A wide Caucasian Chalk-Circle could have come up out of the Alkap performances. But it did not.

Translation: Sujaan Mukherjee

Note

1 Syed Mustafa Siraj, 'Alkap Natyariti o Third Theatre', in *Nirbachita Rachana*, Nitai Basu (ed.), Kolkata: Punascha, 2006, pp. 1085–1094.

29 Qazi Motahar Husain: State language and language issues in Bangladesh

Introduction

Qazi Motahar Husain (1897–1981), born in Lakshmipur village in Kushtia District, was an eminent scientist, literary critic, and social commentator. He had a dual MA degree in Physics and Mathematics from Dhaka College and the University of Calcutta. He got his doctorate degree in Statistics from the University of Dhaka, and, after a teaching career at the University, went on to become the first Director of the Institute of Statistical Research and Training at the University.

Qazi Motahar Husain was associated with 'Muslim Sahitya Samaj' (Muslim Literary Society 1926) and for a short period was the editor of its mouthpiece *Shikha* (Issues II – III). The journal played an important role in advocating rationalism and freedom of thought.

Qazi Motahar Husain's publications include *Sancharan* (1937), *Nazrul Kavya Parichiti* (1955), *Ganit Sastrer Itihas* (1970), and *Alok Bigyan* (1974). His first book Sancharan is a collection of essays on various topics such as 'The Religion of an Atheist,' 'The Relation between Art and Religion', and 'Religion and Society'. The text stands out as an example of the work of a liberal modernist writer striving to establish a strong foundation for a non-communal approach to education, literature, and culture, while the title suggests the deep need to disseminate the same awareness among the people.

The essay selected for this volume, 'State Language and Language Issues in Bangladesh' (1947), takes up the all-important question of what the state language of East Bengal should be. The language debate had begun before partition when, in 1937, supporters of Bangla had opposed the idea of making Urdu the lingua franca of Muslims in India in the Lucknow session of the All India Muslim League. After partition, several measures were taken by the central government of Pakistan to make Urdu the sole state language of Pakistan, resulting in widespread protests by students and intellectuals in East Bengal. The historic Bhasha Andolan or Language Movement that ensued linked language with the fundamental rights of the people and hence their overall development. Qazi Motahar Husain played an important role

DOI: 10.4324/9781003224686-30

in this movement. The essay selected for this volume brings out his rational, pragmatic, and historical perspective on the necessity of making Bangla one of the state languages of Pakistan.

*

State language and language issues in Bangladesh[1]

Qazi Motahar Husain

The language that people of a country speak is its natural language. Why then are there issues with the language of Bangladesh? Strangely enough, what is normal is not often easily understood by a complex intellect. Let me try to clarify this further.

Let us assume that ninety-nine percent of people in a country speak in Bangla and the remaining one percent in English, Urdu, Hindi, etc. Again, let us assume that this one percentage of people had come to the country as rulers or for trade, become powerful, and started dominating the less educated or poorer people. Hence, they are disrespectful towards the people and their language. They consider it a waste of time to learn their language and to enter into transactions with them, and that hurts the self-respect of the people. That is not proper either. It is also true that learning the language of the conqueror or those in power, establishing contact with them, and hence pleasing them can also lead to greater opportunities for earning one's livelihood. And what is more important is that a sense of considerable pride emerges from remembering and maintaining one's great distance from the common people. Those fortunate enough to receive the grace of the conquerors are the ones who acquire the right to be the leaders of the country and partake of all kinds of advantages in the name of the people. This is normal in today's situation, for there is nothing to fear in depriving the 'deaf and the dumb', and in fact to desist from doing so is a sign of stupidity.

This, in broad terms, is the intellectual background of issues of language in contemporary East Pakistan.

The official language was Pashto during the Pathan rule, and in Mughal era it was Persian. The Mughal and the Pathan were foreigners, but they accepted this land as their own and greatly encouraged the native language in order to know the condition of the people. It was under the patronage of the Pathans in Bangladesh that the *Ramayana* and the *Mahabharata* were translated – and the *Bhagavata* and other puranas composed. Bangla before this was not a very robust language and was disrespected by pandits as the language of the masses. The pandits of those days maintained their purity and supremacy under the cover of an artificial Sanskrit language. The Pathan subedars of Gauda with a noble generosity disregarded the opposition of Brahmins, and for the welfare of the common people (and probably also to satisfy their thirst for stories) got the puranas, the *Ramayana*, and the *Mahabharata* composed. Needless to say, these texts are unparalleled for the faithful preservation of cultural traditions and for upholding ideal, moral characteristics before the people. It is for this to some extent that even common Indian peasants have appeared as philosophers and have evoked the wonder of Western scholars. In fact, it was because their language was encouraged by foreign rulers that Bengalis remained stable and took many fine elements from Islamic civilisation and strengthened their own. On the other hand, Islamic rulers and the people came into contact with Hindu tradition and brought in new and relevant developments in Islam demonstrating the capacity for acceptance and the general compatibility of the religion in the practical sphere.

In the Mughal period, the ministers of the Arakan court in particular did not hesitate to allocate wealth for the upgradation of Bangla. Muslim court poets Daulat Qazi and Syed Alaol gained immortal fame by composing Bangla poetry. They had in their repertoire a large number of words from Sanskrit, Arabic, Persian, Urdu, and other languages; but they did not try to impose heavy words from any particular language forcefully and instead composed their works in the language used in everyday life by contemporary people or in one that was easily understood by all. The Mughals and the Pathans were foreigners, but they made this country their own land. Their state languages Pashto or Persian did not try to wipe out the ideals of the people in ruthless freedom, and the Mughal and Pathan kings and subedars provided royal encouragement to the language of the land in order to establish relations. Hence, the people of the land learnt the foreign language and yet retained their national freedom and enhanced its qualities by drawing upon foreign traditions.

Then came the British. After a while, English became the official language. The Hindus happily accepted their new masters and their language, but the Muslims could not due to various reasons. We know from Rammohun's statements that between the middle-class Hindus and the Muslims, the Muslims were superior in their courteousness, their practical intellect, and in their performative and administrative skills even during his time. But within a few days and due to reasons stated earlier, along with the divisive policies of the rulers, the Muslims fell in status in economic, social, political, and all other spheres, and a strange hatred and envy appeared between the Hindus and Muslims. The Bangla language itself was split. The highly educated pandits made it Sanskrit-oriented and hence a carrier of Hindu civilisation alone, and the semi-learned Muslim munshis created an Islamic literature full of Arabic and Persian words. Each side took recourse to excess. But the Bangla of pandits survived because of its link with education, intellect, and social talent, while that of munshis was lost. Of course, today with the rise of mass society, the Bangla of pandits has also gradually become simplified.

But now British rule has come to an end. After the defeat of the Battle of Plassey in 1757, the failure of the Wahabi Movement in 1830–1840, and the terrible consequence of the Sepoy Mutiny of 1857, the national flag of victory was raised surmounting all barriers in 1947. Now Hindus and Muslims and the leaders are vested with great responsibilities. One may hope that in the next few years, there will be an end to poverty, ill-health, illiteracy, and internal conflicts in a well-planned manner, with the help of all citizens irrespective of creed and religion, and our cherished East Pakistan will regain its seat of glory. To eradicate poverty, it will be of utmost importance to do away with social disparities, prevent foreign exploitation, and circulate whatever wealth there is through industrialisation. It will not be enough to curb the British influence to some extent, one would also have to ensure that its place is not taken up by people from other countries or regions. The leaders and the people will have to be vigilant so that conspirators do not bring in various obstructions in education through language and with many lame excuses create obstacles for the intellectual development of East Pakistan.

India's Hindus and Muslims and particularly Muslims of East Bengal are examples of the crippling effects of bringing in impediments in the use of language. English became the official language and the medium of education. One spent ten years of great mental energy to master knowledge that could ordinarily have been mastered in five years; even then such knowledge gained through a foreign language remained superficial or vague. Students would resort to unassimilated huge quotations or an inflated vocabulary. The education policy of the British in India also caused great harm. Prescribed textbooks for science and the subjects selected led to a kind of superficial text-book-oriented knowledge that did not serve any practical purpose. Hence, the number of graduates and post-graduates in science with degrees in law is not too small in the country, but scientific industrial organisations are almost non-existent. Of course, one cannot deny that English education did have a few advantages of its own.

Apart from this disabling factor among the Indian Hindus and Muslims, there were two others that led to the ineptitude of Muslims from East Bengal. The first was the neglect of the mother tongue Bangla, and the second was the association of language with religion that led to an undue attraction and fascination for Urdu instead of Bangla. Hence, the Bengali Muslim forgot the Persian culture of the Badshah and did not try to keep alive the Islamic tradition through Bangla. However much one may argue for Urdu, it cannot be denied that it was a foreign language. It was impossible to retain religious traditions with the help of Urdu as it did not have any relation with the pulse of the people. A few vague utterances cannot maintain national or religious traditions. The intellectual hunger of the Muslim peasant was to some extent satisfied by all that had been rescued through manuscripts. But due to the educated elite's disrespect and neglect of such manuscripts, they were almost lost to the community. The situation therefore was such that it seemed the Bengali Muslim had no real culture to call his own, and his only wealth consisted of borrowed words or those taught by another. He was a stranger in his own country, and the foreign land seemed to be his own and hence his indifference, his helpless dependence on the west, and his desperate lack of self-confidence. The clever Western people had taken advantage of the situation. They knew that going to Bengal and wearing large turbans would make them *pirs* or at least they could become *maulavis* and make some money. This is similar to the urban shopkeeper making profit by cheating the village consumer. In reality, the Bengali Muslim was a *Bangal*[2] to be laughed at and exploited not just by the Westerner alone, but by all in east–west–north and south.

The poverty and low self-esteem result from the neglect of our mother tongue Bangla and our habitual practice of repeating empty and vague words. These words are not saturated with the rasa of our hearts and we do not feel their strength. Now, the influence of English has lessened, and the time has arrived to create a Bangla literature in East Pakistan nurtured on Hindu–Muslim traditions with the joint effort of all Muslims free from excessive Hindu influence. The onus now is on us to fill the lack of Islamic traditions, nurture our mother tongue, and bring glory to the nation. So far, Muslims had comfortably laid the blame on Hindus stating that they were responsible for filling the language with Hindu ideas, but that will not work in East Pakistan. Muslim writers will now have to predominantly bear the responsibility of bringing in the Islamic tradition. The time has come for Muslim intellectuals to create good Bangla literature in place of the punthi or the manuscript tradition and introduce the people to Muslim culture and civilisation; it is only then that Bangla language will be fully enriched, and the Islamic tradition will, in the right manner, become the substance of the people's heart and remove their poverty and lack of self-esteem. Knocking at the doors of Urdu will not serve any real purpose. It is not as if Urdu has more esteem in the eyes of Allah than Bangla. It is also not true that Urdu is the religious language of Muslims because it is derived from Arabic. Originally, Urdu was a mixed language created by native soldiers from many countries in the Mughal period, but it is not to be disrespected. It has been enriched by words from many languages such as Arabic, Persian, and Prakrit. In course of time, because of the tussle between the maulavis and the pandits, Urdu became divided into Arabic-Urdu and Sanskrit-Urdu. Then, too, Urdu is used differently in different places – in Lucknow, Delhi, Lahore, and Hyderabad. Urdu does not have a large body of great original literature, but it is very rich in translations. I do not disrespect or critique Urdu, but I do think that the Bengali Muslim's fascination for Urdu is dangerous particularly when I see an obscene love song in Urdu evoking great feelings in the common Bengali gentleman who takes it as a glorification of Allah and derides a good *Brohmosangeet* as being *haram*. I then realise that this senseless devotion and derision are both bereft of value: it is a mere matter of infatuation with sound. How long will we remain mesmerised by this illusion? We have to look at the world and press forward in tune with the movement of life. Hence, instead of moving ahead like one in a dream or like a puppet, we have to move like a human being. We must free ourselves of illusions, open our eyes, and examine issues and matters. That would be our real independent step forward. The only way to do this is to engage with one's mother tongue and through it gain complete access to whatever is beautiful, enticing, or noble. No development can be possible for us without our mother tongue.

Of course, a reference to a complete life does not imply a self-centred existence but a life led in the company of many. Hence, one must learn different languages to maintain relations with others. But this learning should take place against the background of a holistic mother tongue-based education and definitely not as a substitution of the mother tongue. Those who live near us, or those with whom we live, are the people closest to us and first we have to attend to their demands, and then of those who are at a distance. Hence it is only after acquiring a strong foundation in one's mother tongue that one should start learning whichever language one needs. So primary education must only be in the mother tongue, and then later in the pre-matriculation period, a student may be asked to acquire knowledge of one or two other languages for three or four years as required. This would make learning the second or the third language relatively easy and fast.

The medium of instruction should definitely be the mother tongue. English would perhaps be most advantageous for us to maintain relations with the world. But it is completely unnecessary to lay a lot of stress on this at the moment. To remain in touch with people of other regions in the country and with our neighbours, a kind of Urdu that traverses the middle path between Arabic-Urdu and Sanskrit-Urdu would be suitable. Contemporary Urdu should also be reformed from this angle. Doing away with false pride and blind prejudice and working together may reduce the difference between Urdu and Hindi and a strong and easy lingua franca responding to the needs of Pakistan and India or a commonly accepted language may be created. Students learning the language in the last three or four years before matriculation would gain access to a large cultural area. And those who finish their education after primary or middle school can remain free of the burden of language learning and through their mother tongue alone can get the required knowledge and taste their own culture.

Apart from issues related to the medium of education and the common language, there is the other question related to what the state language should be. So far, with the English people as the rulers, English was the official language, which meant that the language of the ruler was the official language. State language implies the language in which verdicts are given in court – knowledge of which leads to high positions in government service and which is used for the state's correspondences, its documents, etc. In other words, it is the language for which the government allocates the largest sum, and if one receives education in that language one is considered to be better educated than most by the nation.

Hence, it is natural and just for Bangla to be the official or the state language. A few Bengalis relying on others are already taking recourse to Urdu. But one cannot applaud their judgement. We have already talked about the false attraction for Urdu and its reason. All such utterances are the unmindful, immature expressions of 'mechanical dolls'. This will lead to the collapse of Bengal's national backbone. What this means is that Bengali Hindus and Muslims gaining independence from the British will immediately fall into the hands of the rulers of Punjab, Sindh, and Balochistan. People are clamouring for Urdu out of a blind religious madness. But we have already stated that a true sense of religion or tradition will never seep into the heart of the Bengalis except through Bangla. For this it is important to set up translation committees immediately to translate all key texts of religion and culture. To ignore this duty and partake of the left-over food of others will neither satisfy hunger nor lead to any gratification. This will never serve the purpose of sustainable well-being for the country. One can no more work with the conceit evident in projecting Urdu as the best language, the language of religion, or an aristocratic language. The newly awakened people will no more be duped by a few impostors or the tricks of the so-called elites. Aspirants for government jobs should instead be required to prove their proficiency in Bangla up to the secondary school level. Those who do not qualify will become ineffective after their training period, and their unsympathetic approach to the common people will lead to their dismissal.

In the whole of Pakistan, Bangla-speaking Muslims are greater in number. Yet, we are not in favour of making Bangla the state language in West Pakistan because that will be a hindrance to the normal growth of the common people in the region. Hence, Urdu or Pashto in West Pakistan and Bangla in East Pakistan will be the state languages. This is not at all unacceptable; there are several modern and developed countries like Russia and Canada with multiple state languages. If adjacent regions in Russia can have more than one state language, Punjab and East Bengal situated a thousand or a thousand and five hundred miles apart in West Pakistan and East Pakistan can surely have two different state languages, and that is also natural. Russia gives importance to the dictates of the people – they are the rulers, and hence the tendency to impose the language of a different region as the state language cannot emerge. In our country, in the new Pakistan, people will prove that they are the rulers – persons in positions of authority will not be allowed to exploit them for long. If attempts are made to impose Urdu forcefully on Bengali Hindus and Muslims as the state language, it will not work. This is because a flaming discontent cannot remain suppressed for long. That would then lead to the break-up of relations between East and West. The duty of a far-sighted politician is to acknowledge the views of the people and take up principles and practices that are just and that can help in the progress of the entire nation.

Translation: Subha Chakraborty Dasgupta

Notes

1 Qazi Motahar Husain, 'Rashtra-Bhasha o Bangladesher Bhasha-Samasya', in *Qazi Motahar Husain Rachanabali*, Vol. I, Abdul Haq (ed.), Dhaka: Bangla Academy, 1984, pp. 218–226. The essay was first published in *Saugat*, 1947.

2 People of West Bengal refer to those who have come from East Bengal or Bangladesh as 'Bangal'. Similarly, people of West Bengal are often referred to as 'Ghati'.

Index

www.ingramcontent.com/pod-product-compliance
Lightning Source LLC
Chambersburg PA
CBHW071752110726
47908CB00006B/1779
* 9 7 8 1 0 3 2 1 2 4 7 0 4 *